# ASQUITH

H. H. Asquith was prime minister through eight tumultuous years. No modern statesman has matched his record for controversy and continuity. His was a pivotal career that has since cast a long shadow over partisan and historiographical debate, particularly with regard to the decline of British Liberalism.

Here is a biography of Asquith, a lively appraisal based upon a selection of previously unavailable sources. Written with greater candour than its predecessors, it portrays a complex personality and illuminates the important events in which he was a key participant. New light is shed on his apprenticeship under Gladstone and Rosebery, his preparation for power, the policies of his long premiership, and his mutually destructive rivalry with David Lloyd George. Taking equal account of Asquith's unfailing ambition and his fidelity to principles, this book offers an interpretation that will carry greater conviction to a critical generation of readers.

Acknowledged as one of the most distinguished historians of his generation, Stephen Koss wrote many books including an outstanding two volume work on *The Rise and Fall of the Political Press in Britain*. At the time of his tragically early death in 1984 he was Professor of History at Columbia University in New York.

# HAMISH HAMILTON PAPERBACKS

*In preparation*

Alan Campbell-Johnson
## MISSION WITH MOUNTBATTEN

Robert Rhodes James
## ALBERT, PRINCE CONSORT

Robert Rhodes James
## LORD RANDOLPH CHURCHILL

Priscilla Napier
## A LATE BEGINNER

Jasper Parrott
with
Vladimir Ashkenazy
## BEYOND FRONTIERS

Margot Peters
## MRS PAT
## THE LIFE OF MRS PATRICK CAMPBELL

Constance Babington Smith
## JOHN MASEFIELD

A. J. P. Taylor
## BISMARCK

Emlyn Williams
## GEORGE

Cecil Woodham-Smith
## THE GREAT HUNGER

*For a complete list of available
titles see the end of this book*

# ASQUITH

*by*

## STEPHEN KOSS

A HAMISH HAMILTON PAPERBACK
London

First published in Great Britain 1976
by Allen Lane
First published in this edition 1985
by Hamish Hamilton Ltd
Garden House 57–59 Long Acre London WC2E 9JZ

Copyright © 1976 by Stephen Koss

ISBN 0-241-11500-0

Printed and bound in Finland
by Werner Söderström Oy

# CONTENTS

*Introduction  vii*
*1. From Herbert to Henry  1*
*2. From Back Bench to Front Bench  18*
*3. From Rosebery to Campbell-Bannerman  41*
*4. From Relugas to Biarritz  64*
*5. From the Old Liberalism to the New  89*
*6. From the Budget to the Curragh  111*
*7. From Agadir to the Dardanelles  142*
*8. From Coalition to Compulsion  175*
*9. From Downing Street to the Wilderness  208*
*10. From Defeat to Defeat, 1918–24  239*
*11. From the Peerage to Posterity  270*
*Bibliographical Notes  285*
*Index  293*

# ILLUSTRATIONS

Asquith as a young man by Spy, 1891 (Mansell Collection)

Margot Asquith, 1897 (BBC Hulton Picture Library)

The Exchequer Bird and the Little Economists by F. Carruthers Gould (British Library)

'Porro Unum Est Necessarium', caricature by Max Beerbohm (by kind permission of Mrs Eva Reichmann)

'Supporters' Rampant, cartoon by Bernard Partridge, *Punch* 29 December 1909

The Treasury Bench, 1911 by Max Beerbohm (By kind permission of Mrs Eva Reichmann)

Mr Asquith in office, by Max Beerbohm (By kind permission of Mrs Eva Reichmann)

Under his Master's eye, cartoon from *Punch*, 21 May 1913

Asquith by F. Carruthers Gould (National Portrait Gallery, London)

An Asquith to the Rescue! Cartoon by Bernard Partridge, *Punch*, 9 April 1914

Asquith by A. Cluysenaar, 1919 (National Portrait Gallery, London)

Lord Oxford by David Low (cartoon reproduced by permission of *The Standard*)

# INTRODUCTION

How can one justify yet another appraisal of the public life of H. H. Asquith, whose memory – for better or worse – has suffered no neglect? The author of two weighty twin-volume sets of reminiscences, which he unconvincingly disclaimed as autobiography, Asquith has been the subject of periodic biographical reassessments. Of these the most significant are an authorized *Life* by J. A. Spender and Cyril Asquith (2 volumes, 1932), an unjustly forgotten portrait by R. B. McCallum (1936), and, most recently, an elegant and eulogistic study by Roy Jenkins (1964). Why another?

With varying degrees of formality, each of the previous biographies was written under the aegis of the Asquith family, who made available unpublished material to which they held copyright and who thereby and otherwise exercised a measure of editorial control. While not without certain obvious benefits, this arrangement tended to work to the mutual disadvantage of author and subject: questions were left unanswered, and the impression was created, perhaps unfairly, that punches were being pulled. Then, too, each of these works was inspired, at least in part, by a devotion to the political tradition (if not necessarily to the party) with which Asquith was identified. Consequently, these biographers were further inhibited in their critical judgements and disappointingly reticent in their respective approaches to controversial issues. 'It is not the function of a biography to be a magnified epitaph or an expanded tract', Asquith declared in 1901 in a lecture to the Edinburgh Philosophical Institution. Yet, curiously enough, that is the sort of biographical treatment he himself has hitherto received.

In his later years, Asquith – or the Earl of Oxford and Asquith, as he was dignified in 1925 – was already a cult figure, adulated as 'the last of the Romans', and favourably contrasted with the 'hard-faced men' who had conspired to depose him from the premiership, to exclude him from Parliament, and to deny him his rightful influence in national and world affairs. Idealistic young intellectuals and disillusioned veterans, equally appalled by the moral bankruptcy of the Lloyd George ascendancy, clustered around Asquith's pedestal and pressed his claims with the nostalgic fervency of latter-day Jacobites. Unable to restore him to power, they nevertheless succeeded in fostering an image of him which has only lately come into open dispute.

Celebrated as a martyr to the forsaken cause of principle in politics, Asquith commanded sympathy and respect as the repository of prewar virtues and, still more vaguely, as the embodiment of a 'serene dignity', as it was admiringly described by Harold Nicolson. For many, Asquithianism was more a sentimental attachment than a reasoned commitment to any programme or electoral strategy: Nicolson, for example, professed a disbelief in Free Trade, yet confided to his sons that 'by nature' he was 'an Asquithian Liberal'. These enthusiasts (some of whom, ironically, had been among Asquith's most vigorous critics during earlier decades) accepted and propounded a view of their hero which they then proceeded to project backwards over the whole of his long career. To Lord Haldane, whose friendship Asquith acknowledged as 'one of the most intimate and valuable . . . of my life', it was no less amazing than amusing to observe the way that the residents of The Wharf, the Asquiths' retreat on the upper Thames, had been transmogrified into the 'Holy Family'.

After his death in 1928, Asquith was – more than ever – venerated for his 'classical' qualities. His daughter, Lady Violet Bonham Carter (after 1964 Lady Asquith of Yarnbury), was the zealous and often obsessive guardian of her father's reputation. She brooked no criticism of him and replied with stinging rhetoric to anyone who dared to defame his memory as she upheld it. Unwilling and perhaps unable to entertain the possibility of any incapacity or moral failing on his part, she worshipped him and expected posterity to do like-wise. Not surprisingly, her defensiveness gave rise to suspicions that Asquith was no more than a plaster saint, and there came an inevit-able reaction against the hagiographical interpretation which she so strenuously attempted to impose. Even before she died in 1969, a new orthodoxy had begun to challenge the old. Since that time, there has been an outpouring of books, informed by new evidence and encouraged by a new frankness in scholarly writing, in which Asquith has been variously depicted as an incorrigible opportunist, a dotard, a pantaloon, and a drunk. The present work is an attempt to steady the pendulum which, too long held in check, has rebounded with a vengeance.

It is argued here that Asquith's memory is better served by a dis-interested investigation of the facts of his career than by the recita-tion of outworn myths. For this reason, it has been deemed necessary to confront situations and allegations which previous biographers felt obliged either to ignore or, at best, to treat allusively. This can-dour, which need not work to Asquith's detriment, is made manda-tory by the recent opening of archives which neither Mr Jenkins nor any of his predecessors was able to consult. Like their accounts, this study has made extensive use of the Asquith Papers, now on deposit at the Bodleian Library, Oxford. It was also possible, with the permis-sion of Mark Bonham Carter and the co-operation of Michael Brock, to make reference to Asquith's correspondence with Miss Venetia Stanley (later Mrs Edwin Montagu), which Michael and Eleanor Brock had then begun to edit for eventual publication. In addition, a special effort has been made to incorporate material from the private papers of Asquith's principal colleagues and antagonists and from the biog-raphies and monographs that have appeared in such profusion over the last few years. Particular attention will be paid to those episodes or aspects of Asquith's career on which new information has come to light. It is hoped that this revisionist approach will result in a more balanced view of Asquith's aims and achievements, an illumination of the context in which he operated, and, not least, a political biography that carries greater conviction to a more critical generation of readers.

In the Bibliographical Notes that conclude this volume, grateful acknowledgement is made to the individuals and institutions who allowed me access to manuscript materials in their keeping. Those who gave me permission to quote documents to which they hold copyright have received my private thanks.

Many librarians and archivists have facilitated my research; to discriminate among them would be invidious, if not impossible. Various scholars provided information and suggestions: in addition to Mr Brock, they include W. J. Reader, H. R. Tinker, and Chris Cook, an exemplary editor. Lady Elliot of Harwood helped to clarify intricate family relationships. Jill Craigie afforded me a preview of her dedicated labours on the women's suffrage movement. Keith Devlin gave genial advice on matters of jurisprudence and terminology.

Peter Stansky and P. F. Clarke each read and rigorously criticized the greater part of this manuscript in draft. Portions were also scrutinized by Bentley B. Gilbert, A. M. Gollin, Melvin Richter, and A. J. P. Taylor. Mark Bonham Carter perused the whole and tellingly disputed various points of interpretation. Needless to say, the responsibility is mine for any errors of fact or judgement that survive.

I had the benefit of many spirited conversations with the late Ivan Yates, whose premature death robbed me of a valued friend and a trusted counsellor.

As always, my wife contributed her unstinting encouragement and expertise.

Finally, it is my privilege to record a debt of gratitude to the director and staff of the Netherlands Institute for Advanced Study, whose generous support and gracious hospitality are deeply appreciated.

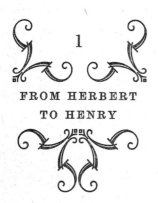

# 1

## FROM HERBERT
## TO HENRY

All public lives are edifices, custom-designed and tenanted by a private personality. Some are more elaborate than others, reflecting the tastes, the resources, and sometimes the imagination of the particular individual who dwells within. Some are built on a solid foundation of social antecedents, while others – no less durable – hang suspended, as if by cantilever, above ground. A few examples will testify to the distinction: in modern British politics, the careers of W. E. Gladstone, David Lloyd George, and Winston Churchill figure prominently among those in which class origin and/or family tradition exercised a dominant influence; by contrast, that of Benjamin Disraeli offers perhaps the most notable case in which the factors of birth and background were disregarded, indeed even defied. Whereas Gladstone or Lloyd George or Churchill may each be convincingly portrayed as the product of his respective circumstances, Disraeli seemingly willed himself into existence: it was by adoption and not by inheritance that he derived not only his principles but, more conspicuously, his political style.

The career of Herbert Henry Asquith belongs, on balance, to the second category. With far less affectation than Disraeli, but with no less ingenuity, he successfully cast himself in his own image. His modest upbringing, while never repudiated, was effectively transcended, especially after his second marriage in 1894. Born and cradled in an atmosphere of northern Congregationalism, he quickly outgrew the Puritan ethic and theology of his forebears. With no apparent difficulty, he eventually took communion with the Established Church. In time, with equal ease, he obtained admission to the *salons* and country houses of the high born and the well bred. Although it is technically correct to designate him as the first 'middle-class' Prime Minister, he did not conceive of himself in that light and would have keenly resented the epithet. Once he arrived, he had no reason to recollect his point of departure, which had proved more an irrelevance than a liability. In his *Memories and Reflections*, posthumously published in 1928 in two volumes, he devoted a mere five pages to his ancestral background and 'early years'. The story is told that his daughter Violet, campaigning as a Liberal candidate at Colne Valley in 1951, neither welcomed nor reciprocated the embrace of her long-lost Yorkshire cousins, who reminded her of the Nonconformist stock from which she was recently descended.

It can be argued that Asquith, who came to lead a party in which Nonconformity was one of the main components, lost something by cutting himself off from his roots. From all indications, however, those roots had never run very deep. Certain influences were inescapable, but these tended to be of a negative quality. The deprivations of his boyhood left him with a thirst for luxury, a weakened ability to resist temptation, and a financial recklessness that, fortunately, did not carry over into his policies as Chancellor of the Exchequer. Orphaned at the age of eight, and thereafter shuttled between the homes of relatives and strangers, he was forced to develop habits of self-reliance and self-assertion. Later, he acquired a reputation as the servant of a vaulting ambition. It was neither undeserved nor the least surprising. Without a supreme belief in his innate ability, what hope would he have had for storming the citadels of late-Victorian Oxford and Westminster?

Because Asquith's early development did not contribute materially to his mature outlook, it does not warrant a detailed investigation in these pages. The little that is known about his family and youth has been told and repeated elsewhere. Admittedly interesting for the more general purposes of a full-scale biography, these fragments are largely irrelevant to the more specific purposes of a political biography.

To his credit, Asquith was inclined to treat with mild scepticism the legend (which his official biographers reported as established fact) that he was the direct descendant of seventeenth-century Cromwellians, perhaps even sixteenth-century mayors of York. His surname was common enough in the West Riding of Yorkshire, where he was born on 12 September 1852. Leaving aside more remote branches on his family tree, Asquith was able to describe his father only by recourse to 'local and family tradition'. Joseph Dixon Asquith, who made his living from the omnipresent woollen mills at Morley, died suddenly in his thirty-fifth year, leaving a widow, two sons (Herbert being the younger), and two daughters. Asquith's mother, of whom he retained fond and vivid impressions, was a chronic invalid who, from the sofa on which she lay, inculcated a love of books and a respect for learning. Like her husband, she was an ardent Congregationalist: their social life had revolved around the Rehoboth Chapel in Morley. Yet, typical of many Nonconformists during this period, her Puritanism grew more relaxed, if only to the extent that she guiltily allowed her son to teach her to play whist after taking the moral precaution of substituting chessmen for cards. Asquith's own conscience, already more sophisticated, required no such deception. For him, coming as he did from so strict a home, card-playing and theatre-going were to hold an irresistible attraction.

His mother's family, who assumed responsibility for him and his siblings when Joseph Asquith died, were relatively affluent. Asquith's maternal grandfather, William Willans, was a woolstapler at Huddersfield, where he was an active participant in civic affairs. An ally of Cobden and Bright in the Anti-Corn Law crusade of the Forties, he had stood for election to Parliament in 1851 and, as his grandson oddly put it, 'narrowly escaped being returned'. Willans, for whom Nonconformity and Radical politics were mutually supportive, belonged to what one historian has described as 'an urban governing class which, through intermarriage and business and political associations, had national ramifications'. His eldest son, for example, was married to the daughter of Edward Baines, M.P. for Leeds (1859–74) and a strict Congregationalist and teetotaller whose family owned the *Leeds Mercury*. Its self-righteousness confirmed by material success, this was a tightly knit society, but one whose ties were already beginning to loosen.

At their grandfather's expense, Asquith and his brother were enrolled as day-scholars at Huddersfield College. Then, for reasons which are not clear, they were transferred to a Moravian boarding school in a suburb of Leeds; the Baines connection may have had something to do with it. The next disruption occurred soon afterwards in 1863, when William Willans died. Emily Asquith, following her doctor's standard prescription, moved south to St Leonards on the Sussex coast. Her daughters accompanied her; but her sons, whose education had to be considered, were entrusted to the care of her eldest brother, John. Conveniently domiciled in London and without children of his own, he received his nephews into his home and generously paid their fees at the City of London School, which they entered as day-scholars in 1864. But the happy arrangement was short-lived. Within the year, John Willans returned to the north, and the Asquith brothers were boarded out first to a family in Pimlico and then to another in Islington.

Huddled into premises in Milk Street, off Cheapside, the City of London School had little to offer in the way of tradition or facilities. Yet it boasted some admirable teachers, whose dedication partly compensated for the grievously overcrowded conditions. With a total enrolment of approximately 650, the school had a Dickensian appearance that was mirrored in its curriculum. Commercial subjects were emphasized, and it was only through the intervention of Edwin Abbott, the new headmaster, that Asquith was spared the fate of penmanship and book-keeping in the fifth form. He received a similar dispensation from mathematics in the sixth. With Dr Abbott's invaluable encouragement, which did not go unacknowledged in later years, Asquith instead applied himself to the study of English and the Classics, the only subjects (according to the recollection of one of his classmates) in which he showed interest. He had little time and even less inclination for games, and spent his leisure hours browsing at the nearby Guildhall Library, listening to the proceedings at the Courts of Law, and comparing the pulpit performances of the leading metropolitan divines. He joined the throng at the Crystal Palace to welcome Garibaldi, and there were occasional outings with Uncle John to the gallery of the House of Commons, where, at the tender age of twelve, Asquith learned to differentiate between 'a true Liberal' (i.e. a Gladstonian) and one like Robert Lowe, who resolutely opposed Baines's 1865 Bill for the extension of the borough franchise. Almost intuitive in his grasp of the forms of parliamentary debate, if not yet the content, he was well equipped to participate in the school debating society; a mature seventeen, he carried off the prize for an unusually precocious memorial to John Carpenter, whose ancient bequest had been used to endow the institution. To quote his official biographers, 'the distinctive qualities of his oratory in manhood and middle life seem to have been present not merely in their germ, but almost in their maturity in his debating débuts at the City of London School and the Oxford Union'.

So, too, was the appearance of intellectual effortlessness, sometimes tantamount to arrogance. He did not suffer fools gladly, if at all, and the academic subjects that did not engage his attention – German, for example – were dismissed as second-rate. He 'perused' his sister's 'interesting scrawl' with the same condescension (his official biographers label it 'humorous objurgation') with which he later noted the mis-spellings and errors of syntax in his colleagues' Cabinet memoranda. Without taxing himself unduly, he was made captain of the school, and became the first boy in its relatively brief history to win the 'blue ribbon' of a classical scholarship to Balliol College, Oxford, where he began his undergraduate studies in October 1870. A few weeks earlier, Napoleon III had surrendered to the Prussian commander at Sédan. Had Asquith perhaps been too hasty in his dismissal of German culture?

His arrival at Balliol was also coincident with the election of Benjamin Jowett as master of the college. 'The greatest of Oxford tutors', as Asquith paid tribute to him many years later, Jowett had passed the period of his greatest influence and accessibility, leaving Asquith to regret that he had come too late to avail himself of 'the privilege, such as St Paul enjoyed, of sitting at the feet of Gamaliel'. It is interesting to note that, in private conversation and correspondence, Asquith was a good deal less reverential. His comment that Jowett's talk 'had more bouquet than body' scandalized St John Brodrick (later the Earl of Midleton), who nevertheless had to admit that Jowett's 'summary judgements' were often wide of the mark. 'In my own time', Asquith wrote candidly to Lady Horner in 1891, Jowett 'was already looked upon, by the more advanced spirits, as an extinct volcano, and even a bit of a reactionary.'

Although his personal contacts with the master were only occasional and never intimate, Asquith was susceptible to his ethic, which reinforced his own predilection. The emphasis was on excellence and individualism. Of Jowett it has been written that 'Ineffectiveness was for him no mark of spiritual distinction.' His Balliol was infused with a spirit of 'resolute modernity', and, according to Jenkins, 'its intellectual climate was eclectic, humanist, and a little worldly'. Asquith was in his element.

The senior common room at Balliol was well stocked with eminent scholars and commanding personalities, among them T. H. Green, whose 'spiritual philosophy' and spellbinding pedagogy inspired fierce loyalty in his students and distrust on the part of Jowett. His strong commitment to Liberal politics, no less offensive to the master, served to endear him to Asquith, with whom he further shared a taste for theological disputation coupled with a resistance to religious orthodoxy. Yet Asquith, while acknowledging a debt to 'Green's gymnastics, both intellectual and moral', did not count himself among the disciples who 'worshipped at the Temple's inner shrine'. He took a detached view of all philosophic systems, including those to which he was attracted, and, from the beginning, gave no mentor his unqualified support.

The antagonism between Jowett and Green generated a tension that electrified the atmosphere at Balliol and stimulated those who passed through its cloisters. In retrospect, Asquith was able to reconcile, even to synthesize, their rival influences: when he became Prime Minister, he expressed sorrow 'that Jowett and Green had not lived to see their belief in him justified'. His ability to merge the two men can be taken to suggest that neither had touched him very deeply. One cannot imagine him saying, as did the fifth Marquess of Lansdowne, that 'had it not been for [Jowett], I would have done little with my life'.

'Does it matter to anyone who is Master of Balliol?' Arthur Balfour asked with characteristic cynicism when a successor to Jowett was being considered. Balfour, a bachelor who was educated at Trinity College, Cambridge, amused himself almost as much by belittling Oxford as by pitying his married friends. Brodrick, a loyal son of Balliol, offered a wager of £50 that Balfour could not name four men educated at Cambridge in the years between 1870 and 1880 who qualified as the equals of those whom Balliol had produced during the same decade. To prove his point, he rattled off the names of Asquith, Alfred Milner, George Curzon, and Edward Grey. Balfour, always gracious in the face of defeat, declined the bet.

Was there ever a constellation that shone more brilliantly? Curzon and Grey came to Balliol shortly after Asquith's time, just as Lansdowne had preceded him. But Milner was his contemporary and a close associate. Other friends within the college community included Herbert Warren, the future president of Magdalen, Andrew Bradley, who was to attain eminence as a Shakespeare scholar, and Charles Gore, the progressive and (perhaps for that reason) controversial High Churchman. W. H. Mallock, who made a name as an anti-socialist publicist, Arnold Toynbee, the social philosopher who inclined in the opposite direction, and A. R. Cluer, the distinguished jurist, also belonged to Asquith's circle of Balliol acquaintances. Herbert Paul, eventually to become an acerbic journalist and a Liberal backbencher in the 1906 Parliament, was an interloper from Corpus. Asquith's older brother, whose studies had been interrupted by poor health, followed him to Balliol. For the sake of economy, they shared a single set of rooms.

The distinction Asquith attained and, still more, the 'assured serenity' with which he attained it make one forget the difficulties which he faced and overcame. Milner, another avowed 'scholarship hunter' who possessed neither wealth nor social credentials, achieved scholarly eminence; but, as his biographer pointedly reminds us, it 'drew tremendously on his reserves of vitality and nervous energy' to the point of endangering his health. Asquith's 'academic successes', as described by Jenkins, were by contrast 'achieved on the basis of a moderate and controlled amount of work', leaving him ample time for other pursuits. As early as the first month of his first term, his voice was heard in the Union debates. Elected treasurer in 1872, he was defeated in his first bid for the presidency and had to wait until his final term to capture that prize. There was time for rowing and for 'the unknown and outlandish game of golf' (as he facetiously called it), which became something of an addiction. Studying for 'Greats', he put aside his books to speak at Woodstock for Brodrick, who was bravely standing against Lord Randolph Churchill. It was the least that one Balliol man could do for another.

These extra-curricular activities, although time-consuming, do not appear to have detracted significantly from his scholarly performance. His official biographers, both Balliol men of later vintage, proudly enumerate that he attained 'easy first classes in "Mods" and "Greats", the Craven Scholarship, and a Prize Fellowship at his own College. The chapter of accidents denied to him both the classical University Scholarships', they quaintly relate, 'but the margin by which he missed them was so narrow as to be quite unimportant.' In 1872, he was *proxime* for the Hertford Scholarship; in 1873 and again in 1874, he was *proxime* for the coveted Ireland, which, a generation later, was awarded to his oldest son, Raymond. Jenkins, yet another biographer who has imbibed the rarefied air of Balliol, has concluded that Asquith's record was 'striking without being sensational'. His judgement, which itself smacks of Balliolity, neglects to take into account the background from which Asquith had emerged. A 'striking' success for an Etonian perhaps, it was nothing less than a 'sensational' one for a day-boy from the City of London School who had passed his early years in the shadow of the mill and the chapel.

'Life', Herbert Samuel declared aphoristically, 'is one Balliol man after another.' And so it must have seemed to him, a graduate of the same college and later an honorary fellow. During the last hundred years, other Oxford and Cambridge colleges have sometimes rivalled Balliol in the competition for first-class degrees, but never in the sweepstakes for worldly success. Certainly none has established a comparable aura. 'Balliol men are marked not only by their achievements', Anthony Sampson has observed, 'but by their awareness of Balliol, which (like Winchester) gives the impression of being more a cult than a college.' The Balliol Mind, although obviously an abstraction, has been regarded by those who either admire or reject it as an immutable phenomenon: public-spirited, but somewhat aloof; cultivated, but not necessarily cultured; earnest, but never strenuous in its exertions; and methodical, but often tinged with an unfeeling sterility. Asquith, if only by virtue of his pre-eminence, later came to be regarded as its embodiment. 'He creates confidence and carries conviction', A. G. Gardiner knowingly wrote in the *Daily News* on 29 February 1908, when Asquith's ascent to the premiership was imminent,

but he does not inspire men with great passions . . . Mr Asquith does not utter great thoughts. No Balliol man of the Jowett tradition does. The Balliol mind distrusts 'great thoughts' even if it thinks them . . . Balliol, in fact, is really atrophy of the heart. It is exhaustion of the emotions. It has produced the finest mental machines of this generation, but they are sometimes cold and cheerless . . . We admire them, we respect them: we do not love them, for we feel that they would be insulted by the offer of so irrational a thing as love.

It was not simply that Asquith ran true to stereotype; in large measure, he was responsible for creating it. He exuded an air of superiority, and, in time, fell victim to an overweening self-confidence.

There was a brief but significant hiatus between the time that he took his degree and his tenure as a fellow. At Jowett's nomination, he served as tutor to Lord Lymington, heir to the earldom of Portsmouth, when the youth was en route from Eton to Balliol. For three months, he lived with the Portsmouth family on their estates in Hampshire and North Devon. 'I thus obtained a glimpse of a kind of life which was new to me', he ingenuously recorded, and, needless to say, he did not find it the least unappealing. The Earl, 'a considerable landowner', abstained from direct political involvement, but nursed the sentiments of 'a strong Liberal'. His brother-in-law, Lord Carnarvon, was a frequent visitor that summer, and a source of malicious anecdotes about Disraeli, from whose second government he had recently resigned. Another notable guest was Richard Monckton Milnes, Lord Houghton, 'a fertile and picturesque *raconteur*' and the father of the future Lord Crewe, one of Asquith's most trusted Cabinet colleagues.

Like Disraeli before him and Ramsay MacDonald (among others) after, Asquith was strongly attracted to the comforts and graces of country-house society. Intellect was his ticket of admission, and not one to be despised; but it could take him only so far: to a chair at the foot of the dining table, but never at its head. Despite the kindnesses he received, he could not mistake the fact that he was being patronized. Having supped from Lord Portsmouth's silver spoon, he was shaken in his ambition to pursue an academic career, which, whatever its rewards, would exclude him from the circles of affluence and influence in which he aspired to move. To Jowett, for whom donnishness was next to godliness, wealth offered only the temptation to dissipate one's talents. To Asquith, however, material success promised a means to obtain security and status. A late-Victorian Julien Sorel, he had limited choices. In June 1875, after six months in residence at Balliol, he quit Oxford and moved to London. Twenty-four years old, he became a student at Lincoln's Inn and began the long and arduous preparation to practise at the bar.

'A penniless barrister' (as his official biographers have described him), Asquith could always bank upon his Balliol connections. He was taken on as a pupil by Charles Bowen, the future Lord Justice, who had been a scholar and fellow of Balliol as well as president of the Union. His penury, which may have been exaggerated, did not prevent him from settling into rooms at a fashionable address in Mayfair; nor did it deter him from marrying when he was only twenty-five and virtually without a practice. It has been further noted that 'most of the five children of his first marriage were born before his means had materially increased'. There was a tinge of Disraelian audacity in his make-up: 'a surprising but strong streak of recklessness', as Jenkins has alliterated it. It manifested itself in a level of expenditure which, at the best of times, he could not quite afford. Yet, having learned to live with financial anxiety, he refused to allow it to cramp his style. In the early 1880s, for example, he lavished £300 of scarce savings on a diamond necklace for his wife, whose modest tastes and retiring nature do not suggest that she encouraged the gift.

He remained as a pupil in Bowen's chambers in Brick Court for about a year, until his call to the bar in June 1876. Looking back, he admired Bowen's 'unerring knowledge of law', but took him to task for an inability to 'avail himself adequately of other people's labours . . . To know what you must do yourself, and what you can let others do for you, is one of the secrets of efficiency', Asquith asserted, 'and it was a secret which Bowen never succeeded in mastering.' This criticism is especially interesting in the light of charges subsequently levelled at Asquith that he left too much in the hands of his subordinates, over whom he failed to exercise effective control.

From Brick Court, Asquith moved to chambers which he shared with two other struggling barristers at 6 Fig Tree Court. There followed, his official biographers tell us, 'six or seven of the most disheartening years of his life', when briefs were few and far between, and when the gamble seemed unlikely to pay off. Fortunately, his Balliol fellowship continued until 1881, and helped him to make ends meet. All the same, this modest sum was hardly sufficient for the obligation which he assumed in 1877.

In 1870, he had met Helen Melland, the daughter of a Manchester physician, who came to spend her holidays with cousins at St Leonards. He was then eighteen, and she fifteen. Four years later, they were secretly engaged. No sooner had he been called to the bar than Asquith sought to formalize the relationship. He pleaded his case before his prospective father-in-law, who waived his initial objections after 'certain enquiries' had afforded him 'the fullest conviction that your industry and ability will procure for you in due time that success in your profession which has attended you in your past career'. Dr Melland, who lived to the ripe age of ninety-eight, saw his belief in Asquith more than justified. His daughter, who died in 1891 in her fourteenth year of marriage, did not live to see her husband attain Cabinet rank.

The wedding took place in August 1877. With her own income of a few hundred pounds a year, Helen Asquith paid her own way, and neither relieved nor increased her husband's financial burdens. He earned a livelihood by examining for the Oxford and Cambridge Board at various public schools, by lecturing for the Law Society and on the staff of the newly formed Society for the Extension of University Teaching, and by contributing articles to the *Spectator* and the *Economist*. His legal career did not catch fire until 1883, when R. S.

Wright (another Balliol man) succeeded Bowen as Junior Counsel to the Treasury and invited Asquith to 'devil' for him. 'Until then', Jenkins has written, 'he was short of money, under-employed, and full of surplus intellectual energy'.

Even so, the young couple were able to afford a large house in Hampstead, across from where Keats had lived. The attractions of the West End were not beyond his reach either geographically or economically, and there was room alike in the house and the budget for friends to come to stay. Another expense was foreign travel: with his wife, Asquith made visits to Germany and Switzerland; accompanied by old Oxford friends (including Milner), by R. B. Haldane, or by Mark Napier, with whom he shared chambers in Fig Tree Court, he crossed the Alps to Italy and the south of France. According to the official biography, 'the extreme simplicity of the Asquiths' manner of life' made possible these occasional indulgences. Nevertheless, the impression persists that Asquith, although doubtless frustrated by this prolonged period 'of knocking at closed doors', did not forgo any of the usual comforts or recreations.

Nor did his straitened circumstances, such as they were, dictate that he and his young wife should defer or limit their family. Raymond was born in 1878, and he was followed by Herbert ('Beb') in 1881, Arthur ('Oc') in 1883, Helen Violet (better-known as Violet and best-known as Lady Violet Bonham Carter) in 1887, and, lastly, Cyril ('Cis') in 1890. They were, 'without exception, a constant and unfailing source of pride and happiness' to their father. At the time of their mother's premature death, Raymond was twelve and Cyril eighteen months.

Not yet a successful barrister, Asquith had begun to entertain political ambitions and, for this purpose, to establish contacts. His rise to prominence was facilitated by his apprenticeship to Wright, who, at a more exalted level, served the Attorney-General in much the same capacity as Asquith served him. Thus, at second hand, Asquith was the assistant to Sir Henry James (later Lord James of Hereford), a law officer of eminent reputation whose political advancement was continually checked by his Whiggish tendency to put the dictates of conscience above those of party. In 1883, Asquith prepared for James a detailed memorandum on the theory and practice of the Parliamentary Oath, which was the focus of an interminable and debilitating dispute involving Charles Bradlaugh, the 'Radical atheist' M.P. for Northampton. Asquith's manuscript was forwarded to Gladstone, the Prime Minister, who warmly commended the effort although it failed to provide the basis for any legislative solution. 'From that time onwards', Asquith recalled, 'I was a frequent visitor and worker at the Attorney-General's room in the Law Courts.' He helped to draft the Corrupt Practices Act of 1883, and afterwards, at James's suggestion, he wrote a guide to its provisions which was published by the Liberal Central Association and distributed among election agents.

To an even greater extent, his interest in Liberal politics was stimulated by his friendship, which dated from 1881, with Haldane, a portly Scotsman four years his junior. Educated at German universities, Haldane had come to London to practise law at about the same time as Asquith, and with equally discouraging initial results. They dined together regularly at Lincoln's Inn, offering each other pointers and commiseration. Lady Violet Bonham Carter, writing in *The Times* on 30 July 1956 to commemorate the centenary of Haldane's birth, recalled an occasion from her early girlhood when Haldane, who had got a brief at last, journeyed to Hampstead and consulted until the early hours of the morning with her father, who had not been similarly blessed for months.

As this incident would suggest, Haldane was the first to see his way to professional success. He was also the first to win a seat in the House of Commons. In December 1885 he was elected for East Lothian (or the Haddington Division), where his family owned a comparatively small estate, but exercised a considerable influence. Six months later, the Liberal Party split over Gladstone's Home Rule Bill, and Parliament was dissolved. Haldane, defending his seat, persuaded Asquith to stand at neighbouring East Fife, where the sitting Liberal member had been repudiated by the local association for his refusal to follow Gladstone's leadership. The contest was a close one, with Conservative electors throwing their weight behind the renegade Liberal in an effort to discredit Gladstone's Irish policy. Asquith, who proclaimed himself an 'uncompromising' defender of that policy, was adopted less than a fortnight before polling. An unknown quantity, he suffered the further disadvantage of being an unknown *English* quantity. Under the circumstances, he was extremely lucky to garner a majority of 375 votes.

Disbelieving his own youthful presumption, Asquith is later reported to have jested 'that most of the rash decisions he had taken in the course of his life had been due to the malign influence of his friend Haldane'. But the latter, in his *Autobiography*, made it clear that Asquith's arm did not require too much twisting: 'From the beginning he meant to be Prime Minister, sooner or later.' And, on balance, Haldane thought him admirably equipped for the position.

Well aware of his own deficiencies, which included a reedy voice and a penchant for abstruse oratory, Haldane was an intensely political animal, but one with a difference. As Beatrice Webb staunchly defended him, 'his intrigues are always to promote a cause, never to push himself'. As a strategist, he was supremely useful to Asquith, whom he assisted not only in finding a seat, but also in giving valuable counsel and encouragement. He served much the same function in the case of Sir Edward Grey, who was elected in 1885 for Berwick-upon-Tweed. 'If it were not for you, I do not think I should have even the hold on public life which I have now', Grey wrote to him in 1890. 'I should say . . . that Asquith owed some of the very best in himself to you.'

The triumvirate of Asquith, Haldane, and Grey was formed early in the lifetime of the 1886 Parliament, and it survived, more in shadow than in substance, into the period of the First World War. Ten years younger than Asquith, Grey had come up to Balliol too late to meet him there, and just as well: his lacklustre academic performance and reputation for idleness could have been guaranteed to evoke Asquith's disdain. In 1884, Grey was ignominiously sent down from Oxford; eighteen months later, he entered the Commons as its youngest member. The inheritor of his grandfather's baronetcy, which went with a 2,000-acre estate in Northumberland, he was spared the financial worries that plagued Haldane and especially Asquith, but he possessed neither their self-discipline nor their consuming interest in party politics.

It was through Haldane that Grey came to know Asquith, whose maiden speech on 24 March 1887 impressed him as 'about the best 35 minutes I've ever heard, well delivered and fresh and strong to a degree'. In other respects, too, Haldane was the link between them. A bachelor who dined out most evenings, he got on well with both his friends' wives, who were altogether unlike each other. With Asquith, to whom he was closer in age, he shared a dedication to the subtleties of jurisprudence. With Grey, he shared a love for the countryside of Northumberland, where he had roots through his mother's family. As Keith Robbins has pointed out in his recent life of Grey, it was 'hardly surprising that no social friendship with Asquith developed', given the differences between them in age and interests.

In temperament and political style, all three men were conspicuously dissimilar. Asquith was a Radical by descent, if not quite by instinct, Grey was the product of a Whig tradition, and Haldane kept close ties among the Fabian socialists. Asquith, no sportsman ('I don't run much,' he protested, as his second wife hurried him to catch a train), relaxed upon the golf links, Grey knee-deep in a trout stream, and Haldane on marathon hikes through Perthshire. Haldane had a passion for Wagnerian opera, Asquith preferred Gilbert and Sullivan, and Grey's ear was finely attuned to Northumberland bird-song. At Westminster, Asquith had a reputation for diligence, Haldane for indefatigability, and Grey for indolence. The party chiefs knew they could count on Asquith, but they regarded Haldane as something of a troublemaker, and Grey as unreliable. 'A great Member of Parliament', Gladstone once said of Grey, 'but then, no one knows when he will not be going fishing.'

This triangular relationship, more isosceles than equilateral, transcended the usual political alliance. It was a source of strength to each of them in times of emotional need. In 1890, Haldane came to Asquith distraught and shaken when, after five weeks, his fiancée had terminated their engagement. He spent an extended period of convalescence in Hampstead, where the Asquith children took delight in his company and roly-poly figure. G. M. Trevelyan, Grey's earlier biographer, has testified that 'it would be difficult to overestimate what Haldane did for Grey' when the latter's wife died early in 1906. Grey, newly appointed to the Foreign Office, came to live for a time at Whitehall Court with his bachelor friend, and he returned to Haldane's new address at Queen Anne's Gate for periodic visits until he remarried in 1922. For his part, Asquith required no comparable consolation when his first wife died suddenly of typhoid during a summer holiday on the Isle of Arran. He did, however, unburden his soul in a letter which Haldane treasured.

A premier-in-the-making, Asquith was, by then, already caught up in his own ambitions, social as well as political. In 1894, he married the irrepressible Margot Tennant, horsewoman and socialite, whom he had met years earlier at a dinner at the House of Commons ('I had never heard of him before', Margot later confessed, 'which gives some indication of how much I was wasting my time') and whom he had frequently encountered in his unaccompanied excursions into high society. She deduced 'from something he said . . . that he was married and lived at Hampstead', and properly arranged for him to bring his wife to dinner. 'I do hope, Mrs Asquith', she greeted her predecessor, 'you have not minded your husband dining here without you, but I rather gathered Hampstead was too far away for him to get back to you from the House of Commons. You must always let me know and come with him whenever it suits you.' Helen Asquith rose to the occasion. She forthrightly informed her hostess that 'she did not think that she would ever care for the sort of society that I loved, and was happier in the circle of her home and family'. In reply to assurances 'that she had married a man who was certain to attain the highest political distinction', Helen declared 'that that was not what she coveted for him'. Poor Margot was left wondering whether 'my ambition for the success of her husband, and other men, was wrong'. In her celebrated *Autobiography*, she professed unbounded admiration for the first Mrs Asquith: 'a wonderful mother and a devoted wife, always a rare combination'. Her private verdict was more severe and, unfortunately, more characteristic: Helen, she declaimed, was 'no wife for him. She lives in Hampstead, and has no clothes.'

As usual, Margot wildly overstated her case, but her impressions were not wholly without substance. Asquith had fallen in love with Helen Melland when he was eighteen, and had married when he was twenty-five. His wife belonged happily to a world that no longer suited his tastes or accommodated his ambition. 'She was always perfect, loyal, sympathetic, devoted', he wrote on the first anniversary of her death to Frances Horner, one of the first of his many confidantes and eventually mother-in-law to his eldest son; but, he complained, she was 'not the least anxious for me to "get on"', never sanguine or confident, and as a rule inclining to take a less hopeful view of things'. Indeed, he went so far as to suggest that, had she lived, he would have been unlikely to accept Gladstone's offer of the Home Secretaryship in the 1892 Liberal Government. A disturbing assertion, it has been charitably dismissed by Jenkins as 'permissibly exaggerated'. (A sentimentalist might regard such an exaggeration as completely impermissible.) At the time it was written, Asquith was feverishly courting Margot, and her extravagant views probably coloured his own.

In the late summer of 1892, Dorothy and Edward Grey paid a 'funny visit' to Cloan, Haldane's house in Perthshire, where Asquith and Miss Tennant were among the other guests. Lady Grey was embarrassed by the utter frankness of Margot's conversation. Asquith, she reported to Mrs Sydney Buxton, looked 'worried and sad, whether about Margot or the Home Office I don't know'. Haldane, too, noticed the change that had come over his friend. Although he was best man at Asquith's second wedding – a splendid affair held at St George's, Hanover Square – it is apparent that the two men had already begun to drift apart. Deeply devoted to the memory of the first Mrs Asquith, Haldane preferred to blame Margot for corrupting Asquith rather than to recognize how much Asquith yearned to be corrupted. 'London society came . . . to have a great attraction for him', he reminisced in his *Autobiography*, 'and he grew by degrees diverted from the sterner outlook on life which he and I long shared.' It is noteworthy that Haldane lifted this passage, word by word, from an autobiographical memorandum which he had written three years earlier, and from which he tactfully expunged the phrase 'particularly after his second marriage'. He might have reflected that, in their choice of wives no less than in their choice of political comrades, public men usually reveal some hidden aspect of their private characters.

Asquith's second marriage signalled a transformation in his attitudes and conduct; but it did not cause it. The old patterns of behaviour had been strained, if not yet broken, before Margot's advent. She brought him into the centre of a more glittering – some would say a more meretricious – social world, but its features were neither unknown nor unacceptable to him. She introduced him to the habit of after-dinner brandy (and came to regret it), but he already fancied himself a connoisseur of clarets and champagnes. She encouraged his tendency to live beyond his means, and gave him ample excuse for the frivolous expenditure of time as well as money. Far from resisting, there is every indication that he welcomed these temptations.

In Margot, Asquith acquired a spur to his ambition, but, at the same time, a distraction from official duties. Margot, in turn, acquired a husband who was a minister of the Crown, and a ready-made family of five young and gifted children who competed with her for his attention. 'You have a great and noble work to perform,' Gladstone told her. 'It is a work far beyond human strength. May the strength that is more than human be granted you.' She was more offended than inspired by his sanctimoniousness: 'Gladstone thinks my fitness to be Henry's wife should be prayed for like the clergy – Almighty and Everlasting God, who alone workest great marvels!'

But the Grand Old Man had taken the proper measure of Asquith's marital situation, just as he had been quick to appreciate and reward Asquith's parliamentary skills. He had known the bride, in fact, longer than she and the bridegroom had known each other: during his short-lived third premiership, he was invited to luncheon in Grosvenor Square at the house of her father, a Liberal Party stalwart, and afterwards he had allowed himself to be led upstairs to her room for a tête-à-tête. He was inspired – not by her personality, his daughter strenuously insisted, but by the challenge of the rhyme – to write four stanzas of doggerel that revolved around her name (e.g. 'Though young and though fair, who can hold such a cargo / Of all the good qualities going as Margot?'). This distinction notwithstanding, Margot was as much a creature as a leader of fashion, superabundantly vital, yet frequently irksome. Her candour easily gave way to rudeness, her wit to acidity, and her pride to haughtiness. On people, her judgements were most often acute; on events, they were almost invariably faulty. Those closest to her, including her husband, knew when to pay her heed and when to discount her categoric pronouncements. Those who knew her less well were alternately fascinated and appalled by her indiscretions.

Asquith was forty-two years old at the time of his marriage to Margot, and his evolution was now complete. Hampstead, like Yorkshire before it, receded irretrievably into the background; once he had left it, he did not look back. Christened 'Herbert Henry' and nicknamed 'Bertie' by his parents, he was addressed by his second wife as 'Henry', and it was from her that his intimate associates henceforth took their cue. 'Any reference to "Herbert" by the time of his premiership came as a faint echo from a distant past', Jenkins has tellingly observed. In this respect, Asquith resembled a host of Eminent Edwardians who sheltered publicly behind a pair of initials while they were known privately by their middle names. But neither in his case nor in most others was this peculiar practice without significance. 'H. H. Asquith', as he officially designated himself, was a composite of 'Herbert' and 'Henry', each of whom represented a rival set of attributes. By 1894, the former had been superseded – indeed, obliterated – by the latter. It is 'Henry' to whom we must now turn.

## 2

## FROM BACK BENCH
## TO
## FRONT BENCH

In the general election of 1886, Asquith was inauspiciously launched on his parliamentary career. Neither his slender majority at East Fife – which was reduced substantially when he next defended the seat in 'a hardish fight' six years later – nor the ramshackle condition of the Liberal Party could have inspired him with confidence. Yet he represented this Scottish constituency for thirty-two consecutive years, eight of them as Prime Minister. Who, at the time, could have predicted the triumphs that lay ahead?

Going against the national tide, which ran distinctly in an anti-Gladstonian direction, he secured his election in the aftermath of the

first Home Rule crisis. The previous Parliament, its lease on life
barely begun, came precipitously to an end in June, after Gladstone's
Irish Bill had been defeated in the Commons by a margin of thirty
votes: on that occasion, the parliamentary Liberal Party had
formally split, ninety-three of its members voting in the Opposition
lobby. Gladstone had weighed the alternatives. Well aware that 'a
dissolution is formidable', he had concluded that 'resignation would
mean for the present juncture abandonment of the cause', which was
unthinkable. He therefore decided to take his case to the electorate,
from whom he vainly expected an endorsement of his controversial
Irish formula.

The result was a Liberal rout. Gladstone neither received the
mandate for which he had hoped, nor did he shake more than a few
of the Liberal Unionists (as they now called themselves) out of their
resolve to spurn his leadership. Asquith, in his survey of *Fifty Years
of Parliament*, lent credence to the orthodox Gladstonian view that
'the Dissentient Liberal members . . . belonged, for the most part, to
the Right Wing of the party', and that their insurgency constituted
'what was to all intents and purposes a "Whig revolt"'. The situation, as others saw it more clearly at the time, was a good deal more
complicated. Liberal party organization in the constituencies had
fallen into disrepair, and the rank and file could not be roused to
support a policy that offended the anti-Papist sensibilities of the
Nonconformist communities, frightened the landholding classes, and
left many Radicals bitterly resentful. There was widespread abstention at the polls among traditionally Liberal voters, whose response to
Home Rule fluctuated between tempered indifference and acute
hostility. In the final reckoning, only 191 Gladstonian Liberals
successfully negotiated their passage to Westminster, where the
assurance of support from a phalanx of eighty-five Irish Nationalists
was insufficient to tilt the balance against a preponderance of 316
Conservative M.P.s. In addition, there were seventy-eight Liberal
Unionists who, on the crucial question of Ireland, could be expected
to side with the Conservative majority.

The Liberal Party had foundered – and, to all appearances,
irrevocably – on the rock of Gladstone's Irish policy, which he had
failed to explain to the satisfaction of his supporters either in Parliament or outside. It remains a moot point whether Joseph Chamberlain, whose defection from the Liberal camp had the most disruptive
effect, could have been conciliated: was the party's commitment to
Home Rule the cause or the pretext for his disaffection? When
Asquith took his seat in the House of Commons, Chamberlain's

apostasy had not yet come to be regarded as final, and feverish attempts were being made to bring him and his followers back into the fold. These negotiations continued, at one level or another, well into the next year, and it was against this background of shifting alignments – intra- as well as inter-party – that Asquith rose steadily to prominence.

Given the campaign he had waged at East Fife, his Gladstonian allegiance was never in dispute. Yet he retained close connections among the Unionist dissentients through Sir Henry James, who had once been his conduit to Gladstone and was now one of the leaders of the 'Whig revolt'. Parliament had no sooner convened in August than Asquith was brought into the thick of things by James, who invited him to dine at his house in Greenwich in a small party that included Chamberlain, Jesse Collings, Sir William Harcourt, and Henry Broadhurst. The event was ostensibly social, but the guest list indicated an effort at *rapprochement*. On the boat ride from Westminster and, better still, at his host's table, Asquith enjoyed a singular opportunity to acquaint himself with the personalities and issues that divided the Liberal Party. There were few novices who found themselves accepted so quickly, or indeed so effortlessly, by the men at the top. It is therefore not surprising that, as his official biographers have pointed out, 'from the start he assumed the manner of a front bencher and the House accepted him at his own valuation'.

Nine months passed before his maiden speech, a carefully worded indictment of Lord Salisbury's Government for its intention to deal with the 'manufactured crisis' in Ireland by means of coercion. The delay can be taken to imply that he was waiting to see how the political situation would crystallize; more probably, however, he was biding his time until he found the particular occasion that would exhibit his talents to best advantage. In either case, the strategy worked. On 24 March 1887, addressing the Commons for the first time, he professed himself 'a loyal member of my party and a faithful follower of my leader', whom he went out of his way to defend against Tory imputations of having been a coercionist in 1881. 'I was listened to very well & everyone said it was a great success,' he proudly recounted to his wife. It went without saying that Haldane was effusive. But 'Joe Chamberlain who followed was very polite and complimentary'. It was not every débutant who spoke on a major topic before a crowded House, who was rewarded with words of encouragement from an opponent of Chamberlain's stature, and, not least, who had obtained sufficient intimacy to refer to the member for West Birmingham as 'Joe'. It could be said of Asquith, as Carlyle had said of Gladstone, that he had 'gone irrecoverably into House of Commons shape', and in record time.

There was, of course, no compelling reason why political differences should have been allowed to impair personal relationships. Throughout the greater part of his long career, Asquith displayed a conspicuous ability to sustain private friendships among those from whom he divided publicly. A case in point was his intimacy with A. J. Balfour, who, as Chief Secretary for Ireland, bore responsibility for the Crimes Bill which Asquith made the target of his maiden speech. Other adversaries with whom he enjoyed extra-mural contacts included James, Curzon, Alfred Lyttelton, and Lord Randolph Churchill. Chamberlain, who moved in different social circles, nevertheless qualified for respect. 'Though he was an unsparing he was always a generous antagonist', Asquith reminded the House of Commons on 6 July 1914, the day of Chamberlain's funeral, 'and I rejoice to remember that we never ceased to be friends.'

The terms of their friendship did not deter Asquith from taking a strong stand against any deal with Chamberlain, presumably at the expense of the Home Rule policy. On 25 May 1887 he wrote to *The Times* in vigorous defence of the decision to exclude Chamberlain and other turncoats from membership in the Eighty Club, which several of them had helped to found in commemoration of Gladstone's electoral victory seven years earlier. More imperative was the need to purge the National Liberal Federation of its lingering Chamberlainite connections: since its creation in 1877, it had been familiarly known as 'Joe's caucus', after its first president and moving force. To this purpose, Asquith journeyed to Nottingham for its annual meeting in October. There he issued a stern warning against any further concessions to the Unionists: 'Henry IV had said that Paris was worth a Mass. But they might pay too high a price even for the capitulation of Birmingham.' In keeping with the spirit of the occasion, he closed with a paean to Gladstone, who sat behind him on the platform, and 'whose presence at our head is worth a hundred battalions'. Harcourt considered it 'a really remarkable speech . . . the only speech of the afternoon'; and John Morley concurred that it was 'eloquent and powerful'.

What was it that entitled Asquith to speak with such obvious authority, let alone to receive a respectful hearing from his party superiors? With little more than a maiden speech to his credit, he possessed a self-assurance which in other cases might well have been taken for presumptuousness. Unlike Lord Rosebery or even Grey, he did not boast a family tradition or territorial influence at his disposal. Unlike Harcourt or James, he had not arrived at Westminster with a distinguished reputation at the bar. From all accounts, his physical presence was not commanding, and his academic laurels had been gathering dust for a decade, and therefore did not count for much.

Doubtless the value of his arguments was enhanced by his forthright manner, clear exposition, and, ironically perhaps, by his comparative youth. His was a fresh voice, and one in which the elder statesmen of the party were disposed to hear the resonances of informed opinion on the back benches. Paradoxically, his words were given added weight by the infrequency with which he uttered them. He 'succeeded from the first', Jenkins has neatly put it, 'in making the maximum of impact upon the parliamentary scene with the expenditure of the minimum of effort'. This ought not to imply laziness on his part so much as a deliberate husbanding of limited resources. Had he interposed more often in debate, speaking on any and every subject, Asquith would have dissipated in ineffectual drizzle the oratorical power which he saved for periodic thunderclaps.

The basis of his devotion to Gladstone is more easily ascertained. Inspired partly by self-interest (the Liberal association at East Fife would neither have adopted nor tolerated him otherwise), it was more sentimental than tactical. The hero of his boyhood, Gladstone was more than twice his age, but still capable of Herculean feats. Asquith's personal contacts with the Grand Old Man, as yet few, were uniformly inspiring. He was introduced to him in 1883, after preparing a 'magnificent statement' as background for an Affirmation Bill to extricate the Liberal Government from its entanglement in the Bradlaugh case. Gladstone's speech on the second reading of that Bill, which he himself described without false modesty as 'rather Alexandrian', made a profound impression on the young Asquith, who allotted nearly five pages in *Fifty Years of Parliament* to a recapitulation of its 'most moving passages'. Soon afterwards, they met again at the Eighty Club, where Asquith was brought by Haldane, and where Gladstone heard him deliver an after-dinner address. Each admired the other as rhetorician, and the bond between them was forged during the 1886 Home Rule debate, when Gladstone gave indisputable proof of his status as 'the most consummate parliamentarian of his own or perhaps of any time'. Asquith could bestow no higher tribute.

Gladstone was not, however, the most readily accessible of party leaders; nor was he particularly responsive to younger talent. As a self-styled 'parliamentary novitiate', Asquith usually had contact with him at second hand through John Morley, who, he hastened to explain, was 'not one of the "greybeards"' who dominated the Liberal front bench. Morley had entered Parliament as recently as 1883, leaving behind a distinguished career in literature and journalism; three years later, as Irish Secretary in Gladstone's third administration, he established his reputation as Gladstone's principal lieutenant, and he confirmed it in 1903 by writing a massive biography of his late mentor. Morley, who had his own difficulties with the 'greybeards', was grateful for the presence in the 1886 Parliament of men of Asquith's stamp, faithful to the Irish cause and promising to infuse it with new vitality.

Along with Asquith, the 'younger generation of Liberals' to whom Morley accorded his patronage included such members as Haldane and Grey, A. H. D. Acland, Sydney (later Lord) Buxton, T. E. ('Tom') Ellis, and Ronald Munro Ferguson (later Lord Novar). 'They were a working alliance, not a school', Morley recorded in his *Recollections*; 'they had idealism but were no Utopians. They had conscience, character, and took their politics to heart.' All of them under forty years of age (Acland by a shade), they had arrived in the House more or less at the same time, and in some cases had known each other beforehand. Munro Ferguson, for example, was Haldane's neighbour in Perthshire, the brother of his erstwhile fiancée, and an influential property-owner in Asquith's constituency. Of the seven, five were destined to attain Cabinet rank: the exceptions were Ellis, who distinguished himself as Chief Whip before his premature death in 1899, and Munro Ferguson, who served as Governor-General of Australia from 1914 to 1920. According to Haldane, Asquith qualified as the *de facto* leader of the group. But Asquith himself was inclined to regard Acland as 'our corporate conscience'. The latter would appear the more likely in view of Acland's seniority, his family connection with Gladstone, and his proficiency in the social questions that concerned the others. All the same, there is reason to doubt the existence of the 'coherent parliamentary team' which Cyril Asquith and J. A. Spender have described. Although the seven frequently consulted with each other about ideas and strategy, they tended to act without discipline. Asquith's participation in the group's activities was more often private than public, and he declined to join Haldane and Grey in their defiance of the whips over the 1888 Land Purchase (Ireland) Bill. As a Welshman, Ellis had competing claims on his allegiance, and, as private secretary to Sir John Brunner, he was also linked to Radical manufacturing interests; Haldane was already engaged in collaboration with the Webbs and their Fabian friends; and Munro Ferguson, a protégé of Rosebery, anticipated the imperial enthusiasm eventually shared by most – but not all – of the others.

During these politically formative years, Asquith was seen to greatest advantage not in the committee rooms at Westminster but in the more relaxed atmosphere of the Savoy Hotel, the National Liberal Club, or the Blue Posts, a public house that stood sheltered in a mews behind Cork Street. With Haldane, who belonged to many such coteries, he co-hosted the annual dinners of the Articles Club, to which he referred inadvertently – but ominously – to the actions of and another of non-parliamentary public figures. The harmony on these occasions was intentionally broken by the dissonant topics introduced for discussion. Morley, always a spirited conversationalist, was among the regulars. On one of the evenings, he joined Arthur Balfour, Sir Edward Carson, Charles Bowen, and Grey in evaluating the merits of possible successors to Tennyson as Poet Laureate, Asquith taking the view that the office should be suspended. Usually, however, the proceedings were more explicitly political, although scrupulously non-partisan. Haldane recalled a dinner at which Chamberlain ill-advisedly intruded into an exchange between Rosebery and Lord Randolph Churchill, who summoned the waiter and asked for a flower pot to be placed between himself and Chamberlain.

The dinners of the Articles Club, which continued until Asquith took office in 1892, testify to the fact that he and Haldane were assiduously cultivating new acquaintances and seeking to widen their respective horizons. That they were successful in capturing, if only for an odd evening, so many of the political lions of the day is likewise an indication of their growing stature. In this respect, it must be conceded, they were helped along by the fluidity of the political situation, where various personalities were casting about for allies.

The man on whom they fastened, Haldane more securely than Asquith, was Rosebery. Only thirty-nine years of age, he was appointed Foreign Secretary in 1886 by Gladstone, who designated him 'the man of the future'. Already he was widely regarded as the probable successor to the Grand Old Man, who was nearing eighty and showing signs of debility. Rosebery, whose peerage was considered no liability, had much to commend him: baronial patronage, vast wealth, a certain wayward charm, a brilliant platform style, and a masterly grasp of the imperial themes that had begun to excite public interest. Most important, he boasted a reputation for progressivism which he had deservedly earned as chairman of the London County Council. It was this last attribute that won him the respect and admiration of Asquith and his friends, who found Morley sadly deficient with regard to education and social reform. Imperialism, which Jenkins and others have cited as the crucial ingredient, 'played little part in establishing these relationships', H. C. G. Matthew has forcefully argued in *The Liberal Imperialists*. 'It was, if anything, a divisive factor.'

With Munro Ferguson pointing the way, the others moved, one by one, into Rosebery's orbit. In 1889 Asquith joined the Imperial Federation League, in which Rosebery was a dominant force. Lord Spencer, one of the party's 'greybeards', was reportedly 'very angry . . . and . . . greatly disappointed in him'. Harcourt, who shared Spencer's apprehension, was marked out by Haldane as 'the *bête noire*' of the pro-Rosebery movement. A Gladstonian fundamentalist like Morley, he had neither intellectual breadth nor social graces to redeem him. Harcourt was a House of Commons man in the classic sense, and, as such, he disapproved of those who spent their time and oratory out of doors. It especially infuriated him that Asquith, whose speeches in the House could then be counted on the fingers of one hand, had elsewhere called upon the party elders to outline the Irish scheme they intended to introduce when they came back into power. Vowing to resist 'Asquithism', which could only lead to embarrassment and recrimination, he fumed to Morley that 'Asquith, *who will never do a day's work for us in the House*, goes about the country, doing mischief, and gladdening the hearts of the Unionists . . .'

Morley's own position was, as always, somewhat ambiguous. On the one hand, he received Harcourt's confidences; on the other, he co-operated with the Roseberyite clique against him. Notoriously thin-skinned, he was repeatedly wounded by Harcourt's gruff demeanour. Both were popularly characterized as 'Little Englanders', but the similarities between them were more apparent than real. Morley doubted the strength of Harcourt's commitment to Home Rule, while he persisted in the delusion that Rosebery could be depended upon to honour Gladstone's historic promise. Furthermore, there were personal considerations which could not be separated from ideological ones: he reasoned that Rosebery, who would lead the party from the House of Lords, would presumably assign a more prominent place to him and implicitly to the Irish programme with which he was identified. Morley was therefore willing, perhaps even eager, to assist the young men who flocked to Rosebery's standard.

Asquith, who had far less either to gain or to lose from these manoeuvres, was essentially concerned with the formulation of party doctrine. The Liberal front bench had maintained a guarded silence, with the result that Henry Labouchere and other extremists had captured the limelight, possibly with Harcourt's connivance. Asquith had 'been talking' with Haldane and Morley, he told Sydney Buxton on 10 November 1889, about

> the practicability of independent action from behind the front bench, which may put an end to the assumption that the Jacobyn [sic] tail is the only vital part of the party dog.
>
> There is, so far as I know, no idea of starting a new party organisation, but there are many of us who feel (1) that the better kind of Radicalism is not articulate enough and is unduly backward in putting out constructive proposals, (2) that, to remedy this, we need concerted action and distribution of labour, and (3) that in everything that is done it is well to be in touch with the worthier elements in the front bench.

There was a fundamental logic to Asquith's position but, at the same time, a vagueness that implied no threat to the *status quo*. It is noteworthy that he classified himself, according to the nomenclature of the day, as a Radical, although not one of the Labouchere persuasion. A constructionist in the sphere of domestic legislation, he did not go so far as Haldane in the direction of collectivism. In May 1891 he accompanied Haldane, Grey, Buxton, and Acland to a 'queer party' at the home of Alice Stopford Green, where a corresponding number of Fabians had been invited. 'Asquith spoilt it', Beatrice Potter (soon to become Mrs Sidney Webb) complained in her diary. 'He was determined that it should not go.' Prepared to engage in a 'free interchange of views', Asquith discountenanced anything more far-reaching or formal. Yet he placed himself firmly in the 'section' of the Liberal Party 'which had a definite leaning to the "Left" . . .'

One of Asquith's infrequent interventions in parliamentary debate was to speak on behalf of a 'trivial proposition' to provide modest salaries for M.P.s; it was not until 1911, when he was Prime Minister, that this policy was finally enacted. Had such a stipend been available a quarter of a century earlier, Asquith would have been free to devote greater attention to parliamentary business. Under the circumstances, however, he was obliged to keep up his law practice, on which he depended for sustenance. Fortunately, it had grown more prosperous as he established himself as a public figure. In 1887 he defended (albeit unsuccessfully) R. B. Cunninghame Graham, the 'socialist' M.P. for North-West Lanarkshire, who was indicted with

John Burns – later Asquith's Cabinet colleague – for unlawful assembly in Trafalgar Square on 'Bloody Sunday', 13 November; it was Haldane, incidentally, who stood bail for the defendant. The next year, Asquith achieved a greater success at the expense of his liberal image as prosecuting attorney in the case of Henry Vizetelly, who was charged with obscene libel as the publisher of the 'realistic' novels of Zola and other depraved Continentals; he opened the case by reading aloud to the jury, whose Victorianism was suitably offended, a string of 'the most objectionable passages', which he had assembled 'with scissors and a pot of paste at hand'. (A French newspaper, reporting the trial, referred to *'la pudeur effarouchée de l'avocat Asquith'*.) He had a better opportunity, although an unanticipated one, to assert his forensic ability as junior counsel to Sir Charles Russell before the Parnell Commission, which sat for 129 days and, by his own account, witnessed 'scenes of poignant and unforgettable drama'.

During the spring of 1887, while the Irish Crimes Bill was being heatedly debated in Parliament, *The Times* dutifully took the ministerial side by running a series of articles on 'Parnellism and Crime'. On the morning of 18 April, hours before the vote on the second reading, it sought to clinch its case by publishing a facsimile of a letter in which the Irish Nationalist leader gave back-handed condonation to the 1882 Phoenix Park murders. Parnell denounced the document to the House as a forgery, but his reluctance to take proceedings seemed to give substance to the allegations. It was left to another Irish member to take up the legal challenge; he lost the case, but afforded *The Times* an opportunity to introduce other incriminating letters. Parnell, more convinced than ever that he could not expect a fair trial in an English court of law, appealed to the House of Commons for a Select Committee to ascertain the authenticity of the evidence. The Government refused, and moved instead to set up a Statutory Commission of three judges, who were to be empowered to conduct a more general inquiry into the charges and counter-charges that were circulating. The Liberal and Irish parties, with backstairs assistance from Lord Randolph Churchill, protested against this unusual procedure and, still more, the appointment of a trio of Unionists as commissioners; but there was no choice. The Attorney-General, Richard Webster (later Lord Alverstone), was counsel for *The Times*: law officers of the Crown were not then prohibited from private practice. Parnell retained the services of Russell and Asquith, the latter having impressed him by his fiery attack on the province and personnel of the Commission.

The proceedings dragged on for six months before Richard Pigott, who had sold the spurious letters to *The Times*, was called as a witness. After two days of cross-examination by Russell, he fled first to Paris and then to Madrid, where, like a character out of a Zola novel, he shot himself in a shabby hotel-room. He had, however, left behind a confession that confirmed his guilt and Parnell's innocence. *The Times* stood discredited and, with it, the Conservative Government that had been all too willing to trust the veracity of its disclosures.

The forgery exposed, there remained another important question to be answered. How had a newspaper with the pre-eminence of *The Times* allowed itself to be taken in by such a scoundrel as Pigott, whom Churchill decried as 'a man, a thing, a reptile, a monster'? C. J. MacDonald, the manager at Printing House Square, was put in the box, where he detailed the circumstances involving the acquisition of the letters. It was, Asquith later recalled, an 'amazing tale ... which remains almost unique in the annals of infantine simplicity and malevolent credulity'. Russell, who was scheduled to begin his cross-examination of MacDonald after lunch, turned to his junior counsel and said: 'I am tired: you must take charge of this fellow.' Asquith, who professed to have been 'never more surprised in my life', protested, but to no avail. Unprepared, he assumed 'the critical task of conducting the cross-examination: a task all the more formidable because my leader, the greatest cross-examiner at the English Bar, sat there throughout and listened'. When he had finished, he had demolished the witness and, in the process, had assured his own professional acclaim.

The effect of the Pigott exposure on national politics was immediate and profound. 'The stars seemed at last to be fighting in their courses for Home Rule,' Asquith wrote in retrospection. The attempt to destroy Gladstone's Irish policy by discrediting Parnell had backfired, and, for the time being, the Irish leader appeared less a sinner than a man grievously sinned against. Successive by-election victories confirmed the Liberals in their optimism, and the pundits were predicting 'a substantial Home Rule majority in Great Britain (apart from Ireland) at the General Election which could not be long delayed'. To John Roskill, whom he had taken on as a pupil, Asquith confided his ambition to become Home Secretary when his party returned imminently to office.

The effect of this episode on his personal life was no less notable. Now, for the first time, he was overwhelmed with briefs and had to turn away prospective clients. During the winter of 1889–90, at the inevitable instigation of Haldane, who himself led the way, he applied to the Lord Chancellor to take silk. As a Queen's Counsel, he was entitled to append a pair of initials to his name, to wear lace ruffles, and to raise his fee accordingly. His annual income was calculated at £5,000.

But the euphoria soon gave way to public humiliation and private anguish. In November 1890 there was a second and more celebrated inquiry into Parnell's associations. Captain William O'Shea, a conniving Irish politician who had taken belated cognizance of his wife's infidelity, sued for divorce and named Parnell as co-respondent. He triggered off a scandal that shook the Home Rule alliance to its foundations. 'A week or so before the final crash', Asquith chanced to meet Parnell, who was on his way to see a lawyer, and who proffered assurances that there was no cause for worry. But the luck of the Irish had run out. Gladstone, under strong pressure, broke with the reprobate, who was repudiated by a majority in the Irish parliamentary ranks. Nevertheless, Parnell refused to step down, and it remained for him to be removed from his command by a higher authority. His sudden death in October 1891 – 'an uncovenanted mercy for his opponents', F. S. L. Lyons has called it – left the Irish Nationalists savagely divided and their Liberal allies deprived of the three-figure majority which had seemed within their grasp.

Asquith, who knew better than to confuse questions of personal morality with those of political fitness, held unrepentantly to the opinion that Parnell had been 'one of the half-dozen great men of action of this century'. To the outrage of some of his 'excellent friends', he averred that, 'if I had been an Irish Nationalist Member, I should have been more than tempted to be also a Parnellite'. Yet he could not deny that irreparable damage had been done by Parnell's 'incredible follies and vulgarities'. Ten days after Parnell died, Asquith had an assessment of party prospects from John Morley, who recounted a remarkably accurate prophecy by the Chief Whip that the Liberals 'will probably be a small majority, and without the Irish a minority' in the next Parliament.

Weeks before the death of Parnell, Asquith suffered a more personal loss. In mourning for his first wife, he was unable to attend the October meeting of the National Liberal Federation at Newcastle, where Morley had hoped to have his support 'to hold up the hands of our veteran'. In the event, Gladstone proved more than capable of holding up his own hands. In his address to the Federation, he signified his acceptance of the comprehensive programme on which the delegates had voted the day before. A collection of 'bits and pieces', the Newcastle Programme effectively catalogued the diverse areas of concern within the party: Irish Home Rule (on which Grey moved the motion), Welsh and Scottish disestablishment, local option, House of Lords reform, the abolition of plural franchises, employers' liability, land revaluation, triennial parliaments, the extension of small holdings, payment for M.P.s, and much else besides. Although Asquith had played no part in its formulation, it represented in front-bench minds the policy of 'Asquithism' to which Harcourt had previously taken strong exception. By laying down guidelines for any future Liberal administration, the National Liberal Federation had unwittingly exacerbated underlying tensions and, more seriously, had formally acknowledged the extent to which the Liberal Party had become a composite of mutually exclusive pressure groups.

Most obviously, the Newcastle Programme was a signal that the parties were preparing to confront each other in electoral combat. Asquith, who was defending a marginal seat, girded himself for battle with an election address that focused on the Irish problem, but included references to many of the items in the Newcastle package: small holdings, the abolition of plural franchises, and, most revolutionary in its implications, 'the ending of a hereditary second chamber'. Parliament was finally dissolved at the end of June, and polling took place at East Fife in mid-July. Asquith, his majority shaved by eighty-two votes, claimed to take less satisfaction in his own return than in his eldest son's election to a scholarship at Winchester. 'Between you and me (tho' as a hardened optimist I scarcely admit it to myself) I am not in high spirits about the future – the country's, the party's, my own,' he wrote to Mrs Horner. 'To save others, even if one cannot save oneself, is something', he reasoned; 'but to fail in both would be a poor result.'

There were 273 Liberal members in the new House, who, combined with eighty-one Irish Nationalists and a lone Labourite, ensured 355 votes for Home Rule; on the opposite side, there were 269 Conservatives and forty-six Unionists, a total of 315. Gladstone thus had a working majority for which several of his more recent successors would have been grateful. Yet from the perspective of Harcourt and others it was tantamount to a defeat. Morley and Asquith, who were of the same mind, 'agreed that a worse stroke of luck than such a majority has never befallen political leaders'. Under the circumstances, however, there was no choice but to persevere.

The Parliament of 1892 assembled in August to find the Tories still occupying their ministerial places. To dislodge them was a formality, but not one to be taken lightly. Following the precedent of January 1886, when Collings had rallied the Liberal Opposition against Lord Salisbury's previous Government by moving an amendment to the Address, Gladstone called upon Asquith to move a similar motion of no-confidence to consist, 'as far as possible, in a single operation avoiding extraneous matter'. On 8 August Asquith discharged his obligation, and with the dexterity expected of him. Carried by a majority of forty, his amendment brought down the second Salisbury Government and opened the way for Gladstone to take office for a fourth and final time.

Asquith interpreted his selection for the assignment as a guarantee of high office in the new administration. While his assumption was entirely correct, it is not clear on what he based it. As Jenkins has pointed out, Collings, for performing the same service in 1886, had been rewarded with nothing better than a parliamentary secretaryship to the Local Government Board, with a salary reduction to add injury to insult. The previous April, Asquith had had a 'vague talk' with Morley about the possibilities of a Cabinet position; but Morley, who tended to imply greater authority than he had at his disposal, had spoken on his own account. The next month, Rosebery had met with Gladstone, whom he found 'averse to giving Asquith Cabinet office'. What, then, gave Asquith the presumption to canvass Balfour and Harcourt on the relative advantages of a political office over one of the law officerships?

With even greater presumption, Asquith specified that he was not prepared to affiliate with a government 'in which there was not a strong infusion of new blood'. To this end, he consulted with Morley and, more intimately, with the other 'young men' with whom he had joined forces during the previous Parliament. Tactics were mapped out that foreshadowed the 1905 Relugas Compact, by which he and his confederates tried to bring pressure to bear on a subsequent Liberal Premier. Asquith had set his sights on a political department, the Home Secretaryship being his first choice. He urged the appointment of Acland as Chief Whip, and, for what it was worth, had the backing of Grey, who vowed to stand aside unless 'some such arrangement were made'. Grey himself, his disclaimers notwithstanding, was not averse to the prospect of a junior office, the most for which he could reasonably hope. Haldane, who described himself as 'a sort of referee', was characteristically more intent upon advancing the claims of others.

Asquith got his wish: on 14 August Gladstone wrote to offer him the Home Office, and he 'replied at once, gratefully accepting the

Prime Minister's proposal'. When an attractive opportunity presented itself, he was never one to hold out for terms. Acland joined
him in the Cabinet as Vice-President of the Council with responsibility for education. At a lower level, Grey was appointed to the
parliamentary under-secretaryship at the Foreign Office, and Buxton
to the corresponding place at the Colonial Office. Ellis was named
second whip; and Munro Ferguson, with a degree of disappointment,
resumed his duties as private secretary to Lord Rosebery, who was
coaxed back to the Foreign Secretaryship. Haldane was the single
member of the group to find no accommodation, but he harboured no
resentment. Grey, on the other hand, confessed to certain misgivings:
'We shall lose our freedom and may be turned into clerks', he wrote
to Buxton, 'instead of people who are doing something to develope
and expand Liberal principles.'

Any doubts which Asquith may have entertained were quickly
dispelled by the delights of office. 'When I was a boy', he told Mrs
Horner, 'I used to think that to get into the Cabinet before one was
40 was, for an Englishman who had to start on the level of the crowd,
the highest height of achievement.' Still a few weeks short of his
fortieth birthday, he scaled that height, securing a seat in a Cabinet
of which he was the youngest member: of his sixteen colleagues,
eight were over sixty-two, and only two others were under fifty-four.
A privy councillorship attached to the seals of office. The mood of
melancholy that had dogged him during the summer was dissipated
by early autumn, when he mused to the same confidante about 'the
Theban, somewhere in Herodotus, who says . . . that of all human
troubles the most hateful is to feel that you have the capacity of
power and yet you have no field to exercise it. That was for years my
case', he reflected, 'and no one who has not been through it can know
the chilly, paralysing, deadening depression of hope deferred and
energy wasted and vitality run to seed.' This deeply revealing statement was pronounced as an epitaph to a situation that had passed,
presumably for ever. A quarter of a century later, 'the chilly,
paralysing, deadening depression' was to return with a vengeance.

The Government formed, its first business was to travel *en masse* to
Osborne for the customary royal audience. Queen Victoria, none too
pleased to exchange her trusted Tory ministers for troublesome
Liberals, maintained a stony silence throughout the ceremony. She
recorded afterwards that the new Home Secretary had struck her as
'an intelligent, rather good-looking man', which was more than she
had to say in favour of most of the others who kissed hands. Later
that month, Asquith paid a return visit to Osborne in the more

acceptable company of Sir Henry James. On that occasion he found the Queen more communicative. 'Had a conversation with Mr Asquith whom I thought pleasant, straightforward, and sensible', she recounted in a letter of 26 August.

The qualities discerned by his sovereign were those that most readily characterized Asquith during his early ministerial years. There was one other: a prodigious efficiency. 'He became the best Home Secretary of the century,' Sir Philip Magnus has written (perhaps a trifle hyperbolically), and that in a Government more conspicuous for its failures than its achievements. Dependent in the Commons on Irish support, which was itself divided, the Liberals could expect their measures to meet with implacable resistance in the House of Lords, where the Conservatives were entrenched. There were also problems of personnel. At eighty-four years of age, the Prime Minister was, more than ever, 'an old man in a hurry', who did not welcome distractions from his preoccupation with the Irish question. To make matters worse, Harcourt and Rosebery (with Morley flitting between them) were constantly at loggerheads. Embattled from without and disrupted from within, the ministry's most impressive feat was to survive as long as it did. 'The continuance for three years of the two Liberal Governments which held office from 1892 to 1895 is indeed one of the miracles of Parliamentary history', Asquith knowingly asserted.

As Home Secretary, Asquith was essentially more concerned with administration than with legislation. He took advice from his civil servants, with whom he enjoyed excellent relations, from Harcourt, a former tenant at the Home Office, and from a wide range of contacts in the legal profession; yet, in the last analysis, he invariably acted as his own man. 'He liked to move,' Jenkins has shrewdly observed, 'but in well-tried directions.' Given the inherent instability of the Government and the potential explosiveness of the social situation, his moderation was as much a necessity as a virtue. It was immediately manifest in his handling of the vexed question of the right of assembly in Trafalgar Square, which was technically Crown property. Long a subject of passionate dispute, it had been peremptorily settled by his Tory predecessor, who had sanctioned a police ban on all meetings at this historic site. It may be recalled that Asquith was not unfamiliar with this controversy, having defended Cunninghame Graham against charges that arose from a Trafalgar Square rally in 1887. This fact did not go unnoticed by Radical champions of free speech and by indignant socialists who, within days of his arrival at the Home Office, appealed to him to redress their grievance. To give impetus to their arguments, they scheduled a mass demonstration for November. Asquith, after due consultation and calm deliberation, promulgated a compromise solution. Henceforth, meetings in Trafalgar Square were to be permitted during daylight hours on Saturday afternoons, Sundays, and Bank Holidays (when they would neither disturb commerce nor disrupt traffic), provided that the police authorities had received proper notice and had approved the route of procession. With the exception of Queen Victoria, there was universal satisfaction with these arrangements.

It was not always so easy for Asquith to acquit himself and to reconcile his past record with his present responsibilities. John Redmond, who led the Parnellite rump in the House of Commons, pressed for the release of fourteen convicted dynamiters, who had been incarcerated for a decade. Could his plea be resisted by a Home Secretary who had discredited allegations in *The Times* of a link between 'Parnellism and Crime', and who belonged to a Government that continued on the sufferance of its Irish allies? 'A weak Minister might well have snatched at this occasion for the exercise of a facile politic leniency, and shrunk from the immediate penalties of a long-sighted firmness,' Asquith's official biographers have rotundly stated. 'But there was a vein of iron in the Home Secretary's composition'. Confirmed in his belief that all of the fourteen sentences were just, he refused to cancel or commute them. His first ministerial performance in the House was a staunch defence of his position, which Redmond had made the subject of an amendment to the Address. With enthusiastic Conservative support, which was not altogether reassuring, the amendment was defeated and the Government sustained.

Labour unrest, intensified by high unemployment and a simultaneous decline in real wages, added to Asquith's problems, if not necessarily to his esteem. A violent colliery dispute in the West Riding of Yorkshire, not far from his birthplace, rampaged beyond the control of local constabulary forces. Police reinforcements were brought in from London and as far afield as Wiltshire, but they could not restore order. Finally, at the persistent request of the local authority, troops were dispatched. In a fracas at Featherstone colliery, near Wakefield, they opened fire and two men were killed. Two coroner's juries reported contradictory findings. A Special Commission – consisting of Bowen, Haldane, and Sir Albert Rollit, a Tory backbencher – was appointed to investigate the incident, and it concluded that the use of troops had been warranted and their action justified. The Home Secretary was among those vindicated by his three Special Commissioners, two of whom were known to be his own special friends. He might have taken greater care to establish the impartiality of the inquiry and to protect himself against accusations of having perpetrated a cover-up. For years thereafter, his public speeches were interrupted by shouts of 'Featherstone'.

This unfortunate incident, in which Asquith is said to have played 'an almost mechanical part', ought not to obscure the fact that his three-year stint at the Home Office ranks as a period of cautious but constructive reform from which labour was the chief beneficiary. Few politicians have left this department, a notorious graveyard of reputations, with their credentials intact, let alone enhanced: Sir Robert Peel was one; Harcourt possibly another; and, most recently, Roy Jenkins has proved a happy exception to the rule. Asquith's success, in view of the difficulties that beset him, was particularly striking. During his secretaryship, significant advances were made to strengthen the factory inspectorate, to improve penal methods, and to deal with working conditions in the so-called dangerous trades, including chemical industries. An Employers' Liability Bill, which he had painstakingly drafted in 1893, came to grief in the Lords, where it was amended to permit 'contracting out' of its provisions. He had better results with an omnibus Factory Bill, which he introduced in March 1895. Among other things, it provided extended protection for the work force, empowered the Home Secretary to conduct formal investigations into the circumstances of accidents, required the installation of fire escapes in factories, restricted overtime, and brought laundries and the docklands (where some of the worst offences had occurred) within the scope of factory legislation. Before the Bill could be piloted through the House of Commons, the Liberal Government had capsized, and Asquith was succeeded by Sir Matthew White Ridley. But, according to an official Home Office account, his 'most skilful handling . . . secured the passing of his Bill through the remaining stages in the Commons', and saw it safely lodged on the statute book.

Sir Robert Ensor, summing up the record of the Liberal Governments of 1892–5, has singled out Asquith as 'one of three ministers who achieved notable administrative progress in their departments', the others being Acland at the education ministry and Sir Henry Campbell-Bannerman at the War Office. In addition, H. H. Fowler merits recognition for his work at the Local Government Board; and Harcourt, with his 'death duties' Budget of 1894, effected a fiscal revolution. Generally, however, the record was one of disappointment and frustration. Nowhere was this more apparent than in the sphere of Irish affairs, where the Liberals had assumed a special mission.

Until his belated retirement in March 1894, Gladstone applied his waning powers to a second Home Rule Bill. It emerged from Cabinet committee on 13 February 1893, and Morley moved its first reading four days later. The following September, after eighty-five gruelling sittings, the Bill squeaked through the Commons on its third reading by a margin of thirty-four votes, six less than the combined Liberal-Irish-Labour majority. Thereupon the Bill went to the upper house, where it was considered for fewer days than the Commons had taken months. After a week of declamation, the Lords rejected Home Rule by a resounding vote of 419 to forty-one.

Asquith, whose name appeared on the back of the Bill by virtue of his departmental position, spoke in April, when the measure had its second reading. He had not been a member of the six-man committee that drafted it, and he was not intimately involved with its parliamentary defence. Nevertheless, his position and outlook were profoundly affected by its fate. He had taken office, much as he had entered the House, a confirmed Home Ruler: his 1892 election address was unequivocal on that score. Morley, in a 'long talk' with Lord Acton which Sir Algernon West recorded in his diary on 17 December 1892, criticized the majority of his colleagues for insincerity, and complained bitterly that 'none of them cared for Home Rule but he, Asquith, and Mr Gladstone'. But gradually Asquith's position began to shift.

It disturbed him that so many opportunities for constructive action, including his own Employers' Liability Bill, were sacrificed at the altar of Home Rule. Without wishing to repudiate his leader's Irish policy, he advocated its extension into 'a general plan of devolution' that might appease other national interests and facilitate the conduct of business at Westminster. He believed that the Government's tactics were self-defeating, and that the issue, as Gladstone had narrowly defined it, was too 'local, exceptional and anomalous'. By making Home Rule for Ireland the *sine qua non* of Liberal policy, he complained to Lord Rosebery, the party threatened to become 'hopelessly shut in'.

Meanwhile, precious time and public support were being wasted on a forlorn enterprise. So long as Gladstone remained at the helm, any modification of principles or strategy was out of the question. 'It's brutal to put into words,' Asquith admitted to Morley, 'but really, if Mr G. stood aside more, we might get on better.' Could he have seriously expected that Gladstone, at eighty-five, could stand aside without stepping down? By the early days of 1894, the majority of the Cabinet – Asquith included – had come to the conclusion that (in Morley's pious words) the 'appointed hour for our Chief's resignation' had arrived. The immediate cause was Lord Spencer's naval estimates, on which Gladstone stood opposed to an overwhelming number of his colleagues; but that was merely the last in a series of confrontations that testified to the Prime Minister's inflexibility and eroded authority.

Strictly speaking, 'Mr Gladstone's resignation was entirely his own act', as Asquith legalistically described it. That, however, is not to deny that it came after considerable wrangling and with extreme reluctance. He chaired his final Cabinet on 1 March, sitting unmoved through the 'blubbering' tributes that were paid him. Asquith was present, but saved his eulogy for a private letter which was more appreciated. '. . . I am glad that the prolongation of my political life has given me an opportunity of helping the arrangements under which you have taken your stand in political life', Gladstone replied warmly, if a shade defensively. Betraying a faulty memory, he recalled

the impression made upon me by your speech at the Eighty Club, the first time I ever saw or heard you. It has since been, of course, deepened and confirmed. Great problems are before us: and I know no one more likely to face them, as I hope and believe, not only with a manly strength, but with a determined integrity of mind. I most earnestly hope that you may be enabled to fulfil your part, which will certainly be an arduous one.

The most immediate of the 'great problems' to engage Asquith's attention was that of the Liberal succession.

As the long imminence of Gladstone's retirement had drawn to a close, party spokesmen had lined up behind either Harcourt or Rosebery, the two major claimants for the party leadership. In the ensuing struggle, Asquith played a secondary role, but a symbolic one. In retrospect, he was assumed to have been a fervent Roseberyite from the start. But at the time his position was more ambiguous and his motives more complex.

He was not yet – and perhaps never was – the Liberal Imperialist that he was subsequently taken for. In 1892, on the question of the establishment of a protectorate in Uganda, he had strongly sided with Harcourt and the 'Little Englanders' against Rosebery, who nevertheless prevailed. In the area of foreign affairs, he criticized Rosebery as too Francophobe. On domestic issues, to which he gave precedence, his views were – on balance – closer to Harcourt's. With regard to

Home Rule, there was not much to choose between the rivals, neither of whom was firmly wedded to Gladstonian tenets. Granted, Asquith was on better social terms with Rosebery, but that does not appear to have made the difference. Sir Edward Hamilton, formerly Gladstone's private secretary and now a keen Rosebery enthusiast, wondered whether Asquith was 'running quite straight with Rosebery . . . I sometimes have doubts which are shared by others who know him better than I do.'

There was no ignoring the fact, however, that Rosebery was by far the more attractive figure. *Persona gratissima* to the Court and the press, he offered a standard beneath which the party might appeal more successfully to the electorate. Harcourt, 'to tell the naked truth, . . . was an almost impossible colleague, and would have been a wholly impossible chief', Asquith wrote years later. The choice, then, was essentially one between personalities and principles, the two factors not easily separable. Fortunately, as Asquith's opinion was not decisive, he was not required to declare it emphatically, and could allow others to draw their own conclusions. 'Loulou' Harcourt, canvassing support for his father, asked Morley if Asquith 'was *very* Roseberian', and Morley 'said he did not know'. Morley, who was himself veering away from Harcourt and towards Rosebery, affirmed 'that Asquith was very thick with Rosebery . . . but that he was very discreet . . . He was a young man with a future, and wise to hold his tongue.'

It was Morley's espousal of Rosebery, soon admitted to have been a miscalculation, that made possible a Rosebery premiership. The reward he had expected was denied him, and he returned dejectedly to his 'back kitchen' at the Irish Office. Harcourt, ever more disgruntled, remained at the Exchequer, but was compensated with the leadership of the Commons. Asquith stayed put at the Home Office; although he did not demur, there were intimations that he would have liked to follow Lord Kimberley as Secretary of State for India. Herbert Gladstone, who had been his under-secretary, graduated to become First Commissioner of Works. He was replaced by George Russell, who, Haldane informed the Webbs, 'couldn't be worse'. Like the continued exclusion of Haldane, the 'dreadful appointments' of Russell to the Home Office and J. G. Shaw-Lefevre to the Local Government Board were regarded as an act of revenge by the 'old guard' against 'the little gang of collectivist Radicals (which included Asquith, Acland, Sydney Buxton and Grey) [that] had forced Rosebery on the parliamentary Radicals' of the Harcourt–Labouchere school. Mrs Webb's account of the Cabinet formation, inscribed in her diary on 12 March, was obviously coloured by her own sympathies. Yet H. W. Massingham, who had assisted the 'successful Rosebery intrigue' in the columns of the *Daily Chronicle*, confirmed to her that 'Asquith and Haldane . . . are hated by the House of Commons Radical, who feels the ground slipping from under him without knowing why'.

The 'old gang' were not the only ones who felt the ground slipping. Rent by dissensions, the Rosebery Government staggered on for sixteen months, during which it performed the excruciating feat (in Harcourt's pungent phrase) of 'hanging on by the eyelids'. The Prime Minister, plagued by insomnia and by incessant quarrels with and among his colleagues, left no doubt of his incapacity, physical and otherwise. His statements on Ireland were ill-considered. His colonial policy, avowedly expansionist, was anathema to the rank and file. His personal conduct was too often gratuitously offensive. In the sphere of domestic reform, where Asquith (along with Haldane and the Webbs) had looked to him to provide a lead, he proved distressingly vague. 'I have no confidence in Lord R.', Haldane wrote to his mother on 10 August 1894 after a colloquy with Asquith, who purportedly shared his disillusion. 'He is so anxious to please everybody that he ends up by doing things which please nobody. We none of us have the least idea of what he is at just now.'

In his official capacity, Asquith continued much as he had under Gladstone. Not directly involved in the party's internecine feuds, he was preoccupied by his departmental routines and, after May 1894, by his new marriage. A meeting of the Cabinet, scheduled for his wedding day, was thoughtfully postponed to allow Rosebery to be on hand to sign the register with Gladstone and Balfour. A gala occasion, it gave the Government – as Jenkins has wryly noted – 'one of its few hours of harmony'.

In the House of Commons, Asquith took charge of the abortive Welsh Disestablishment Bill. On 15 February 1895 David Lloyd George listened attentively from the back benches 'to a fine duel between Chamberlain & Asquith. Chamberlain', he reported to his wife, 'delivered a tremendous onslaught on the Government . . . Asquith simply smashed Chamberlain up. He was all Welsh Disestablishment & tripped Joe up fairly over that. Joseph looked abashed & sat down.' (Harcourt, more picturesquely, told his son that Asquith 'knocked Joe into a cocked hat'.) Lloyd George was a good deal less admiring after Asquith had brushed aside his proposed amendment to stiffen the Bill. 'The episode', Kenneth O. Morgan has written, 'did not serve to endear Asquith towards Welshmen in general or Lloyd George in particular.' Asquith recalled it as a 'thankless task'; and (according to Rosebery's biographer) his 'lack of interest in the measure was ill-concealed'. He was relieved of the burden in June, when the Government, defeated on a snap vote, gratefully seized the opportunity to surrender office.

Rosebery and Harcourt, in rare accord, considered that resignation was preferable to dissolution. Asquith favoured the second alternative, which he 'never doubted was strategically the right course', but he was carried along. Possibly he had been stunned by the spectacle of the two warriors for once acting in unison. On 24 June Harcourt accordingly announced to the Commons the Government's decision. It was thereupon Lord Salisbury's obligation to form an administration and to call a general election. Asquith, preparing to defend his seat at East Fife, had reached the turning-point: his own prospects were now incomparably better than those of the party to which he belonged.

# 3

## FROM ROSEBERY
## TO
## CAMPBELL-BANNERMAN

In the general election of 1895, the Liberal Party went into the fray disunited, and came out an absolute shambles. None of its spokesmen had anticipated any better and, quite fittingly, none was pleasantly surprised. Its complement in the new House reduced to 177 M.P.s, the party's distress was reflected most acutely in the number of its standard-bearers – including Harcourt and Morley – who were rejected by their constituents. Asquith at East Fife, like Campbell-Bannerman at the Stirling Burghs nearby, was among the more fortunate, and even managed to increase his majority from 293 to 716. Lord Rosebery, who took sanctuary on a rented yacht, observed the 'smash up' with grim detachment. 'My only interest has been in individual elections like yours', he wrote to Asquith, 'for the general catastrophe was under the circumstances certain and inevitable.' These were unconventional sentiments for a party leader to profess; but, then, Rosebery was hardly the archetypal party leader.

With 340 Conservative seats, Lord Salisbury won a commanding majority. It was further swelled by the formal adherence of seventy-one Liberal Unionists, four of whom – including Sir Henry James (now Lord James of Hereford) – took office under him. A decade of uninterrupted Unionist rule had begun. Asquith had never doubted that his erstwhile Liberal colleagues, who had affixed a Unionist label to themselves, would gradually merge indistinguishably into the Tory mass. A few months earlier, he had upbraided his old friend Alfred Lyttelton, who announced his intention to stand at Leamington as a Liberal Unionist:

The experience of the last few years has shown that there is only room for two great English parties. If, as is not unlikely, we are defeated in the next General Election, it is clear that there will be a going government, and you & the rest, who are returned as Liberal Unionists, will have to support it in the Division Lobby with the same fidelity as the Conservatives. You will be quickly fused into one party, and time only can show which will be the leaven & which the lump.

A prophetic statement, it elucidated Asquith's fundamental antipathy to breakaway parties, whether Liberal Unionist or Coalition Liberal or (by his definition) Labour; more immediately, it helps to explain the limits he scrupulously set on his participation in the Liberal Imperialist movement.

Asquith was firmly identified with the wing of the Liberal Party that took its signals, when it could discern them, from Rosebery. Yet he enjoyed a reputation within the party as a whole that transcended his Roseberian connections. In the wake of electoral defeat, Rosebery was – more than ever – ready to retire to the shadows, where he found a natural haven. He could contemplate no worthier successor than Asquith, whose undeclared candidacy received warm endorsement in certain quarters. But, at this particular juncture, Asquith was not regarded as seriously as Roy Jenkins has suggested. Lord Kimberley went no further than to speculate that, 'If H[arcourt] were out of the way, C. Bannerman or Asquith could lead.' And Harcourt, of course, had different ideas. His assurance to Margot Asquith that 'your man is the man of the future', which Jenkins has adduced as a declaration of support, came five years later, during the Boer War.

All the same, Asquith's position in party councils was unassailable. Morley, temporarily outside the Commons, advised Lord Spencer that 'you will be able to steady our poor derelict ship – or perhaps I should call it our *raft*' – on the basis of 'a firm understanding between you, C.B., Asquith, and in a secondary degree' Fowler and Acland. It was as a member of the team that Asquith was invariably mentioned, and, significantly, usually in the same breath as Campbell-Bannerman, who was to precede him up the greasy pole. No less patently, it was as a member of the team that he acted. With tact and dexterity, he worked to restore relations between Rosebery and Harcourt, who had meanwhile secured election as member for West Monmouth. He spent alternate weekends at Mentmore and Malwood, appealing to each antagonist to forgive and forget in the interest of Liberal unity. The best that he or anyone could manage was a sort of armed truce that left Rosebery in possession of the titular leadership, while Harcourt held sway in the Commons. A wholly unsatisfactory arrangement, it lasted until October 1896, when Rosebery suddenly announced his resignation, ostensibly in response to the party's disagreements over Turkish atrocities in Armenia. In a private letter to Asquith, he lamely explained his position, and closed with the hope that, 'very soon, you will replace me'.

One of the more interesting aspects of this protracted episode was Asquith's extraordinary ability to keep credit with both sides. 'Every effort has been made by mischief makers to cause ill blood between me and Asquith, but I have steadily refused to listen to them', Harcourt wrote on 4 November 1896 to Morley, who by then had found a constituency elsewhere on the Celtic fringe. 'Don't you wish you could open a paper', Morley asked Campbell-Bannerman eleven months later, 'without reading that you and I and Asquith are all ready to cut one another's throats – all for the sweet privilege of *leading* the Liberal Party?' Young enough to be able to wait patiently on events, Asquith did nothing to force the pace, which might have prejudiced his future claims.

Besides, he was in no financial position to pursue a full-time political career. In the autumn of 1895, he returned to his practice at the bar, which netted him between £5,000 and £10,000 a year. In the opinion of Henry Lucy, better-known to readers of *Punch* as 'Toby, M.P.', he had committed 'an act of political suicide unparalleled in recent history'. But, deprived of his ministerial income, Asquith had had no choice. His second wife, the daughter of a wealthy manufacturer and sometime Liberal backbencher, had to be kept in the style to which she was accustomed. And Asquith thoroughly enjoyed keeping her – and himself – in that style. Her father gave them an annual allowance of £5,000, which, however generous, did not go far to indulge Margot's extravagant tastes. Asquith took a lease on a large house in Cavendish Square, where he maintained a staff of no fewer than fourteen servants, including the requisite pair of footmen. He entertained lavishly and, until 1906, kept a stable for his wife, who had resumed her equestrian pursuits. There were also fees to be paid for the education of his four sons from his first marriage. Even without Margot, Jenkins has calculated, Asquith 'could never have afforded to be a full time politician in opposition'; with her, the idea was totally out of the question.

His closest friends took the view that his legal career, which was not especially distinguished, was an unfortunate distraction from his true calling. Twenty-six months after Harcourt had succeeded Rosebery as *de facto* party leader, he too resigned in a pique, and again the position was open. The front-runners were Campbell-Bannerman, who betrayed a characteristic diffidence, and Asquith, who in many ways appeared the logical choice. 'The best thing for us, far and away . . . would be for Asquith to give up the Bar & take the lead in the House,' Grey wrote to Haldane on 16 December 1898. 'If he could throw everything else to the winds and throw himself into this position and the work of it, his qualities & powers would develop and by the next Election he would have gained an influence far greater than he has ever yet had.' The party strategists and most of the 'bright young men', as Peter Stansky has felicitously dubbed them, concurred.

There is some indication that, this time, Asquith gave serious consideration to the proposition. Haldane was entrusted with the assignment of getting Balfour and Rosebery to put in a good word with Sir Charles Tennant, Margot's father, who might be induced to render additional assistance in the event that his son-in-law assumed the leadership of the Opposition. Haldane was authorized to say that Asquith 'is ready, and so is she, to make sacrifices to accept'. But 'the Bart' was evidently not forthcoming. At the age of seventy-five he had just remarried, and had his own domestic responsibilities. Furthermore, according to Haldane, he was partial to Campbell-Bannerman as a fellow Glaswegian. On 19 December Asquith wrote to Campbell-Bannerman 'to say at once, & without any ambiguity, that I earnestly hope you will see your way to take the lead, & that if you do you will receive from me – and I believe from all of us – the most loyal & energetic support'. Three days later, Asquith's eldest son shed further light on the situation in a letter to R. C. K. (later

Sir Robert) Ensor, whom he told that his father 'defers to C.-Bannerman, being a poor man and dependent on his practice at the Bar'. Campbell-Bannerman, pronounced fit by his doctors, left no doubt of his willingness to serve. On 6 February 1899 there was a meeting of Liberal M.P.s at the Reform Club, where he was duly elected. 'It did not necessarily follow that he would become Prime Minister if the party were returned to power,' his most recent biographer has pointed out, and many people – including Asquith – were inclined to regard him as a *locum tenens*. In any case, the advent of the Liberals to office was then the dimmest of prospects.

These were painfully difficult years for the Liberal Party, which was internally divided and out of temper with the prevailing national mood. In rapid succession, it had been spurned by two leaders, with Morley – to Asquith's intense annoyance – following Harcourt into retirement from the front bench. Rosebery, now a free agent, hovered enigmatically in the background, but was widely expected to re-emerge when the opportunity presented itself. As opposed to those who held nominal control, he personified a 'policy', which he articulated in a series of statesmanlike speeches that aimed to purge the party of the vestiges of Gladstonianism and to attune it to new currents of thought. While loyal (in varying degrees) to Campbell-Bannerman, the members of Asquith's circle were fervent Roseberians, and continued to look to their lost leader for a 'constructive' programme to overcome class and sectional differences within the party and beyond. Collectively, these individuals were known as Liberal Imperialists; but that was a designation that raises many more questions than it answers.

A Roseberian before he was a Liberal Imperialist, Asquith shared his mentor's determination to equip Liberalism with a new ethic and, in the process, a new image. Too long dominated by faddists and cranks, whose handiwork was the cumbersome Newcastle Programme of 1891, the party needed to have its horizons broadened and its spirit revived. To this purpose, Rosebery proposed a 'system of guiding principles . . . a great systematic and comprehensive concept that unified and guided the conduct of Liberals in many hitherto unco-ordinated areas of policy'. In the words of D. A. Hamer, 'much of the idealism and enthusiasm which is called forth especially among younger Liberals stemmed from its satisfying a craving for order and system in Liberal politics. It released energies that had hitherto been held in check or even paralysed by the absence of any over-all sense of direction and purpose.' Liberal Imperialism was, therefore, conceived by its proponents as a means to an end, which was to be achieved within the ideological context and organizational framework of the existing party. It promised to harness – and possibly to rechannel – the dynamism of popular sentiment, to provide an alternate philosophy to socialism, and – as Asquith saw it – to stimulate greater creativity in the sphere of social reform. As far as Morley was concerned, Liberal Imperialism was only 'Chamberlain wine with a Rosebery label'; but to those who imbibed at the fount, it was an altogether distinctive elixir, at once refreshing and nourishing.

The Liberal Imperialists, as Morley's quip would illustrate, incurred fierce enmity among the Gladstonian fundamentalists within their party, who were stigmatized as 'Little Englanders'. To these stalwarts, Rosebery and his disciples threatened to betray shamefully a proud tradition in an opportunistic bid for public favour. Anxious to dissociate themselves from this backward-looking school, the Liberal Imperialists had to beware of becoming apologists for the Unionist Government, which was engaged in these years in far-flung campaigns to extend the boundaries of empire. Some managed more adroitly than others to steer a middle course, to profess their imperialism without impugning their Liberalism. That a formal split was averted was largely to the credit of Campbell-Bannerman, who weathered the storm by perceiving its transitory nature. But Asquith, who had no wish to follow in the path of the Liberal Unionists, helped by providing a bridge between the two camps and, not least, by restraining some of his more impetuous associates.

No sooner had Rosebery relinquished office, though not yet the party command, than imperial controversies began to flare up. In the closing days of 1895, Dr Leander Starr Jameson (familiarly known as 'Dr Jim') launched his abortive raid on the Transvaal, allegedly in response to an appeal from the Uitlanders, the foreign community in Johannesburg, to rescue them from the iniquities of Boer rule. Instead of precipitating an uprising against President Kruger's Boer republic, Jameson was ignominiously captured and handed over to the British authorities for trial. 'An adventure more childishly conceived or more clumsily executed it is impossible to imagine', Asquith wrote years later, and he continued to marvel at the way the culprits 'were, on their arrival in England, acclaimed and fêted by a section of London society as the worthy successors of Drake and Raleigh'. A shade disingenuously, he neglected to mention that his own wife was among the hostesses who 'acclaimed and fêted' Dr Jim, who dined at Cavendish Square on the night before he went to prison.

Jameson's culpability, and that of Cecil Rhodes behind him, created less of a furore than suspicions that Joseph Chamberlain, the Colonial Secretary, had countenanced if not instigated the venture. It made no difference that Chamberlain, quickly and categorically, disavowed Jameson. 'That repudiation by itself', Jeffrey Butler has stated, 'did not satisfy all his contemporaries that the British Government was innocent of the charge of complicity at worst, connivance at best.' A Select Committee of the House of Commons was appointed to inquire into the circumstances of the raid. After some delay, it held the first of its thirty-five sittings on 6 February 1897. Five members of the Liberal Opposition – Campbell-Bannerman, Harcourt, Buxton, Labouchere, and J. E. Ellis – participated in the investigation. Margot Asquith could 'remember opening the front door of 20 Cavendish Square to Mr Chamberlain one morning' during the preceding summer, 'and showing him into my husband's library'. Afterwards, she asked what Joe had wanted. 'He asked me if I would serve on the Committee of Inquiry into the responsibility of the Jameson Raid – they call it "the Rhodes Commission" – and I refused,' Asquith told her. 'I asked him why he had refused,' Margot continued, 'to which he answered: "Do you take me for a fool?"' There is no reason to doubt the veracity of her recollection, especially as her husband was alive when it was published. Jenkins, citing the fact that Asquith disbelieved in Chamberlain's guilt, has taken it to mean that he 'was merely reacting against spending six months upon an enquiry which he thought likely to be politically disappointing'. More probably, however, Asquith was able to perceive the discredit that would attach to the members of the Select Committee, and especially those from the Liberal side, who would be saddled with responsibility without having had the opportunity to satisfy their consciences.

While the South African Committee conducted its proceedings, the country was celebrating Queen Victoria's Diamond Jubilee. On 25 June 1897 Beatrice Webb returned to London, and noted in her diary: 'Imperialism in the air – all classes drunk with sight-seeing and hysterical loyalty.' Neither Jameson's escapade nor the humiliation it incurred in any way dampened public ardour. Further imperial exploits only served to raise the pitch of excitement. 'Khartoum and Fashoda', Harcourt predicted to Morley with gloomy accuracy, 'will rally the popular sentiment as much as Trafalgar and Salamanca . . . We shall either see the submission of France which will be popular or a war with France which will be more popular still.' Early in 1899, the French withdrew their expeditionary force from the area of the upper Nile. *The Times*, in a leader on 18 January, trumpeted that the British Empire 'is now the mainstay of civilisation and progress, the refuge of freedom, intellectual, political, and commercial, in every part of the globe'. The stage was set for the war in South Africa, which was declared the following October.

Like Mrs Webb, but essentially for different reasons, Asquith was profoundly impressed by the way in which imperialism helped to promote social solidarity as well as an ethic of national efficiency. He did not, however, foresee the 'jingo' excesses to which it would lead. For information on the precarious state of affairs in South Africa he relied on frequent and lengthy communications from his old Balliol friend Alfred Milner, who had been dispatched in March 1897 as High Commissioner. A Liberal by his antecedents, if no longer by his proclivities, Milner was guest of honour at a farewell dinner that Asquith had given on the eve of his departure, at which the speakers had included Chamberlain, Balfour, and Morley. As High Commissioner, it was his assignment to negotiate with the recalcitrant Boers over Uitlander grievances and other subjects of dispute. Addressing his constituents on 2 September, weeks before the outbreak of hostilities, Asquith inveighed against the 'irresponsible clamours which we hear from familiar quarters for war', and put his trust in 'firm and prudent diplomacy'. But Milner, more firm than prudent, only stiffened Boer resistance.

Asquith's response to war, when it came, was one of calm resignation. 'I was much interested by your news,' he replied to John Roskill, who relayed word on 8 October that the Transvaal government had drafted an ultimatum. 'Smuts's cable reads as if the Boers had finally made up their minds to fight. I am afraid there is nothing more to be said or done.' Thereafter, he adhered religiously to the view 'that war was neither intended nor desired by the Government and the people of Great Britain, but that it was forced upon us without adequate reason, entirely against our will'. Others within the Liberal fold thought differently, and ascribed the conflict to Milner's inflexible diplomacy and Chamberlain's unrepentant expansionism. When Parliament convened on 17 October, Philip Stanhope, an outspoken critic of the South African Committee report, moved an amendment to the Address expressing 'strong disapproval of the conduct of the negotiations with the Government of the Transvaal which have involved us in hostilities with the two South African Republics', the Transvaal and the Orange Free State. Although it could not have been expected to carry, the motion afforded the occasion for a full-scale debate on South African issues, and made an impact by the number and prominence of its supporters. Campbell-Bannerman abstained along with seventy-seven others of his party; but Ellis, Labouchere, and Harcourt were among the 135 M.P.s, including no fewer than eight future Liberal Cabinet ministers, who accompanied Stanhope into the lobby. Predictably, most of the Liberal Imperialists, including Grey and Haldane, voted with the Government. Asquith, however, was not among them.

Consonant with his resolve to lead from the centre, Campbell-Bannerman declined to affiliate either with the truculent 'pro-Boers', who demanded peace at any price, or with the Liberal Imperialists, who wished the war to be fought to a successful conclusion. Taking the position that Liberalism was a mansion with many rooms, he was not prepared to deny accommodation to any viewpoint, however extreme. Unfortunately, some of his followers refused to extend him the same toleration. To Morley and his ilk, Campbell-Bannerman was insufficiently militant against the war; to the Rosebery brigade, he counted as an irredeemable 'pro-Boer'. In fact, he was neither, but merely an astute politician, feeling his way. Writing to Grey on 21 October 1899, Rosebery mischievously gloated that the Liberal Party 'is nearing its final cataclysm. The Rump will break with the Imperialist section and ally itself with the Irishry. All this in the long run must tend to do good.' But Rosebery had misjudged the situation and, in particular, the quiet resourcefulness of Campbell-Bannerman.

It is noteworthy that Rosebery anticipated that the 'Rump' would break with the Imperialist faction, and not vice versa. He knew full well that Asquith, Grey, Haldane, Fowler, and the others did not dare to sever their ties with the official leadership. They hoped to permeate or capture the party, not to estrange themselves from it. Asquith, doubtless the most circumspect among them, tried to focus attention on those questions on which Liberals could still agree. 'The difficulty is that for the moment people will listen to nothing but talk about the war,' he complained on 27 November to Herbert Gladstone, the Chief Whip. 'As you wd. see', he recounted,

I had to deliver myself about the war on Sat. In one way the result was very satisfactory. I had on the platform [Robert] Spence Watson, [Charles] Fenwick, & others who belong to the extreme peace party. They all spoke, & while of course not agreeing wholly with me as to the causes of the war, they all declared that they agreed absolutely with what I said as to our future line, & that the differences in the party were merely as to the right interpretation of past facts, & not as to the principles of our action.

On the vexed question of Home Rule, to which the Liberal Imperialists were generally less committed than other Liberals, he again took a conciliatory line. 'I agree with Sir H. C-B,' he averred to Gladstone on 8 January 1900. 'There is no question, as I understand, of those of us who have for 13 years advocated HR abandoning our position.' The 'sole question' was a tactical one: 'is it to be raised as an "issue" at the next election, in the sense that the Liberal party, if victorious, would be under an obligation to bring in a Bill?' To this specific question, an academic one to be sure, he was disposed to reply 'in the negative'. He put his case most clearly in a letter to James Bryce, whose vote for the Stanhope amendment did not disqualify him as a faithful supporter of Campbell-Bannerman. 'The great object at the moment', he stated on 20 January, 'obviously shd. be to choose & frame an issue on wh. the whole party can unite. As no one among us has a good word to say for the Govt. this ought not to be impossible. But it is undoubtedly a delicate task.'

As the months passed, and the rift within the party widened, Asquith came to doubt whether Campbell-Bannerman would be able to discharge this 'delicate task'. In May, the relief of Mafeking, where British infantry had withstood a siege of 217 days, unleashed a frenzied exultation which the Unionists did not hesitate to exploit. Voters in a by-election at Manchester South were implored to 'let their first message to gallant Mafeking' be the news of a Liberal defeat. 'Khaki' methods of electioneering were proved spectacularly successful and, by the time that M.P.s returned from the Whitsun recess, it was apparent that the Government were set to go to the country at an early date.

Of all people, it was Lloyd George, who was to call an election under similar circumstances eighteen years later, who rose in the Commons on 25 July to denounce the Prime Minister for seeking 'a judgment of the people in the very height and excitement of the fever'. Sir Wilfrid Lawson, who shared his 'pro-Boer' indignation, moved a stinging censure of the Government. Finding himself in an embarrassing position, Campbell-Bannerman appealed for 'a general abstention' on Lawson's amendment, but his advice was disregarded. Thirty-five Liberals, including Asquith, walked out; thirty-one voted with Lawson; and forty voted against the amendment and, to all intents and purposes, in support of the Government. Late that evening, Haldane gave Rosebery a detailed account of the proceedings:

Asquith (who was with us but did not vote) and Grey think that CB was riding for a fall. He may change his mind in the morning, but our impression is that he means to resign & set off for Marienbad on the advice of Maclagen, his good physician.

If so what has happened has merely anticipated what later on would have happened & it is now necessary to see what should be done.

The party is not likely to agree on any leader in the House. Grey & I think that there will be 2 sections now. Asquith is pretty sure to be the *de facto* leader. He took me aside tonight & from what he said I think he is ready to act as the chief of our group should CB not go on . . . But if you choose to emerge & lead those Liberals who may be called 'Lord R's friends', with Asquith & Grey as lieutenants in the House, I think things will work out.

But Rosebery, whom Morley delectably described as 'a dark horse in a loose box', stayed pent up; and Campbell-Bannerman, with encouragement from Bryce, stayed on in his thankless job.

As expected, an election was called for early October. The Liberals were in utter disarray, leaving the Unionists as confident of victory at the polls as in the South African *veldt*. Bryce alleged to Campbell-Bannerman that their opponents were using as ammunition quotations from the speeches of Asquith and Fowler. The Liberal Imperialists, trying to protect themselves from the 'pro-Boers' on one flank and from the Unionists on the other, set up a Liberal Imperialist Council, with Lord Brassey as president. Its driving force was R. W. Perks ('Imperial Perks', Beatrice Webb disdainfully nicknamed him), the member for Louth and a prominent Wesleyan lay leader. Irreparable harm was caused by Brassey's 'slip' that the Council was designed to provide the nucleus for a new party. 'My notion has always been to secure sufficient power to capture & control the old', Perks hastened to assure Rosebery. Nevertheless, it was possible for Harcourt and Labouchere to castigate the 'Limps' as seceders, at the same time as Chamberlain attacked them as lukewarm patriots. Fowler, who was connected to Perks through business and religious contacts, and Grey took an active part in Council affairs; but Asquith was not directly involved. Perhaps for that reason the 'pro-Boers' were more muted and sometimes even respectful in their attitude towards him: Lloyd George, in a speech at Conway on 27 September, paid him tribute as 'an abler man intellectually' than Chamberlain. Despite this encomium, Asquith was among the fifty-six Liberal candidates whom the Council deemed worthy of its backing in the election that got under way the next day.

Polling was spread out over more than a fortnight, and one Liberal reverse followed another. Chamberlain, taking no pains to distinguish between his adversaries, smeared them all with the same brush:

'A seat lost to the Government', he crudely put it, 'is a seat gained (or sold) to the Boers.' Not surprisingly, anti-war candidates fared badly: Stanhope lost Burnley (a seat that had not gone Conservative since 1868) by 600 votes; Lawson was defeated by 209 votes at Cockermouth; and Lloyd George was returned for the Caernarvon Boroughs with a shaky majority of 194. By various estimates, between one and two dozen of the 'pro-Boers' in the last Parliament were rejected.

Thirty miles from the Stirling Burghs, where Campbell-Bannerman's previous majority was halved, Asquith at East Fife increased his majority from 716 to 1,431. '... My people behaved splendidly', he reported to Gladstone on 7 October. 'The rot, which had devastated Glasgow & invaded Edinburgh, did not affect them in the least, & at the end the pro-Boers, Socialists, &c, &c, worked as hard as the rest, with the result that we doubled our majority.' Yet he could not deny that, on the whole, the election was proving a 'damnable débâcle' for the Liberals. 'We have seen the worst fit of political debauch since 1877–78, with the difference that the orgy was then presided over by a man of genius [Disraeli], whereas now the master of the feast has the manners of a cad & the tongue of a bargee.'

*The Times*, without specifying the criteria on which it based its tabulation, was pleased to observe that the Liberal Imperialists had increased their representation in the Commons from sixty-three to eighty-one. In addition, it counted 106 'Radical and Labour members' whose opinions on the war were either negative or 'doubtful'. Although Harcourt, for one, considered 'the result ... better rather than worse than [one] would have expected', the Liberals mustered only 184 seats, giving the Unionists an overall majority of 134. And, in the course of a gruelling campaign, personal relations had been subjected to intensified strain. 'We heard a great deal of the election bringing Liberals together', Campbell-Bannerman reminded Spencer on 6 November. 'I doubt it.' Jenkins's protestations to the contrary, Campbell-Bannerman was now, for the first time, inclined to look with suspicion on Asquith, whom he identified as a member of a 'Balliol set' and one of the high priests of the *religio Milneriana*.

Asquith, for his part, was initially more critical of Rosebery: 'He was afraid to plunge, yet not resolute enough to hold to his determination to keep aloof.' Grey, equally disillusioned with their phantom hero, threatened to 'chuck it' sooner than continue under Campbell-Bannerman's feeble leadership. Munro Ferguson, to whom Grey communicated his threat on 18 October, did 'chuck it' by resigning as Scottish whip. The Liberal Imperialist Council, convinced that the judgement day had dawned, issued a manifesto that called for a new leader 'in whose policy with regard to Imperial questions patriotic voters may justly repose confidence'. Campbell-Bannerman countered in a speech at Dundee on 15 November in which he referred inadvertently – but tellingly – to the actions of 'the Liberal Unionist Council'. For a time, he seemed to have reasserted his authority. In December, Grey and Haldane spoke and, with the other Liberal Imperialists, voted in support of a resolution moved by Lloyd George, who faulted Chamberlain for assigning war contracts to firms in which his family held investments. But the intra-party truce was short-lived.

It was broken in the spring of 1901 by the return of Milner, who came home on leave. Opponents of the war held him personally responsible for its origins and, still more, for having sanctioned the decision to respond to Boer commando raids by farm-burnings and civilian concentration camps, where the mortality rates were shockingly high. The Liberal Imperialists, on the other hand, defended him as a dedicated public servant, who had taken on a difficult assignment and, under the circumstances, had done it well. On 24 May, when he disembarked at Southampton, Grey was on hand to join in the tumultuous welcome. Fowler went further, and accepted Chamberlain's invitation to a dinner in Milner's honour at Claridges. As one faction of Liberals eulogized Milner, another was correspondingly moved to denounce him. As A. M. Gollin has explained, 'Chamberlain regularly drove the "Milner wedge" into the Liberal ranks', and 'Campbell-Bannerman could do little to heal the divisions in his party in the face of these tactics.' At first, like Asquith, he refused to be drawn into the public debate. But, in a speech to the National Reform Union at the Holborn Restaurant on 14 June, he came off the fence, and took his place on the anti-Milner side.

With Morley, Harcourt, and Stanhope in attendance, Campbell-Bannerman reviewed the military tactics to which the British had resorted in their desperate effort to quash Boer guerrilla resistance. 'A phrase often used is that "war is war"', he temperately began, alluding to a recent statement by St John Brodrick, the Secretary of State for War; 'but when one comes to ask about it one is told that no war is going on, that it is not war. When is a war not a war?' he asked rhetorically. 'When it is carried on by methods of barbarism in South Africa.'

The effect was slightly delayed, as befitting a thunderclap. The

next day's newspapers passed over Campbell-Bannerman's passionate peroration and, like Asquith, instead took issue with Morley's
'impromptu' that offered the 'challenging description' of true
Liberals as those in accord with the sentiments of the evening.
Within a few days, however, it was the 'methods of barbarism'
phrase on which everyone fastened. The Unionists denounced it as
an inadmissible slur on British soldiery. The 'pro-Boers', welcoming
Campbell-Bannerman belatedly to their ranks, applauded it as a
noble affirmation of Liberal humanitarianism. Alternately celebrated
as a stroke of genius and criticized as an unpardonable blunder, his
speech gave the anti-war agitation a new slogan and a new direction:
it was not necessary to condemn British diplomacy in 1899 in order
to condemn the prosecution of the war in 1901. That, it seems, may
have been unintentional. Many years later, Asquith recalled to
A. G. Gardiner, the Liberal journalist and biographer, that Campbell-
Bannerman had 'often admitted to me' that the 'methods of barbarism' phrase 'was his worst *gaffe*'.

At the time, Asquith was stung into action. 'The banquet of last
Friday', he wrote to Perks on 19 June, 'with its incidents and consequences, seems to me to suggest that it is time for those of us who are
not willing that the official and propagandist machinery should be
captured by Lloyd George and his friends, to bestir themselves'. The
previous day, when Campbell-Bannerman supported Lloyd George
in a censure motion on the concentration camps, Asquith was among
fifty Liberals who abstained. In retaliation for Campbell-Bannerman's after-dinner remarks on the 14th, he dined six days later at
the Liverpool Street Hotel with members of the South Essex Liberal
Association, whom he told 'in the plainest and most unequivocal
terms' that neither he nor his associates had 'changed our view, that
we do not repent of it, and that we shall not recant it'. To Gladstone,
he wrote 'disingenuously' (in the opinion of Campbell-Bannerman's
recent biographer) to the effect that the second dinner had been 'no
idea of mine, but it was put to me in such a way that I did not feel
able to decline'. Unconvinced, Gladstone thought it imperative 'to
save A. from his friends'. Henry Lucy was better able to see the
humour in the situation: 'To dine or not to dine, that is the question', he parodied. 'Whether 'tis nobler to suffer the slings and arrows
of the outrageous John Morley, or, to take a room at the Hotel Cecil,
invite Asquith to dinner and make things hot for our pro-Boer
brethren.' First, the National Reform Union had savoured Campbell-
Bannerman's comestibles at the Holborn Restaurant; then, the
South Essex Liberals had had their hunger appeased by Asquith at

the Liverpool Street Hotel. 'Now the hot bloods of the party are for war to the knife – and fork.' It remained to be seen which of them would land in the soup.

With sharpened cutlery, Asquith's friends planned another dinner in his honour at the City Liberal Club on 19 July. Its announcement, coupled with the fact that Rosebery was invited to preside, dropped a bombshell. Forty M.P.s, led by Reginald McKenna and Charles Hobhouse, both of whom were eventually Asquith's Cabinet colleagues, protested that, despite their esteem for him, they could not attend such an inflammatory event. Nine days before it was to be held, Campbell-Bannerman appealed to him for its postponement 'to a later time when all the Party will join in, and when it will have lost all that tinge of sectional feeling which undoubtedly will cling to it now'. After consulting 'with those who are responsible for the dinner', Asquith officiously replied that 'the arrangements are too far advanced to make postponement possible except at the cost of enormous inconvenience to people in all parts and countless explanations and misunderstandings'. Campbell-Bannerman was prepared to ascribe the difficulty to 'weakness' on the part of Asquith, whom he held less culpable than 'those gentry' – particularly Grey and Haldane – who 'have made A. their tool in a great plot against me'. But according to Grey, Asquith was 'very annoyed' at Campbell-Bannerman's intrusion, and entirely his own master. It was obvious that he did not mean to leave his imperialist friends in the lurch; and, as Jenkins has reasonably inferred, he 'was not averse to using the dinner as a show of his strength as against that of Campbell-Bannerman'.

For all the controversy that anticipated it, the dinner on the 19th fell strangely flat. For one thing, Campbell-Bannerman had stolen its thunder by hastily summoning a meeting of Liberal M.P.s and peers at the Reform Club ten days earlier. There, where he had been elected to the party leadership, he secured a resounding vote of confidence. But the real damage was done by Rosebery. Having declined to appear at the City Liberal Club either for Asquith's dinner or for a luncheon meeting the same day (he would 'never voluntarily return to the arena of party politics', he declared in a letter to *The Times* on the 17th), he changed his mind and materialized that afternoon. Pre-empting attention from the dinner that followed, he made a provocative speech which, by its timing as much as by its contents ('I must plough my furrow alone'), was taken to imply disapproval of Asquith.

With Grey in the chair, the dinner went off as planned, with thirty-nine M.P.s among the guests. In the main speech of the evening, Asquith took a moderate line that contrasted with Rosebery's sullen bellicosity: on the one hand, he stressed the need for the Liberals to serve as 'a national party to which you can safely entrust the fortunes of the Empire'; on the other, he proclaimed that 'I have never called myself a Liberal Imperialist. The name of Liberal is good enough for me.' He could not, however, dispel the mood that lingered from the lunch-time session. Mrs Webb heard from her husband, whom Haldane had 'enlisted . . . on the Asquith side', that it was 'a scratch assembly'. It was Asquith who was being honoured, but Rosebery to whom all thoughts turned. What had his outburst signified?

Grey, who had taken it as a veiled attack on Asquith, reproached Rosebery the next day in (for him) forthright terms:

You are going to plough your furrow. Some of us too are setting to work to plough a furrow, which goes in the same direction. We ought not therefore to come into conflict, but the situation needs delicate handling and for the present there is some soreness. In the first place, Asquith has come through a very trying time and has in my opinion saved the situation, as far as the 'centre' of the Liberal party is concerned. Without him, and if he had not stood by us, there would have been a secession of myself and a few, but *very few*, others from the Liberal party before you had come back. Now, if there is a split, it will be a much less one-sided affair. Asquith has been very staunch to us & we are very chivalrously disposed towards him.

Haldane, after a conversation with Asquith on the 21st, carried word to Rosebery that their friend regretted 'the loss of prestige which arose from the *appearance* of the great sacrifice & effort of his life being jumped upon'. He seconded Grey's request that Rosebery should show greater 'consideration' for Asquith's motives and predicament. By this time, Asquith had presumably received a disarming letter from Rosebery who, oblivious to any rebuke he may have administered, professed glowing admiration for Asquith's speech at the City Liberal Club and, in fact, 'all your speeches'. Not knowing what to make of Rosebery's behaviour, Asquith replied in a nostalgic vein, expressing 'hope . . . that your "furrow" will prove not to be divergent, or even parallel, but sooner or later (& the sooner the better) to be one in which E. Grey & I & all your real friends & associates can lend a hand'. There was no use remonstrating with Rosebery, whose instability had to be accepted as a fact of political life.

During the summer and autumn of 1901, Asquith assumed an

unrivalled command over the Liberal Imperialist troops. His speech in late August on belligerent rights was interpreted by Campbell-Bannerman to show 'a vicious determination to stick at nothing in his, and his friends', separation from us'. But Campbell-Bannerman, far off at Marienbad, only vaguely suspected what was afoot. Professing himself 'most anxious that we should not dissipate our forces or lose (thro' inactivity, or unorganized movement) any of the real & solid ground which we have gained during the last two months', Asquith presided over a series of meetings of what Haldane called 'the Asquith committee'. In secret conclave at Cavendish Square and, with the change of season, at various Scottish retreats, the group – which included Grey, Haldane, Munro Ferguson, and Perks – met to lay down 'the lines of the speeches in October when we begin work'. There was to be a co-ordinated campaign for 'efficiency' with reference to domestic reform, the empire, and Ireland. Haldane primed the Webbs, and Perks kept in touch with Rosebery, who confided his 'doubts' as to whether 'Asquith can succeed in his endeavour to influence the party from within'.

'The timing of the Asquith committee's autumn campaign was excellent', H. C. G. Matthew has written, pointing out that it followed hard upon a by-election at North-East Lanark, where a split Liberal vote had delivered the seat to the Unionists. The Liberal Imperialist Council, which, at Rosebery's suggestion, had been rechristened the Liberal (Imperialist) League – 'The design of the brackets', Rosebery helpfully explained to a follower, 'was to imply that the Liberal Imperialists were the real Liberal Party, which should naturally imply Imperialism' – was now shorn of its clumsy brackets and reconstituted as a vehicle for the Asquith committee. Grey replaced Lord Brassey as president, Haldane and Perks took charge of organization, and William Allard, who had distinguished himself as secretary of the Home Counties Liberal Federation, was brought in as secretary. Asquith delayed until 25 November before he became, with Fowler, an 'honorary member' of the League. 'I wonder how Asquith's new move strikes you', Morley asked Harcourt. 'To me it seems rather grave for C.B. . . . It was certain he [Asquith] would have to do something, but this looks like the worst thing he could have done – to join a sectional organization formed inside the party, with the avowed design of countering the leader of the party.'

On 16 December Rosebery delivered a much heralded speech at Chesterfield. Not even Asquith and Grey, who graced the platform, had had any intimation of what he would say. To their consternation,

Rosebery took issue with Milner's demand for 'unconditional surrender' and, while deriding the 'methods of barbarism' mentality,
advocated a negotiated settlement to the South African war. More
satisfactorily, he called for a 'clean slate', which meant dismantling
the planks of the Newcastle Programme and, in particular, jettison-
ing Home Rule. Campbell-Bannerman, more bemused than irritated,
saved his outrage for 'Master Grey', who had threatened dire consequences if Rosebery's message went unheeded. 'But Asquith', he
recognized, 'is the man of real importance', and on 31 December (and
again on 6 January) Campbell-Bannerman instructed Gladstone to
ascertain his position.

Although Asquith was stinting in his praise for Rosebery's
Chesterfield performance, he thought that it had presented 'a real
chance for united & reconstructed action' that had gone begging. Of
his own intentions, he revealed little. 'I never hear anything of or
from him', Campbell-Bannerman admitted. Rosebery could not have
said the same. During the early weeks of 1902, he and Asquith were
meeting with the officials of the Liberal Imperialist League, who
decided on yet another change of name and an intensified campaign.
Challenged by Campbell-Bannerman to define his 'definite separation', Rosebery replied in a letter to *The Times* on 21 February in
which he declared himself 'outside [Campbell-Bannerman's] taber-
nacle, but not, I think, in solitude'. Three days later, at his London
house, the Liberal League was founded. Rosebery was president,
with Asquith, Grey, and Fowler (joined by Haldane at a later date)
as vice-presidents, and Perks as treasurer. Among the supporters for
the venture was Sir Charles Tennant, 'the Bart', whose assurances,
according to Haldane, made it 'not unlikely' that Asquith would
'leave the Bar at once to devote himself to the attempt to work
something out of what is reasonable in our party'.

At the inaugural meeting, Rosebery warned his colleagues of the
risks, to which Asquith was fully alive. Asquith, his own being one
of the 'one or two prominent careers . . . which might be gravely
affected by the course they took', voiced a preference that those
M.P.s 'who agreed with Lord R. . . . should remain in the House of
Commons without forming a separate organization, though acting in
connection on important questions'. The League was to concentrate
its energies in the constituencies where (as in North-East Lanark)
Liberal Imperialist candidates had been disavowed. Purportedly a
defensive operation, it disclaimed any schismatic tendencies, although
there was loose talk that it might on occasion field its own candidates.
The League attracted a good deal of attention in the press, but less

at Westminster, where, Campbell-Bannerman was pleased to report, it was 'laughed at'. Elsewhere, Asquith's eldest son was among those who sniggered: Rosebery, he wrote from Oxford to John Buchan in South Africa, 'has started a thing called the Liberal League, which appears at present to consist of three persons – himself, my father, and Grey – backed by a squad of titled ladies'.

Vague in its purpose, the League suffered most from its reliance on Rosebery, whose national appeal was offset by his inconstancy. The wind was taken out of its sails, which had never billowed to any great extent, by the restoration of peace in South Africa and, still more, by Balfour's Education Bill of 1902. Nonconformists, who had flocked to the League largely through the initiative of Perks, were adamantly opposed to the legislation, which allocated state funds to Church and even Roman Catholic schools. Finding the League divided in its response to the measure, they mounted their own agitation, separate from and, to some extent, in conflict with the League.

Asquith, a Nonconformist by background, took a more militant stand against the Education Bill than Rosebery or certainly Haldane, who incurred odium by supporting it in Parliament as a major step towards 'national efficiency'. Sir Robert Ensor, who concurred with Haldane's view, has ranked it as 'among the two or three greatest constructive measures of the twentieth century'. Nonconformist opinion, too inflamed to see any merit in the Bill, solidified in opposition to it. As it proved, education was one of those rare issues that permitted Liberals of different persuasions to join in concerted activity: at the Queen's Hall on 10 June, Asquith shared the platform with, among others, Lloyd George; at the Alexandra Palace on 1 November, he and Campbell-Bannerman jointly addressed a demonstration sponsored by the Liberation Society. Reconciliation was made easier by the fact that Rosebery, like the Cheshire Cat, had once again faded from the scene.

Chamberlain, without a war to occupy him, and with a view to winning back support alienated by the Government's education policy (for which he was no enthusiast), hit out in the spring of 1903 with a scheme of protective tariffs. 'On the morning of 16th May, 1903,' Margot Asquith recalled, 'my husband came into my bedroom at 20 Cavendish Square' – she never tired of reciting her address – 'with *The Times* in his hand. "Wonderful news today," he said, "and it is only a question of time when we shall sweep the country."' If there was one thing on which all Liberals could be expected to unite, it was the defence of their Free Trade principles. Asquith, although he had taken part in the education campaign, had not been on his home ground. Now a second and, to his mind, an overriding issue presented itself that exerted a more direct appeal to his intellect and experience.

In a speech at Doncaster on 21 May, Asquith replied assuredly and authoritatively to the Tariff Reform proposals which Chamberlain had unveiled at Birmingham six days earlier. He resumed the battle in the autumn, after Chamberlain had resigned from the Government (was Asquith as instrumental as Jenkins has implied?) to stump the country on behalf of his fiscal policy. At each whistle-stop, he had Asquith at his heels, challenging his statistics, and disputing the logic of his case. Steeped in economic theory and historical precedent, Asquith displayed a prodigious knowledge, which, as his official biographers proudly observed, 'was producible on the instant, in black and white, without blur, indecision, or inaccuracy'. It was not without irony that, a self-professed imperialist, he made his mark as the trenchant critic of a scheme to unify the empire.

So far as Asquith was concerned, 'it is all important to defeat J.C., & for the moment to concentrate on that'. To this end, he advocated an alliance, preferably a formal one, with the Free Traders (including, incidentally, Lord James of Hereford) on the ministerial side. Inconveniently, the leading Unionist 'Free Fooders' had identified themselves as fervent supporters of the Education Act, and therefore the Nonconformist element would have no truck with them. However agile, the Liberal chiefs could not pick up the support of these disaffected Unionists without dropping their own Nonconformist parcels. On this score, Perks and Lloyd George stood in rare agreement, and the latter wrote to his wife on 23 December that 'Asquith . . . must be stopped at once'.

It was here that Campbell-Bannerman showed his mettle. Firmly of the opinion 'that Education is far before Tariffs in the public mind', he accepted Bryce's recommendation that 'It would not do, when we are going into battle, to blunt the edge of the Puritan sword.' Nevertheless, he warmly commended Asquith's 'wonderful speeches', which he appreciated as a contribution to the common cause that neither he nor anyone else was equipped to make. Off the record, he evaluated party personnel in a conversation about this time with Gardiner of the *Daily News*. 'Asquith?' he replied pensively to Gardiner's interrogation. 'Asquith *qua* Asquith is a fine fellow, an honest man & a sincere Liberal. But Asquith *cum* Margot is a lost soul.' By 'Margot' he meant not only Asquith's wife, but also the social and political ambitions with which her glittering name was synonymous.

And what, at this stage, did Asquith think of C.B. *qua* C.B.? On the one hand, he grudgingly admired the way the beleaguered veteran had held his ground against more clever men. On the other, he nursed serious doubts as to whether Campbell-Bannerman had either the stamina or the resolve to lead the Liberals successfully back into office. In his late sixties, Campbell-Bannerman's health was indifferent, and his wife was ailing. Herbert Gladstone, after 'a long talk about the future' with him, wrote to Asquith on 29 October 1903 that, 'in the event of a change of government', Campbell-Bannerman 'did not think that he would be able to take any part which involved heavy and responsible work'. He would probably be satisfied with a peerage and some honorific post – perhaps the lord presidency of the council – in the next Liberal administration. Gladstone's news, Haldane told his mother two days later, put Asquith 'in good spirits'. The way seemed paved for a Roseberian restoration or, more probably, an Asquith premiership. Rosebery, who did nothing to facilitate the first prospect, was ambivalent about the second. After indicating to Haldane 'that he is going to work with all his strength for an *A*. Ministry', he sulked to Munro Ferguson that 'shd. an Asquith Govt. be formed he might go abroad'.

Campbell-Bannerman's renewed activity during the next parliamentary session belied the sentiments he had expressed privately to Gladstone. Yet Gladstone's disclosure continued to weigh heavily on Asquith's mind and to influence his strategy. In the light of what had been reported, it appeared less urgent to dislodge Campbell-Bannerman, who might be expected to abdicate, than to harry the Unionists from office. Asquith conveyed back-handed congratulations in October, when Lyttelton was appointed to the Balfour Cabinet: 'I should of course try (as would you, in a similar case) to make the days of your Government as few & as uncomfortable as possible.' In order to expedite matters, he moved to dissociate himself from Milner and 'Milnerism'.

On the same day as Gladstone wrote to him, Asquith dined with Milner, who afterwards 'talked a good deal to Asquith, Grey and Haldane'. Already the Liberal Imperialists had retreated from their earlier position of uncritical support for Milner's South African policies, but it was not yet clear how far they intended to go. The break came the following February, during the uproar in the Commons over Milner's decision to permit the importation of Chinese indentured labour to work the mines on the Rand. Aside from Haldane, who tactfully abstained from the vote and did not speak, the Liberal Imperialists joined in the condemnation of what less responsible elements in the party branded as 'Chinese slavery'. Asquith's opposition to the scheme, although couched in procedural terms, came as a particular blow to Milner, who was under the impression that he had obtained the assent of 'the moderate section' of the Opposition during his visit to England the previous autumn. '. . . I did think you had got Asquith straight on the point,' Leo Amery wrote to assure him on 26 February, 'but I am afraid the temptation, with office looming so near and wall paper for 10 Downing Street already selected by Mrs A., was too much for him, and his performance was as bad as anyone else's, if not worse'.

Amery, then a young journalist on *The Times*, was not mistaken. Asquith had set his sights on office, and high office at that. If Margot's wall paper was not yet to adorn Number Ten, it might complement the decor at Number Eleven, next door; in any case, it would not go to waste. Haldane reported that 'the general feeling', when Parliament assembled in February, was 'that the Govt. cannot last long'. A string of by-election defeats presaged its imminent fall. But Balfour, playing for time, held on tenaciously, forcing the Liberals to revise their timetables. On 11 August Asquith wrote to St Loe Strachey, editor of the *Spectator*, that he thought 'a dissolution in the spring a moral certainty'.

Margot was another of Strachey's correspondents. 'I long for my husband to have his chance while he is young & keen', she declared on 4 January 1905. Behind Asquith's shoulder (and sometimes behind his back as well), she participated in the idle pastime of assigning places in the next Liberal Cabinet. Rosebery, she told Strachey 'in great confidence', had taken himself out of the running. 'I want you in your paper not to talk of a Rosebery administration now but an Asquith one.' Spencer was not to be lightly dismissed, either on his own account or in tandem with Campbell-Bannerman, but 'if Henry is the person written & spoken of as the obvious man it might help Ld. Spencer to see whether it might not be better for him to be foreign secretary & H. P.M. & leader of the House'. These calculations, she emphasized, were 'only my own idea'. As such, they were no more far-fetched than those that preoccupied other Liberals, including her husband, while they waited to leave the wilderness and enter the promised land.

Before proceeding to the formation of the 1905 Liberal Government, it is appropriate to ask what continued relevance the doctrines and agencies of Liberal Imperialism may have had. Although the Liberal League remained in existence until May 1910, when it was unceremoniously disbanded, its senior members were already pursuing separate strategies, often at cross purposes to each other. Back in September 1901, Sidney Webb had brilliantly illuminated the underlying contradictions of the movement in a famous article, 'Lord Rosebery's Escape from Houndsditch', in the *Nineteenth Century*. The ambiguities and inconsistencies he perceived thereafter became more pronounced. A *fin de siècle* phenomenon, more memorable for its rhetorical flourishes than for any distinctive policies, Liberal Imperialism never effectively resolved its allegiances. As the intrigues of 1905 were to demonstrate most conclusively, it was a halfway house without political foundations, which its tenants accordingly abandoned when more regular accommodation was made available to them. Perhaps, in Asquith's case, that had been the intention all along.

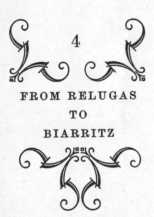

# 4

## FROM RELUGAS
## TO
## BIARRITZ

        With little else going for him, Balfour staved off electoral defeat by clinging to office as long as possible in the hope that the delay might exacerbate and bring to the surface the divisions on the Liberal side. His opponents, as they waited impatiently, came perilously close to fulfilling his cynical expectation.

As the weeks passed and party prospects brightened, top-ranking Liberals amused themselves and infuriated one another by drawing up elaborate blueprints for the construction of the next administration. Every conceivable ministerial combination was aired. Some party strategists pressed the claims of Lord Spencer, whom Gladstone had nominated as his successor back in 1894, but whom Queen

Victoria had passed over: could Campbell-Bannerman and Rosebery be persuaded to serve under him, the latter possibly at the Colonial Office, its status enhanced by Chamberlain's recent tenancy? Others strenuously urged a Campbell-Bannerman premiership, if only until a general election had confirmed the party in possession of power: in that case, Spencer might go to the Foreign Office, and either Morley or Asquith might take the Exchequer. Not a few held out for a Roseberian restoration, although Lord Rosebery's closest associates privately admitted that the cause was 'hopeless'. And there was some talk, not limited to Margot's rarefied social circle, of an Asquith government, with Rosebery standing benevolently aside, and either Spencer or Campbell-Bannerman leading in the Lords.

The crystal ball was clouded by Rosebery's habitual aloofness, by Campbell-Bannerman's renewed determination, and finally by Spencer's sudden and serious illness that took him out of the running. It was against this confused background that Asquith joined with Haldane and Grey to formulate a concerted policy. Rosebery was neither a party nor an accessory to their plan: 'his interest', Haldane warned Asquith, 'would be to wreck it'.

In previous conversations with Morley, upon whom they could depend to convey their message to Campbell-Bannerman, the trio had made clear their extreme reluctance – though not yet their absolute refusal – to affiliate with any administration led by Campbell-Bannerman from the front bench of the House of Commons. The possibility was thus held open that they might, individually or collectively, accept an arrangement by which Campbell-Bannerman was transplanted to the upper House. For reasons that invite speculation, others too had come to the conclusion that Campbell-Bannerman might best serve party interests by taking a peerage; the idea was one that merited and received serious consideration.

With this purpose in mind, Asquith and his two friends ratified their curious 'Relugas Compact'. Framed in the early weeks of September, it took its name from the remote fishing-lodge in Morayshire where Grey had gone in pursuit of the season's catch. Conveniently, Haldane and Asquith were also relaxing in Scotland, gathering strength for the coming session, which they had good reason to suppose would be Balfour's last as Prime Minister. At one or another of their respective retreats, the three Liberal Imperialists met informally to formalize their position. Their movements, which escaped detection by the press, cannot be ascertained with any degree of precision: an abortive *coup* is never as easily documented as a successful one.

But the terms of the 'Compact', if not its circumstances, are well enough known. Asquith, Haldane, and Grey pledged to deny Campbell-Bannerman the benefit of their services or reputations unless he first obliged them by removing himself to the Lords and surrendering the leadership of the Commons – with the Exchequer attached – to Asquith. It further stipulated that the Foreign Office (or alternatively the Colonial Office) should be reserved for Grey, that Haldane (with no prior ministerial experience) should be made Lord Chancellor, and that suitable accommodation should be found for such subordinates as Fowler and Buxton. Haldane was deputed to acquaint the Court with these deliberations, and, if possible, to bring royal pressure to bear on Campbell-Bannerman; *persona grata* to the King, whom he had advised on constitutional and educational questions, he had been recently honoured by invitations to Windsor. It was Asquith's assignment to negotiate directly with Campbell-Bannerman on behalf of the triple alliance; an equally appropriate choice, he was the most persuasive, the strongest politically, and the one who knew Sir Henry best. Unfortunately, as it proved, Asquith was also the most susceptible to personal blandishments.

Haldane went promptly into action. On 12 September he communicated the terms of the 'Relugas Compact' to Lord Knollys, the King's private secretary. A fortnight later, when Edward VII returned from Marienbad (where Campbell-Bannerman was also staying), Haldane saw him at Balmoral. The King, who had made known his intention 'to do the strictly constitutional thing & to send for C. Bannerman whenever he had to change his Govt.', declared himself anxious to see these 'most able and moderate men' in the forthcoming government as a counterbalance to 'men holding extreme views'. He therefore agreed that, when the time came, he would guardedly express to Campbell-Bannerman his royal doubts, 'from recent observation, whether anyone but a young man can be both P.M. and leader in the H. of C.'

Campbell-Bannerman did not return from the Continent until 11 November, and Asquith tackled him two days later. Margot provided a polished account of the encounter, as she had heard it that morning from her husband. Steeled for the confrontation, Campbell-Bannerman was in perfect control. 'What would you like? The Exchequer, I suppose?', he pointedly asked his caller, who thereupon lost the initiative. Far from delivering an 'ultimatum', Asquith gently gave advice, and came away with 'the impression . . . that it would be with reluctance and even repugnance that Campbell-Bannerman would ever go to the House of Lords'. The 'Relugas

Compact', like the title – Earl of Belmont – which had been selected for Campbell-Bannerman, was a dead letter. Its failure resulted not from the fact that its demands were exorbitant, but that they had been pressed so half-heartedly.

After a perfunctory defence of Grey and Haldane, Asquith agreed unconditionally to become Chancellor of the Exchequer in a Campbell-Bannerman ministry. His place assured him the deputy leadership of the Commons and, to all intents and purposes, the right of reversion. Campbell-Bannerman was a tired man, old at the age of sixty-nine, who was not expected to retain power very long. In the spring of 1908, which had not been too long to wait, Asquith inherited from him immeasurably more than he could have obtained by threats in 1905.

It cannot be denied, however, that he had abandoned his friends, particularly Haldane, who had taken literally the terms of the Relugas agreement. In self-defence, Asquith pleaded that the situation had altered to such an extent since early September that the Relugas strategy had become irrelevant. At that time, it had been presumed that Balfour would dissolve Parliament, leaving the next government to be formed after a general election. But Balfour, seeking to capitalize on Liberal quarrels, had decided instead to present his opponents with the unenviable task of forming a government before the country went to the polls. Asquith remonstrated that, under the circumstances, his conscience did not permit him to hold aloof: 'If the election were over, and Free Trade secure, different considerations would arise', he assured Haldane on 7 December. But, as A. M. Gollin has pointed out, Asquith's argument ignores chronology. He had accepted the offer of the Exchequer, and thereby 'crippled, or at least seriously weakened, the Relugas Compact', on 13 November, three weeks before Balfour's intentions were known.

The 'Relugas Compact' was later written off by Haldane as 'a private agreement of a purely defensive character', and Asquith similarly asserted in his memoirs that 'from first to last there was nothing in the nature of an intrigue'. Yet the frequency with which the phrase 'putting a pistol to C.B.'s head' appears in their correspondence makes one wonder. Perhaps the only intrigue that qualifies as such is one that attains a measure of success. An unmitigated failure, the 'Compact' achieved none of its primary objectives: Campbell-Bannerman stayed put in the Commons; Asquith did not become leader of the House; Haldane, denied the woolsack, consoled himself with the War Office; and Grey was appointed to the Foreign Office only after it had been refused by Lord Cromer.

In a lengthy autobiographical memorandum he prepared in 1916, Haldane acknowledged that Asquith's *volte face* in November 1905 had dealt a fatal blow to the Relugas policy that rendered his position (and to a lesser extent Grey's) untenable. His criticism of Asquith's behaviour was not simply the product of subsequent disappointments which he had suffered at his friend's hand. There can be no doubt that neither he nor Grey had suspected Asquith's withdrawal until the last moment. Although each of them professed to understand and sympathize with Asquith's predicament, they were vastly more appreciative of each other's qualities. Living together at Haldane's flat in Whitehall Court, Grey and Haldane were left pretty much to their own devices. 'Asquith was not easy to get hold of for constant communication', Haldane recalled with a tinge of bitterness.

His own place secure, Asquith assumed a statesmanlike air. He tried to convince Campbell-Bannerman, who was ready to take office as soon as the opportunity presented itself, that the Unionists ought to be forced to dissolve rather than to resign. 'Far better that we should fight the election when everyone is full at any rate of hope', he wrote on 25 November to Herbert Gladstone, who was of like mind. That day, Rosebery delivered a speech at Bodmin in which he repudiated the policy of Home Rule. In substance, if not in tone, it did not differ materially from a speech Asquith had made at Earls-ferry on 11 October. Yet Asquith, whom Morley had 'come across' at the Athenaeum, was 'most *furious* at the "bombshell"', and 'ridicule[d] the notion of R *now* being able on any terms to come into a Liberal Govnt.' Morley, who had responded angrily to Asquith's Earlsferry speech, was delighted. So, too, was Campbell-Bannerman, to whom Morley dutifully reported the chance encounter, and who received a letter from Asquith ('not in the least actuated by personal & still less – if possible – by sectional considerations') in which Haldane's suitability for the lord chancellorship was advertised. 'C.B. must have smiled when he read this', his latest biographer has speculated. 'He ignored the appeal. Now that he was sure of Asquith, he did not have to worry too much about Haldane, nor did he propose to be dictated to by those who had been doing their utmost to neutralize him.'

Rosebery's speech, which threatened to embroil the Liberals in troubles with their Irish allies and with one another, increased the probability of Balfour's resignation. In response to urgent telegrams from Gladstone and Morley, Campbell-Bannerman left Belmont, his estate in Perthshire, and took the night train to London on Sunday, 3 December. The same night, similarly enjoined by Asquith, Grey travelled south from Northumberland. As his recent biographer has observed: 'He held himself bound by the "Relugas Compact" without realizing how frayed it had become.' Before leaving Fallodon, Grey unburdened himself in a letter to Rosebery:

Asquith, R.B.H. & I have gone too far to refuse office unconditionally & I go to hear whether the conditions, which I consider the essential minimum, are conceded; but I go very sadly. Our talk at Dalmeny has been much in my mind; now the time has come I wish I was staying out more than ever. It isn't yet certain that I shall not, but I guess & fear.

Yet another railway passenger was King Edward, who returned from Sandringham to accept Balfour's resignation at four o'clock on the afternoon of the 4th.

Within the hour, the King sent word to Campbell-Bannerman, whom he summoned to Buckingham Palace the following morning 'at a quarter to eleven o'clock'. By then, Campbell-Bannerman had seen Asquith and Grey, both of whom struck him as 'very amicable & reasonable'. But, unaccompanied, Grey reappeared later that evening, and left a different impression. Appearing to the premier-elect as 'all buttoned up and never undoing one button', he stood firm by the terms of the 'Relugas Compact', and added that Rosebery should be paid the courtesy of an invitation to join the new government. Although Grey had not consulted Asquith, and did not claim to speak for him, Campbell-Bannerman could not be sure whether Asquith shared these sentiments. Grey, however, had acted independently, and wrote to absolve Asquith of any collective responsibility in the matter.

During these hectic days, Asquith was staying with the Salisburys at Hatfield House, hardly an appropriate address for a Liberal Chancellor to make his début. On Tuesday morning, the 5th, shortly before Campbell-Bannerman left his house in Belgrave Square for his audience with the King, Asquith called on him. According to Margot's diary, they 'had a moving interview', which they continued at leisure after Campbell-Bannerman returned from the Palace as Prime Minister. Once again, Asquith expressed concern for C.B.'s physical welfare, pointing to the heavy burden that would have to be shouldered by any man who combined the duties of the premiership with the leadership of the Commons. Moreover, he cited the 'personal pain' he himself would suffer in being separated from Grey, 'his dearest friend as well as supporter'. From Belgrave Square, he proceeded to Whitehall Court, where he found Grey 'in an uncompromising three-cornered humour'. With no progress to report on either front, he motored back to Hatfield to join Margot, who 'admired him more than I could say for throwing himself into the social atmosphere of a fancy ball, with his usual simplicity and unselfcentredness'.

On Wednesday morning, he came back into town, and 'went at once to see C.B.', whom he addressed in the most forthright terms: 'It is no use going over the ground again, my dear C.B. I make a personal appeal to you, which I've never done before; I urge you to go to the House of Lords and solve this difficulty.' *The Times* that morning and, more ominously, the *Westminster Gazette* that afternoon had spoken in the same vein. Campbell-Bannerman was non-committal, but promised to consult his wife, who was due to arrive from Scotland at seven that evening. It was supposedly her declaration of 'no surrender', delivered over the dinner table, that made him determined to stand his ground.

Well into the night, however, the intrigues and counter-intrigues continued. Earlier in the day, Gardiner had arrived at his office at the *Daily News* to find a message from Gladstone, who asked him to 'be good enough to ring me up as I wish to speak to you on an urgent matter'. Gladstone gave cryptic instructions that Gardiner was to telephone a private number at precisely 10.15 p.m., and that at no time in the conversation was he to pronounce the name of the person to whom he was speaking. Gardiner rang the specified number at the appointed time, and Gladstone himself answered. He asked whether Gardiner had seen the leader in *The Times* that endorsed the proposal of a peerage for Campbell-Bannerman and the designation of Asquith as leader of the Commons. Presuming that the *Daily News* meant to reply, he advised its editor 'that you should not dismiss the idea too absolutely'.

This 'singular request' mystified Gardiner. 'Gladstone', he later minuted, 'was one of the most loyal of C.B.'s supporters & had already accepted the Home Secretaryship' under him. On whose behalf was Gladstone acting? 'If H.G. was in favour of C.B. going upstairs,' he reasoned, 'then C.B. himself must have given way.' With a press deadline fast approaching, Gardiner decided 'to put the question bluntly to C.B. himself'. He dashed off a note 'referring to *The Times* leader, but not, of course, to the telephone communication, and asking for a word of guidance'; his secretary took it round to Belgrave Square. Campbell-Bannerman, who had retired for the night, came downstairs in his dressing-gown to sanction 'a reply to *The Times* [that] was not wanting in vigour & firmness'. His confidence had ceased to wobble, and his mind was made up.

On Thursday morning, Asquith returned to Belgrave Square for Campbell-Bannerman's decision. There are two contradictory accounts of their exchange. In Margot's published version, Asquith reported that Campbell-Bannerman 'looked white and upset and began like a man who, having taken the plunge, meant to make the best of it. He spoke in a rapid, rather cheerful and determined manner: "I'm going to stick to the Commons, Asquith, so you will go and tell Grey he may have the Foreign Office and Haldane the War Office."' But Campbell-Bannerman presented a wholly different version to Mrs T. R. Buchanan, the wife of his old friend, who came to tea at Belgrave Square on Friday. By his telling, it was Asquith who had been filled with anguish. 'We must come to business', Campbell-Bannerman peremptorily opened the interview. 'I have duties as Prime Minister. I am not going to the House of Lords. You must say definitely whether you are coming in or not.' Mrs Buchanan recorded that Asquith, who had not yet bound himself to take office, 'was in a great state, walked up and down the room', and weighed the alternatives. 'See what a position I am in', he was said to have protested; 'if I refuse and go to my constituents they will ask why, was it on policy? I must say no. Were you not offered a good post? I must say "the best", then it was on personal grounds that you stood out and were prepared to break up the party? What answer have I?' (In such circumstances, Campbell-Bannerman calculated, Asquith 'would lose his seat'.) For these reasons, Asquith 'evidently was willing to come in', but yet did not dare. 'If I come in and Grey stands out they will say at once this man deserted his friends and crawled back into office', he reasoned. As Mrs Buchanan described it, 'C.B. contented him with saying that it was not he that had put Asquith in this dilemma.' Finally, 'Asquith said he would go and tell Grey and see if he could bring him in.'

Each of these highly coloured accounts of the meeting on 7 December must be taken with a grain of salt. Margot, always better at reporting opinion than events, asserted that her husband had been instructed to offer the War Office to Haldane; but the Prime Minister, communicating directly with Haldane that afternoon, tried to fob him off with the attorney-generalship, which involved 'what are practically Cabinet responsibilities, though not Cabinet rank'. And it would have been uncharacteristic of Campbell-Bannerman to treat Asquith like an errand-boy. Similarly, it is difficult to credit Mrs Buchanan's suggestions either that Campbell-Bannerman continued to doubt Asquith's allegiance, or that Asquith stood in dread of his constituents' reaction. Each lady, eager to glorify her hero, was inclined to exaggerate the perturbation and the vulnerability of his antagonist.

Asquith made a personal appeal to Grey, and wrote to Haldane. The first remained intransigent, but the second, after a lecture on patriotism from Lady Horner, began to waver. Late that afternoon, Haldane returned to Whitehall Court, where Asquith had called in his absence, to find Grey 'lying on a sofa in the library' and contemplating the sunlit days that awaited him among the ducks at Fallodon. At seven o'clock, they left for dinner at the Café Royal, stopping on the way to keep an appointment with Acland, who had retired from active political life and who implored them not to follow. Dining in a private room, Haldane and Grey subjected themselves and each other to intense soul-searching. It was after they had finished the fish course that Grey agreed to retract his refusal to serve in the new Cabinet, provided that he and Haldane could enter it as colleagues. Haldane, despite his reputation as a gourmand, was sufficiently excited to interrupt his dinner and bring the news to Campbell-Bannerman, who confirmed that Grey could have the Foreign Office, and offered Haldane first the Home Office (which Gardiner believed had already gone to Gladstone) and then the War Office, which no one else would 'touch . . . with a pole'. Left alone to finish his dinner, Grey had relapsed into a self-abnegatory mood; but, with further exhortation from Haldane and Acland, he was persuaded to accept. 'Now I have come in I will be loyal to you,' he sullenly told Campbell-Bannerman the next morning. 'If you will forget what I said I will forget what you said.' He had already mastered one of the fundamental techniques of diplomacy.

Back at Hatfield, Asquith knew nothing of these nocturnal developments. Believing that Grey's 'closed door' was firmly bolted, he took time out from the revelry to recommend Lord Crewe, Rosebery's son-in-law, for the foreign secretaryship. On Friday morning, aboard the train to King's Cross, he read unsuspectingly a report in *The Times* that Grey had spurned office. Arriving at Cavendish Square, he was handed a note from Haldane to the effect that their mutual friend had consented to 'reconsider'. Leaving Margot on the doorstep, he went to chase after Haldane, from whom he learned that Haldane and Grey had seen Campbell-Bannerman and accepted places. At noon, Gladstone burst into Margot's boudoir, 'his face shining with happiness', to tell her the good news. 'It's all right, Margot!' he exclaimed. 'Not possible!' she answered incredulously. Later, when the shock had worn off, she wryly reflected: 'So we are all in, and not *one* of us had got what we wanted!'

By contrast, Campbell-Bannerman had got precisely what he wanted. Still a commoner, he presided over an administration that accommodated the widest range of talents and personalities within the framework of a viable Government. 'All the possible actors have been included', Mrs Webb noted approvingly, 'and the parts have been skilfully allotted.' The Prime Minister, whose genial exterior concealed a core of iron, had managed to detach the four vice-presidents of the Liberal League – Asquith, Grey, Haldane, and Fowler – from its president, Rosebery, who was forsaken even by Crewe. Granted, the Relugas covenanters were awarded custody of three vital organs of state; but they conferred an aura of respectability on the new Government, and allowed its leader to go before the country as the spokesman for a united Liberalism. That, at the moment, was the dominant consideration.

Asquith was too profoundly relieved to harbour any regrets for the greater prize that had eluded him. He penned a glowing tribute to Haldane, whose influence on Grey he recognized: 'No words of mine can express what I feel', he wrote on the 8th; 'by your action during the last two days you have laid the party and the country and myself (most of all) under an unmeasured debt of gratitude.' Asquith had good cause to be grateful. He was now acquitted of the charge, which he had brought against himself, of having thrown over his associates in his haste to reap personal advantages. 'More could not have been accomplished', he assured Haldane. That, however, was extremely doubtful, as no one knew better than Haldane, who was on his way to the War Office at the same time as Sir Robert Reid (now Lord Loreburn) was ensconced on the woolsack.

In addition to Reid, the Radical 'pro-Boer' element was represented in the new Cabinet by Lloyd George (who had fancied himself for the Home Office, but went happily to the Board of Trade), and John Burns (who, proud as a peacock, took up lodgings at the Local Government Board). Morley, whose Radicalism had faded from its earlier hue, had set his sights on the Foreign Office, but went instead to the India Office, which he derided as 'a gilded pagoda'. Along with him, the Government contained such Gladstonian fundamentalists as Bryce (Chief Secretary for Ireland), Ripon (Lord Privy Seal and leader in the House of Lords), and Herbert Gladstone (Home Secretary), who, his paternity notwithstanding, proved the least distinguished apostle of the creed. The Whig contingent consisted of Lords Elgin (Colonial Secretary), Carrington (Minister for Agriculture), and Crewe (Lord President of the Council). Of the lesser Liberal Imperialists, Buxton was named Postmaster-General and

Fowler became Chancellor of the Duchy of Lancaster. Lord Tweed-mouth (First Lord of the Admiralty), Augustine Birrell (President of the Board of Education), and John Sinclair (Secretary of State for Scotland) brought the new Cabinet to a full complement of nineteen members. Among those who filled vacancies at the junior level, Lewis ('Loulou') Harcourt, Sir William's son, was assigned the post of First Commissioner of Works; and Winston Churchill, Lord Randolph's son, was rewarded for his apostasy from Unionist ranks by being made under-secretary at the Colonial Office.

There were the inevitable disappointments, but there was no gainsaying that Campbell-Bannerman had done a masterly job. The King was well disposed, the press was generally respectful, and Rosebery accorded the enterprise his public blessing. It remained to be seen whether the electorate, which had not returned a Liberal majority since 1892, would respond with comparable satisfaction. Asquith, confident that it would, wound up his legal practice: according to Haldane, he 'gave up a brief of £10,000 to defend the Khedive's property that very week'. As deputy leader of the House, his position was pivotal, and his critics no less than his friends promptly realized as much. 'If Mrs Asquith can be prevailed upon to release her husband from the treadmill of society', W. T. Stead wrote caustically in the *Review of Reviews*, 'Mr Asquith may have enough energy left in two years' time to lead the House of Commons'. Stead, an unrepentant 'pro-Boer', need not have worried. Asquith was determined to make the most of his chances, and applied himself to parliamentary business with an assiduity that could not have been anticipated.

He quickly established his reputation as the most forceful and incisive debater on the Government front bench. His speeches, while rarely startlingly original or especially eloquent, were invariably succinct, incisive, and to-the-point. ('Asquith's lucidity of style is a positive disadvantage when he has nothing to say', Balfour tartly quipped.) They were delivered, Leo Amery has testified, in a voice that was 'resonant, clear and pleasantly modulated'. And, to an extent that was virtually unrivalled among the party chieftains of the day, his pronouncements were firmly grounded in a bedrock of empirical argument. Less memorable than the literary exercises of Morley and Birrell, the weighty historicism of Bryce, the meta-physical didacticism of Haldane, or the incendiary fulminations of Lloyd George and Churchill, his interventions in parliamentary debate were none the worse for verging on the platitudinous. 'Strong in argument, but weak in imagination, his terse Latinized oratory

had never in itself the magic which compels attention', Sir Robert
Ensor has shrewdly observed. 'But when there was attention already
(as for an important minister there must be), its exceptional precision
and concision told on men's ears and minds with monumental effect.'
As Walter Bagehot had said of Gladstone, so one may justly say of
Asquith:

it was not till he busied himself with finance, – *i.e.*, with very definitely marked-out subject-matter, in which there was no room for
subtleties, though much for explanatory and expository dissertation,
– that his remarkable faculty as an orator, his artistic power of planning out his subjects, his ease and vivacity in making them interesting
to others, his skill in illustrating principles, his animation in re-
counting facts, began to be generally understood.

In the inner sanctum of the Cabinet, Asquith served a comparable
function. He assumed the responsibility, which came naturally
enough to someone of his professional training and temperament, of
summarizing his colleagues' ideas, synthesizing them, and giving
them focus. Morley subsequently complained that Asquith, 'although
he discussed every proposition advanced by others with great intelli-
gence and force, . . . never submitted any ideas of his own for our
consideration'. In his feline way, Morley meant to imply that
Asquith lacked content and possibly conviction as well. But the
explanation is at once more obvious and less damaging. Perceiving
the acute differences that persisted within the Liberal fold, Asquith
sought to isolate and reduce the areas of disagreement. His was to be
the guiding hand that kept the creative forces in juxtaposition. There
was no dearth of intellectual talent among his associates, who com-
prised a team of uncommon – perhaps unsurpassed – distinction; yet
the most esteemed among them often seemed to lack a sense of
proportion. As heir apparent to Campbell-Bannerman, no less than
as Prime Minister after April 1908, Asquith acted as a fulcrum,
balancing discordant opinions, and mediating between them.

For the time being, the novelty of office, coupled with the pressures of electioneering, diverted attention from the party's lingering
dissensions. With polling scheduled to begin on 12 January 1906,
Campbell-Bannerman officially launched the campaign on 21 December with a speech at the cavernous Albert Hall. Cataloguing the
abuses of the late administration, he made only the most vacuous
statements about his own projected policies. Largely inaudible, his
remarks have been charitably described by his recent biographer as
'comparatively pedestrian'. No matter: they were rapturously
received, and served their intended purpose.

War was declared, but electoral combat did not begin in earnest until after Christmas. On 29 December Asquith took to the road and delivered a series of hard-hitting speeches in Yorkshire, the north-east, and Scotland before winding up in his own constituency, which the party pundits had deemed sufficiently safe to dispense with his full-time presence. At each stop, he inveighed against the evils of protectionism, which he saw as the inevitable result of a Unionist victory, and he took his stand as a staunch defender of Free Trade principles. With well-rehearsed arguments, he concentrated on this single issue, which he emphasized almost to the exclusion of any others. On the educational and licensing policies of the Balfour Government, which so much exercised Nonconformist opinion, he had little to say. On the vexed question of Irish Home Rule, he affirmed his philosophic commitment, but cautiously asserted that the subject lay temporarily beyond the pale of practical politics.

The same insistence on 'practicality' dictated his response to the emotive issue of 'Chinese slavery' – the importation of indentured labour to South Africa – which his 'pro-Boer' allies were keen to exploit. Campbell-Bannerman had promised in his Albert Hall address to call a halt to 'the recruitment and embarkation of Chinese coolies', and Asquith reproved him for ignoring the legal complexities of the matter. Such a step, he pointed out to his chief, would require legislation that 'would rouse a tremendous hubbub both here and there'. Furthermore, 'it would involve the British taxpayer (who is without available funds) in infinitely large claims for compensation and', strictly speaking, 'would not be necessary to fulfil your pledge.' At a meeting of the Cabinet on 3 January, Campbell-Bannerman was persuaded to qualify his promise to apply only to those cases in which import licences had not yet been issued by the South African authorities. 'It was an early example', Jenkins has observed, 'of the power within the Government of the Chancellor of the Exchequer.' Likewise, it was a striking example of Asquith's legalistic approach and his characteristic tendency to interpret moral issues, Free Trade included, in terms of pounds, shillings, and pence.

Confident of a modest success, the Liberal leaders did not dare to anticipate the spectacular triumph that awaited them at the polls. With the exception of the venerable Lord Ripon, none of them had known the satisfaction of holding office in a strong Liberal ministry. Morley, whom the passing years had conspired to rob of his mid-Victorian optimism, wearily forecast 'a tie, as in 1885: *i.e.* Liberals = Unionists + Irish'. Grey, writing to Perks, one of the Nonconformist

stalwarts, expressed the hope that 'the size of the majority . . . will
be large enough to carry a reform of the Education Act; if we aren't
strong enough to do that we shall do very little good'. The magnitude
of the Liberal victory exceeded the most sanguine expectations. It
began, tentatively enough, on 12 January, with the gain of a seat at
Ipswich. The next day, the Liberals swept Lancashire, with Balfour
heading the long list of Tory casualties. At the end of nearly three
weeks of polling, the Liberals had amassed 400 seats (including those
'Labour' members who, as Asquith put it, 'were to all intents and
purposes Liberal'). Given the fact that the Liberals could generally
muster support from eighty-three Irish Nationalists and thirty
Independent Labour M.P.s, they commanded a staggering 513 votes
against the Opposition's feeble total of 157.

The Liberal floodtide carried to Westminster an assortment of
candidates who, having stood against all odds, were astonished at
their own success. Among them was the eccentric Arnold Lupton,
who captured Sleaford. 'We didn't win it', his agent told those who
proffered congratulations; 'it was an act of God.' Gladstone, whose
years of painstaking work with constituency organization had not
been in vain, kept a watchful eye on the returns. What impressed
him most, he informed Campbell-Bannerman on 21 January, was
'the predominance of the "centre"' in the parliamentary party as
it was taking shape: 'There is no sign of any *violent* forward movement in opinion . . . The dangerous element does not amount to a
dozen.'

Gladstone was not in the least ruffled by the 'emergence' of an
independent Labour Party on the left of the parliamentary spectrum;
indeed, his controversial electoral pact with Ramsay MacDonald in
1903 had paved the way for this development. Nor, for that matter,
was Morley daunted by the appearance of the fledgling party: 'The
wonder is that it did not come earlier', he proclaimed matter-of-
factly to Lord Minto, the Viceroy of India. More portentous in
retrospect than it appeared at the time, the Labour showing in the
1906 general election gave the Liberals no cause for fright. As L. T.
Hobhouse had confidently professed in his treatise *Democracy and
Reaction* (1904), 'the breach of principle' between Liberalism and
Socialism 'is much smaller than might appear on the surface'. That
Asquith shared this attitude goes far to explain his relations with
Labour not only during the 1906 Parliament, but also during the
postwar years, when Labour's emergence was an incontrovertible
fact.

If this 'mild and gentle Labour Party', as Asquith's daughter wistfully recalled it, failed to revolutionize policy, it nevertheless helped to transform the atmosphere in the House of Commons, which was no longer, as Disraeli had found it, the 'smartest club in town'. Morley complained to his private secretary that, 'when he walked about the lobbies, he hardly knew the H. of C. – so changed were its whole appearance, tone, and manners'. Margot Asquith experienced a similar sensation when she attended the State Opening on 19 February: 'The new House is sadly unfamiliar to me, fearfully overcrowded and full of strangers.' Her husband, who had fewer pretensions, could console himself that the overcrowding was on his own side. Besides, the social composition of the Liberal majority, far from being representative of the nation at large, was drawn overwhelmingly from the interests and classes with which he naturally identified. There was a bumper crop of sixty-four practising barristers in the parliamentary Liberal Party, which was weighted with businessmen and manufacturers. More than a third of Liberal M.P.s had been to Oxford or Cambridge. Asquith was in his element.

Having obtained its unprecedented mandate, the Government got down to business. The King's Speech, which opened the session, gave notice of the intention to introduce twenty-two bills, a dozen of them guaranteed to spark controversy. Along with proposals to restore self-government to the Transvaal, the ministry was pledged to revoke the galling provisions of the 1902 Education Act, to remove disabilities from trades unions, to end the anomaly of plural voting, to ameliorate Irish conditions, and to offer various measures related to employment procedures and commercial activity. Above all else, the Government was determined to uphold Free Trade.

South African affairs took priority, and afforded Campbell-Bannerman a success which, for reasons he could not have foreseen, has been alloyed by time. First and foremost, procedures were laid down to bring gradually to an end the infamous system of Chinese indentured labour. The next task was to devise a constitutional settlement. In that particular case, the principle of gradualism was soundly repudiated. A Cabinet committee, chaired by Lord Loreburn and with Asquith among its five members, collected testimony from colonial officials and from such Boer spokesmen as J. C. Smuts. The Prime Minister duly informed the King that 'the desire of the Cabinet was to introduce fully responsible government into that Colony at the earliest possible time'.

Smuts, who had made a direct appeal to Campbell-Bannerman, was convinced that Campbell-Bannerman deserved paramount, perhaps even exclusive, credit for the bold policy that conceded autonomy to the Transvaal and, soon afterwards, to the Orange River Colony. Lloyd George later took the same view in various conversations. 'The South African constitution was the biggest thing established in our day. Who was responsible?' Sir George (later Lord) Riddell asked him in 1913. 'Oh, C.B.!' Lloyd George replied without hesitation. 'In ten minutes he brushed aside all the checks and safeguards devised by Asquith, Winston and Loreburn.' Asquith, however, dismissed as 'a ridiculous fiction' the suggestion that Campbell-Bannerman was the architect of the South African settlement. 'Between ourselves,' he protested to J. A. Spender in 1912, 'he had little or nothing to do with the matter and never bothered his head about it. The Transvaal Constitution was worked out by myself, Loreburn, Elgin, Winston, and Sir R. Solomon with the help of [Sir John] Lawson Walton', the Attorney-General. To A. G. Gardiner, Asquith wrote in 1923 that Campbell-Bannerman, fatigued by his wife's long illness, had 'slept placidly' through the meetings at which South African problems were discussed. Whichever version one accepts, and obviously one cannot accept them both, the fact remains that the young Government had proved itself capable of resolute and principled action.

Asquith, despite his Liberal Imperialist antecedents, was more prominently associated with matters of domestic policy and, specifically, with the annual budgets which it was his responsibility to produce. With the exception of Peel and Gladstone, in whose fiscal tradition he followed, he showed greater technical competence at the Exchequer than most of his predecessors or, for that matter, than his successor, whom he himself appointed. Traditionally, the chancellorship has been regarded more as a political plum than as an administrative department: the story is told that, in 1852, when Disraeli knowingly pleaded his incapacity to deal with financial affairs, Lord Derby assured him 'You know as much as Mr Canning did. They [i.e. the Treasury officials] give you the figures.' Asquith, however, was not content to serve as the mouthpiece for anonymous bureaucrats, whom he respected, but occasionally overruled. He eventually recalled his stint at the Exchequer as his most gratifying ministerial experience. By his own description, he proved 'a financier of a respectable and more or less conservative type', resourceful without being particularly innovative, orthodox without being hidebound.

His three budgets – the third presented shortly after he had exchanged official residences in Downing Street – gave substance to the Liberal catch-phrase of 'Peace, Retrenchment, and Reform'. That of

1906, introduced on 30 April, was fairly perfunctory. Circumstances did not allow him much choice. As he candidly admitted to a sympathetic House, he had 'to deal with the finances of one year for which he was hardly at all responsible', having arrived in office when it was nearly over, 'and with the finances of another year for which, although he had direct responsibility, yet when he assumed it, he found the field of possible action already to a very large degree limited and circumscribed'. The most notable feature of his first budget was a cut in naval expenditure, made possible by Sir John Fisher's admiralty reforms. It came as a sop to Radical opinion, groaning under the weight of inflated defence appropriations which were the legacy of the Boer War.

During the ensuing year, Asquith had better opportunity to take stock of the financial situation, and the measure of the men with whom he had to deal. He outmanoeuvred his permanent officials by means of an all-party Select Committee on tax procedures, which returned a report favourable to his predetermined position. His second budget, introduced on 18 April 1907, marked a departure sufficiently subtle to go unnoticed in some quarters: Peter Rowland, in his investigation of *The Last Liberal Governments*, has glibly remarked that it was 'as unexciting as the first'. It contained the significant provision by which the rate of taxation, which was calculated at a shilling in the pound, was reduced to ninepence in the case of those taxpayers whose earned incomes fell below a yearly level of £2,000. It stood to reason, Asquith declared, that the tax-paying capacity of a man who derives an unearned income from landed or other investments is necessarily greater than that of a man who derives a comparable income from his own labour. This differentiation between the rates of taxation on earned and unearned incomes, which Gladstone had thought 'impracticable', has since remained a fixture of the British tax structure.

The budget of 1907 was also important for other reasons. Haldane, contrary to expectation, had effected savings at the War Office that contributed to a healthy surplus of over £5,000,000. Ordinarily, this sum would have been partly remitted in taxation, with the remainder applied to the Sinking Fund. Taking a long-range view, Asquith decided to set aside a portion of the surplus for non-contributory old-age pensions, which were introduced the following year. Here was a welcome indication that Retrenchment was pursued not for its own sake, but as the concomitant of Reform: it did not mean, as some critics alleged, simply the curtailment of expenditure, but specifically the curtailment of expenditure on armaments and the consequent reallocation of revenues to programmes to promote social welfare, however modest at their inception.

On this score, Asquith has received less than his due, even from Jenkins, whose deferential biography preceded his own progressive tenure at the Exchequer. It has been variously suggested that Asquith's interest in the question of old-age pensions was either a capitulation to demands from the Liberal and Labour back benches or, more cynically, a defensive response to Labour by-election victories in the spring of 1907. Either argument, besides tacitly impugning the sincerity of Asquith's reformist convictions, ignores important evidence. In July 1906, his private secretary was already collecting information on alternative pension schemes, and a definite proposal was submitted in December to the Cabinet, which gave its endorsement in the following April. 'It is unlikely that Asquith's initial decision to prepare material on old age pensions owed much to outside pressures, though the Cabinet decision to go ahead may have done', J. R. Hay has persuasively reasoned:

> Old age pensions were, to some extent, a product of statistical investigation which proved the extent of poverty among the old and the impossibility of attributing it solely to moral failing. Humanitarian considerations were probably stronger in the case of pensions than in any other Liberal measures, though Asquith and many of his colleagues saw pensions more in terms of the duty of the state towards its citizens, as redefined by T. H. Green and his successors.

This duty was not to be confused with socialism which, as Asquith declared in a commemorative address at the London School of Economics in 1922, was an abstract theory rooted in the 'fallacy that human nature is indefinitely modifiable by extraneous circumstances, artificially produced and imposed'. Old-age pensions, as conceived and implemented, were intended to take account of the diversity of the human condition, not to abolish it.

The 1907 budget provoked grumbling from various sources. Labour members, while they applauded the scheme for old-age pensions and the lowering of the tea duty, would have wished the Chancellor to reduce the duty on sugar (which was done in the following year); disappointed, many of them opposed the budget on its second reading. Cobdenite traditionalists, on the other hand, remonstrated that the Government was threatening to endow indolence and to undermine the Victorian ethic of thrift; Rosebery spoke to this effect in the Lords. But the most bitter and sustained criticism came from Conservative politicians and propagandists who, with strong backing from certain naval and military authorities, argued that the paring of service estimates left the empire incapable of defending itself. Like Haldane, Asquith was pilloried as a traitor to his imperialist principles, a practitioner of 'penny-in-the-slot' politics (to quote Leo Maxse's phrase), more concerned with buying votes than with maintaining national strength and prestige. There was no use in replying that economy was achieved as the result of increased efficiency, not at the expense of it.

The issues were fast developing that dominated political debate during the Edwardian age and carried into the wartime period. Asquith was caught in the crossfire. As a Liberal Chancellor, he willingly assumed budgetary responsibilities that made it impossible for him to satisfy fully either his former imperialist allies or his newly acquired Radical friends. Rosebery, who privately nursed a burning resentment against the Government ('If you accept C.-B.'s invitation' to second the motion for the Royal Address in 1906, he told his elder son, 'you are no son of mine'), was not half so contemptuous of Asquith as were some of the Roseberian loyalists. On 15 May 1906 Munro Ferguson reported to his chief 'that Asquith was over genial, again, at Ld. Wimborne's the other night. I can stand the bottle, but I can't stand that.' He recounted that he had baited Margot on the subject of the Relugas strategy: Haldane, he had told her,

had given me a false impression as to the line to be taken with C.B., in common, on forming a Govt. She hastened to place the whole blame on her own man and said there had been an acute difference between them as to the terms of their agreement. Arthur Acland evidently ranged himself with Asquith against R.B.H. and E.G. The fact is that none of us came very well out of the last ten years and the less one thinks of them the better . . .

Among unreconstructed Roseberians, no less than among hard-line Conservatives, Asquith was resented for having successfully played both ends against the middle. He had ostensibly joined with the Radicals, who had made him their captive, and who exploited his dignity for their own pernicious purposes.

Divided among themselves, the Radicals were not nearly so confident that they could count on Asquith, who was with them, but not of them. Although he voted in support of Churchill's resolution to censure Lord Milner (21 March 1906) and, seven years later, refused to reconsider the matter, he continued to be suspected as a crypto-Milnerite. Margot, who spoke for herself, disapproved of this action, and could 'not see Henry's chance in this House of Commons under Campbell-Bannerman in spite of our huge majority'. The awkwardness of Asquith's position was soon clearly revealed in the episode of the Government's attempt to introduce a Trades Disputes Bill that would lift the liabilities which had been imposed on organized labour by the judicial decision in the Taff Vale case of 1900. Asquith opposed the line, taken by Burns and a minority of Cabinet members, that trades unions ought not to be held accountable for actions committed by their agents. The law officers agreed, and a bill was accordingly drafted which, in its convoluted way, restricted the law of agency to exclude actions of the Taff Vale type. Confused and dissatisfied, trades unionist spokesmen in the Commons countered with a private member's Bill that categorically exempted trades unions from all actions for tort. Campbell-Bannerman, professing himself not 'very intimately acquainted with the technicalities of the question, or with the legal points involved in it', voted for this alternative Bill on its second reading, and reportedly clashed with Asquith within the Cabinet. The Trades Disputes Act of 1906, as it reached the statute book, represented an alliance between the Prime Minister and his backbench supporters over the heads of the ministerial majority.

Wary of antagonizing organized labour, the House of Lords did not oppose the measure. But it was less accommodating in other instances, beginning with Birrell's Education Bill of 1906. Promulgated on 9 April, the Bill was conceived as an attempt to relieve Nonconformists of the disabilities which had been inflicted upon them by the 1902 Education Act. It met with a mixed response from its intended beneficiaries, the more militant of whom decried it as a paltry return on their recent investment of electoral activity. Asquith favoured Birrell's compromise, expecting it to remove the more glaring injustices of Balfour's Act without impairing the system which it had created. Unlike Lloyd George, who had emerged as a defender of Nonconformist interests, he did not attach much importance to the issue of tests, by which non-Anglican teachers were often excluded from employment.

Before irate Nonconformists could be reconciled to the Bill, it proceeded to the Lords, where it was amended beyond recognition. The controversy thereupon widened into a constitutional dispute: it was no longer a question of whether the Bill had been satisfactory, but whether a non-elected chamber of territorial and (worse) ecclesiastical magnates had the right to defy the will of the nation's accredited representatives. In a forlorn effort to salvage the Bill and the Government's reputation among outraged Nonconformists, the Cabinet decided to delegate one of its members to negotiate with Balfour, the leader of the Opposition. Lloyd George revealed to Herbert Lewis, with whom he enjoyed 'a walk along the Plage' at Biarritz on 29 December, that Asquith's name was proposed,

but I was determined that he should feel suspect, so I said, 'No, I suggest the Foreign Secretary'. Asquith turned round to me with a smile and said, 'You are afraid that I shall give way on the question of the teachers'. 'That is just what I am afraid of', I said. The result was that in the negotiations, Grey fought hard on the question of teachers. He had previously been willing to give way (and the Chancellor heartily agreed with him) to the extent of allowing all the teachers to give denominational education, which would have been absolutely fatal to us.

Lloyd George's seaside testimony, intended as much to regale as to impress Lewis, offers some illuminating sidelights on Asquith's relations with his Cabinet colleagues and, in particular, with Lloyd George. One would not wish to suggest that he was distrusted; but he was watched attentively, and especially by those who saw themselves as agents of competing interest groups and communities from which he stood aloof.

There were those who urged the Prime Minister to dissolve Parliament and go to the country sooner than capitulate to the House of Lords. Instead, the Education Bill, which had inspired little enthusiasm in the first place, was ignominiously dropped, and the Government got on with the task (in the parlance of the day) of 'filling the cup'. One after another, measures were proposed that passed through the Commons with massive majorities, only to come to grief in the Lords. A Plural Voting Bill, designed to remove the anomaly of multiple franchises, was thwarted. Bills for English and Irish land reform were emasculated, and two similar bills for Scotland were summarily rejected. A Licensing Bill, predictably enough, suffered the same fate. The Liberal rank and file seethed with indignation, which, it was hoped, would mobilize the electorate.

Campbell-Bannerman's strategy was transparently clear: he depended upon the peers to discredit themselves by the irresponsible and unmistakably partisan use of their inherited prerogatives. Taking up where Gladstone had left off in 1894, he called for legislation to trim the overweening powers of the House of Lords, which operated 'as a mere *annexe* of the Unionist party'. His own solution, which he persuaded his colleagues to accept, was a suspensory veto, which would leave intact the composition of the upper House, but would limit its right to that of delaying – for two sessions – the implementation of any bill that had met with approval in the Commons. Asquith, although he 'coquetted' with the notion of holding a referendum in cases of constitutional deadlock, sanctioned the procedure which the Prime Minister elaborated. It seemed to him more workable than Ripon's cumbersome scheme by which a hundred peers would be invited to sit in deliberation with the Commons; and it was, to him, preferable to more revolutionary schemes either to abolish the second chamber or to reconstitute it on a non-hereditary basis. As he had assured Lyttelton on 24 December 1894, he had never aimed 'at the substitution of a single-chamber for the present system', but was

perfectly content to acquiesce in, & to advocate, a system of two chambers, provided that . . . the 2nd chamber shall act . . . impartially . . ., whatever, for the time being, the party complexion of the first chamber may be . . .

Personally, I should have no objection to giving a 2nd chamber, *so acting*, the power (not of dissolution) but of referring a specific question of difference to the popular judgment.

In the Cabinet (where he helped to overcome objections from Grey and others) and more conspicuously in the Commons (where he closed three days of passionate debate), Asquith rallied support for Campbell-Bannerman's resolution, which was to inform the policies of his own premiership.

Having bared its teeth, the Government inexplicably declined to bite. The Prime Minister's resolution of 24 June 1907, carried by a majority of nearly three to one, failed to give issue to any immediate legislation for constitutional reform. Instead, the King's Speech at the opening of the 1908 session gave pride of place to a comprehensive Licensing Bill, which was doomed to end up on the dustheap. The House of Lords, declining to take seriously the Government's undated ultimatum, continued on its collision course. In Parliament and the country, Liberal morale was at a low ebb. Against a background of worsening economic conditions, a string of by-election defeats demonstrated that the party was losing public favour. Its leaders, whatever excuses they might legitimately offer, could point to embarrassingly few positive achievements. Lloyd George, whose Merchant Shipping Act (1906) and Patents Act (1907) were exceptions to the rule, feared that 'the Liberal Statute Book' would resemble 'a bundle of sapless legislative faggots fit only for the fire'. To Herbert Lewis, with whom he 'walked part of the way from Nice to the Villa Pastorelle' on 29 December 1907, he described 'the natural tendency of each individual Minister' to pull in a separate direction, with no collective sense of destination. The controversy with the House of Lords epitomized the problem. 'If I were only sure', he told Lewis, 'that C.B. and Asquith had talked the matter over and had arrived at a definite policy, I would not mind, but I fear that the general outlines of policy have not been considered.'

The ship of state, to the distress of its passengers, was drifting aimlessly. Its captain, who had suffered recurrent heart attacks, had gone to Biarritz for an extended convalescence. He had set off on 27 November 1907 and, apparently refreshed, returned on 20 January. But the strength he had gathered was quickly sapped. Although he chaired eight meetings of the Cabinet over the next three weeks, he was not in his accustomed place when Parliament convened on the 29th. Haldane, noting his absence, was disconsolate. 'The session opens in a doubtful fashion', he wrote to his sister three days later. 'C.B. is the only person who can hold this motley crew together & he is not there ... I should like to liquidate the concern and start afresh. That is just what I fear HHA will never do.'

On 12 February the seventy-one-year-old premier met his Cabinet for the last time, and put in a final appearance at Westminster. The next day, he had a prolonged seizure, absurdly diagnosed by the King's personal physician as influenza. He retired to his residence in Downing Street, never to emerge. Asquith took leave of him on 27 March. 'You are the greatest gentleman I ever met', Campbell-Bannerman complimented his lieutenant. 'This is not the last of me', he defiantly added; 'we will meet again, Asquith.' He died on 22 April.

Even after the grave nature of Campbell-Bannerman's illness was known, his doctor had discouraged any talk of resignation, fearful of the psychological effect it might have on the patient. Besides, the King had advertised his disinclination to interrupt his Continental sojourn for the purpose of transferring the seals of office. As the weeks passed, Asquith grew impatient with the charade. 'It is, I think, clear ... that the status quo cannot go on,' he wrote stiffly on 22 March to Lord Knollys, the King's private secretary: 'There is absolutely no hope of a return to public life, and the prolongation of the present uncertain[ty] is having very demoralising results. The House of Commons has become a gossip shop ... It has become my opinion, which is shared by all my leading colleagues, that whatever reconstruction has to be done should be done at once, & once for all ...' There was some talk that, at the eleventh hour, the Prime Minister might ease the transition by taking a peerage, but that would have seemed a belated capitulation to the men of Relugas. By the early days of April, there was no longer any hope or choice. The Prime Minister pathetically tendered his resignation to the King, who, as he had previously indicated, invited Asquith to form an administration.

Since the previous autumn, when Campbell-Bannerman's health had broken down, there had been widespread speculation about the succession and, especially, about the changes in personnel and policy that it would bring. The inevitability of Asquith's ascent had been assumed, but not without demur. Lord Knollys confided to Austen Chamberlain his preference for Grey, who, in turn, regarded Haldane as '*the* Prime Minister'. Bernard Shaw, too, plumped for Haldane, whom he gamely urged to 'seize the crown'. Certain Nonconformist journals had the temerity to nominate Fowler. Morley, who could claim seniority of service on the front bench, jested to Lord Esher that 'he would *like* to be Prime Minister himself'; resigned to the impossibility, he told his private secretary that it would be unpleasant for him '(who had been a Home Ruler all his life) to join' a Government led by Asquith, who was lukewarm on the subject. Like Morley, the *Manchester Guardian* found it difficult to forgive Asquith for his stance during the Boer War and, no less, for his machinations during the formation of the Government in 1905. On 17 February it implied its support for Lloyd George, taking the precaution not to mention him by name. Its editor privately conceded that Asquith 'was a sort of natural successor, and his claim is reinforced by his readiness and force as a leader in the daily Parliamentary scrimmage'; even so, C. P. Scott insisted to Goldwin Smith on 15 March, 'his political record is bad, and the present Cabinet with Asquith simply substituted for Campbell-Bannerman could not command confidence in the country, and will, I hope, never be accepted by the genuine Liberals in the Cabinet'.

Further support for Lloyd George's undeclared candidacy came from the most unlikely source. 'Asquith's line is so decided as to the 2nd Chamber & to the [Scottish] Land Bill that it is very desirable to have an alternative successor to C.B.', Munro Ferguson wrote to Rosebery on 21 December 1907. 'I like Lloyd George for the job as well as anybody.' Five days later, he had switched his backing to an even darker horse, Lord Loreburn:

He is, of course, a great impostor in many ways – but . . . he is the most effective instrument that I know to keep Asquith out of the Leadership, which is to my mind worth the trying. He, Asquith, is at heart a raw English middle class radical, with a character deteriorated by a vulgar society of another sort & by a free use of wine which he cannot carry. He has come to be quite unreliable, for he would accommodate himself to any line of policy to secure the enticements of office . . . Asquith is evidently playing the understudy with great care & it will take equal diplomacy to check the political disaster that his success would go far to secure.

In this extreme case, as in the others, it is apparent that rival contenders were being promoted (one suspects without their encouragement) not so much out of consideration for their intrinsic qualities as out of a determination to stop Asquith at the last ditch. Yet the incongruity and, in no small measure, the petulance of these complaints was itself the best proof that the rise of Asquith was irresistible. As Morley put it in a letter to Lord Minto on 12 March, the matter had been 'decisively settled by circumstances'.

At the insistence of the King, whose whims had to be indulged, Asquith broke precedent and crossed the Channel to kiss hands in a hotel room at Biarritz. On the morning of 8 April, he 'put on a frock coat' and went through the brief ceremony, which was followed by a royal breakfast in an adjoining room.

Fifty-five years of age, Asquith had arrived. It amused him to reflect with mock solemnity that he was the first practising member of the bar to become Prime Minister since Spencer Perceval, who was assassinated in 1812: '*Absit Omen!*' More distinctively, he was to occupy his high office for eight and a half years, a longer continuous period than anyone else in modern British political history. With a tempered enthusiasm, which would have been difficult to imagine two years earlier, the party submitted to his command. Again to quote Ensor, 'His loyal service under Campbell-Bannerman had filmed over the old sores.' Winston Churchill and Walter Runciman, who were to advance to Cabinet membership under the new premier, had long agreed 'that Asquith must be the heir. I am sure', Churchill had written to Runciman in the closing days of 1907, 'no better workman will have been installed since the days of Sir Robert Peel. As to the work which he will choose – that lies in the mists.'

The parallel with Peel is an intriguing one. Asquith shared many of his characteristics: a dogged commitment to 'practical reforms', a disdain for mob enthusiasms, a high sense of public rectitude, an inability to respond to personal abuse, and a somewhat glacial exterior. Neither deigned to cater to sectional interests (as he defined them), or concerned himself unduly with the contingencies of party management. And, most obviously, Asquith was toppled in December 1916 under circumstances that bore a striking resemblance to those that had brought Peel's ministerial career to a premature close seventy years earlier. *Absit omen.*

5

## FROM THE
## OLD LIBERALISM
## TO THE NEW

Asquith's ascent to the premiership, however
much a foregone conclusion, marked a watershed in his private life,
in the history of the Liberal Party, and in the course of modern
British politics. With equanimity and self-assurance, he succeeded a
man whom he could not presume to replace. 'CB leaves a gap which
is not easily, or perhaps at all, capable of being filled,' he admitted to
Bryce on 28 April, the day after Campbell-Bannerman's funeral:
'He was to the last, by negative as well as by positive gifts, an
emollient & unifying factor in our party, & indeed in public life. One
can only trust that the great measures we have in hand, & the growing feeling among our followers that they must close their ranks, will

keep the ship well afloat. (Rather a mixed metaphor!)' Given the emotional significance of the occasion, it is perhaps less surprising that Asquith should have mixed his metaphors than that he should have self-consciously called attention to his stylistic lapse.

Despite the length of time he had spent in public life and the prominence he had attained, Asquith was very much an unknown quantity when he came to power in the spring of 1908. What was he like, and what did he believe? Not yet Prime Minister, he was the subject of one of Gardiner's celebrated character sketches in the *Daily News*. A remarkably perceptive and prophetic portrait, it depicted Asquith as 'an ingenious mechanic', somewhat 'handicapped by . . . the sense of remoteness and hardness which those who know him best declare is unjust to the real man'. As Gardiner saw him, Asquith was not 'a popular figure' and 'perhaps does not seek to be' one: 'To be a popular leader', after all, 'one must be expansive and self-revelatory, and Mr Asquith is neither.' Unlike his avuncular predecessor (or, one might add, his dynamic successor), Asquith did not project or generate warmth. 'He is the constructive engineer of politics', Gardiner continued,

not the man of visions. He leaves the pioneering work to others and follows after with his levels and compasses to lay out the new estate. No great cause will ever owe anything to him in its inception, but when he is convinced of its justice and practicability, he will take it up with a quiet, undemonstrative firmness that means success . . . If he is wanting in any essential of statesmanship, it is a strong impulse to action. He has patience rather than momentum.

Margot Asquith, recuperating from the ordeal of her fifth and final pregnancy (the baby died a day after the delivery), responded on 21 March, three weeks after publication, that Gardiner's article had been 'quite xcellent' (her spelling). To a less sympathetic journalist, Leo Maxse of the ultra-Tory *National Review*, she proffered assurances on 24 April that her husband was 'a cold hard unsympathetic man loved by none admired by a few'.

From the wife of any other politician, such words might be construed as a flagrant act of conjugal disloyalty; from the inimitable Margot, however, these were effusions which informed individuals knew better than to accept at face value. Subject to periodic bouts of insomnia and nervous exhaustion, she spent her sleepless nights scrawling innumerable letters with a blunt pencil. Festooned with exclamation marks and multiple underscorings, her correspondence was usually embarrassingly frank, sometimes unintelligible, yet rarely without flashes of wit or insight. In the spring of 1913, when she was again afflicted, she described her malady to Haldane's aged mother as 'anaemia of the brain', and she explained that, 'when tired, which is nearly always, I speak quite indistinctly'.

Any appearance to the contrary, Margot adored her husband, and dedicated herself to the furtherance of his career. Like Trollope's Lady Glencora Palliser, whom she resembled as much in her youthful indiscretions as in her adult ambitions, she was convinced that to be Prime Minister of Britain 'is to be the greatest man in the greatest country in the world'. On occasion, she might criticize Asquith with an acerbity which she would never brook from anyone else. All the same, she worshipped him, even to the point that she would interrupt one of her own rambling monologues to command imperiously 'Just listen to Henry!', who was holding forth across the room.

Incorrigible as she sometimes seemed, Margot boasted strong loyalties to match her strong prejudices. She doted on her children, Elizabeth (born in 1897) and Anthony (born in 1902), whose creative talents she carefully nurtured. As Princess Antoine Bibesco, the wife of a Rumanian diplomat, Elizabeth came to enjoy a minor literary reputation and inherited her mother's facility for scintillating conversation; no less an authority than Marcel Proust paid her tribute as 'probably the most intelligent woman in the world'. Anthony, known to his family and friends as 'Puffin', became a distinguished film director. As Asquith's official biographers (one of them his son Cyril) put it, 'The children of his second family suffered from fewer inhibitions than those of his first, and grasped firmly by the leaf the nettle of their father's reserve.'

Margot, whom the young Oswald Mosley recognized as 'the match of any woman in wit and more than a match in audacity', felt increasingly uncomfortable in the company of her five maturing stepchildren, who shone with a less glittering brilliance. Deeply religious in a fundamentalist way (she had once knelt to pray with General Booth in a railway carriage), she was appalled to learn that her charges neither had been baptized nor seemed to care. She could remedy this particular deficiency, but sadly acknowledged her powerlessness to mould their characters. In varying proportions, the children of Asquith's first marriage combined their father's sang-froid with their mother's quiet simplicity. Margot found them 'modest and motionless', and complained: 'If you had appeared downstairs in a ball-dress or a bathing-gown they would never have observed it – and would certainly never have commented upon it if they had.' They, in turn, did not know quite what to make of her. 'She was never of course the least like a mother', Violet Asquith later recalled: 'Nor was she like a stepmother, wicked or otherwise. She just flashed into our lives like some dazzling bird of paradise, filling us with amazement, amusement, excitement: sometimes with a vague uneasiness as to what she might do next. We realised, of course, that she was a law unto herself – but would other people do so too?'

Margot encouraged and admired her stepchildren. Yet they stubbornly remained ducklings, who afforded her less satisfaction than her own graceful cygnets. The four boys had left the nest by the time that the family moved to more constricted quarters at 10 Downing Street: Raymond, a practising barrister, was married in 1907 to Katharine Horner, the daughter of old family friends; Arthur and Herbert were at Oxford; and Cyril, soon to join them there, was away at Winchester. There remained only Violet to compete with her stepmother for Asquith's attention. More politically engaged than any of her siblings, she was her father's confidante and the lifelong champion of his cause. More hard-headed than Margot, she was equally strong-willed and quick-tongued. Both women prided themselves in knowing what was best for the man to whom they were each fiercely devoted. In 1915, at twenty-eight years of age, Violet married Sir Maurice Bonham Carter, her father's private secretary. By then, Margot had nearly given up hope that she would be allowed to raise her own family without the formidable presence of Asquith's first daughter.

For the sake of comfort, the Asquiths had declined to occupy the compact house at 11 Downing Street, which was one of the perquisites of the chancellorship; instead they had stayed put at 20 Cavendish Square for the duration of the Campbell-Bannerman premiership. There was no question, however, that they would avail themselves of the opportunity to reside at Number Ten when it fell vacant. Violet inspected the premises, and was not impressed: 'There was one bath in the whole house, and that was in my father's bedroom ... and there was not a single bookshelf except that containing Hansard in the hall. Therefore, I asked myself, has no Prime Minister in the past ever washed or read?' Margot's response was similar: she found it 'an inconvenient house with three poor staircases', where, she quickly decided, she 'could only entertain my Liberal friends at dinner or at garden parties'. That, to her, mattered a good deal. She entertained constantly, and on a lavish scale, partly because she thought her husband's position demanded it, and partly because she accepted it as her *métier*. 'I shall be giving a series of political dinners wh. I always enjoy', she wrote early in 1909 to Sir John Brunner, whose opposition to the Government's naval estimates ensured him a special invitation. 'The only form of entertainment that exhausts me is a "crush" where there is no room to breathe and nothing amusing that I can see neither conversation nor ventilation possible.' No expense was spared by the hostess, who, all her life, was as prodigal in matters of household expenditure as in her opinions. 'Money! no more to me than almonds and raisins!' Sir Maurice Bowra once heard her exclaim after the war, when he stayed at The Wharf, a house that 'was governed on Edwardian principles. There was an air of extravagance about everything,' Bowra recorded in his memoirs, 'and whenever I came away from it, I felt that I should go at once and spend money, so infectious was its spirit.'

Asquith gave his wife licence to spend freely, and took her assorted eccentricities in his stride. Far from being the helpless captive of 'the Margot set', which Lytton Strachey disdained as 'rich, smart, showy, and self-indulgent', he entered unprotestingly into the *beau monde* which she (with, later, the assistance of some of the children) assembled around him. He 'looked on, apparently with a detached tolerance,' Jenkins has observed, 'but in fact with a good deal of placid enjoyment'. Easily caricatured as a *bourgeois gentilhomme*, he basked in the attentions he received from titled hostesses (many of them Margot's relations) and from an array of literary and artistic people. And, in turn, he was accepted warmly, but sometimes uncomprehendingly, by the *literati* whose *salons* he frequented: Vanessa Bell, whose indifference to public affairs was legendary, once turned to him at a dinner party and asked 'Are you interested in politics?' Some of those with whom he consorted were considered not quite respectable. 'There is no getting away from the fact that ours is a Nonconformist Party, with Nonconformist susceptibilities and Nonconformist prejudices', Edwin Montagu (himself a Jew) reproved the Prime Minister, who had invited a lady of dubious virtue to a reception at Downing Street. More seriously, Asquith's friendship with 'Robbie' Ross, the companion and literary executor of Oscar Wilde, was to rebound against him.

Like the books he read voraciously, his social engagements afforded him a welcome distraction from official cares, and refreshment at the end (and occasionally in the middle) of an arduous day. 'My father's thinking was done in strict privacy, almost behind locked doors, as though it were an indecent act', Lady Violet revealed; when it was finished, he craved diversion. Unlike Lloyd George, who lived and breathed politics around the clock, Asquith felt a compulsive need to unwind in lighthearted company at the

dinner table, at the theatre (though never the opera), on the golf
links, at bridge, or in his voluminous correspondence with a succession of admiring young ladies. In times of crisis, which recurred with
accelerating frequency, his need became all the greater. That, however, ought to imply neither a dereliction of duty nor necessarily
marital infidelity. Yet, on both scores, he inevitably created an
impression that counted against him.

Just as many of his habits and attitudes were the product of his
background, so too were a number of the more unreasonable criticisms levelled at him. In professional no less than personal terms,
Asquith's premiership marked a transition from the ascendancy of
the Cecils, Salisbury and Balfour, to the age of Lloyd George. Those
traditionalists who resisted the dominant trend towards social
democracy asserted that Asquith lacked the credentials, and therefore the inclination, to keep in check the forces of disruption and
decay. 'The plain truth is [that] no man in England ought to be
Prime Minister except a man who either from wealth or from position
does not depend on office for distinction', Professor A. V. Dicey
declared to St Loe Strachey on 25 September 1909, when the budget
crisis was heating up. Sounding less like a distinguished jurist than a
disgruntled apostate from Liberal ranks, Dicey speculated that 'if
Asquith were to be driven from office he might soon be practically a
nobody. In such a case, the temptation to retain office at all costs is
too great.'

Later, during the wartime years, it was frequently alleged that
Asquith had mortgaged his principles for an emolument, that he had
been corrupted by the fast company he kept ('The middle class legal
don became a *voyeur*', Lytton Strachey mocked), and that he had
gradually gone to seed. But it was not the case that Asquith had lost
either his scruples or his grip, so much as that the world had tilted on
its axis. Qualities which previously had been revered as supreme
virtues had come to be misprized as liabilities. From the proud
beginning of his premiership to its ignominious termination, he
evinced the same essential strengths or weaknesses, depending on
one's perspective. His contempt for demagogy was as constant as his
scorn for the sentimental. Striving continuously to maintain party
unity, he interpreted Liberalism as a latitudinarian creed. He
adhered religiously to the concept of political balance, even after he
could no longer find the makings for such a balance within the ranks
of his own party. In the conduct of Cabinet and parliamentary
business, he held to the same guiding principles and administrative
procedures. Above all else, he was profoundly convinced of his own

'natural inevitableness' (to borrow Gardiner's phrase) for the lofty place he occupied.

At the beginning of his tenure, few could doubt the tenacity of his grasp and the surety of his command. The first business on the agenda that awaited him was to reshuffle the cards in the ministerial pack. He proceeded with a dispatch that in a few cases smacked of savagery. Prudence dictated that he should hold changes, especially those at the senior level, to a minimum, so as not to disrupt the equilibrium of tensions which Campbell-Bannerman had evolved. But there were organizational imperatives which could not be ignored. 'The first essential for a Prime Minister is to be a good butcher', he quoted Gladstone to Churchill, whom he informed that there were several colleagues 'who must be pole-axed now'. Like the Lord High Executioner in Gilbert and Sullivan's *Mikado*, one of his favourite entertainments, he had 'a little list'. Heading it were Lords Elgin and Tweedmouth, the first of whom had failed to carry weight in either Cabinet councils or House of Lords debates, and the second of whom had proved a recurrent embarrassment by his indiscretions. Elgin was dropped altogether; Tweedmouth was shunted to the lord presidency of the council. 'I venture to think', Elgin wrote resentfully to his fellow-victim on 20 April 1908, 'that even a prime minister may have some regard for the usages common among gentlemen . . . I feel that even a housemaid gets a better warning.' At the lower echelons, Edmund Robertson, who presumed that he might continue in office with a peerage, was removed from his junior place at the Admiralty. Likewise, Lord Portsmouth, whom Asquith had tutored during the summer of 1874, was dismissed from his under-secretaryship at the War Office; the King, in his interview with Asquith at Biarritz, had professed himself 'anxious to get rid of' Portsmouth, who, Asquith had to agree, would not be missed. And Thomas Lough, who had served without distinction as under-secretary at the Board of Education, was pensioned off with a privy councillorship.

Not all the dead wood was chipped away immediately. Lord Ripon, out of respect for his age and experience, remained Lord Privy Seal (although he relinquished the leadership in the Lords) until the summer recess, when he resigned in the aftermath of a dispute with the Home Secretary. Fowler continued as Chancellor of the Duchy of Lancaster until the following October, when, as Viscount Wolverhampton, he was kicked upstairs to replace Tweedmouth, whose 'cerebral malady' had entered its terminal phase. Of far greater consequence was the decision to give Burns – an obstacle to innovation

– a renewal of his lease on the Local Government Board; it took nothing less than the outbreak of the First World War to dislodge him from office.

Grey was left undisturbed at the Foreign Office, Haldane at the War Office, Gladstone at the Home Office, Loreburn on the woolsack, Birrell as Irish Secretary, and Morley as Secretary of State for India. Always a difficult piece to fit into the puzzle of Cabinet-making, Morley had threatened to retire to the calm of his library, but was persuaded to reconsider by a personal appeal from the new Prime Minister, whom he surprised with a request to be sent to the upper House. 'Why on earth should you go there?' Asquith (by Morley's telling) asked incredulously. 'Because,' Morley reportedly replied, 'though my eye is not dim, nor my natural force abated, I have had a pretty industrious life, and I shall do my work all the better for the comparative leisure of the other place.' To Lord Minto, the Viceroy, whom he tantalized with hints of his intentions, Morley rendered an equally improbable account of his negotiations with Asquith, who, he said, had dangled the Exchequer before him; according to this version, Morley had protested that he was 'too old to learn a new trade' and, besides, was committed to the Indian reform scheme on which he and Minto had begun work. One may infer, however, that Morley took a peerage for political reasons that owed little, if anything, to departmental factors: he was resolved to escape the moral as well as the physical burdens that attended a place on the Government front bench, and to be absolved from any obligation to defend policies which, he had good reason to suspect, would not meet with his Gladstonian approval. Although he, like Burns, lingered until the declaration of war, he found frequent cause to lament his continued servitude and, still more, his 'grand glorification' as Viscount Morley of Blackburn.

Lord Crewe, displaced from the lord presidency in order to accommodate the doddering Tweedmouth, succeeded Elgin at the Colonial Office and, in addition, assumed the thankless task of leading in the Lords. Asquith reposed tremendous confidence in his sober judgement: writing to Venetia Stanley (the future Mrs Edwin Montagu) on 26 February 1915, he rated Crewe first in his 'tripos' of Cabinet colleagues on whom he depended. Reginald McKenna, another protégé, was appointed to follow Tweedmouth as First Lord of the Admiralty. He had recently shown his mettle as financial secretary to the Treasury and, to somewhat less advantage, as minister for education. In the 1915 'tripos', McKenna was placed third, behind Grey but ahead of Lloyd George. Asquith shifted him to the Home

Office in 1911, and advanced him to the Exchequer four years later. Unlike Crewe, who returned briefly to office during the political convulsions of 1931, McKenna never resumed his ministerial career after the fall of his mentor in December 1916.

The Admiralty was assigned to McKenna after it had been refused by Churchill, who, being Tweedmouth's nephew, hesitated to go there. It was a difficult decision for Churchill, who was peculiarly attracted to the position which he was to hold in two world wars. Another 'Asquith man', although he eventually declined to classify himself as such, he was then an *enfant terrible* of thirty-three, with strong claims for promotion to Cabinet rank. Asquith, entreated by Violet to 'make the most of Winston', assured her that she 'need have no fear on W's account'. According to her published reminiscences, Churchill stated his preference for the Local Government Board, where Burns was firmly entrenched, but went willingly to the Board of Trade, where a vacancy was created by the transfer of Lloyd George to the Exchequer. Randolph S. Churchill, his father's official biographer, politely – but tellingly – took issue with Asquith's daughter on this point. In a letter of 14 March 1908, Churchill made clear to Asquith not only his desire to continue at the Colonial Office (preferably as the first in command, but, if necessary, as deputy to the 'unassertive' Elgin), but also his aversion to the Local Government Board: 'There is no place in the Government more laborious, more anxious, more thankless, more choked with petty & even squalid detail, more full of hopeless and insoluble difficulties.' No mention was made at this juncture of the Board of Trade, about which much the same could have been said. Asquith, to give him his due, had a better idea than Churchill of the latter's penchant for social administration. He sometimes criticized him for want of tact or party loyalty, but always gave him credit for 'a zigzag streak of lightning on the brain', and took a paternal interest in the progress of his career. 'He was always very kind to me and thought well of my mental processes', Churchill wrote without false modesty nearly three decades later.

The greatest stir was made not, as one might suppose, by the inclusion of Lord Randolph Churchill's son in a Liberal Cabinet, but by the elevation to the Exchequer of Lloyd George, the Welsh firebrand and 'pro-Boer'. It was not initially Asquith's intention to make such an appointment. At Biarritz he had solicited and obtained royal approval for the idea of combining the duties of the chancellorship with those of the premiership, if only temporarily. Peel and Gladstone had provided precedents for this arrangement; and, from

May to August 1923, Stanley Baldwin was also to serve as his own chancellor. Asquith had prepared the 1908 budget, so it made sense for him to present it himself. And, one may argue, he had a tendency to play Pooh Bah: in March 1914, when J. E. B. Seely hastily departed from the War Office as a result of the Curragh 'mutiny', the Prime Minister doubled as War Secretary until the following August; two years later, in the aftermath of the Easter rebellion in Dublin, Asquith took on the job of Chief Secretary until late July.

On this occasion, however, tactical considerations ultimately prevailed. In a conversation on 10 April, Morley (a notorious purveyor of backstairs gossip) told Lord Esher (whose appetite for secondhand intrigue was insatiable) that 'Lloyd George "put a pistol" to Asquith's head, and *asked* for the Ch. of the Ex. with a threat of resignation'. Was Morley attempting to excuse his own failure to win the prize? In any case, Asquith had no wish to dispense with Lloyd George, whom he justly valued for his superior qualities and as a counterpoise to the Liberal Imperialists, who would otherwise monopolize the high offices of state. On receiving Asquith's 'flattering proposal', Lloyd George promptly replied: 'I shall be proud to serve under your Premiership and no member of the Government will render more loyal service and support to his chief.' Despite Morley's disclosure that Lloyd George had spoken 'deprecatingly' of Asquith, let alone what eventually transpired, there is no reason to doubt the sincerity of Lloyd George's pledge.

Vaughan Nash, whose services as private secretary Asquith gratefully inherited from his late predecessor, marvelled at the speed and efficiency with which the new premier went into action. 'Asquith is A1 to have dealings with', he wrote to Arthur Ponsonby on 13 April. 'Mrs A. I find an effort.' Others, too, were inspired with confidence by the dexterity with which Asquith achieved harmony and cohesion without introducing too many new faces (Churchill and Runciman were the only débutants in the Cabinet) or, for that matter, banishing too many familiar ones. In the exchange of offices, which was completed in time to greet the King on his return from the Continent on 16 April, an unusual attempt was made to allocate places with a due regard for an individual's talents, interests, and reputation. Unlike Campbell-Bannerman, who had had only his own Scots instinct to guide him, Asquith had the benefit of having seen most of these men on the job. Some of his appointees, invited to remain at their posts, interpreted the renewal of their ministerial leases as evidence of his personal support and, more problematically, as confirmation of their departmental sovereignty. Others were afforded the opportunity for more creative enterprise. 'There is, I am glad to say, a complete absence of anything like personal jealousies or intrigues,' the Prime Minister reported with justifiable satisfaction to Bryce after the task was done, 'and I think that the reconstruction of the Government has appreciably added to its fighting & administrative resources.'

If not, strictly speaking, the 'Ministry of All the Talents' which some would have it, this was indisputably a highly capable administration. Having taken such elaborate care to assemble a viable team of men whom he could trust and respect, Asquith was disposed to treat his subordinates as colleagues, and to concede to them a generous measure of discretionary freedom. Secure in his place in the driver's box, he could afford to relax his grip on the reins of power. Robust and wilful, the horses would inevitably pull in different directions, but he expected them to keep one another on an even course; and, as a last resort, he was prepared to shift his weight in order to ensure that the stagecoach did not lurch too violently either to the left or right.

His admirers have traditionally assigned him paramount credit for the skill (and, less relevantly, the grace) with which he kept so many high-strung thoroughbreds in collective harness. That, in effect, is to minimize his function and thereby to discount his accomplishment. More recently, his detractors have dismissed him as 'a braking influence', no more and no less. That is even more fanciful and unjust. Asquith was no reincarnation of Lord North, who told the House of Commons in 1778 that he 'should never be so presumptuous as to think himself capable of directing the departments of others'. Rather, if one had to choose the precursor Asquith most closely resembled in terms of executive style, one would have to go back beyond Gladstone and Peel to Lord Liverpool, whose contribution to the premiership, subtle but substantial, has too often gone undetected. 'Liverpool was never a mere chairman presiding over a Cabinet of superior talents', Norman Gash has convincingly asserted: 'the guiding lines of policy were always firmly in [his] hands, in consultation with an inner ring of ministers . . . Liverpool himself kept a close supervision of all the main departments, including the Foreign Office; and in matters of trade and finance was always the dominating figure.' As Gash has said of Liverpool, so one may say, word for word, of Asquith. And, just as Liverpool was pilloried by Disraeli as the 'Arch-mediocrity', Asquith has been significantly reduced in stature by well-meaning panegyrists who have acted in unwitting alliance with ungenerous critics.

For his own part, Asquith adamantly rejected the view that he was a fainéant Prime Minister, 'a mere figurehead', as he protested to McKenna in an interview on 20 October 1911, 'pushed along against his will and without his knowledge by some energetic colleagues', namely Lloyd George and Churchill. At the same time, he would not have been insulted to be regarded primarily as a mediator in Cabinet councils. That he did not, as a rule, impose his ideas on his associates does not mean that he lacked ideas to impose. So long as men and measures proceeded along the lines which he set down, he was content to hold his hand. As before, he could depend upon the men around him to bring an ample supply of grist to the legislative mill. His task, as he saw it, was to regulate the input and to keep the gears in motion. 'His powerful brain', Birrell recalled from intimate experience, 'operated directly upon questions as they were put before him, and he never seemed to go in search of them.' What Birrell doubtless intended as a tribute to Asquith's conduct of Government business and to the fecundity of Liberalism has since been misconstrued as evidence of alleged indolence and neglect. To those who would captiously assert that Asquith was no innovator, let it be asked whether, under any other auspices, the administration would have survived half so long or accomplished half so much.

Many resignations were threatened, no fewer than twenty-three of them by Morley, whose private diatribes and published innuendoes about Asquith's incapacity must therefore be taken with a grain of salt. But until the outbreak of war none of these threats was carried out. There can be no better testimony to Asquith's effectiveness in reconciling divergent viewpoints and disparate personalities. To accomplish this feat, he sometimes found it necessary to obfuscate issues and to resort to a studied ambiguity; but that would hardly set him apart from others who have held his office. More distinctively, he proved unfailingly loyal to his colleagues, which J. A. Spender considered 'a very rare virtue in Prime Ministers'. He did not mind if they reaped the laurels for the Government's achievements, though he was quick to shield them from the blame for their own misjudgements. The question remains: to what purpose was he dedicated?

The period of Asquith's premiership has been alternately celebrated and derided: on the one hand, it has been depicted as one of purposeful and progressive reform; on the other, as one of unfulfilled promise, more impressive for its rhetoric than for any positive attainments. While it has been generally conceded that the prewar Liberals broke with tradition to establish new principles of social justice and state responsibility, it has been pointed out that they did not go far enough to satisfy the demands of more advanced contemporaries, still less the consciences of later generations. Apologists have cited extenuating factors, particularly the recalcitrance of the Tory-dominated House of Lords: the Edwardian climate of opinion, they have pleaded in defence of the Liberal record, was not conducive to more far-reaching changes. Others have put the countervailing case that the Liberals went about as far as their ideology would safely permit, and that their limitations were basically intrinsic.

Neither argument can be discounted. Under Asquith's leadership, the Liberal Government made notable strides in the direction of the modern Welfare State. Considering the intellectual and institutional frameworks in which they operated, many of their reforms were indeed remarkable, however meagre they may appear by latter-day standards. In the course of drafting, promulgating, and implementing their various proposals, the Liberals encountered formidable obstacles, not all of them confined to the parliamentary arena, and not a few of them self-imposed. It would be only half facetious to suggest that, had the House of Lords not existed, some elements within the Liberal fold might have been tempted to invent it as a scapegoat. Asquith, most assuredly not of their number, nevertheless appreciated their apprehensions and felt obliged to take them into account. Given his position, which was exemplary as well as pivotal, it would be helpful to examine the general attitudes that governed his responses to events as they unfolded.

For all the attention that has fixed on Asquith's inconclusive allegiance to Rosebery, his most profound debt was to Gladstone, under whom he had served his apprenticeship. Jo Grimond, without pretence to objectivity or non-partisanship, has declared that 'no summing up of Asquith should forget that he carried on the Gladstone tradition of politics as a heroic and endless engagement in trying to translate moral attitude into practice and raise the standards of aesthetic and intellectual as well as economic life.' There were numerous superficial characteristics which Asquith shared with Gladstone: an 'astringency' in public manner, a meticulous attention to administrative detail, and a weakness for aristocratic company. In addition, there were certain common assumptions about the emergent forces of democracy, which each in his way helped to stimulate.

In 1865, as a boy of twelve, Asquith had paid his first visit to the House of Commons to hear Edward Baines, a relation, propose his annual motion on the widening of the borough franchise. Baines, no out-and-out democrat, was the advocate of 'household suffrage', which he studiously differentiated from the more sweeping schemes propounded by extra-parliamentary agitators. The previous year, when the same ritual had taken place, Gladstone had revealingly addressed the House. His speech, which adumbrated his position in the Reform Bill debates of 1867, rested on a calculated equivocation: affirming his sympathy for the principle of universal manhood suffrage, he went on to renew 'the protest I have previously made against sudden, or violent, or excessive, or intoxicating change'. With due allowance for the passage of time, Asquith's mature views were much the same. Like Gladstone, he feared any drastic or potentially disruptive change, and he conceived of the representation of the community in terms of constituent classes, not individuals. Specifically, as an 'avowed antagonist' of the campaign for women's votes, he argued along Gladstonian lines.

'The number of people who really think in any age and country is very limited, and still smaller is the number of those who think for themselves', Asquith declared in his 1918 Romanes Lecture. These are not the sentiments which one would normally expect from a fervent democrat, much less from a leader of a mass political party. On a personal level, there was an unfortunate tendency to under-value men of more humble background (his refusal to take seriously Andrew Bonar Law, whom he likened to a 'chimney-sweep', was to his own peril), and to ignore their sensibilities. For example, he accused Lloyd George of leaking Cabinet secrets to the press, exactly as Gladstone had accused Chamberlain and Dilke. 'Men whose promotion is not sustained by birth or other favouring conditions are always liable to be assailed with unkind suspicions', Lloyd George protested smartingly.

On a more basic level, Asquith adhered to the Gladstonian belief that popular agitation ought not to be confused with public opinion. Confronted by suffragettes, anarchical trades unionists, and rebellious Ulstermen, he jealously upheld the principle of parliamentary supremacy. Obviously, events 'out of doors' would affect proceedings at Westminster; but they should not be allowed to dictate them. By the same token, such extra-mural developments should not be allowed to exacerbate fissiparous tendencies within the party or Cabinet.

There were, of course, several important respects in which Asquith differed markedly from Gladstone. As Chancellor of the Exchequer, he had pioneered new methods of taxation. In contrast to Gladstone, who had assented only grudgingly to the Newcastle Programme of 1891, he was firmly committed to policies of social reconstruction. Conversely, he was more pragmatic in his espousal of Free Trade, which orthodox Gladstonians continued to regard as an article of faith. 'I have realised from the first', he wrote in the early weeks of his premiership to St Loe Strachey, 'that if it could not be proved that Social reform (not Socialism) can be financed on Free Trade lines, a return to Protection is a moral certainty.'

The priorities which Asquith thereby set for himself and his Government were palpably un-Gladstonian. Determined to give the Free Trade system every opportunity to vindicate itself (as he trusted it would), he was prepared, if necessary, to sacrifice it on the twin altars of social welfare and national efficiency. 'This has been one of the mainsprings of my policy at the Exchequer', he explained on 9 May 1908 to Strachey, against whose imputations in the *Spectator* he defended his fiscal transactions:

I prepared the way by steadily reducing the principal of the debt – at the cost of the taxpayer & by means of the war taxes – till I shall have brought it at the end of this year to the level of 20 years ago.

1½ millions is permanently saved in *annual* interest – just as truly as if it had been taken off the Army or the Navy: and the capital of the debt, having regard to our increased wealth & population, is nothing like as burdensome as the same load was 20 years since.

To talk therefore of 'raiding' the Sinking fund, & improvident finance, when after setting aside out of it the whole additional cost of old age pensions (about £1,200,000) . . ., seems to me to be the height of absurdity.

Old Age Pensions were inevitable: I have secured an ample fund to meet them without any extra taxation.

As a Unionist Free Trader, Strachey remained sceptical on two scores: he disputed Asquith's budgetary computations and rejected as chimerical the distinction between social reform and socialism. Writing to Rosebery on 22 May, he deplored Asquith's loss of 'firmness': 'It is surrender after surrender.' Rosebery, in his reply the next day, showed greater tolerance: 'Perhaps I appreciate more keenly than you do the concrete and complicated embarrassments of a prime minister that lurk behind the scenes.' Nevertheless, he too wondered if it would be 'possible for the chief of this ill assorted and tumultuous host to keep his legs'.

Despite 'the concrete and complicated embarrassments' which Rosebery foresaw, Asquith's reign began auspiciously. On 29 April his leadership was formally endorsed by a party conclave at the Reform Club, where many of the participants had gathered nearly a decade before to elect Campbell-Bannerman their leader. The chair was taken by Sir John Brunner, a self-styled 'sturdy Radical', who paid a nostalgic tribute to 'C.B.' and extended a cordial welcome to

Asquith. He expressed confidence that the new premier 'would prove as admirable a leader of the House of Commons as Sir Henry had proved', and no less 'determined' than his predecessor 'to maintain the dignity and the power' of the elected chamber, increasingly challenged by presumptuous peers. He enjoined Asquith to pursue a foreign policy consonant with Campbell-Bannerman's election promise to put Britain 'at the head of a league for peace', and, more contentiously, renewed his appeal for the party to repudiate the shibboleths of *laissez-faire*. Morley, who had been conspicuously absent on political grounds when Campbell-Bannerman was elected in 1899, drafted the resolution in support of Asquith, who had been kept away on the earlier occasion by influenza. Carried unanimously, it spoke of 'his strong sense in council, power in debate, and consummate mastery of all the habit and practice of public business'.

In a cascade of metaphors, Asquith – obviously deeply touched – reminded his supporters that 'There is a lot of country still to traverse, steep hills to climb, stiff fences to take, deep and even turbulent streams to cross before we come to the end of our journey'. It was neither the time nor the place, however, to map out too detailed a route. Yet something had to be done quickly to revive party morale, which was badly shaken by a combination of blows dealt by the Lords on one flank and successive by-election reverses on the other. Although their overall majority remained an imposing one, the Liberals had, since the previous general election, lost six seats to the Conservatives and four to Labour; in the ensuing months, the Tories were to capture four more, portending a victory for them when the country next went to the polls. With the wisdom that comes of hindsight, there were some party strategists who regretted that the Government had not dissolved Parliament back in 1907, after the Lords had torpedoed the Education and Plural Voting Bills and before economic conditions had worsened.

The durability of Asquith's premiership has tended to camouflage the severity of the problems that beset it. Punctuated by prolonged bouts of discomfort, even distress, it has only in retrospect come to seem assured of its survival. It is against this background of fading electoral enthusiasm and attenuating self-confidence that its actions, particularly with regard to questions of social reform, must be projected. As Henry Pelling has perceived, 'the progressive legislation of the period was in great measure sponsored by middle-class reformers, partly for humanitarian reasons, partly because they thought that social reform would be electorally popular'. Neither factor should be underestimated, and neither should be allowed to eclipse the other.

The endemic ministerial difficulty was money. Each department pressed for a bigger allocation, necessitated as much by rising costs as by increased commitments. Concurrently, there was strong back-bench pressure in favour of the sacred maxim of retrenchment. Asquith, in the preparation of his third and last budget, tried as best he could to reconcile these competing claims. By mutual agreement, it was he rather than Lloyd George who announced its provisions to the House of Commons on 6 May. Pointing to a surplus of £4,726,000 for the 1907–8 fiscal year, he anticipated a surplus of £4,901,000 for the year under way. These savings made it possible to proceed with old-age pensions, and permitted a partial remission of the sugar duties, for which Labour members had agitated. Lloyd George, wait-ing in the wings, admitted to Austen Chamberlain that he would have preferred 'to keep the sugar duty on and use it for pensions'. But, on the whole, he was pleased with his inheritance. 'Budget over. Asquith spoke for over two hours – a very fine performance', he wrote to his brother on the 6th:

Old Age Pensions at 70. Five shillings a week and half the sugar tax off. Very great satisfaction to our side and it leaves the coast clear for me to initiate my own schemes. It is time that we did something that appealed straight to the people – it will, I think, help to stop the electoral rot, and that is most necessary. If it failed it might react in the House and bring us down prematurely.

The Old Age Pensions Bill, which Asquith assured the King was a 'modest and tentative measure', was introduced three weeks later. The Conservatives opposed it in principle, and unsuccessfully moved an amendment against it. Labour criticisms of its inadequacy were largely met by Lloyd George's concession of a sliding-scale to deter-mine the rate of coverage. The second reading was carried without a division, and the House of Lords acquiesced. Opinion on the Labour benches was also gratified by legislation to reduce to eight hours the working day in the mines. Critics feared the effects on the price and production of coal. This pious invocation of the laws of supply and demand was enough to cool the ardour of Gladstone who, as Home Secretary, took charge of this measure. Lord Ripon, soon to run foul of him on another issue, called upon the Prime Minister 'to infuse a little firmness into Herbert Gladstone about the Miners' 8 Hours Bill'. With the help of some gentle prodding from Asquith and some rousing oratory from Churchill, the Bill reached the statute book the following December as the Coal Mines Regulation Act. Less comprehensive and binding than its sponsors would have wished, it represented the first successful attempt to limit the working hours of men as well as women and children.

Other questions that preoccupied the Government were also those which Asquith had found in the pipeline when he came to power. At the Board of Education, Runciman tried (no more successfully than Birrell or McKenna) to devise a formula that would prove acceptable to uncompromising Churchmen and aggrieved Nonconformists. For the second time within the year, an Education Bill was introduced, only to be left stillborn. Infuriated Free Churchmen charged the Government with ingratitude, and, more by their abstentions than by their votes for other parties, seriously impaired the Liberal performance in a number of by-election contests.

A Licensing Bill, which might have been expected to assuage the Nonconformist Conscience, failed to clear the House of Lords. Given the predictability of its defeat, it was unfortunate that the Government lavished so much time and attention upon it. For this, Asquith was not entirely to blame. In the King's Speech of the previous January, top billing went to the Liberals' intention to supersede Balfour's Licensing Act of 1904, which was said to have overcompensated the brewers and, implicitly, to have endowed drunkenness. On 27 February Asquith had dutifully presented to the Commons a Bill that provided for a graduated reduction in the number of public houses as well as more stringent licensing hours. From all appearances, it was not a measure by which he set great store. Until the moment of its defeat, even the various temperance bodies were divided on its merits, and, needless to say, 'the trade' were implacably opposed. But, in its constitutional ramifications, the abortive Licensing Bill of 1908 acquired a transcendent importance. 'To put the thing plainly', Asquith told Liberal M.P.s, who honoured him with a dinner at the National Liberal Club on 11 December,

the present system enables the leader of the party which has been defeated and repudiated by the electors at the polls to determine through the House of Lords what shall and what shall not be the legislation of the country. The question I want to put to you and to my fellow Liberals outside is this, 'Is this state of things to continue?' We say that it must be brought to an end, and I invite the Liberal Party to-night to treat the veto of the House of Lords as the dominating issue in politics – the dominating issue, because in the long run it overshadows and absorbs every other.

C. P. Trevelyan, newly appointed to the under-secretaryship at the Board of Education, wrote jubilantly to his father:

I think this may be the *real* turning point. Asquith's power of leadership was at issue. If he could not fire a real load now he never would ... He got better as he went on – every sentence interrupted by cheers, getting louder and louder until when he declared 'I invite the Liberal party tonight to treat the veto of the House of Lords as the dominating issue in politics', we all leapt to our feet and cheered ... It is the step I have been longing for. There is no going back now. I have always hoped that Asquith with all his caution would be very formidable, and now he is proving it.

Trevelyan did not exaggerate either the heady emotionalism of the evening or its reciprocal effect on Asquith and the party. The honeymoon period was over, and the rank and file cried out for a forceful and inspiring lead. 'Practically everything that could have been done with the consent of the House of Lords had now been accomplished', Asquith's official biographers conceded, 'and on all the major measures of Liberal policy – education, temperance reform, land reform, Welsh Disestablishment, Irish Home Rule – the road seemed to be hopelessly blocked.' Serious unemployment in the country had given new impetus to the Protectionists, who turned the Government's misfortunes to their own advantage. At Westminster, as well as in many of the constituencies, the Liberals were reduced to an intolerable impotence. Their malaise was intensified by factional strife that surfaced within the Cabinet and, more amorphously, in a tug-of-war between the front and back benches.

These internal conflicts antedated Asquith's premiership, but became more pronounced as time passed and the field for decisive action seemed to contract. 'There is a crisis impending', Haldane had written to his sister on 5 February 1908. 'On naval & military expenditure the H. of C. may turn us out . . : In fact our party is hopelessly divided & I am not sure where the majority is.' Backbench 'economists' and their Cabinet allies waged a fierce battle to slash Admiralty estimates, even at the cost of forsaking the Two-Power Standard by which Britain was pledged to maintain a fleet larger than the combined navies of any two potential enemies. Their offensive repulsed, they sharpened their axes for an assault on Haldane's army estimates. Asquith, preparing to wrap himself in the mantle of leadership, was instrumental in frustrating these moves, and inevitably incurred resentment from both sides. As *The Times* complained on 3 March, he was 'compelled to play the not very enviable part of Mr Facing-both-Ways', which was not one for which he lacked rehearsal. When the controversy flared again the following autumn, he responded to the challenge from Arthur Lee, the Unionist member for Fareham and a zealous guardian of the

Two-Power Standard, with no fewer than 'three ambiguities'; and he cautioned McKenna on 14 November that it would be best if the Government's intentions 'may continue to lurk in convenient obscurity'.

A perennial conflict, it was one that increased in scope and heat with each repetition. Although it was not until later years that it reached a climax, its reverberations were already acutely felt. Asquith staved off the showdown by arranging a series of artful compromises and, no less adroitly, playing off one department or colleague against another. On his arrival in office, greeted by vehement demands for a curtailment of military expenditure, he appointed Lloyd George, Churchill, and Harcourt – all Radical 'economists' – as a committee to review War Office estimates. Churchill proposed a 'scheme', Haldane later recalled, which 'would have meant ruin and confusion to the Expeditionary Force, and I fought against it tooth and nail'. Lord Esher, at Asquith's bidding, brought home to Churchill 'the difficulty of forcing Haldane's hand and the undesirability of breaking up the Government'. By the last days of June, the reductionists had relented, and, for the time being, trained their artillery elsewhere.

In a matter of days, public opinion was inflamed by reports of German naval expansion, and there was a clamour for Britain to accelerate her Dreadnought programme. McKenna, as First Lord, seemed to have forgotten the slogans of economy which, only recently, he had been heard to preach. 'As you know,' the Prime Minister reproved him on 4 July, 'I have for a long time been increasingly sceptical (in the matter of shipbuilding) as to the whole "Dreadnought" policy . . . There is much money in it – and more than money.' Sir John Fisher, with enthusiastic backing from the jingo press, pulled out all stops in his campaign to commit the Government to laying down eight ships in the forthcoming estimates. Lloyd George and Churchill, with support from Morley in the Cabinet and 'the Brunner party' (as Fisher dubbed his antagonists) outside, insisted that four would be sufficient. And McKenna struck a balance by holding out for six. The Cabinet was divided down the middle; but Fisher was fortified by an endorsement from Grey, who minuted on 31 July: 'If the Germans continue to execute their naval programme at a rapid speed, we shall certainly have to ask Parliament to vote a considerable increase to our expenditure: no Government of either party could avoid doing so.'

The dispute smouldered through the autumn and winter, and was finally resolved in March 1909 by a typically Asquithian compromise: four Dreadnoughts were to be laid down immediately, with an option for four more if the situation seemed to warrant it. 'It is merely a question of phraseology', Asquith had cavalierly assured McKenna, whom he undertook to provide with 'a form of words which will be universally accepted'. Although McKenna was led to understand that the Prime Minister 'would instantly resign' if he failed to secure parliamentary assent, that contingency never arose. Asquith was confident of his verbal skills, which did not fail him. 'You alone can save us from the prospect of sterile & squalid disruption', Lloyd George had told him on 2 February in a thirteen-page appeal. Who was Asquith to disagree?

The 'economists' or 'pacifists', as they were variously designated, emerged from the fray with the shadow of victory, the 'Big Navy' men with the substance. 'It ends an era – the era of Gladstonian retrenchment', Morley grumbled to his private secretary on 18 March, after the collapse of Radical resistance in the Commons. 'The Liberal League has beat us.' Lloyd George, at a Cabinet meeting the next day, reportedly waxed indignant. But there were no resignations, and a semblance of unity was restored. In 1923, when Asquith published his reflections on *The Genesis of the War*, he recalled with egotistical satisfaction his *coup de grâce*:

> Estimates presented upon the authority of a Cabinet in which the advocates of peace and economy and the enemies of militarism were known to have a predominant voice . . . could not, in principle and as a whole, be opposed by the Liberal Party.

It was in the midst of this wrangle over naval estimates that the House of Lords rejected, by a vote of 272 to ninety-six, the Government's Licensing Bill. Liberals of antithetical persuasions, including those who had been lukewarm about the measure, were uniformly incensed. Dining at the House of Commons with the Buxtons on 26 November 1908, Lucy Masterman, whose husband was then parliamentary secretary to the Local Government Board, found herself seated next to Churchill. 'He was perfectly *furious* at the rejection of the Licensing Bill by the Lords, stabbed at his bread, would hardly speak', she recorded in her diary. 'We shall send them up such a Budget in June as shall terrify them', he thundered; 'they have started the class war, they had better be careful.' Others, too, had been driven to the conclusion that the way to circumvent the obstruction of the Lords was by recourse to money bills. Haldane, as early as 9 August, had volunteered to Asquith a

suggestion . . . over which you have probably already thought much –

that we should boldly take our stand on the facts and proclaim a policy of taxing, mainly by direct taxation, such toll from the increase and growth of . . . wealth as will enable us to provide for (1) the increasing cost of Social reform; (2) National Defence; and also (3) to have a margin in aid of the Sinking Fund. The more boldly such a proposition is put the more attractive, I think it will prove.

With the defeat of the Licensing Bill, there was the further incentive to strike back at aristocratic prerogatives. Brunner reported to a constituent that he had seen the Prime Minister on 2 December as a member of a deputation on naval policy; after the interview, he had lingered because 'I had something to say on my own behalf', and had counselled Asquith

that if he and his colleagues would now enter upon the fight with the Lords, his followers would back him with enthusiasm and that the stronger he showed himself the greater would be that enthusiasm. His only comment was 'The House of Commons has never received a greater blow in its existence than it did last week.'

Nine days later, Brunner was gratified to recount, Asquith attended the dinner of Liberal M.P.s at the National Liberal Club, where he delivered a 'memorable speech with which I am heartily contented'.

One would be mistaken to conclude that the struggle with the House of Lords was initiated as a diversionary tactic. But Asquith, for one, had no cause to complain if, incidentally, it fulfilled that function. The rapturous ovation accorded to his declaration of war against the Lords' veto has been noted. But special attention must be paid to his proclamation on the same occasion that 'the Budget of next year will stand as the very centre of our work, by which we shall stand or fall, by which certainly we shall be judged in the estimation both of the present and of posterity.' By this solemn affirmation, he had coupled the passage of the 1909 budget (which had yet to be drafted) with the fate of the House of Lords. The Lords themselves, by their foolhardy intransigence, were to solder this historic link. Asquith could not have anticipated, of course, the chain of events that led, through two general elections, to the Parliament Act of 1911. All the same, he galvanized his party, with tremendous political and constitutional repercussions.

# 6

## FROM THE BUDGET
## TO
## THE CURRAGH

'The truth is', Disraeli confided to the readers of his novel *Coningsby* (1844), 'the peers were in a fright. 'Twas a pity: there is scarcely a less dignified entity than a patrician in a panic.'

Sixty-five years after these sardonic words were written, history improved upon literature. The House of Lords, with a bellicosity that bordered on the pathological, threw caution to the winds and, with it, the Lloyd George budget of 1909. There followed a crisis that reached its climax, two years later, in the belated curtailment of aristocratic powers.

Far from being the straightforward dispute which contemporaries usually found convenient to define, the controversy of Peers *v.*

People – as it was popularly characterized – was a kaleidoscope of mutually impinging issues. Seen from one angle, it signified a collision between two irreconcilable theories of constitutional representation, each embodied in one of the rival Houses of Parliament. Seen from another, it was a contest between the claims of the transient Liberal majority in the one place and the pretensions of the perpetual Tory regime in the other. To some, it symbolized nothing less than a pre-destined clash between the emergent forces of social democracy and the entrenched interests of privilege. To others, it marked the culmination in a long and acrimonious struggle over the future of Ireland. It was at their various points of intersection that these discrete issues evoked the strongest feeling. To treat them separately would be to divest them of the cumulative impact that helps to account for the blind fury with which the battle was waged on both sides.

Historians have effectively disposed of the legend that the Chancellor of the Exchequer, with the tacit compliance if not the active connivance of his chief, cunningly framed his proposals so as to ensure their rejection and thereby to goad the Lords into sealing their own doom. From all indications, the budget of 1909 was conceived as a means to circumvent the obstacle of the upper House, not as a frontal assault on its prerogatives. There was the precedent of 1860–61 to inspire the belief that the Lords would ultimately back down: the Palmerston Government had carried through the Commons a measure that abolished the excise duties on paper, only to see it defeated in the Lords; resuscitated and wrapped in a larger parcel, the measure was passed into law. Not since the seventeenth century had the House of Lords dared to challenge the supreme authority of the Commons over the provisions for annual expenditure, and a Finance Bill had come to be regarded as more than the sum of its parts. The peers, as self-appointed guardians of established custom, were expected to fume and to fulminate, but nevertheless grudgingly to submit.

Rather, the 1909 budget was intended to cope with the 'unprecedented financial strains' which Asquith described to an audience at Glasgow a few weeks before its introduction on 29 April. The industrial and commercial boom of the early Edwardian years had subsided at the same time as Dreadnought construction and old-age pensions had imposed new burdens on the exchequer. Increased taxation was necessary if the Government were to meet a projected deficit of sixteen millions, and if (in Lloyd George's ringing phrase) it were to fulfil its promise to 'wage implacable warfare against poverty and squalidness'.

The Cabinet considered the Chancellor's detailed recommendations at a series of fourteen meetings, sometimes at the rate of three a week, that began in mid-March and continued after the brief Easter recess. In later years, when Lloyd George was anxious to impugn the Liberalism of those from whom he had since broken, he was wont to reminisce how, virtually singlehandedly, he had carried his bold proposals in the teeth of opposition from his timorous colleagues. But these retrospective complaints, like the second thoughts which Asquith eventually enumerated in his memoirs, were obviously coloured by the antipathies that had developed in the interim. Various ministers may have quailed at the inflammatory rhetoric in which Lloyd George habitually indulged; but remarkably few of them took serious exception to the principles at stake. In fact, there is evidence of only one occasion – a Cabinet session on 19 March – when the Chancellor was actually overruled.

The Prime Minister, Lloyd George recalled, 'was as firm as a rock'. His co-operation, Jenkins has explained, 'took the form more of the deft turning of difficult corners than of argumentative assistance'. It was an invaluable service, and one which he was uniquely equipped to perform. In the Cabinet he worked sedulously to promote a consensus: 'Once, when nearly everyone around the table had raised objections to a certain proposal,' Lloyd George testified many years later, 'Asquith summed up with the words, "Well, I think there is substantial agreement on this point."' In the Commons, where his attendance was sporadic (he voted in only 202 of the 554 divisions on aspects of the Finance Bill), he came to Lloyd George's rescue in early-morning debates. In a few well-timed speeches, he broadcast his support to the country at large. On the whole, his interventions were limited, although carefully weighted to achieve the maximum effect. It was wholly characteristic of his style of premiership that he should have deliberately allowed Lloyd George, who had taken a back seat the previous year, to monopolize the limelight. And, needless to say, Lloyd George gloried in the opportunity.

Asquith and Lloyd George were indispensable to each other, and, at this juncture, both recognized as much. Temperamentally, they were poles apart. But that, perhaps paradoxically, made them all the more redoubtable as a team. As Kenneth O. Morgan, one of Lloyd George's more recent biographers, has stated,

Asquith's judicious leadership, backed by stern partisanship, Lloyd George's radical passion, supported by tactical flair, provided a massively effective partnership. It brought Liberal England, not to its 'death' as once was mistakenly claimed, but to its glorious high noon. Those who try to seek a rift between Asquith and Lloyd George before the new strains of the war years will do so in vain.

It was Churchill, not Lloyd George, whom the Prime Minister rebuked on 21 July for 'purporting to speak on behalf of the Government' on the question of tactics. Asquith may have been critical of the way in which Lloyd George juggled statistics; and he, like others, was not particularly impressed by the Chancellor's meandering Budget Day speech. Nevertheless, he valued Lloyd George for his creative spark and boundless energy. And Lloyd George reciprocated with a high regard for Asquith's parliamentary authority.

There are some pairs of politicians (Harcourt and Rosebery, to cite one example) who collaborate best in opposition. There are others who require the responsibilities of office to cement their relationship. Asquith and Lloyd George belong to the second category. In earlier years, they had stood apart over the Welsh Disestablishment Bill of 1895 (when Asquith, as Home Secretary, encountered backbench resistance from Lloyd George, 'a natural *frondeur*'), during the stormy days of the Boer War, and again in the agitation over the 1902 Education Act. In later years, they were to face each other in bitter rivalry and recrimination. Yet, as colleagues in the prewar administrations, they shared a common purpose and a mutual respect.

After forty-two days (and nearly as many nights) in the committee stage, the Finance Bill passed its third reading in the Commons on 4 November. In the event, the Irish Nationalist M.P.s, who had opposed the new direct taxes on spirits, abstained, resulting in a final vote of 379 to 149. The agitation out of doors, organized by the Budget Protest League, an adjunct of the Opposition front bench, continued through the summer and autumn months. Lloyd George responded in kind to the vitriolic attacks made upon himself and the Government. But, as yet, he gave no indication that he expected the Lords to reject the budget, still less that he welcomed such a deadlock, which could only retard the welfare programmes he had in mind. And Asquith, addressing an audience of 13,000 at Birmingham on 17 September, declared emphatically: 'Amendment by the House of Lords is out of the question. Rejection by the House of Lords is equally out of the question . . . That way revolution lies.'

Was it wilful self-delusion or astute political sense that led the Prime Minister, at any rate publicly, to discount the likelihood of an intransigent stand by the peers? As early as 16 July, Lord Lansdowne had obliquely warned that his Unionist legions in the upper chamber 'would not swallow the Finance Bill whole without wincing'. To

Churchill, for one, that had conveyed an unmistakable threat. Writing to his brother on 17 August, Lloyd George first contemplated the possibility of rejection and, flushed with excitement, 'rejoice[d] at the prospect'; he soon convinced himself that he had worked towards this objective all along. On 8 September and again on 5 October, the Cabinet met to consider the contingency. 'It was agreed', Asquith informed the King after the second of these conclaves, 'that until the course of events shapes itself more clearly it would be premature to decide on any definite course of action.' In other words, Asquith was resolved to wait on events, which he did not wish to accelerate by any bold pronouncement or even by an acknowledgement of the gravity of the situation. His policy, which can be characterized as 'Wait and see', was one with which his name became synonymous. To an admirer like A. P. Ryan, here was an example of his 'massive common sense and refusal to be stampeded into the excitement of the moment'; to his critics, however, this was an early indication of his congenital tendency to slackness and sloth.

On this particular occasion, Asquith's caution can be ascribed to a multiplicity of factors. For one thing, he had serious doubts whether it would serve the Liberal cause to drive his antagonists to the point of desperation: the Government had been geared for a general election in the autumn of 1910, at the earliest, and did not relish the idea of going to the polls at short notice and on a stale register. Furthermore, he had reason to suspect that the responsible Unionist leaders, whose control over the 'Whole Hoggers' he was inclined to overestimate, were in no greater hurry to confront the electorate. Possibly, as Jenkins has suggested, he was fully alert to the danger, but reasoned 'that the best way to bring the constitutional enormity home to the country was for the Government publicly to stress its impossibility'. But that is to give him the benefit of the doubt. So far as one can tell, he held sincerely to the view that rejection was unthinkable. It was inconceivable to him that men of station would shed their reason, let alone their dignity, and that they were prepared to sabotage the institutions to which they professed devotion.

At the same time, he could not have ignored the divisions among his colleagues on basic questions of constitutional interpretation. United in defence of the budget and the democratic values which they held it to represent, the members of the Cabinet could agree only that it was imperative to 'smash the veto'. How they intended to proceed and what – if anything – they intended to substitute for it were moot questions. Some party leaders revived the plan for joint sittings, which Lord Ripon had advocated in 1907; others proposed an array of reforms in the composition of the second chamber, while a few wished to abolish it completely; another group preferred to leave the membership of the House of Lords intact, but to introduce a 'suspensory veto' of one type or another. Even after the evening of 30 November, when the peers denied their assent to the budget by a massive vote of 350 to seventy-five, the Liberal ministers had yet to find a common ground which they could defend.

One thing, and one thing alone, was certain: if the peers had the temerity to refuse supply, the Government had no option but to dissolve. Other alternatives, including a scheme for the collection of 'extra-legal' taxes on an *ad hoc* basis, were recognized as impracticable, too humiliating, or both. Because the House of Lords had taken so long to vent its spleen and to bring the Bill to a vote, a new register would take effect that was expected to favour the Liberal side. Conveniently, the passionate feeling among Liberals in the country relieved the party chiefs of any obligation to stipulate their ultimate goals. The situation, as Neal Blewett has discerned in a recent study of the general elections of 1910, was fraught with irony: 'Having no agreed Second Chamber policy, they [the Government] now took the extraordinary step of publicly pledging themselves to secure guarantees in order to implement one.'

Within twenty-four hours of the Lords' rejection, the Government retaliated by tabling a resolution in the Commons 'That the action of the House of Lords in refusing to pass into law the financial provision made by this House for the service of the year is a breach of the Constitution and an usurpation of the rights of the Commons'. The next day, Asquith was warmly cheered when he rose to decry 'this new-fangled Caesarism which converts the House of Lords into a kind of plebiscitory organ'. A magisterial speech, it upheld the claims of the elected chamber with mordant wit and cool logic. 'There were to be more effective demagogic assaults on the action of the Lords from the platform, and more erudite attacks in the press,' Blewett has written, 'but for sheer power and cogency no utterance was to equal this in the spate of words about to burst upon the nation.'

On 3 December, 'the best Parliament for the people this country had seen' – as Burns immodestly described it – was prorogued. The campaign, which had already begun, was officially opened by the Prime Minister with an address a week later at the Albert Hall, from which women were carefully excluded to guarantee against suffragette disruption. Again, Asquith was in superb form. In a calculated bid for regional and sectarian support, he renewed his party's commitment to Irish Home Rule, educational and licensing reform,

Welsh disestablishment, Scottish land policies, and 'a costly social campaign'. Explicit in his declaration that 'the absolute veto must go', he did not go so far as to commit himself to the suspensory veto about which he had been lukewarm when Campbell-Bannerman had proposed it two years earlier. In essence, he was asking the electorate for a blank cheque to deal with the constitutional crisis. His reticence can be largely explained by the private intimations he had received that the King was not prepared, 'until after a second general election', to implement plans to overwhelm the House of Lords by the mass creation of new peerages.

It was not until six days after the Albert Hall rally that the Cabinet met to set a timetable for polling. The Prime Minister, unavoidably absent, had deputed Lord Crewe as chairman. That morning, the younger son of Lord Aberdeen – a close friend of Violet Asquith – died from injuries in an automobile accident, and Asquith feared the effects on his daughter's fragile health. Like Balfour on the other side, Asquith was out of commission during much of the prolonged campaign. His colleagues, left to their own devices, vacillated pitiably. Eventually, the decision was taken to schedule the first polls for Saturday, 15 January. The Opposition protested against the delay, but doubtless profited from it as the issues quickly grew stale and Liberal ardour peaked early and ebbed thereafter.

The campaign dragged on for eight gruelling weeks. Asquith spoke twice at Liverpool on 21 December and, after the turn of the year, took to the hustings for ten days. 'But', Blewett has further observed, 'burdened by personal worries, with an exhausting year behind him and difficulties ahead whatever the result, Asquith visibly flagged.' When the ordeal was over, he withdrew to Cannes in such haste as to forget to keep a long-standing engagement at Windsor. He was 'completely knocked up by the election', he excused himself sheepishly to his affronted Sovereign.

Churchill and, especially, Lloyd George filled the vacuum, much to the irritation of Margot Asquith, who complained to Strachey that the Chancellor's 'speeches have been a *disgrace*: vulgar, silly and infinitely bad for us . . . I have given up reading them they are so disgusting.' Perhaps, as she and others alleged, Lloyd George frightened away middle-class support; but he more than compensated by the strength of his appeal to militant Nonconformists on the one hand and to working-class Radicals on the other. Sir Robert Perks, who declined to defend his seat at Louth out of opposition to the 'socialistic' provisions of the budget, was among those who noticed that 'Asquith seems to be taking quite a back place. As I told him

6 months ago ', Perks recounted to Lord Rosebery on 8 January, 'the victory (if it is one) will be Lloyd George's and not his.' Asquith may have been unperturbed, but his wife was absolutely furious at these insinuations. 'I only know one man with the qualities of leadership just now & that is the man who has kept his party & Cabinet together to a man', she told Strachey on the 31st. 'It is only amateurs who say that Henry is led by L. George!'

On 24 January, 'proportionately the worst day of the election for the Liberals', who lost nine out of seventeen contests, party publicists were impelled to contemplate the future with greater candour than the politicians permitted themselves. 'Asquith will, I hope, get through on his pledge by the promise of Royal support for a Bill giving finance to the Commons', Spender of the *Westminster Gazette* wrote apprehensively to Gardiner of the *Daily News*:

But if the Lords check that, we are all right & make our own issue; if not, we recover finance & get the Budget & then advance to the Second Chamber question more at leisure. But the King will not give guarantees on the legislative veto Bill; indeed, on the present showing, it would not be fair to expect it for a Bill which has never been drafted & if we give the other side ground for dragging the King in & saying that we are treating him badly & threatening the monarchy, we shall be playing a very bad card.

Gardiner, whose recent attitude to Asquith had been perceptibly cool, was inclined to agree. 'The great thing to my mind, at the moment, is not to make it difficult for Asquith to go on, or we should not even get the Budget through', he replied the next day. 'The Budget will be a great point gained & after that, I think, must come financial control for the House of Commons as the first step to the whole House of Lords question.'

In the final reckoning, the Liberals held 275 seats as compared to 273 for the Unionists. Shorn of their overall majority, they depended on their Labour and Irish allies to provide them with a working majority of 112 which, as Asquith defensively asserted, 'compared favourably with the majorities which such statesmen as Lord John Russell and Palmerston considered adequate'. Grey, less sanguine, drew 'the moral . . . that neither party had succeeded in gaining the confidence of the country'. Certainly, it was difficult to interpret the result as a mandate for drastic change. Sustained in office on the sufferance of the smaller parties, which promptly made clear that their votes could not be taken for granted, the Liberals were in an unenviable predicament. On the assumption that another appeal to the electorate could not be long postponed, they had to clarify their policies without alienating any of the factions on which they depended.

Given the ambiguities of the situation, how was the Government to proceed? John Redmond, the leader of the Irish Nationalist M.P.s, pressed for amendments to the budget and for the immediate abolition of the Lords' veto. Radical and Labour backbenchers enthusiastically supported his second demand. Within the Cabinet, however, there was a countervailing movement in favour of a more limited scheme of second chamber reform. To those who had had weighty reservations about the Campbell-Bannerman formula – including Haldane, Grey, and Crewe – were added the voices of Churchill and Lloyd George, who came to see it as an electoral encumbrance. The Chancellor, still 'very, very tired', returned from a holiday at Nice 'very bitten with the reform idea', although he kept repeating to Masterman that 'I cannot see what we are to do'. Loulou Harcourt, ordinarily no champion of popular causes, stood alone against the tide. 'There is a deal of loose thinking *inside*, as well as outside, the Cabinet just now', he admonished the Prime Minister on 7 February. 'We must stick tight to principles and not go a-whoreing after false constitutions.'

Asquith floundered with the rest, and his own indecision contributed substantially to the Government's incapacity. 'For several weeks after his return to London on February 9th', Jenkins has acknowledged, 'he exhibited less sureness of touch than at any other stage in the long constitutional struggle.' Mrs Masterman, writing in her diary, put the matter more bluntly: 'Asquith, so far as anyone could discover, came back with no ideas and no plan of any kind.' It was recalled that, in his Albert Hall speech, he had stated categorically that 'We shall not assume office and we shall not hold office unless we can secure the safeguards which experience shows to be necessary for the legislative utility and honour of the party of progress.' This declaration was widely taken to mean that he had obtained an assurance of royal support for the creation, if necessary, of hundreds of new peerages. Yet, when he appeared before Parliament on 21 February, it was his bounden duty to confess 'quite frankly' that he possessed no such 'guarantee'. Alexander Murray, the Master of Elibank and Chief Whip, considered Asquith's speech on this occasion 'the very worst I have ever heard him make'. Even his official biographers conceded that 'it came as disillusion and disappointment to a multitude which was looking for immediate spirited action, and the ringing emphasis with which it was stated was too much in the Aristides manner'.

'The seams in the Cabinet ran very queerly', Mrs Masterman reflected soon afterwards. 'Asquith', she noted, 'personally dislikes the Irish in spite of the Parnell Commission and the *Times* case', and he was unwilling to accept – still less to appear to accept – dictation from Redmond. By his canons, the settlement of the financial crisis should take precedence over more general constitutional issues. His principal colleagues concurred in this view, but those upon whom he depended for support in the Commons and outside were dead set against him: the Nonconformists, as self-conscious heirs to the Puritan tradition, were adamant that grievance should precede supply so as to remove the aristocratic obstacle to educational and licensing measures; Irishmen, recalling the defeat which the peers had dealt them in 1893, demanded a Veto Bill in order to clear the way for Home Rule; and Labour leaders, fortified by their egalitarian slogans, sought the destruction of the veto as a means to secure the reversal of the Osborne judgement, by which trades unions had been deprived of the right to dispense funds for political purposes.

By its studied vagueness, the King's Speech preserved a semblance of ministerial unity, but at the expense of party morale. Divided on its budget strategy, and particularly on how far they should go in order to appease Redmond, the Government were at sixes and sevens over the fate of the House of Lords. Harcourt, who could count only on Lord Pentland (formerly John Sinclair) to accompany him, threatened to resign if the Government defaulted on Campbell-Bannerman's solemn pledge. At the other end of the spectrum, Grey indicated his intention to 'go out' if the Government persevered with its veto resolutions. Runciman, with some misgiving, proposed to inform Asquith 'that Grey is not speaking or acting alone'. He did not know whether Haldane and Crewe were prepared to follow suit; but McKenna, to whom he wrote on 27 March, assured him that 'if Grey goes out I go too'. Not to be outdone, Morley renewed his request for release from the trammels of office. The previous autumn, he had inveighed to his private secretary against 'the failure of this Government: want of courage, nerve, and knowledge of what they were driving at'. Recent developments had merely strengthened his impression. But, for all his complaints, 'Radical John' had nothing to offer save his equivocations. Lloyd George, who found him 'no use at all', purveyed Harold Spender's jest that Morley 'really behaved (at the idea of creating peers) as an orthodox Christian might if it were proposed to add a fourth person to the Trinity'. On 14 April, when the Parliament Bill had its first reading, Morley wrote to the

Prime Minister: '*You had better let me go after Monday's crisis, if we survive it.*'

As it transpired, the Government survived the crisis and, needless to say, Morley survived with it. For several weeks, it had looked as though its break-up was imminent: if it managed to withstand internal pressures, it seemed likely to succumb to external ones. Gradually, however, Asquith began to recover his impetus and to reassert his mastery. The potential backbench revolt was averted by an announcement on 28 February that the budget would take second place to the promulgation of veto resolutions which a Cabinet committee was delegated to draft. The potential revolt within the Cabinet was effectively quelled by a compromise, framed by Haldane, by which ministers temporarily agreed to differ on the vexed question of reform *v.* veto. In mid-March, the committee recommended the Campbell-Bannerman plan with minor modifications. On the understanding that an organic change in the House of Lords might follow 'hereafter', Grey and other recalcitrants went along. Once a decision was reached, the Cabinet closed ranks in support of it. Churchill was a case in point: dining *à deux* with Masterman, he had sworn 'that he would resign sooner than accept the Veto policy again . . .: "No, no, no; I won't follow [Lloyd] George if he goes back to that d—d Veto"'. But, as Mrs Masterman was amused to observe, 'three weeks later he was making passionate speeches in favour of the Veto policy'.

At long last, the Government was ready to grapple with Redmond. 'After full consideration', it was decided that there could be no tinkering with the budget. Asquith could not conceal either from himself or the King that this refusal made it 'possible and not improbable' that the Irish Nationalists would combine with the Unionists to turn out the Liberals. But he gambled that Redmond and his followers would not endanger Home Rule for the sake of reduced liquor duties. As a reassurance to apprehensive Irishmen, among others, he informed the Commons on 14 April that 'in no case would he recommend Dissolution' without obtaining the 'guarantees' that had eluded him the previous time. It was 'a grand Parliamentary triumph for the Prime Minister', the Chief Whip recorded with no less relief than jubilation. 'All his lost prestige has been recovered.' With majorities ranging from ninety-eight to 106, the Cabinet's resolutions on constitutional reform were easily carried. Within the fortnight, the budget was passed by a majority of ninety-three votes (including sixty-two of the eighty-two Irish M.P.s), and sailed through the upper House without a division. Parliament, which had sat through its usual Easter recess, now adjourned belatedly for a well-earned respite of ten days.

Elated by his success, Asquith stopped at the Palace for an audience with the King, whom he found 'very reasonable', before going on to a celebration dinner given by Lloyd George at the Savoy. Early the next morning, he set sail from Portsmouth for a cruise aboard the Admiralty yacht *Enchantress* in the congenial company of the 'McKennae': Reginald and his young wife Pamela, the daughter of Asquith's old friend Lady Jekyll. The first port of call was Lisbon, where he was entertained by the Portuguese royal family and met 'a lot of Portuguese so-called "statesmen"'. On 6 May, as the ship neared Gibraltar, the wireless brought a message that King Edward was dying. Without delay, the *Enchantress* changed course for Plymouth. At 3 a.m. on the 7th, there came 'the terrible news' that, shortly before midnight, the King had died. 'I went up on deck', Asquith later wrote, 'and I remember well that the first sight that met my eyes in the twilight before dawn was Halley's comet blazing in the sky . . . I felt bewildered and indeed stunned.' He disembarked on the evening of the 9th and, the next day, tendered his condolences to the new monarch, George V.

The succession to the throne, although assured, was attended by a welter of difficulties, some more tractable than others. A well-meaning proposal to alter the phraseology of the Royal Declaration sparked a furore among Nonconformists, who favoured the traditional repudiation of Roman Catholic tenets, and who bristled at the modified wording that committed the Crown to an explicit recognition of the principle of establishment. More seriously, the sudden death of King Edward had thrown into confusion matters which, weeks earlier, had appeared to be settled. As Asquith himself told the House of Commons when it reassembled in mid-June, events had 'completely transformed the political situation'. Doubtless he exaggerated; but it was more convenient to profess loyal consideration for the newcomer to the throne, who was in mourning for his father, than to admit to one's own misgivings. It did no harm, after all, to make a virtue of necessity.

There was no further talk of a summer election, which no one had particularly wanted. Instead, expressly to postpone indefinitely any electoral contest, the leaders of the two major parties resorted to the aberrant procedure of a constitutional conference. If successful, a wide range of outstanding issues (including, it was hoped, Home Rule) might be settled on a bipartisan basis without embroiling the King. Liberal stalwarts and their Irish and Labour allies, unwilling to see great matters decided over their heads, protested vigorously. Dissident Unionists waxed even more furious at the thought of their nominal leaders trafficking with the enemy. The front-bench 'mandarins', although derided, were not deterred. Between 17 June and 10 November there were fifteen clandestine sessions at which the Government was represented by Asquith, Lloyd George, Birrell, and Crewe, and the Opposition by Balfour, Lansdowne, Austen Chamberlain, and Lord Cawdor.

Unlike Balfour, who was fighting to save his political skin, the Prime Minister's position within his party was impregnable. His participation in these proceedings was therefore all the more enigmatic and, to some minds, reprehensible. At the least, as Jo Grimond has deigned to comment, 'Asquith showed almost too much forbearance'; at the most, he seemed willing, even perversely eager, to sacrifice the momentum and legislative gains of the previous session. Unduly reluctant to put pressure on the King, who could not be counted upon to issue the requisite 'guarantees', he was swayed by his Liberal colleagues, who preferred to obtain – if possible – some measure of inter-party accommodation. Lloyd George, who did nothing by halves, urged a full-scale coalition, an arrangement to which he was instinctively attracted. His proposals received unexpected backing from Grey, who cowered from the 'explosive and violent forces which will split our party', and from Crewe, who calculated that 'we have not got far from the end of our tether as regards the carrying of large reforms'. There is some evidence that the Chancellor floated his scheme for a 'National Government' with the intention to displace Asquith; but, however hyperbolically, he averred his own willingness to stand aside if the higher interest demanded it.

Neither Lloyd George's altruism nor Asquith's compliance was put to the test. On 8 November a 'meeting of the Conference brought matters to a head', the Prime Minister notified the King. 'The result showed an apparently irreconcilable divergence of view.' Two further meetings were held in quick succession before failure was conceded. Balfour, already estranged from his rank and file, did not dare to give further ground: 'I cannot become another Peel in my party', he concluded. Asquith 'had a rather intimate talk with him' before the ultimate session on the 10th, and recounted to Margot: 'He is very pessimistic about the future, and evidently sees nothing for himself but chagrin and a possible private life.' For his own part, Asquith would have found it awkward to justify to his Liberal supporters any compromise with the Unionists, let alone a decision to coalesce with them.

A second election, staved off for five months by the 'Truce of God' (as J. L. Garvin scornfully called it), again loomed large. Cabinet opinion was divided between those who favoured an immediate dissolution, so as to exploit Unionist disarray, and those who wished to delay until January, when the Parliament Bill would have been piloted through the Commons and a new register would take effect. Before any decision could be taken, the Prime Minister was obliged to redeem his promise of 14 April to procure from the Crown contingent guarantees that the royal prerogative would be used 'if and when the occasion should arise'. On Friday, 11 November, Asquith journeyed to Sandringham for an audience with the King, with whom he discussed the situation in general terms. Unfortunately, the terms were too general for the literal-minded monarch, who was left with the mistaken impression that he would not be compelled to commit himself until after an election, if then. The King persisted in his delusion through the weekend, only to suffer a rude shock on Monday, the 14th, when Lord Knollys informed him that Asquith '*now* advocates . . . that you should give guarantees *at once* for the next Parliament'.

With a sense of deep distress and possible betrayal, the King instructed Sir Arthur Bigge (later Lord Stamfordham), his private secretary, to telegraph a stringent reply: 'His Majesty regrets it would be impossible for him to *give contingent guarantees* and he reminds Mr Asquith of his promise not to seek for any *during this Parliament.*' The Government and the Crown were at loggerheads, and it remained to be seen which would back down.

As a conciliatory gesture, the Cabinet decided on the morning of the 15th to assure the King that any guarantees would not be made public until the need actually arose. At the same time, the controversial guarantees were now formally solicited. Unappeased, the King received conflicting advice from his private secretaries: Bigge, who had served him for a decade, deplored the request as 'not English'; Knollys, whose services he had inherited at his accession, considered it one which the Crown could 'safely and constitutionally accept'. In the end, Knollys prevailed, but by means which were slightly disreputable. Misrepresenting Balfour's position, he alleged that the Unionists were not prepared to form a minority administration, leaving no choice but to capitulate to the ministerial demand. The King, when he subsequently learned that Knollys had knowingly misled him, was justifiably incensed. But there can be no doubt that, in his ignorance, George V was allowed to save face and to preserve the image of the monarchy as an institution above politics.

Accompanied by Crewe, Asquith saw the King on the afternoon of Wednesday, the 16th. During the course of what he celebrated as 'the most important political occasion of his life', he obtained the vital commitment. The King, less euphoric, chronicled the interview in his diary:

> After a long talk, I agreed most reluctantly to give the Cabinet a secret undertaking that in the event of the Government being returned with a majority at the General Election, I should use my Prerogative to make Peers if asked for. I disliked having to do this very much, but agreed that this was the only alternative to the Cabinet resigning, which at this moment would be disastrous.

This guarantee in hand, the Liberals persevered with their election plans. Buoyed by their showing in a recent by-election at Walthamstow, they were confident of victory. Two days later, Asquith announced that Parliament would dissolve on 28 November, with the first polls fixed for 3 December.

The second campaign of 1910, as brief as the law would allow, was more narrowly focused on the constitutional issue. In this round, Asquith manifested a dominant presence. He confined himself to the House of Lords question, which, in its infinite complexity, tapped unsuspected reserves of power and eloquence. His speeches, artfully cool and restrained, contrasted with the wild irresponsibility of other principal belligerents on both sides. On 19 November he opened his campaign at the National Liberal Club, where he ridiculed the 'constitutional jerry-builders' who improvised assorted blueprints for second chamber reform. Six days later, he assailed the contradictions of Unionist policy and the gyrations of Unionist politicians in the keynote speech to the National Liberal Federation, gathered at Hull for a truncated annual meeting. On the 29th he shared a platform at Reading with Rufus Isaacs, the Attorney-General, who was running hard to retain his local seat. Churchill, himself no slouch at electioneering (and certainly no sycophant), could not praise too highly Asquith's contribution. On 3 January 1911, after the dust had settled, he surveyed 'the general position of our affairs' – taking time out between paragraphs to lay siege to a 'gang' of suspected anarchists in Sidney Street, Stepney – and told his chief

what everyone feels – that your leadership was the main and conspicuous feature of the whole fight. It is not always that a leader's personal force can be felt amid all that turmoil. You seemed to be far more effectively master of the situation and in the argument than at the Jan election, and your speeches stood out in massive pre-eminence whether in relation to colleagues or opponents ... I noticed that Liberal audiences responded to your name with increasing enthusiasm as the days wore on. The result was decidedly a victory, and decidedly your victory.

It was a valid assessment. Without personal difficulties to distract him, Asquith had recovered his old flair. Possibly, too, he was stimulated by his acquaintance with Miss Venetia Stanley, the youngest daughter of Lord Sheffield (otherwise known as Lord Stanley of Alderley), with whom he was then beginning a celebrated correspondence.

What sort of victory was it? The second election of 1910 pretty much confirmed the verdict of the first. On a reduced turnout, the Liberal and Unionist parties were evenly balanced, each with 272 seats. Labour and the Irish Nationalists each registered a gain of two seats, thus increasing the anti-Unionist majority to 126. Given the clear lines on which the battle had been fought, there was no gainsaying the decisiveness of the result. Various Unionists might wail that the election had ended in another 'dead heat', but their mutual recriminations gave conclusive testimony to the magnitude of their defeat. Asquith, who had led his party to its third successive win, was reasonably satisfied with its modest proportions. 'I think that our election here has cleared the air, and made the way fairly plain, if not exactly smooth', he wrote on 17 January to Bryce at the Washington embassy:

When history comes to be written, it will surely declare the rejection of the Budget by the Lords to have been the most stupendous act of political blindness in our time. It is a little more than a year ago, and you have to-day both parties in agreement that the House of Lords, as we have always known it, is as dead as Queen Anne.

He spoke too soon. To his periodic disadvantage, he was inclined to gauge the opinions of his opponents by the private sentiments of a few leaders. His abiding respect for Balfour, whom he considered 'head and shoulders above his colleagues', induced him to discount the right-wing attacks on Balfour's waning authority. Consequently, he was persuaded that the storm had passed when, in fact, it had not yet broken.

It was his idle hope that the Unionist majority in the House of Lords, having speedily validated the budget as a result of the January election, would likewise interpret the December result as a 'referendum' on the Parliament Bill; in that event, he reasoned, it would be gratuitous for him to threaten the creation of 'puppet peers' (to use another of Garvin's blistering epithets). The Unionists, however, proved stubbornly resistant: in the lower House, where the Bill finally received its third reading on 15 May, passage was slowed by more than 900 amendments; in the upper House, similar obstructionist tactics were employed. On 5 July Churchill gave his wife an account of how 'the Lords go on tearing the Veto Bill to shreds'. The next day, Asquith drafted a memorandum in which he tactfully reminded the King of his 'Constitutional duty' to use his prerogative for the creation of an adequate number of peers. The King agreed in principle, but proposed to wait until the Commons had received, considered, and presumably rejected the Lords' amendments.

Formally requested by Lansdowne to specify his intentions, Asquith replied on 20 July (with a duplicate letter to Balfour):

> In the circumstances, should the necessity arise, the Government will advise the King to exercise his Prerogative to secure the passing into law of the [Parliament] Bill in substantially the same form in which it left the House of Commons; and His Majesty has been pleased to signify that he will consider it his duty to accept, and act on, that advice.

Four days later, when Asquith rose to address the Commons, he was raucously shouted down. 'It was', Churchill angrily informed the King, 'a squalid, frigid, organised attempt to insult the Prime Minister.' The clamour, lasting half an hour, was fomented by Lord Hugh Cecil, the original 'Hooligan', and F. E. Smith, on whom Asquith (over Balfour's objections) had recently conferred a privy councillorship. Unable to make himself heard over the din, Asquith sat down, 'declining to degrade himself further'. Grey, implored by Margot (who watched from the Ladies' Gallery) to 'defend him from the cats and the cads', received a respectful hearing. The damage, however, had been done.

The chant 'Divide, divide' was punctuated by choruses of 'Traitor', and by the refrain that Asquith, Redmond's lackey, had hounded King Edward to the grave. Jenkins has chosen to regard this outburst 'merely as the yelping in defeat of some sections of the Unionist Party', namely the 'Ditchers', who vowed to go down fighting. But the tumult was too great to be dismissed as a death rattle. In large part, it was a hysterical reaction against what many Unionists took to be Asquith's unscrupulous methods: his high-handed treatment of the monarchy, his unholy alliance with Irish separatists (financed by 'American dollars'), and, above all else, his casuistical statements. Even after his reply to Lansdowne on 20 July, uncertainty lingered: did the Government propose to create only so many peers as would be necessary to carry this particular measure (following the precedent of 1711–12, when Queen Anne created a dozen Tory peers in order to ensure the ratification of the Treaty of Utrecht), or did it mean to shift permanently the political balance in the upper House? That question was ultimately answered on 10 August, when Morley, deputizing for the ailing Crewe as Liberal leader in the Lords, announced – with the King's 'entire approval' – the royal concurrence in 'the creation of peers sufficient in number to guard against any possible combination of the different parties in opposition by which the Parliament Bill might be exposed a second time to defeat'. The 'safety valve', as Bagehot had labelled this residual power, was to be used.

The threat, as Asquith had hoped all along, obviated the need for its implementation. By a vote of 131 to 114, their lordships stripped themselves of their historic veto. A preponderance of Unionist peers followed Lansdowne's example and abstained, while Curzon played Pied Piper and led a pack of thirty-seven 'rats' into the Government lobby. The Prime Minister, whose vocal cords and temper were alike badly frayed, expressed tremendous relief. The King thanked the Almighty that 'I am spared any further humiliation'. Balfour, hours before the crucial vote, departed for the Continent, where he tried to clear his mind of politics. The Unionist diehards, robbed of their effective constitutional veto, proceeded to substitute an anti-constitutional one.

Paradoxically, although Morley had shrunk from the creation of peers, it fell to him (as he picturesquely put it to Minto) to 'denounce the House of Lords to their noble faces'. His Indian reform scheme safely lodged on the statute book, he had applied for a discharge from public service. In late October 1910, Asquith granted his request, only to discover that Morley had had no wish to be taken at his word. By then, however, Crewe had already been assigned to the Indian secretaryship. Churchill, in a letter to the Prime Minister on 22 October, hoped that it might prove possible to retain Morley's 'services in some great office without administrative duties', and suggested the Privy Seal. Instead, Morley was appointed Lord President of the Council. In that capacity, he displayed a new vigour and administrative zeal. When Crewe collapsed from exhaustion, he uncomplainingly resumed his India Office duties and, in addition, took charge of the Parliament Bill in the House of Lords. He also filled in at the Foreign Office when Grey went on holiday, and participated in the deliberations of the Committee of Imperial Defence.

'Morley and I were now the only two members of the Gladstone-Rosebery Cabinet of 1892–95 who remained in the Government',

Asquith later recalled. Fowler (raised to the peerage as Viscount Wolverhampton) had retired in June 1910. Lord Beauchamp, who had succeeded him as Lord President, became First Commissioner of Works in November, displacing Harcourt, who was raised to the colonial secretaryship. Churchill, who had replaced Gladstone at the Home Office the previous month, traded places in October 1911 with McKenna, who, in turn, had been succeeded at the Board of Trade by Buxton. In June 1912 Haldane (already a peer) realized his ambition to become Lord Chancellor, replacing Loreburn, who resigned for reasons of health. Colonel J. E. B. Seely was appointed to the vacancy at the War Office and, at the same time, Isaacs (remaining Attorney-General) was raised to Cabinet rank. A year later, as Baron Reading, Isaacs became Lord Chief Justice, making way for Sir John Simon. These, and other minor changes, saw the Government through the prewar period.

There was hardly time for ministers to congratulate themselves on their parliamentary victory before they were plunged into a series of crises in other spheres. During the autumn of 1910 there was an intensification of industrial turbulence that evinced a new spirit of labour militancy with which neither employers nor governing officials could cope. Churchill, as Home Secretary, dispatched troops to quell disorders in the mining areas of South Wales, and was later hounded by the cry of 'Tonypandy'. The following summer, as temperatures soared, British shipping was ground to a halt by an 'international' dockers' strike which foreign seamen preferred to ignore. The conflict, which Élie Halévy has characterized as 'nothing short of a revolutionary outbreak', was accompanied by appalling violence and fierce class hatreds. G. R. Askwith, who functioned as a professional conciliator, had warned the Cabinet that 'we were in the presence of one of those periodic upheavals in the labour world such as occurred in 1833–34'. To the veterans of the House of Lords crisis, that analogy was real enough.

The Prime Minister, fearing that the Lords would defeat the Parliament Bill, had summoned a Cabinet for 11 August. Instead, the agenda was pre-empted by the topic of industrial disruption. The dockers' strike, settled by wage concessions in mid-August, gave way to the greater threat of a railway shutdown. On the 16th the Cabinet met again in response to a strike call by leaders of the four railwaymen's unions. 'There is no doubt that the men have real grievances', Asquith confided to the King, and he offered a Royal Commission to investigate them. Beyond that he was not prepared to go. The next day, in a tense meeting with union officials at the Board of Trade, he categorically asserted that he would 'employ all the forces of the Crown' to keep the railway lines open. His obduracy served only to stiffen the backs of those around the table. At midnight, the strike began.

At this point, Lloyd George stepped in. As Jenkins has written, 'He employed all the cajolery, all the psychological insight, all the appeals to patriotism which Asquith had disdained to use.' The nation, the Chancellor gravely intoned, was trembling on the brink of a war with Germany, and a railway stoppage would make it impossible to move troops and supplies. Within forty-eight hours, the strike was settled, but not before rioting and bloodshed had occurred. 'The men who have been shot down', Keir Hardie declaimed in a parliamentary debate on 22 August, 'have been murdered by the Government in the interests of the capitalist system.'

Asquith, not in the least jealous of Lloyd George's imposing success, commended him warmly:

I cannot sufficiently express to you how strongly I feel the debt of obligation which I myself, & all our colleagues, owe to you for the indomitable purpose, the untiring energy, and the matchless skill with which you have brought to a settlement one of the most formidable problems we have had, as a Government, to confront. It is the latest, but by no means the least, of the loyal & invaluable services which you have rendered since I came to the head of the Government 3½ years ago.

In a letter to Bryce on 8 September, he continued to ruminate on the danger that had been narrowly averted:

It is curious that, so far, the United States seem to be less affected than Western Europe by the new unrest in the industrial world. It presents . . . some very ugly symptoms. If the railway strike had lasted a few days longer, the strain upon the whole social & political machine would have been unprecedently [sic] severe.

This growing restlessness on the part of organized labour, sometimes diagnosed as syndicalism, coincided not only with the final and most menacing phase of the constitutional struggle, but also with a militant campaign for women's suffrage. Asquith was equipped to handle each of these challenges as parliamentary phenomena: he placated Labour Party opinion by introducing salaries for M.P.s as a provision of the 1911 budget, and he promised to undo the deleterious effects of the Osborne judgement by a system of 'contracting out'; with stinted assistance from the King, he had intimidated the Unionist peers into submission; and he adroitly defused the women's suffrage issue first within the Cabinet, and then within the Liberal Party, Yet, when these conflicts were carried beyond the precincts of the Palace of Westminster, he was at a loss to deal with them.

In his two-volume survey of *Fifty Years of Parliament*, where he relegated the controversy over female suffrage to a chapter of 'Miscellanea', Asquith acknowledged himself to have been an 'avowed antagonist' of that cause. Although it would be comforting to think that his opposition was addressed not to the fundamental issue but to the violent methods by which it was sometimes advanced, one must not forget that he had spoken against the concession of votes to women as early as 1882, when the subject had been essentially an academic one. In 1907, when a Women's Enfranchisement Bill was introduced, he had stood his ground. On this score, he differed not only from Campbell-Bannerman and Lloyd George, but also from Haldane and Grey. It is worth noting that his wife and elder daughter, who did not require the vote to exercise political influence, shared his aversion to 'petticoat politics': at an India Office reception, Margot impetuously boxed the ears of an assailant in a pink dress; and Violet, who wielded her fists to protect her father on the golf links at Lossiemouth (the other side countered that it was Asquith who struck the first blow), recalled that 'In the fierce battle for women's rights I was, alas, a blackleg – a blackleg without even the decent covering of Blue Stocking.'

Doubtless Asquith's well advertised opposition contributed to an exacerbation of tensions. By the end of 1909, many suffragists had come to despair of peaceful tactics, which had got them nowhere, and began to combine heckling with the destruction of property, window-breaking and worse. For much of 1910 an uneasy truce prevailed, during which the Women's Social and Political Union regrouped its forces; after a flare-up of civil disobedience in November, it was extended through most of the following year, while Parliament debated a Conciliation Bill for the limited extension of the vote to women. On 17 November 1911, after an unsatisfactory interview with the Prime Minister, who had done his best to avoid receiving their deputation, the W.S.P.U. resumed its campaign with a vengeance. The subsequent defeat of the Conciliation Bill, and the Government's failure in July 1912 to make specific provision for women in its general Reform Bill (which, it was mistakenly understood, could be amended to include women on the same basis as men), triggered a frenzy of arson, bombings, and arrests. On his way to unveil a memorial to Campbell-Bannerman at Stirling, Asquith was intercepted by suffragettes who stopped his car by lying across the road. He was castigated with slogans and a dog whip, brandished by one of their male comrades.

These were not the sort of 'arguments' to carry weight with

Asquith, who refused, as always, to accept the cries of extremists as an articulation of the public will. For Parliament to bow to such extra-mural pressures would be for it to abnegate its supreme authority. In a debate on 6 May 1913 he put to the House 'in one sentence' – though a cumbersome one – 'the gist and core of the real question':

Would our political fabric be strengthened, would our legislation be more respected, would our domestic and social life be enriched, would our standards of manners – and in manners I include the old-fashioned virtues of chivalry, courtesy, and all the reciprocal dependence and reliance of the two sexes – would that standard be raised and refined if women were politically enfranchised?

To this omnibus question, he replied in the negative. So far as he was concerned, the issue, like the language in which it was enveloped, was outrageously 'exaggerated'. If anything, his own hyperbole tended to exaggerate it further, and his constitutional principles were vitiated by a total want of sympathy, even an intolerance, that extended to those M.P.s ('poor spineless wind-tossed waverers & wobblers', 'fluid flaccid indeterminate elements') who gave 'a rather pitiful exhibition of so-called masculinity' by pledging support to the women's cause. As Mrs (later Dame Millicent) Fawcett, who stood apart from the militant Pankhursts, declared after Asquith had backtracked on his promises: 'If it had been his object to enrage every woman suffragist to the point of frenzy, he could not have acted with greater perspicacity.'

It would have suited him best if the suffragettes, along with other militant agitators, had left their elected representatives free to deliberate (and possibly to act) in an atmosphere of calm; yet he provided no firm assurance that Parliament would proceed on its own initiative. Consequently, with the same desperation as rebellious Ulstermen and discontented industrial workers, the feminists took matters – and weapons – into their own hands.

When the railwaymen had gone on strike in August 1911, it was widely feared that the coal miners, adjudged to be 'in a very disturbed state', would join in. Early the following year, the Miners' Federation balloted in favour of a work stoppage. Accordingly, on 18 February 1912 its executive issued notices for a strike at the end of the month unless it obtained a minimum wage per shift of five shillings for men and two shillings for boys. Ten days later, Asquith and three colleagues – Lloyd George, Buxton, and Grey – met members of the executive at the Foreign Office, where the Prime Minister made (for him) the 'considerable advance' of accepting the principle of a minimum wage, but baulked at the demand for the '5 and 2'. As threatened, the strike was called at midnight on the 29th, bringing the mines to a standstill, and creating havoc in a large number of industries that relied on them for fuel supply. Adding the number of those who had downed tools to the number of those who were laid off, nearly two million were soon out of work.

Further attempts by the ministerial team to negotiate a compromise proved unsuccessful. Finally, it was decided to resort to emergency legislation. In the early hours of 27 March, the Miners' Minimum Wage Bill was pushed through the Commons over opposition from both Unionist and Labour M.P.s; the House of Lords, which made it a policy never to pit itself against the trades unions, quickly gave its assent. Choked with emotion, Asquith had presented the Bill for its third reading. 'I speak under the stress of very strong feeling', he said haltingly and, according to contemporary accounts, almost inaudibly. 'We have exhausted all our powers of persuasion and argument and negotiation. But we claim we have done our best in the public interest – with perfect fairness and impartiality.'

The new Act established a compulsory machinery by which minimum wages would be set by a network of district boards, on which trades unionists would enjoy direct representation. It remained to be seen whether the striking miners would accept this solution, which did not give them the '5 and 2'. During the first week of April, there was another poll of the Federation membership. In the absence of a two-thirds majority in favour of the continuation of the strike, the executive ordered the men back to the pits. 'It is a blessing that the strike is over', Asquith wrote with relief to Miss Stanley on Easter Sunday.

The concession of a minimum wage to miners – Asquith made sure to stipulate that he did not advocate a minimum in every industry – brought to the surface various philosophical differences within the Cabinet. Morley, as a Gladstonian fundamentalist, vehemently opposed even this limited restraint on the system of free enterprise. Grey and Haldane, by contrast, took a more collectivist approach: the former proposed, if necessary, to compensate coal-owners out of the Exchequer for any losses they might incur; and the latter, during the London dockers' strike that followed in May, urged his unyielding colleagues to extend to all employees of the Port of London Authority the wage rates which had been won by unionized dockers. In each of these instances, Asquith adhered to the middle ground, striking a balance between the guardians of the Old Liberalism and the apostles of the New.

It has been calculated that there were 834 work stoppages begun in 1912, thirty-eight fewer than the previous year and 625 fewer than the next. But this figure, taken by itself, is altogether misleading. The stoppages in 1912, longer in duration and affecting more vital industries, resulted in the colossal loss of 40,890,000 working days, more than four times the total for either of the other years, and greater than the total of working days lost through strike action during the previous eight years.

The damage inflicted by rampaging suffragettes was more random, but, in its way, no less destructive. Still more difficult to quantify was the effect of Unionist frustration, which paralleled – and seemingly reverberated with – that of the women and the workers. None of these 'revolts', had it come on its own, would have had such a staggering impact; cumulatively, however, they generated an atmosphere of relentlessly mounting tension.

Of the three simultaneous insurrections, that of the diehard Unionists was the most perplexing and, by any standard, the least rational. An outgrowth of the vindictive struggle over the powers of the House of Lords, its immediate stimulus was the introduction, in April 1912, of a third Home Rule Bill. Redmond was collecting his reward, which could hardly have been denied him. 'If I may say so reverently,' he told the House of Commons, 'I personally thank God that I have lived to see this day.' His Unionist adversaries, who rejected his religion as well as his national cause, responded with blasphemies.

Deprived of the Lords' veto, which had been their safeguard in times past, the Unionist opposition searched anxiously for a means to preserve the Anglo-Irish Union and, if possible, to bring down the Government that endangered it. For want of a better alternative, they decided to play 'the Orange card', as Lord Randolph Churchill had shamelessly referred in 1886 to the sense of betrayed loyalty on the part of the Protestant community in the northern Irish counties. Andrew Bonar Law, the dark horse who had lately replaced Balfour as Unionist leader, possessed neither his predecessor's Irish experience nor his constitutional scruples. 'I am afraid I shall have to show myself very vicious, Mr Asquith, this session,' he nonchalantly remarked to the Prime Minister in February, as they walked back in procession from hearing the King's Speech. Before the session was over, Bonar Law had helped to give a new definition to viciousness.

Allying himself with Sir Edward Carson, a hard-bitten Dublin-born Protestant barrister who sat for Dublin University, Bonar Law sedulously exploited the sectarian hatreds in Ulster. Equating Home Rule with 'Rome Rule', he denounced the Government's policy as a sell-out to the disloyal and unlawful Irish multitudes, who could be expected to rob proud Ulstermen of their birthright, their prosperity, and ultimately their religious heritage. He went further to challenge the very legitimacy of the Liberal regime and the democratic conventions on which it rested. On Easter Tuesday he addressed a monster demonstration at Balmoral, a suburb of Belfast, which he described as 'a besieged city . . . The Government have erected by their Parliament Act a boom against you to shut you off from the British people', he proclaimed to an audience that needed no extra incitement to paranoia or sedition: 'You will burst that boom . . . Help will come, and when the crisis is over men will say to you in words not unlike those used by Pitt – you have saved yourselves by your exertions, and you will save the Empire by your example.' On 29 July, at a Unionist rally at Blenheim Palace, his rhetoric was even more extreme and his message more explicit. He attacked the Government as 'a Revolutionary Committee which has seized upon despotic power by fraud', and he proffered incendiary assurances that he could 'imagine no length of resistance to which Ulster can go in which I should not be prepared to support them'.

Liberal ministers were not impervious to the Ulster problem. Blenheim, where Bonar Law had plied his threats, was Churchill's birthplace and the residence of his cousin, the Duke of Marlborough. Although Churchill had braved personal danger to appear at a Home Rule meeting in the centre of Belfast in February, his family connections and his friendships with F. E. Smith and other truculent Unionists made him an ambivalent Home Ruler. Similarly, Lloyd George could not have underestimated the aversion to Home Rule among large sections of the Nonconformist electorate, who demanded the redress of their own grievances – educational reform and Welsh disestablishment – before concessions to the dreaded Papists. To placate opinion within as well as outside the Liberal fold, the Government proposed to couple the enactment of Home Rule with legislation by which the recalcitrant counties of northern Ireland might temporarily 'contract out' of the jurisdiction of an all-Ireland parliament in the south. These provisions, however, neither allayed the fears of Orangemen nor suited the political interests of their staunch defenders.

Asquith was stupefied. 'I do not believe in the prospect of civil war', he declared 'quite frankly' to a rally at Dublin in July. In the last analysis, he insisted, Ulster patriots, like other subjects of the Crown, would not defy 'the supreme authority of the Imperial Parliament'. Given his recent experience with suffragettes and trades unionists, it is difficult to see where he derived his confidence. But perhaps he was merely whistling in the dark. The distraught Unionists, unable to obtain a majority in the House of Commons or to invoke the House of Lords, tried to persuade the King to dismiss his treacherous ministers or, alternatively, to revive his ancient veto. They contemplated withdrawal from Westminster, the adoption of Irish tactics of parliamentary obstruction, and holding the Government – and the nation – hostage by rejecting the annual defence estimates in the Lords. With virtual impunity, they encouraged the Ulster Volunteer movement, a citizens' army which they covertly helped to supply with arms. Finally, in March 1914, when the Government issued orders to move troops in anticipation of an Ulster uprising, its enemies (as they had unmistakably revealed themselves) sanctioned a 'mutiny' at the Curragh of British officers, who were largely Anglo-Irish by extraction and strongly Unionist by sympathy.

The Curragh incident, which brought the Ulster crisis to an unedifying climax, showed up the weakness of the Government no less than the recklessness of its opponents. The confrontation need never have occurred if matters had not been left to drift indecisively, and if ministers – particularly Churchill and Seely, but to a lesser extent Haldane and Morley – had weighed more carefully their words and actions. What was conceived as a precautionary manoeuvre to reinforce arms depots and other strategic points in and around Belfast was easily misconstrued as a sinister plot to coerce Ulster which, as Bonar Law infamously charged, would be transformed into 'a new Poland'. Churchill repudiated this 'hellish insinuation'; but his own intemperate language, and especially his Admiralty order to deploy the Third Battle Squadron in Irish waters, lent credence to it.

There is no need here to investigate in detail the facts of the episode, through which countless historians and biographers have patiently sifted. It began when Lieutenant-General Sir Arthur Paget, commander-in-chief in Ireland, notified his superiors in Whitehall that the movement of troops into Ulster would touch off civil disturbances and, at the same time, severely strain the loyalty of his officers. As Secretary of State for War, Seely unthinkingly gave those officers who had 'direct family connection with the disturbed area in Ulster' a special dispensation: in the event of conflict, they might 'disappear' without loss of their commissions. Paget, himself disaffected, conveyed to his senior officers the assurances he had obtained from 'those swines of politicians'. Brigadier-General Hubert Gough, commander of the Third Cavalry Brigade stationed at the Curragh ('and the hottest of Ulsterians', according to Asquith), thereupon announced that he and fifty-seven of his subordinates preferred to accept dismissal sooner than to undertake 'active military operations against Ulster'.

The Prime Minister was not unduly alarmed when news of the incident was brought to him at Lord Sheffield's bridge table on the evening of 20 March. In the parlance of the day, he recognized this as a 'strike', not a full-fledged mutiny, and expressed optimism that the whole affair 'will be cleared up in a few hours'. Even so, he realized that 'the permanent situation' would survive 'the immediate difficulty': to Miss Stanley, from whose side he had been suddenly called away, he admitted that 'there is no doubt if we were to order a march upon Ulster that about half the officers in the Army – the Navy is more uncertain – would strike'. That, to say the least, was an unsettling prospect.

In short order, Asquith countermanded Churchill's Admiralty order and took belated steps to co-ordinate Cabinet policy. In an unambiguous speech to the House on the afternoon of the 27th, he disavowed the War Office's concordat with Gough, who had accepted reinstatement at the price of written guarantees that the army would not be used 'to crush political opposition to the policy or principles of the Home Rule Bill'. A new Army Order reasserted the cardinal principle of civilian control over the military. Various resignations followed, including Seely's. Asquith, with the 'emphatic approval' of the King, decided to shoulder the burdens of the War Office along with those of the premiership. 'He is trusted by both sides, and will do his utmost to avoid friction,' Sir George (later Lord) Riddell, the proprietor of the *News of the World*, noted in his diary on the 30th. 'He is a crafty old dog.'

The Government's equivocations and its reluctance to make a clean breast of the Curragh incident were commonly held responsible for several defeats at spring by-elections. Among the casualties was Masterman, who did not acquire another seat until 1923. 'The amount of mud that is being thrown at ministers is wonderful', Haldane wrote to his mother on 23 April. 'But we take these things with equanimity. The P.M. does not turn a hair.' A month later, Asquith was again shouted down in the Commons, 'a form of protest' which the *Daily Express* considered 'proper and justified' in the case of a politician who 'deserves neither respect nor a hearing'. For once, Margot Asquith did not exaggerate when she complained that she had 'never known the Tories so vile, so rude and so futile as now'.

Under strong pressure from the King, who bombarded him with 'hysterical' appeals, Asquith resumed the secret *pourparlers* with Bonar Law and Carson which had been broken off at the turn of the year. Tentative overtures in early May set the stage for an all-party conference, under royal auspices, in July. With the Speaker in the chair, it opened on the 21st and closed, an utter fiasco, three days later. When the Liberal and Unionist representatives had been able to agree, their respective Irish allies had divided against them, and vice versa. All that was achieved was the postponement of Home Rule and the further raising of tensions. At the close of the month, when European events quietly intruded, the threat of civil war continued to hang over Ireland.

Dilatory and insufficient, Asquith's Irish policies have been defended on grounds of practicality. 'The whole technique of his statesmanship was to watch events calmly until he saw an opportunity for effective intervention', Jenkins has contended. Whereas he might have taken criminal proceedings against the agents of sedition, he would have regarded that action as precipitous and possibly as an admission of defeat. As Jenkins has reasoned, 'Asquith's stand was on the inviolability of the parliamentary system. To maintain this stand he had to pretend that the system was working normally, even if it was not – and this meant that, whatever they did, he could not lock up his principal opponents.' Assuming that Jenkins is correct, was Asquith taken in by his own bluff?

Another mitigating factor has often been cited as an explanation – although not necessarily as a justification – for Asquith's tendency to shirk irrevocable commitments. With the profusion of crises that beset him, his most remarkable achievement was to weather them all. The problems that confronted him were as numerous as the heads of the hydra, and as persistent: the prolonged struggle over the People's Budget of 1909; the campaign to curb the House of Lords; the emotive issue of women's suffrage; strife within the Cabinet and the party over naval estimates; the eruption of labour troubles; the Marconi scandal of 1912, in which three ministers and the Chief Whip were implicated; Irish disorders and the Ulster stalemate; recurrent international tensions; and, capping them all, the outbreak of the European war. 'The Prime Minister is fortunately not afflicted with nerves', Haldane wrote to his mother on 22 May 1914.

Others, however, were less admiring. Stephen McKenna, brother and eventual biographer of the Cabinet politician, recalled Asquith's prewar juggling act, adding that 'friends began to wonder whether the highest statesmanship consisted in overcoming one crisis by creating another'. More recently, Cameron Hazlehurst has pugnaciously insisted that 'the record of a prime minister under whom the nation goes to the brink of civil war must be subjected to the severest scrutiny'.

It is fatuous to imply, as some have done, that Asquith was a practitioner of 'brinkmanship' who provoked each crisis – including British entry into the war – as a distraction from the previous one. By the same token, it is absurd to ascribe the many-faceted revolt against the Liberal order to his alleged inertia. Granted, his failure quickly to assert himself often made matters worse; but he cannot be held responsible in any sense for creating the situations that convulsed politics and society during these tumultuous years.

After the second of the 1910 general elections, in which he had participated with renewed energy, he lapsed into a relatively quiescent state, giving rise to rumours that he meant to step aside in favour of Grey or Lloyd George. 'One of the Sunday papers announces that I am subject to fits of severe depression wh. cause my friends much anxiety', he reported on 16 March 1913 to Miss Stanley, whom he teased: 'I hope *you* did not supply this information.' It was not depression from which he appeared to suffer so much as flights of uncontrollable giddiness. On a few occasions, which have inevitably aroused far more comment than they deserve, he turned up at the House visibly the worse for drink. Arthur Lee sniggeringly commemorated the time,

during the Committee stage of a highly controversial Welsh Church Bill, when I was left in charge of the front Opposition bench during the dinner hour. The two Ministers on duty were Herbert Samuel and Rufus Isaacs, and at about ten o'clock Asquith, having returned from dinner, very flushed and unsteady in gait, plumped himself down between them on the bench and promptly went to sleep. Whereupon Balfour, who had been cynically surveying the scene, turned to me and murmured 'I am getting uneasy about this Bill and don't at all like the idea of the fate of the Church being left in the hands of two Jews who are entirely sober and of one Christian who is very patently drunk'!

More in sorrow than in malice, Lloyd George wrote to his wife on 21 April 1911 with an account of the same incident. But, as he told it, Lord Hugh Cecil had made the quip to Churchill during the previous evening's debate on an amendment to the Protestant Succession. Like many a good anecdote, it was embroidered as it circulated. In its innumerable variations, it gave rise to the impression that Asquith was chronically bibulous.

His fast-paced social life fostered the same impression of irresponsibility. With Miss Stanley, an alluring young woman in her mid-twenties, he enjoyed an epistolary relationship in which he grew more garrulous as problems overwhelmed him. He supervised her reading, quizzed her on the classics, and entertained her with sonnets and doggerel verse. For her 'collection', he sent her autographs from various personages, royal and otherwise. Gradually, he began to provide her with political analysis, to regale her with state secrets, and to solicit her recommendations for privy councillorships and other appointments. Like a schoolboy, he playfully nicknamed his associates: Edwin Montagu, her future husband, was (by virtue of his Semitic profile and lineage) The Assyrian; Simon, The Impeccable; Haldane, The Sinless One; Runciman, The Alabaster Statesman; Seely, The Arch Colonel; Beauchamp, Sweetheart; and the leader of the Opposition was Bonar Lisa. A boon to the historian, for whom they provide an invaluable mine of information and opinion, these letters reveal Asquith in another light: he was vain, lonely, sometimes supercilious (as when he mocked Lloyd George's spelling mistakes or Runciman's faulty grammar), and less sportive in his anti-Semitism than Jenkins would have us believe.

In February 1912, more than a year after they had met, Venetia joined the Prime Minister, Violet, and Montagu for a holiday in Sicily. Thereafter, his emotional dependence on her steadily increased. They would meet at parties, often at her parents' house, and made a ritual of Friday afternoon motor drives. Were they lovers? More than one authority has casually identified her as his mistress. His passionate declarations and tender endearments would tend to support such an interpretation. 'It will be 27 years to-morrow since you opened your eyes on this sinful world, and it is not yet 3 since I made my great discovery of the *real* you,' he reminded her on 21 August 1914:

I sometimes wonder, looking back, whether you would rather that I had *not* made it, and that things had continued between us as they were in the early days of the Venetiad. I believe – indeed I know from what you have told me, and you never lie – that it has made a difference to the interests & pleasures (perhaps also at times to the anxieties) of your life. I cannot tell you, for you might think I was exaggerating, the length & breadth & depth of the difference it has made to me.

Connoisseurs of Edwardian literature will instantly recognize the idiom. But, before one jumps to the obvious conclusion, one must consider that Asquith wrote copiously, ardently, and often concurrently to a good many women, among them Margot and her niece, Lillian Tennant; Lady Scott (later Lady Kennet), the sculptor and widow of the Antarctic explorer; Pamela McKenna; and Mrs Hilda Harrisson, to whom Lady Cynthia Asquith (his daughter-in-law) was introduced at The Wharf as 'a neighbour war widow'. His extensive correspondence, Jenkins has remonstrated, 'was both a solace and a recreation, interfering with his duties no more than did Lloyd George's hymn singing or Churchill's late-night conversation'. True enough; but the others, in their respective pastimes, did not make it a practice to divulge Cabinet proceedings or wartime troop movements.

We have, then, two contrasting images of Asquith during the immediate prewar years: on the one hand, he was reserved, dignified, solitary, and exclusive; on the other, he was passionate, mawkish, and more than a trifle frivolous. The last of the Romans, as he appeared publicly, he sometimes behaved privately – as John Grigg has piquantly quipped – like one of the last of the Romantics. Lady Diana Cooper has recalled how, as a girl of seventeen, she 'used to go rather surreptitiously to Downing Street. It flattered my snob side, but also I really loved Mr Asquith. He delighted in the young and the young's conversation, and would talk of poetry and people and weddings and jokes, and he wanted to hold one's hand and feel equal and comforted.' Soon after the war, she and other Bright Young Things helped him to celebrate his sixty-seventh birthday in Venice, where 'we dressed him up as a Doge and hung the *sala* with Mantegna swags of fruit and green leaves and loaded him with presents, tenderness and admiration. I think he was ecstatically happy that day.'

The contradictions of Asquith's personality, however peculiar or even perverse they may seem, faithfully reflected the character of the age to which he belonged, making him at once a more representative and a more arresting figure than one might initially suppose. Far from diminishing his historical stature, they enhance it. 'A great premier must add the vivacity of an idle man to the assiduity of a very laborious one', Bagehot decreed in the *Economist* on 2 January 1875. Better than any example known to Bagehot, Asquith combined both essential qualities in bountiful measure.

# 7

## FROM AGADIR
## TO
## THE DARDANELLES

'It has long been the fashion to disparage the policy and actions of the Ministers who bore the burden of power in the fateful years before the War, and who faced the extraordinary perils of its outbreak and opening phases.' So, with good justification, wrote Winston Churchill in the preface to his three-volume account of *The World Crisis* (1923–31), where he pleaded on his own account for a forbearance which he was not always inclined to extend to his erstwhile colleagues, Asquith included.

There exists a vast historical literature, to which Churchill contributed generously, on the origins of the First World War, the responsibility of British diplomacy, the extent of British preparedness, the qualifications of a Liberal Government to wage a herculean struggle, and, finally, the effect of the ordeal on the personnel and electoral fortunes of the Liberal Party. In each of these fierce controversies, Asquith occupies a dominant position.

For as long as they had held office, the Liberals were confronted with an international threat that sometimes receded but never completely disappeared. A source of perpetual anxiety and periodic alarm, it generated tensions that underlay and compounded the Government's difficulties in other spheres. As the Agadir crisis in the summer of 1911 demonstrated most conclusively, there was considerable overlap between areas of domestic and foreign policy, with the result that ministers collided with one another, with their backbench supporters, and with an array of opponents in Parliament and outside.

No sooner had Campbell-Bannerman assembled his team than there developed the threat of a serious clash between France and Germany over rival interests in Morocco. It was a 'really critical moment', Haldane recalled a decade later: 'a decision had to be taken. For the ways were parting.' To what extent were British statesmen bound to France by the provisions of the Entente Cordiale of 1904, the handiwork of the preceding regime? With the sanction of the Prime Minister, Grey and Haldane assuaged the French ambassador with a promise of talks between the British and French staffs, thus implying that Britain could be counted upon for assistance in the event of German aggression. A conference of the European powers at Algeciras settled the immediate dispute, but not before several important precedents had been established. The Liberal Government, still in its infancy, had tacitly disclaimed neutrality and, in the process, had invested the Entente with new substance and possibly with a new spirit.

The majority of his Cabinet associates, Haldane candidly admitted, 'hardly knew' either the gravity of the situation or, for that matter, the commitment made on their behalf. Asquith, preoccupied with the election campaign, was not among those consulted, although his compliance was naturally assumed. Like Grey, he subsequently regretted the *ad hoc* procedures, and privately deprecated the incident 'as one of the most curious examples in his memory of a concurrence of untoward events working to a conclusion which no one intended and no one could defend'. Yet, after his own ascent to the premiership, such concurrences grew increasingly frequent until August 1914, when untoward events led to a declaration of war.

Foreign affairs posed a special test for Liberalism as an organized political force and as an ethic, and one that it abjectly failed. Here, more conspicuously than elsewhere, party traditionalists found themselves at the mercy of 'vast, anonymous forces' (to borrow Élie Halévy's classic phrase) which they could not fully comprehend, still less control. Positing a rationalism in the conduct of foreign affairs, they were not equipped either by instinct or experience to deal with the parlous circumstances that arose to menace the peace of Europe. Consequently, their responses often proved as tentative and ambiguous as those which they made in the face of agitations at home.

Although Asquith's Radical critics would have been loath to concede as much, the foreign policy of his Government was essentially the same as that pursued under Campbell-Bannerman. That, in itself, is not the least surprising, given the continued tenancy at the Foreign Office of Grey, whom both Prime Ministers tended to leave to his own devices. Asquith, of course, enjoyed a long-standing friendship with Grey, in whom he reposed complete confidence. Not the most communicative of men, Grey treated the Foreign Office as his fief, consulting (besides his permanent officials) only a few intimates, and making it a practice neither to justify nor even to explain his policies.

It was a tribute to Asquith's trust in Grey, but also an illustration of the general manner in which Asquith transacted business, that – within limits – the Foreign Secretary was allowed a free hand in the management of his own department. As elsewhere, Asquith exercised his executive authority indirectly and with discretion; but there can be no doubt that he exercised it nonetheless. When Lloyd George protested that he had been 'kept in the dark in regard to the essential features of our Foreign Policy', Asquith mollified him by setting up – and appointing him to membership on – a Foreign Policy Committee that met from December 1910 until the following July, when it was left quietly to expire. The Committee on Imperial Defence, a legacy of the Balfour years, was another mechanism that achieved greater longevity, but often served a comparable function. The Prime Minister staffed it to suit his immediate purpose, and carefully set its agenda. Tempers flared after a convocation of the C.I.D. on 23 August 1911 to which Morley, Harcourt, and Esher, all potential troublemakers, failed to receive the invitation to which each considered himself entitled. Asquith's assurance that it had been merely a *sub*-committee meeting did not wash with Harcourt, who told Runciman on the 26th that the session had been 'arranged some time ago for a date when it was supposed we should all be out of London . . . to decide on where and how British troops could be landed to assist a

French Army on the Meuse!!!' Morley's indignation in turn infuriated Asquith, who wrote to Haldane on 9 September: 'J.M. has evidently been told of the meeting of the sub-committee: I wonder by whom? He is quite the most impossible colleague that ever entered a Cabinet.' Needless to say, incidents of this type did not inspire mutual confidence.

Depending on the particular topic that took priority, Asquith collaborated with one group of subordinates against another, sometimes going to considerable lengths to withhold information from those outside the charmed circle. Strictly speaking, there existed no 'inner junta' within the Cabinet. Undeniably, however, certain ministers were admitted more freely than others into their chief's confidence: their views were solicited more regularly and carried greater weight. In some cases, they owed their privilege to the portfolio they held; in others, to Asquith's personal regard for their judgement. Grey, who qualified on both counts, was rewarded with direct channels to the Prime Minister. At times even Haldane had to rely on him as an intermediary. Crewe was the recipient of Asquith's favour despite the office he occupied; Lloyd George because of it.

The circuitous methods by which the Government formulated its foreign policy sparked recurrent controversy among members of the Cabinet and, more publicly, within the parliamentary party and the Liberal press. Pledged to the twin ideals of an 'open' diplomacy and a reduction in armaments, Radical fundamentalists sought in vain the fulfilment of Campbell-Bannerman's 1906 campaign pledge to put Liberal England 'at the head of a league for peace'. After the reconstruction of the Government in April 1908, when the Liberal Imperialists assumed command of the heights of power, Radical spokesmen were all the more acutely conscious of their estrangement from the decision-making process. They looked with growing apprehension on the inexorable rise in military and naval expenditure, which they deplored as not only wasteful but also a dangerous and gratuitous affront to German sensibilities. Grey, by doggedly preaching the virtues of 'continuity' in foreign policy, fuelled their suspicions by implying collusion with the Unionists and a disregard for time-honoured Liberal precepts.

Appearances to the contrary, the watershed came not in 1908 but three years later, in the wake of a second Morocco crisis. At that time, with the appearance of a German gunboat at Agadir, the Radical contingent in the Cabinet (nicknamed 'reductionists', 'economists', or, more loosely, 'pacifists') was weakened by the defection of its two most vigorous representatives, Lloyd George and

Churchill. The former, with the approval of Asquith and Grey, used the occasion of a Mansion House dinner on 21 July 1911 to utter a dire warning that, 'if Britain were to be treated where her interests were vitally affected as of no account . . ., peace at that price would be a humiliation intolerable for a great country to endure'. His reputation as a sympathizer with German aspirations and as an opponent of defence spending ensured that his words had a stinging effect in Berlin and, no less, among the Government's exponents of Anglo-German conciliation. Those who neither panicked nor repented of their pro-German sentiments included Morley, Loreburn, Runciman, Burns, and Harcourt, none of whom possessed sufficient stature or stamina to fill the breach. Nursing a strong sense of betrayal, Runciman reminded Harcourt on 24 August that Churchill and Lloyd George, previously the mainstays of 'anti-war feeling', had swung round to 'become the really warlike element in our Government . . . The stability or balance of opinion of the cabinet cannot now be relied on by us'. Accordingly, the Radical initiative now passed to journalists and to a network of extra-parliamentary agencies, the most influential being the National Liberal Federation.

Asquith, for his part, was not the least averse to the possibility of an understanding with Germany. On 24 September 1910, informing a yet unreconstructed Lloyd George of 'the progress of the Anglo-German pour-parlers' then taking place, he reported hopefully that Kiderlin, newly installed as Germany's foreign minister, had intimated that he 'is quite disposed to move (as far as he can) in the direction of an entente with us. But', he cautioned, 'there is always the possibility of some fresh outbreak from the enfant terrible in the Imperial Nursery.' Within the year, the Agadir crisis had given further proof of the Kaiser's instability and the necessity to prepare for armed conflict.

The crisis had also shown up deficiencies of British strategy and, in particular, the lack of co-ordination between War Office and Admiralty. An extensive overhaul of Admiralty organization was imperative, yet could not be accomplished without displacing McKenna, an able administrator but hardly the man to impose a drastic solution upon his hidebound departmental officials. Haldane, convinced that outmoded Admiralty procedures undermined his six years of purposeful reform at the War Office, first threatened to resign, then proposed himself as McKenna's successor. Asquith agreed that 'the time has come (indeed is much overdue) for the creation and organisation [at the Admiralty] of a General Staff', but doubted whether Haldane, a Viscount since March, was a suitable instrument. 'The First Lord ought to be in the H. of Commons,' he asserted to Crewe on 7 October, 'and the Navy would not take kindly in the first instance to new organisation imported direct from the War Office. On the whole', he concluded, 'I am satisfied that Churchill is the right man, and he would like to go. I shall offer the H[ome] Office to McKenna.'

The reallocation of places was handled more expeditiously on paper than in actuality. Despite Asquith's understanding that McKenna 'is not unwilling to go', the First Lord baulked at his transfer to what the Prime Minister assured him was 'one of the most difficult and responsible places in the Government'. There followed a flurry of letters, and, on 20 October, McKenna journeyed to Archerfield House in East Lothian, where Asquith was on holiday. Inveighing against the projected Admiralty reforms and the ulterior motives of their sponsors, he argued that, in the event of a European war, the Prime Minister might find himself overwhelmed or bypassed by insubordinate subordinates. 'Such a thing', Asquith replied imperturbably, 'might be possible in cases like that of the Insurance Bill but not in the case of peace or war.' Finding his host adamant, McKenna yielded, but not without bitterness. 'We had a fight yesterday in the Cabinet over the General Staff preparations', Haldane informed his sister on 16 November. 'McK attacked me rather viciously. But the P. M. steered things through . . . Winston, Ll. G., Grey & I stood firm.'

As Jenkins has shrewdly speculated, Asquith may have had a further reason, besides those he enumerated to Crewe, for appointing Churchill as First Lord: 'If . . . he could permanently detach him (and perhaps Lloyd George as well) from the "economist" wing of the party, the cohesion of the government would be considerably increased.' The gamble, if it was one, paid off handsomely. Ensconced at the Admiralty, Churchill compensated in enthusiasm for what he may have lacked in tact. He was soon pressing for extended commitments and for estimates which Lloyd George, reverting to type, considered grossly inflated.

The threat of war soon subsided as quickly as it had come. But the impression persisted in Berlin, as Grey admitted to the British ambassador there, that, in her 'military and naval preparations', Britain had 'meditated an unprovoked attack on Germany, even if she herself took no warlike step'. Belatedly acquainted with the Anglo-French military conversations that had taken place five years earlier, Asquith issued instructions that they were not to be resumed. 'The French ought not to be encouraged, in present circumstances, to make their plans on any assumptions' of British support, he wrote on 5 September to Grey, who satisfied him by 'ma[king] it clear that at no stage of our intercourse with France since January 1906 had we either by diplomatic or military engagements compromised our freedom of decision and action in the event of war between France and Germany'. That, however, did not preclude further Cabinet consideration of Anglo-French naval co-operation.

Liberals outside the Government were better able to discern the drift of events. The editors of the *Nation*, the *Manchester Guardian*, the *Daily News*, and other organs of party opinion stepped up their campaign for an accommodation with Germany to halt the naval race and to obviate the need for dependence on France. Early in 1912, the executive of the National Liberal Federation adopted a resolution to the same effect, 'with the object of procuring substantial measures of retrenchment'. Various Free Church agencies and chambers of commerce, particularly in Lancashire, echoed the plea. The agitation, co-ordinated with backstairs moves within the Cabinet, raised the spectre of a massive party revolt.

It was against this background of mutinous disquiet that Haldane was dispatched to Berlin in February 1912, ostensibly in connection with 'University affairs'. Educated at Göttingen, he was the obvious person for the assignment. Colonel Repington, the experienced military correspondent for *The Times*, perceived that the mission had a dual function: on the one hand, he explained to G. E. Buckle, his editor, 'the tension between us and Germany' had risen to a level that made it advisable 'to see whether any arrangement of a[n] amicable character was open to us'; on the other, the top men in the Cabinet hoped to demonstrate to their 'Radical tail that all possible had been done to come to such an agreement, so that, if it failed, the party might stomach the national consequences, namely increased [naval] estimates – or at all events not the decreased naval estimates as promised by McKenna'. According to Repington, 'the inner circle of the Cabinet', while far from sanguine, were compelled 'to humour their followers'; this seemed 'as good a way' as any. 'Personally', he confided, 'I do not anticipate any result from the mission except possibly some increased reasonableness among the Radical Left, whom Haldane will purr to sleep when he returns.' Churchill later confirmed that these had been precisely his calculations: his own position would 'be all the stronger in asking the Cabinet and the House of Commons for the necessary monies', he had reckoned, 'if I could go hand in hand with the Chancellor of the Exchequer and testify that we had tried our best to secure a mitigation of the naval rivalry and failed'. To say the least, he did not improve Haldane's chances of success by his disdainful reference to the German fleet as a 'luxury'.

Empowered only to conduct conversations '*ad referendum*', Haldane endeavoured to dispel German fears that Britain was party to a conspiracy to encircle Germany. Arguably, his interviews at Berlin helped to lessen the strain between the two countries. But they failed to lay the groundwork for the naval accord that had been his primary objective. As a gesture, German officials agreed to delay indefinitely the construction of one of the three ships provided in their impending fleet law. Otherwise, Germany accelerated her naval programme, and demanded nothing less than a unilateral declaration of British neutrality in Continental affairs.

Long after Haldane returned to London, negotiations dragged on. Eventually, weeks before the outbreak of war, agreement was reached on the parcelling out of Portuguese colonies and the construction of the Baghdad railway. But there was no progress on the crucial question of naval requirements. Asquith quickly lost patience. 'I confess I am becoming more & more doubtful as to the wisdom of prolonging these discussions with Germany about a formula', he advised Grey on 10 April 1912. 'Nothing, I believe, will meet her purpose which falls short of a promise on our part of neutrality: a promise we cannot give. And she makes no firm or solid offer, even in exchange for that.' Still, to admit defeat publicly would have been to concede the bankruptcy of a distinctively Liberal foreign policy and, more significantly, the inevitability of war.

Party considerations, if nothing else, ruled out such an admission. During the spring and summer of 1912, the Liberals suffered unusually heavy losses in by-election contests. Resistance to the new National Insurance Act was the obvious explanation, but the disaffection of Nonconformists and other sectional interests must be taken into account. It was the contention of many party stalwarts that their leaders were defaulting on their most sacred responsibilities. In seeming defiance of the strongly-worded resolution passed by the National Liberal Federation, the self-styled parliament of Liberalism, Churchill carried out his intention to obtain increased estimates, chiefly for the construction of new Dreadnoughts. Contrary to his confident expectation, the Chancellor of the Exchequer did not 'go hand in hand' with him, but instead fought tooth and nail against any such allocation. Morley leaked an account of the battle that loomed within the Cabinet to F. W. Hirst of the *Economist*, and Lloyd George corroborated it in a pair of talks with Harold Spender, another journalist of unimpeachable Radical credentials. 'You might like to know for your own information how opinion is divided at the moment', Hirst wrote on 15 July to Sir John Brunner, the president of the N.L.F., whom he prodded to address 'a firm letter' to Asquith, 'a party man par excellence': Lloyd George, Harcourt, Morley, and McKenna were all reportedly 'strongly against'; Grey, Haldane, and Asquith 'mildly for Winston'. Hirst counselled Brunner to threaten 'that, if the Government endorses this policy and proposes it to the House of Commons, you would feel conscientiously bound to summon a meeting of the National Liberal Federation in the hope of bringing Liberal opinion to bear upon this fatal and provocative policy'.

However acute their disillusionment with official policy, Radical dissentients could not carry their opposition too far lest they bring down the Government, which, since 1910, had ruled without an overall majority; in that event, they would lose any hope of naval retrenchment, and much else besides. Asquith was well aware of these inhibitions, and capitalized upon them. If his Irish allies wanted Home Rule, they would be forced to sanction welfare measures to which they professed indifference; if Nonconformist militants wished the removal of educational disabilities, they would have to swallow Home Rule, which many of them did only with extreme distaste; by the same token, if Radical 'economists' desired to realize land reforms or Welsh disestablishment or any of the goals to which they were variously committed, they would have to accept, protestingly and under duress, a defence policy that went against their Cobdenite grain. Liberalism was not and never had been a monolithic force, but flourished as an interplay of disparate elements. As party manager, it was Asquith's task to extend the broad areas of agreement that enveloped the pockets of dissension.

Mindful of even greater disarray among his Unionist opponents, Asquith toyed with the idea of a dissolution in April 1913. On Christmas Day 1912, he broached the subject to Lloyd George as something 'worth considering – tho' I have not mentioned the idea to anyone else'. At worst, he reasoned, the Liberals would return to opposition with an honourable discharge from their bondage to the Irish Nationalists; at best:

Assuming we get a majority, we have a direct mandate for the Irish & Welsh Bills *as Bills*, and only the most *enragés* among the Tories can then support or approve violence in Ulster.

We should be free in the new Parlt. to deal with the House of Lords, & Land questions, & Free Trade would be safe for another five years.

The Insurance Act will by April be in full working order, & the present distractions of the Tories are not likely to have been patched up.

There are, no doubt, arguments the other way . . . I do not at all prejudice the matter, but I think it ought to be thought out.

Within twenty-four hours, Lloyd George had considered and rejected the proposal:

I quite agree that there are obvious advantages to be gained by dissolving before the present trade boom cracks up and the working classes drop into unemployment or low wages. Prosperity is fatal to the chances of Tariff Reform. On the other hand one bad winter would revive its prospects and once more render it formidable. That is exactly what happened in 1908.

On these grounds, he argued against going to the country in April, when 'the benefits of the Insurance Act will have hardly made an adequate impression'. Instead he put the case for dissolving at the end of June, with the anticipation that the trade revival and the Tory split would both continue through the approaching year. That the Prime Minister did not persevere with the idea of a spring election was itself testimony to the enhanced stature of Lloyd George in party councils.

There were those who asserted that, for better or worse, Lloyd George had eclipsed his chief. H. W. Massingham, writing in the *Daily News* on 15 July 1912, hinted that the Chancellor, if he failed to get his way in the dispute over naval estimates, would quit the Government and take nine tenths of the parliamentary Liberals into opposition. The next day, the *Daily Express* unearthed 'an active intrigue . . . to depose Mr Asquith and put Mr Lloyd George in his place as Prime Minister'. Either wishful thinking or the fabrications of idle minds, these were reports which Asquith knew better than to take seriously. All the same, he knew that he could not afford to antagonize 'the new Samson' (as the *Express* dubbed Lloyd George), whose strength (with help from the Prime Minister) survived his complicity in the Marconi scandal.

On 22 November 1912 Asquith delivered the keynote address to the annual meeting of the National Liberal Federation at Nottingham. The *Manchester Guardian* found it satisfactory, except with regard to foreign affairs, where the 'sentiment is excellent', but sadly failed to give issue to any constructive policy: 'The understanding with France should lead logically and of necessity to a similar understanding with Germany', it insisted; 'and, if it does not, then there are subterranean forces at work which must be sought out and

defeated, or they will undermine Liberalism.' The next year, the
Federation met at Leeds, and Asquith was again the featured
speaker. To an overflow audience of more than 3,000 ('Yorkshire is
vastly proud of its own Prime Minister', the *Guardian* commented),
he presented a detailed review of the Irish problem. That, however,
was not what most delegates had come to hear. Pride of place was
given to a motion from the chair expressing grave anxiety at the
continued growth in armaments. The *Nation* took Asquith severely
to task for providing 'no substantial offer of relief' on this vital issue:

Mr Asquith at Leeds comforted us with words, but what the
starved spirit of Liberalism wants is deeds. If the world is, indeed,
ruled by the crudest and weakest material calculations – if policy,
the play of common interests, the immense and ever-widening field
of service for humanity that an Anglo-German understanding would
beget are closed for a season or until this madness is overpast – let its
finer intuitions be crushed by Tory, not by Liberal, hands.

Massingham, writing as 'A Wayfarer' a week later, enjoined ministers
not to 'take the anti-armaments resolutions at Leeds as a mere flash-
in-the-pan'. Throughout the country, the cry had been taken up by
local constituency associations, business groups, and Free Church
councils, all determined to resist any 'automatic' increase in estimates. Asquith was not oblivious to the strong feeling that had been
aroused, but neither was he unduly impressed. 'I have spent most of
the day in receiving deputations from anti-armaments MP's, and
Nonconformist divines anxious about "single-school areas"', he told
Miss Stanley on the evening of 17 December. 'They were both rather
trials of patience – people telling you at length things which you
know as well as they do, with a plentiful fringe of banal rhetoric.'
Preoccupied with the fate of a third Irish Home Rule Bill, Asquith
was in no mood to contend with the perennial quarrel over naval
estimates. But the showdown could be deferred no longer. On
8 December he revealed to Miss Stanley: 'We had a Cabinet which
lasted nearly 3 hours, $2\frac{3}{4}$ of wh. was occupied by Winston', who made
his pitch for higher appropriations. Churchill incurred implacable
opposition from, among others, Lloyd George, who daringly proceeded to carry the controversy beyond the confines of the Cabinet
room by giving a New Year's Day interview to the *Daily Chronicle* in
which he decried the 'overwhelming extravagance in our expenditure
on armaments'. Asquith thoroughly disapproved of this breach of
Cabinet etiquette, which might incite rebellion in the ranks or, at the
very least, expose the ministry to ridicule. Lord Esher, a keen student
of political discord, was among those moved to wonder 'whether

there is not, behind the Chancellor of the Exchequer's ostensible objections to high estimates, some personal desire to break away from the Government and to take the lead of the Radical and Labour Party'. Writing to the King on 6 January 1914, Esher recounted Haldane's disclosure that, even with regard to Ireland, the Prime Minister now took the precaution 'to keep his "conversations" secret from all his colleagues'.

For a time, it seemed unlikely that Churchill and Lloyd George could continue as members of the same Cabinet, and John Simon was not alone in taking the view that 'the loss of W.C., though regrettable, is *not* by any means a splitting of the party.' Lloyd George had meanwhile departed for a holiday at Algiers, justly confident that a majority of his colleagues would stand behind him. He was accompanied on his travels by T. P. O'Connor, the veteran journalist and M.P., who wrote on 13 January to John Dillon, the Irish leader, that 'L.G. talks of resigning rather than submit to Ch.'s estimates, but if there be any resignation it must, I think, be Churchill's.'

It was not until the 20th, after Asquith had returned from his own holiday at Antibes, that he brought the two antagonists face to face. 'It was interesting & at moments rather dramatic,' he told his confidante the next day. 'What Mr G. called "bridge building" is going on to-day, but I am not very sanguine about the success of that particular operation.' A week later, 'the air' remained 'more than a trifle thunderous', but passions had begun to cool. Asquith had intimated that he would sooner call a general election than carry on at the helm of a Government weakened by resignations, and this oblique threat proved a surprisingly effective deterrent. In an interview on 2 February, John Redmond found the Prime Minister 'greatly harrassed' [*sic*], by, among other things, the tug-of-war over naval estimates: 'This is not settled,' he told Dillon, 'and tho' he speaks hopefully of averting a split in the Cabinet, he seriously fears a dry rot in the House which might easily lead to accidents.'

Finally, at a Cabinet on the 11th, the feuding colleagues and their respective partisans were reconciled, much to the satisfaction of Churchill, who paid tribute retrospectively 'to the unswerving patience of the Prime Minister, and to his solid, silent support'. Within a few weeks, all was forgiven and apparently forgotten. Morley gave a dinner on 6 March at which 'Winston in a rather maudlin mood' turned to Lloyd George and exclaimed: 'A wonderful thing, our friendship! For 10 years there has been hardly a day when we haven't had half an hour's talk together.' Birrell, another guest, overheard and wryly remarked: 'How awfully bored by this time you both must be.' Asquith, who purveyed the story at second hand to Miss Stanley, informed her of a further Cabinet on the 17th: 'There was great harmony, and Winston preened himself & was stroked by the others . . . And those Navy Estimates, with all the memories which cluster around their cradle, promise to go through on oiled castors, with hardly a murmur of protest. Am I not right in my fixed belief that the Expected rarely happens?'

Birrell came nearer the mark than he probably realized when he jested that Churchill and Lloyd George must have begun to bore each other. Certainly their clashes, as predictable as their *rapprochements*, wearied their associates, Asquith especially. As the war approached, the Liberals were completing their ninth year in power, and Asquith had already spent six gruelling years in the premiership. While far from being 'a range of exhausted volcanoes', as Disraeli had called the Liberal front bench in 1872, the party chiefs nevertheless showed unmistakable signs of fatigue. Their attitudes were often stale, and their responses to certain chronic problems – Ireland, for example – had become mechanical. Personal relationships, an infallible barometer of heavy weather, had deteriorated markedly: McKenna distrusted Churchill and could not abide Haldane; Runciman had fought so bitterly with Lloyd George over university grants in 1911 that the Chief Whip had to interpose himself between them; Burns despised Lloyd George and Churchill as headline hunters and, in turn, was regarded by them as an impediment to social reform; Morley, whose petulance had increased with age, was a constant disappointment to younger Radicals; and Margot Asquith, whose opinions did not necessarily reflect those of her husband, lavished her enmities. Weighed down by unremitting burdens, many Liberal ministers yearned privately for a release from the trammels of office and, more wistfully, for the opportunity to be the dispensers of responsible criticism rather than the recipients of the irresponsible variety.

There were repeated suggestions during the first half of 1914 that a dissolution might 'clear the air' (as the King thought), which had grown stagnant. A relative improvement in the party's performance in by-elections lent credit to the idea. Grey, at a Cabinet on 23 March, professed himself 'strong in favour of a general election as soon as H.R. Bill is passed and before it comes into operation'. His colleagues adapted themselves to the possibility, not sure whether they would have any choice in the matter. As Asquith patiently explained to Miss Stanley on 26 July, it was 'quite on the cards that the King may say he will assent to the Home Rule Bill, provided an immediate

Asquith as a young man by Spy, *Vanity Fair*, 1 August 1891

Margot Asquith dressed as an Oriental snake charmer for a fancy dress ball, July 1897

THE EXCHEQUER BIRD AND THE LITTLE ECONOMISTS
The Exchequer Bird: 'Don't be in too much of a hurry. I'll feed you all in time; but
you must remember I've got to find the worms first.'
*Westminster Gazette,* 16 March 1906

' "Porro Unum Est
Necessarium": Mr Asquith,
having kissed hands on his
appointment, sets to work, with
characteristic industry and
determination, to acquire
personal magnetism.' Caricature
by Max Beerbohm, 1908

'Supporters' Rampant: an heraldic inversion. *Punch*, 29 December 1909. Asquith tottering under the weight of his 'supporters', the outstanding figures of the Liberal party, Lloyd George and Churchill

The Treasury bench, 1911, by Max Beerbohm. Left to right: Lloyd George, Asquith, Churchill, Haldane, L.V. Harcourt, Augustine Birrell, John Burns

Mr Asquith in office, by Max Beerbohm, 1913. The caption reads:
'Come one, come all, this rock shall fly
From its firm base as soon as I.'

UNDER HIS MASTER'S EYE
Scene – *Mediterranean, on board the Admiralty yacht Enchantress*
Mr Winston Churchill:
'Any home news?'
Mr Asquith:
'How can there be with you here?'
– *Punch*, 21 May 1913

Asquith by F. Carruthers Gould

## AN ASQUITH TO THE RESCUE!

WAR MINISTER (*to* PREMIER). "HOLD TIGHT! I'LL SEE YOU THROUGH."

This cartoon appeared in *Punch*, 9 April 1914, when Asquith was doubling as Secretary of State for War and Prime Minister

Asquith by A. Cluysenaar, 1919

Lord Oxford

Lord Oxford by David Low

dissolution follows, and that if we are unable to agree to this . . . he will politely dismiss us & send for Ministers who will agree'. Most Liberals, he acknowledged, would prefer to delay until the anomaly of plural voting had been abolished. But, if the King insisted, the Government would have to comply. 'A general election under such circumstances would be one of the worst things that cd. happen to the country, or (I suspect) to the Liberal Party.'

There were, however, infinitely worse things, yet to reveal their import. In a pendant to the same letter, 'a screed about politics' for which he apologized, Asquith alluded to ominous developments 'in the East of Europe'. On 28 June the Habsburg heir-apparent had been assassinated by Serbian nationalists in the Bosnian town of Sarajevo. The incident, which attracted comparatively little attention in western capitals, was soon pushed off the front pages of the British press by the death of Joseph Chamberlain. Thereafter, nearly a month passed before Austria, on 23 July, delivered an ultimatum to Serbia. 'The news this morning', Asquith wrote to Miss Stanley on Sunday, the 26th, 'is that Servia has capitulated on the main points, but it is very doubtful if any reservations will be accepted by Austria, who is resolved upon a complete & final humiliation.' In any case, he did not anticipate that Britain would get involved, although Russia, as the patron of Slav interests, 'is trying to drag us in'. Nevertheless, he concluded, 'it is the most dangerous situation of the last 40 years, and may have incidentally the good effect of throwing into the background the lurid pictures of "civil war" in Ulster'.

It was by no means unusual for British statesmen to regard the Balkan crisis, in its early stages, as a diversion from their familiar preoccupations. Churchill, Asquith reported half disbelievingly to Miss Stanley on the 28th, welcomed it 'as a way of escape from Irish troubles, and when things looked rather better last night, he exclaimed moodily that it looked after all as if we were in for a "bloody peace"!' By this time, Asquith was taking a more sober view. On the 24th and again, with greater urgency, two days later, Grey had proposed 'a Conference à quatre' at which the so-called disinterested powers – Great Britain, France, Italy, and Germany – might collectively pull Austria and Russia back from the brink of war. But Germany, amenable to this procedure in the recent past, declined to participate. 'The only real hope is that Austria & Russia may come to a deal between themselves', Asquith admitted. 'But at this moment things don't look well, & Winston's spirits are probably rising.' That evening, 'after dinner & a little bridge', he sat up with

Grey and Haldane 'till 1 a.m. talking over the situation, and trying
to discover bridges & outlets'.

As early as Wednesday, the 29th, Asquith already addressed himself to the dilemma which numerous historians, in their attempts to
assign war guilt, have since dwelled upon. 'It is one of the ironies of
the case', he observed to Miss Stanley,

that we being the only Power who has made so much as a constructive suggestion in the direction of peace, are blamed by both Germany & Russia for causing the outbreak of war. Germany says: 'if
you say you will be neutral, France & Russia won't dare to fight';
and Russia says: 'if you boldly declare that you will side with us,
Germany & Austria will at once draw in their horns'. Neither of
course is true.

That morning, the Cabinet met for a long and 'on the whole . . . a
very satisfactory discussion' that resulted in a decision to guarantee
the neutrality of Belgium. The question, Asquith notified the King,
was considered 'rather one of policy than legal obligation', notwithstanding the precedent of Gladstone's commitment in 1870. At
the same time, Grey was 'authorised to inform the German and
French Ambassadors' nothing more than 'that at this stage we were
unable to pledge ourselves in advance, either under all conditions to
stand aside or in any conditions to join in'. British strategy was
therefore left unclear, as indeed it remained in Asquith's own mind.
'Of course we want to keep out of it', he told Miss Stanley in a
lunchtime missive, 'but the worst thing we could do would be to
announce to the world at the present moment that in *no circumstances*
would we intervene.'

As a responsible statesman, Asquith had to weigh the possible
repercussions of any British declaration upon the rival power blocs.
As a practical politician, which he was first and foremost, he had to
consider the possible ramifications among his ministerial colleagues
and within his party. At the close of July, the coherence of the
Liberal Party was as precarious as the peace of Europe. In the knowledge that fully half the Cabinet were fervent advocates of neutrality,
he thought it best to wait on events. Lloyd George, he realized, was
the crucial figure. An 'economist' until the eleventh hour, he gave
solemn assurances on the 27th to C. P. Scott of the *Manchester
Guardian* that 'there could be no question of our taking part in any
war in the first instance'. During the early summer, Asquith had
drawn close to Lloyd George, whom he went out of his way to
acquaint with secret initiatives to devise an Irish settlement. He was
determined not to jeopardize this relationship which, valuable in

itself, was his link to the neutralist camp. Perhaps, as his wife later supposed, he could have isolated and defused the 'peace party' by joining forces with the Unionists; but that would have dealt a crippling blow to his party, savagely divided public opinion, and, in personal terms (which counted least at this juncture), would have been a cynical repudiation of all that he stood for.

The collapse of the European order, a sufficient cause for anxiety, exacerbated tensions within the Liberal fold. On 29 July Arthur Ponsonby presented Grey with a petition signed by twenty-two Radical backbenchers who demanded isolation. The next day he informed the Prime Minister that there had been 'another and larger meeting' of these 'representative men', and he calculated that 'nine-tenths of the party are behind us'. The Liberal press, with the *Westminster Gazette* as the single notable exception, wanted no part of the impending calamity. In a leader on the 31st that won plaudits from Lord Loreburn, a former Liberal Lord Chancellor, the *Manchester Guardian* fulminated against the apparent fact that 'England had been committed, behind her back, to the ruinous madness of a share in the wicked gamble of a war between two militant leagues on the Continent'. That day Asquith confirmed to Miss Stanley that 'the general opinion at present – particularly strong in the City – is to keep out almost at all costs'.

On Saturday morning, 1 August, there was 'a Cabinet wh. lasted from 11 to ½ past 1' at which, 'every now and again', ministers came 'near to the parting of the ways'. Morley and, less definitely, Simon seemed to Asquith to be 'on what may be called the Manchester Guardian tack – that we shd. declare now & at once that *in no circumstances* will we take a hand. This no doubt is the view for the moment of the bulk of the party', he told Miss Stanley, for whose benefit he called the roll: Lloyd George, although 'all for peace', struck him as 'more sensible & statesmanlike, for keeping the position still open. Grey, of course, declares that if an out & out & uncompromising policy of non-intervention at all costs is adopted, he will go. Winston very bellicose & demanding immediate mobilisation. Haldane diffuse . . . and nebulous.' While 'still *not quite* hopeless about peace', Asquith had to admit that he was 'far from hopeful'. Given the stark alternatives, he felt 'sure . . . that we shall have *some* split in the Cabinet. Of course, if Grey went I should go, & the whole thing would break up.' More probably, however, Morley would depart, 'and possibly (tho' I don't think it)' Simon.

The Cabinet, which had 'parted in a fairly amicable mood', was scheduled to reconvene at eleven the next morning for 'an almost unprecedented' Sunday session. In the meantime, Germany delivered an ultimatum to Russia, who had mobilized against Austria in support of Serbia, and another to France. Over breakfast, Asquith received a visit from Prince Lichnowsky, the German ambassador, who 'was very emotionné and implored me not to side with France'. To this appeal, Asquith replied 'that we had no desire to intervene, and that it rested largely with Germany to make intervention impossible, if she would (1) not invade Belgium, and (2) not send her fleet into the Channel to attack the unprotected North Coast of France.' Leaving Lichnowsky 'quite heartbroken', Asquith went on to attend 'a long Cabinet from 11 to nearly 2', where it was 'very soon revealed that we are on the brink of a split'. After considerable wrangling, it was decided 'that Grey should be authorised to tell Cambon', the French ambassador, 'that our fleet would not allow the German fleet to make the Channel the base of hostile operations'. Burns, whom Asquith had discounted, promptly tendered his resignation, which he was prevailed upon to retract for the time being. Lloyd George, less 'sensible & statesmanlike' than the day before, joined Morley and Harcourt as confederates in 'a strong party . . . against any intervention in any event. Grey of course will never consent to this', Asquith assured Miss Stanley, '& I shall not separate myself from him. Crewe, McKenna, & Samuel' were identified as 'a moderating intermediate body'.

Bonar Law, whose own party was virtually free of such discord, sent word to the Prime Minister on Sunday that, as 'it would be fatal to the honour and security of the United Kingdom to hesitate in supporting France and Russia at the present juncture', the Opposition was willing to offer the Government an unsolicited pledge of support. Four years later, Asquith flatly contradicted to St Loe Strachey the 'ridiculous story', propagated by Leo Maxse in the *National Review*, that this communication (for which Maxse claimed responsibility) had forced the Government to commit itself. On the contrary, he insisted on 11 August 1918, it 'had absolutely no influence on the course of events or on the mind of the Cabinet, which was already quite made up. Indeed, I doubt whether I read the letter to them.' Either Asquith's memory played tricks or he remained stubbornly unwilling to publicize the deep divisions that had existed among his colleagues on that fateful Sunday. He had, in fact, replied to Bonar Law that, despite a 'long standing and intimate friendship with France', Britain was 'under no obligation, express or implied, either to France or Russia to render them military or naval help'. He repeated the same assertion in his letter that day to Miss Stanley, although here he averred: 'It is against British interests that France shd. be wiped out as a Great Power.'

Pointedly, he said nothing, even in his most intimate correspondence, about friendship with Russia, a subject that roused his Liberal critics to uncontained fury. To many, the thought of making common cause with the Tsarist autocracy, long the bugbear of constitutionalists and humanitarians, was a shameful act. As much for moral as for the obvious strategic reasons, the Anglo-Russian Convention of 1907 had never acquired the centrality, let alone the respectability, of the Anglo-French entente on which it had been patterned. Even Margot Asquith had shuddered at the prospect of a partnership with Russia. 'Britons never, never will be Slavs', she is said to have quipped in 1905, when the pact was first mooted.

Adjourned at two o'clock on Sunday afternoon, the Cabinet resumed its deliberations that evening at 6.30. Burns affirmed his irrevocable decision to resign, and others – including Lloyd George – signalled their intention to go with him. On Monday morning, before the Cabinet assembled, letters of resignation from Morley and Simon were delivered to Downing Street. Beauchamp, when he arrived for the Cabinet at eleven o'clock, brought the total to four. But, to Asquith's immense relief, Lloyd George held back, his inclination changed by the morning's news that Belgium had rejected the German demand for free passage through her territory and had appealed for British support. Unable to persuade his four 'pacifist' colleagues to rescind their resignations, he nonetheless got them to appear in their accustomed places that afternoon, when the Foreign Secretary addressed the House of Commons.

It was, by all accounts, an intensely moving occasion. With gravity and unexpected eloquence, Grey spoke for an hour. His sober tone, no less than his cogent arguments, made a profound effect on his critics, whom he left with second thoughts about their Government's complicity. Asquith, who marvelled at the performance, boasted to Miss Stanley 'that our extreme peace-lovers were for the moment reduced to silence'. He did not doubt, however, that 'they will soon find their tongues again'.

In the dwindling hours of peace, Asquith strove to pull together his fraying ministry. By Tuesday morning, the 4th, he could report 'a slump in resignations'. Both Simon and Beauchamp were induced to reconsider, and the latter replaced the 'obdurate' Morley as Lord President of the Council. Runciman succeeded Burns at the Board of Trade. A more major change in Government personnel was the appointment on the 5th of Lord Kitchener to the War Office, where

Asquith had been acting as caretaker since the previous March. Initially, as Haldane wrote to his sister on the 3rd, there was to have been a makeshift arrangement: Haldane, while remaining Lord Chancellor, would return to take charge of the military machine which he had created and best understood, with Asquith retaining titular responsibility and 'delegating the work' to him. But that quickly proved impractical. 'It was quite impossible for me to go on, now that war is actually in being', Asquith told Miss Stanley on the 5th; 'it requires the undivided time & thought of any man to do the job properly, and as you know I hate scamped work.' Kitchener, although '(to do him justice) not at all anxious to come in', responded to the call of duty. A national hero, he guaranteed to inspire public confidence and, moreover, promised to stand above politics. 'It is a hazardous experiment, but the best in the circumstances, I think', Asquith wrote with distinctly muted enthusiasm. Later, after various Tory politicians and newspapermen conflictingly claimed that they had foisted Kitchener on an irresolute Government, Asquith proclaimed that Kitchener was 'the only person whom I had ever thought of as my successor' as war secretary. To the extent that he had thought of anyone, that statement was true enough.

With the expiration of an ultimatum to Germany at 11 p.m. on the 4th, the nation was at war. The King, unable to 'stand the tension of last week', appeared to his Prime Minister 'really a good deal relieved' and, literally overnight, 'very anti-German'. Royalty, as was its wont, gave expression to the popular mood, which was instantly one of truculence and exultation. But aside from Churchill, whose boyish glee mystified and embarrassed his associates, the members of the Cabinet were drained of any emotion save an overpowering gloom. 'The whole prospect fills me with sadness', Asquith wrote; 'we are on the eve of horrible things.' Sixty-one years of age, he pronounced himself physically fit, 'tho' at times I feel rather tired'. Still, he was confident that he could supply all the fortitude and stamina that the emergency demanded. Others were not nearly so sure. 'Mark my words,' Morley prophesied to a journalist friend on the Sunday after war was declared, Asquith 'is not the pilot to weather this storm.' For reasons of their own, disgruntled Unionists had the same premonition, which they worked assiduously to translate into fact.

As a peacetime premier, Asquith had had his virtues and also, inevitably, his faults; as a wartime leader, the former came to appear less relevant and the latter vastly more egregious. Neither publicly nor privately did his demeanour change in any significant respect.

Bound more closely to London, he was free to accept fewer invitations to country-house weekends; and there was less time to spare for Friday afternoon carriage rides with his young companion. But, on the whole, he suffered no social deprivation. 'Scratch dinners', as he uncomplainingly called them, took the place of more formal parties; more intimate, they afforded greater pleasure. Some of his friends, not themselves puritans, took a dim view of such merriment. Runciman, after dining with Pamela and Reginald McKenna on 12 January 1915, wrote to his wife that his hostess had gone off 'to a "Jolly" (new name for cards, frolic & frivolity) . . ., where the P.M. and his ladies are dining & other people joining them afterwards. Reggie who disapproves of frivolities during the war refused to go.' Others found it convenient to be more censorious. The same month, the *National Review* tantalized its readers with an allusion to 'political dinner parties about which "all London" has been agog, at which . . . sacred red boxes are produced and matters are discussed which Sir Stanley Buckmaster [the Solicitor-General] would imprison any editor for referring to'.

Asquith, on whom this was a thinly veiled attack, could not have cared less. Despite the intense pressure upon him, he found time to engage in his usual recreations: the theatre, bridge, literature, conversation, and correspondence. 'Looking back' over 1914, he remarked to Miss Stanley that 'I can hardly remember a day out of the 365 when I have not either written to you, or seen you, or often done both'. ('How awfully bored by this time you both must be', Birrell might well have sallied.) His letters to her, which furnish a catalogue of his thoughts and activities, conceivably pay disproportionate attention to the interests they shared. Even so, his general attitude compares to that of his daughter-in-law, Lady Cynthia, who recorded in her diary on 16 April 1915 – the day her husband left for the front – that she found it 'very difficult to believe that history will interfere with one's private life to such an extent'.

In the conduct of Cabinet and parliamentary business, Asquith remained an incomparable technician: no one else could have brought the country into war without political schism or social dislocation. His dominance, while rarely obtrusive and never ostentatious, remained indisputable. Calm and deliberative, he had accurately predicted the way events would unfold, the consequent shift in public opinion, and, in most cases, the reactions of his fellow-Liberals. 'Wait and see' had again proved its logic and efficacy.

But, now that the result was evident, people were no longer prepared to wait. Asquith personified moderation, a discredited ethic, and his steadying hand was increasingly resented as a brake upon effective action. His abiding concern for principles of law and justice, while reassuring to a shrinking band of idealists, was widely interpreted as pedantry or, worse, as an excuse for indolence. Appalled by the 'levity' with which the war was popularly greeted and by the fanaticism that it subsequently evoked, he lacked the instinctive ability to fire men's imaginations. That, perhaps, was as much a defect of his Liberal creed as of his own personality. His admirers, who were more impressive in quality than in quantity, lauded him as a force for morality. His detractors, at least the more literate among them, could riposte that Mr Pecksniff, too, was 'a moral man', whom 'some people likened . . . to a directing post, which is always telling the way to a place, and never goes there'.

To all appearances, Asquith's position was secure, and likely to remain so for the duration of the war. There was no one within his party who yet possessed either the inclination or the resources to challenge his control, which rested on a working parliamentary majority. On 30 July a party truce was proclaimed; extended on 28 August by a formal agreement among the Liberal, Labour, and Unionist whips, it stipulated that – except in Ireland, which lay outside its brief – vacant seats would not be officially contested at by-elections. Bonar Law, propitiated by an assurance that there would be no 'jiggery-pokery' over Irish Home Rule or Welsh disestablishment (both of which had cleared the Commons), was ready to give the Government a clear run. His motives were partly patriotic, partly partisan: firm in the belief that the next general election would yield a comfortable Unionist majority, he meanwhile wished to saddle his opponents with full responsibility for the war effort, which they might otherwise repudiate at great peril to national unity. In any case, there was not much else that he could have done as the leader of a minority party, its normal voting strength at Westminster reduced by the high percentage of its M.P.s who served in the armed forces.

The extremists who stood behind Bonar Law, and to whom he owed his place as Unionist leader, disapproved of his strategy. In their embittered minds, the Liberals were too untrustworthy and, in any case, insufficiently vigorous to be entrusted with the nation's destiny. Could a party that was pledged to dismember the United Kingdom be relied upon to defend its vital interests? More specifically, could one seriously expect men who, only recently, had preached disarmament, who had vouched for Germany's pacific intentions, and who had tottered on the brink of neutrality, to wage a successful struggle against the barbarities of Prussianism? 'Although all hatchets are for the moment buried,' Lord Derby, a prominent Unionist, reminded Grey early in 1915, 'one cannot entirely forget all that went before this war broke out.' Runciman, for one, had no illusions. 'The political truce is very thin', he wrote on 7 February 1915 to an old friend. 'If things go wrong we shall be flayed.'

Thus, prewar passions continued to seethe beneath the surface of bipartisan solidarity, which had been imposed from above. Nor was disquiet by any means limited to the Unionist side. Deep-dyed Radicals, overwhelmed in early August by the onrush of events, had taken refuge in an uneasy silence, which Asquith had known better than to construe as acquiescence. Before long, they refurbished their slogans and resumed their crusade. Painfully aware that they had been unable to arrest the drift to war, they now redoubled their efforts to ensure that the sacrifice would not be in vain. In their view, it was not Liberalism that bore guilt for the catastrophe, but rather the failure to apply, sincerely and systematically, its abused doctrines. With the exception of a relatively small but fiercely articulate band of war resisters, Radicals supported the Government without necessarily exonerating its prewar foreign policy. But, they made absolutely clear, their support was strictly qualified: so far as possible, the war had to be fought under genuinely Liberal auspices, in accordance with Liberal principles, and for Liberal objectives. To this end, they kept a vigilant watch over their political superiors, who might be tempted to stray from the straight and narrow path. The incongruity of their position, pointed up by critics to the right and left, did not deter them. As 'holy warriors', they sanctioned a particular kind of war, distinct from any other, which was supposed to render the world safe for democracy by purging it of the irresponsible agents of destruction, who came in assorted guises: the professional diplomats who conspired behind closed doors; the incendiary journalists who preyed on the irrational fears of their countrymen; the armaments trusts that reaped huge profits by inciting slaughter; the tyrants at Potsdam and (some added) at St Petersburg who appeased their imperial vanities by playing havoc with the fate of mankind; and, at home, the reactionaries who would seize on the war as a pretext to subvert parliamentary rule, to stamp out individual liberties, and to grind down the working classes.

On both sides, mistrust spilled over into paranoia. Radicals, staunch in their defence of the rights of the citizen, branded as pernicious those who urged the implementation of stringent wartime controls, especially conscription. 'If we are to win this struggle,' Gardiner declaimed in the *Daily News* on 7 August 1915, 'we have to prove that Democracy and organisation can co-exist, that political freedom is consistent with material efficiency.' His counterparts in the right-wing press retaliated that Liberal high-mindedness paved the way to national suicide: the defeat of Germany, to which all else had to be sacrificed, required the abandonment of the ramshackle system of voluntary recruiting, the disciplining of labour, the direction of industrial production, and tighter security, including the internment of enemy aliens. 'The great underlying conflict', as A. J. P. Taylor has described it, 'was between freedom and organisation', between those who clung to the shibboleths of *laissez-faire* individualism and those who advocated the extension of the powers of the state into new and hitherto inviolate realms.

The conflict was no less real for the confusion that existed in the minds of contemporaries. Essentially, it was more a question of degree than one of principle. The need for greater social cohesion and augmented governmental authority was almost universally accepted. The formula of 'Business as usual' was, to paraphrase Asquith, as dead as Queen Anne. What was disputed was the extent to which the Government should intervene and in precisely which areas of public and private life. And, as if to complicate matters, opinion did not divide along straight party lines. Within each political constellation at Westminster, there were those who opposed measures of state interference and those who demanded them, both with equal ardour and, at times, ferocity.

Asquith, to give him his due, did not stand Canute-like against the advance of new ideas; but, as much for tactical as for intellectual reasons, he preferred to give the old ones a fair chance before he replaced them. 'He was personally inclined to agree with the arguments of the *laissez-faire*, Free Trade opponents of compulsion, but there seemed to him to be something more important than a clear-cut victory for either side in the controversy', A. M. Gollin has persuasively argued. 'This was the maintenance of that delicate fabric of national unity which he, as Prime Minister, was resolved to preserve.' Consequently, it suited his political purpose as well as his temperament to occupy an intermediary position in national debate, although it left him vulnerable on both flanks. To the wild men of the right, he was too slothful, too lackadaisical, and contaminated by the 'pacifist' company he kept. From the opposite perspective, he seemed too much the cool pragmatist, whose imperialist past did not commend him. In truth, he deserved neither reputation, although he consciously cultivated both of them. It gave him perverse delight to confound his critics with a 'guise of lethargy', and he treasured Lady Tree's query, intended as a witticism, 'Mr Asquith, do you take an interest in the War?' More than competent as an administrator, he was curiously unable to convey that impression. Without fanfare, he supervised the formulation of long-range plans, particularly with regard to postwar reconstruction, for which others would reap the credit.

In the short term, however, he proved less satisfactory. His stoical manner, which impressed some observers but irritated countless others, concealed a core of anguish. In January 1915, at a memorial service for Percy Illingworth, the late Liberal Chief Whip, he uncharacteristically broke down in public, fell to his knees, and wept uncontrollably. He felt deep sympathy for the Lichnowskys, whom he had found convivial company. Grey was obliged to lecture him 'quite seriously' on the need to remove 'Frau', his children's German governess, from his household in Downing Street. 'I hate even the appearance of cruelty, but I don't see how I could do otherwise – do you?' he wrote pathetically to Miss Stanley in the second week of the war.

These chinks in his emotional armour gave rise to rumours that were patently absurd, but nevertheless damaging. His wife recalled in her *Autobiography* how

The D . . . . ss of W . . . . and others continue spreading amazing lies about me and mine; they would be grotesque if they were not so vile. Elizabeth is in turn engaged to a German Admiral or a German General; Henry has shares in Krupps; I 'feed Prussian prisoners with every dainty and comestible', and play lawn tennis with them at Donnington Hall – a place whose very whereabouts is unknown to me.

Margot, it must be said, gave the gossip-mongers plenty of ammunition. 'What — fools we have been believing that Germany would never go for us!' she declared to Lord Rosebery on 1 September 1914, professing pity for 'Poor Haldane and all the pro-Germans among whom I have always counted myself.' One may presume that she repeated this admission to others, who would not have hesitated to give it currency. With even less inhibition, she gave a taste of her 'British candour' to Leo Maxse, who carried on a virulent campaign against top-ranking Liberals. 'I can understand your hating Henry, but why Haldane?' she asked 'dear Mr Leo', to whom she expostulated at length on 1 February 1915. 'I think you are *quite* right to attack Henry. Go on calling him a lazy man', she implored. 'The only men you must not attack are our Generals.' Maxse and his ilk did not require *carte blanche* from the Prime Minister's wife.

The Tory ultras, for whom Maxse maintained a monthly forum in his *National Review*, could never forgive the Liberal Government for its sell-out to the Irish Nationalists. Nor would they credit its disavowals of a plot to coerce Ulster during 'Bloody Week' (as they called it) in March 1914. They soon had fresh proof of Asquith's perfidy, as if any were needed. The party truce, by which they abided grudgingly at best, had implied to them the promise that Home Rule would be shelved, perhaps for ever. If Asquith had made any such promise, which he denied, he broke it on 15 September by an announcement to the House that the Home Rule Bill would proceed directly to the statute book. The pill was to be sugared by supplementary legislation to suspend the operation of the Act until a year had passed or the war had ended, whichever followed the other. In addition, an Amending Bill was to be drafted that would allow Ulster to claim exemption from its general provisions.

The Unionist leadership reacted violently to Asquith's 'quiet, rather humdrum speech, pitched purposely in a low key'. Bonar Law accused the Prime Minister of base deception, and likened his behaviour to the treachery of the Kaiser in invading Belgium. He thereupon led his followers out of the chamber in self-righteous protest. Asquith took it all in good humour. It was, he thought, 'not really a very impressive spectacle, a lot of prosaic and for the most part middle-aged gentlemen trying to look like early French revolutionists in the Tennis Court'. Others better appreciated the deadly earnestness of the charade. 'The universal opinion of our friends', he wrote at midnight to Miss Stanley,

is that B. Law never sank so low in his gutter as to-day . . . The indignation of our people knows no bounds. McKenna left the bench & (as he told me) lay down on his sofa upstairs, lest he shd. succumb to the temptation of going for him – physically & muscularly. Violet & Clemmie [Churchill] were in the Ladies Gallery, and said they felt quite sick.

Redmond, who accepted the compromise as the best he could get, addressed the House, half-empty after Bonar Law's exodus. Facetiously, he declared himself puzzled by the leader of the Opposition, who, 'having told the world that the Government of this Empire is made up of men devoid of honour, devoid of truth, devoid of decency, wound up his speech by saying that his one desire in life was to support the Government in this crisis'. Not himself a signatory to the party truce, although its beneficiary, Redmond saw clearly its hopeless fragility.

Over strenuous objections from the Archbishop of Canterbury, the

Welsh Church Bill was also speedily enacted. Irate clerics might fume and sputter, but did not vacate their pulpits. Once again, the Government laid itself open to charges of mendacity. 'The Opposition has given up contesting by-elections and propaganda work in the country', Walter Long complained on 27 January 1915 in a memorandum to his colleagues on the Unionist front bench. 'The Government', on the other hand, 'pursues its course of domestic legislation, retarded and truncated it is true, but nevertheless by no means entirely suspended.' Exaggerating the extent to which their patriotism was being exploited, the Unionists seethed with sullen indignation. The less scrupulous of them connived with opportunistic journalists to discredit the ministry as a whole by vilifying particular ministers whose backgrounds, personal habits, or ill-considered statements could be held against them. Haldane, a prime target, had once referred to Germany in private conversation as his 'spiritual home'. Simon, McKenna, Harcourt, and Masterman were each, in his way, fair game. By concentrating their energies on a vitriolic campaign of caricature and innuendo, the Government's enemies were able to defy the spirit of the party truce to which they paid lip service.

Although the smaller fry in the Cabinet were the usual victims of newspaper slander, it was obvious to all concerned that these critics were angling for bigger fish. By impugning Haldane's patriotism and accusing Harcourt of employing a German chauffeur, they were able to attack Asquith's honour, if not his name. There was, then, a definite method to the madness as well as a madness to the method. Beatrice Webb was charitably inclined to absolve the 'better class Conservatives' from responsibility for these 'hunts', which she saw as the ugly work of 'such minor MPs' as W. A. S. Hewins, Sir Richard Cooper, and Lord Charles Beresford. To her roster, she might have added the names not only of other backbenchers – William Joynson-Hicks, Ronald McNeill, and Jesse Collings – but also various front-bench personages who either declined to muzzle their supporters or, more culpably, encouraged them with nods of approval. Arnold White, who spewed forth his venom in the columns of the *Daily Express*, sent word to Maxse on 4 February 1915 that he had 'talked at length with Bonar Law, Carson and Long', who indicated 'no desire to abandon the campaign against Haldane just as the scent is burning', but were 'in one way . . . [or] another . . . anxious to be present in Whitehall or St James's Street when the plump body of the Member for Germany swings in the wind between two lamp posts'.

As the war entered its first winter, the euphoria evaporated, leaving a residue of disillusionment and discontent. Despite initial predictions, it was obviously going to be a long struggle that would tax every nerve and muscle of British society. As the nation clamoured for decisive action to break the stalemate on the bloody battlefields of the western front, popular opinion grew more receptive to the newspaper attacks which Asquith affected not to read. The Government's caution was ascribed to incompetence, to pusillanimity, or, more hysterically, to subversion. Runciman, writing to his wife on 6 January 1915, articulated the belief common among his Cabinet colleagues 'that by doing their best we shall succeed if not in a dramatic coup then in a sturdy endurance that will outlast German, or rather Prussian plunges'. A reasonable strategy, it was not one that satisfied the craving either of right-wing publicists or of the man in the street, for whom they were increasingly the mouthpiece. The war of attrition was inflicting more conspicuous damage on British morale than on enemy fortifications. What was urgently needed, Lloyd George minuted to the war council on New Year's Day 1915, was 'a definite victory somewhere' instead of those

long casualty lists explained by monotonous and rather banal telegrams from headquarters about 'heavy cannonades', 'making a little progress' at certain points, 'recovering trenches', the loss of which has never been reported, etc., with the net result that we have not advanced a yard after weeks of heavy fighting. . . A clear definite victory which has visibly materialized in guns and prisoners captured, in unmistakable retreats of the enemy's armies, and in large sections of enemy territory occupied, will alone satisfy the public that tangible results are being achieved by the great sacrifices they are making, and decide neutrals that it is at last safe for them to throw in their lot with us.

Asquith could hardly dissent from this appraisal. Indeed, three days earlier, he had confessed to Miss Stanley that he was 'profoundly dissatisfied with the immediate prospect', which implied 'an enormous waste of life and money day after day with no appreciable progress'. But, as yet, he could see no way out of the impasse. For that matter, neither could Lloyd George.

Short of launching a spectacular military offensive, which could not reasonably be contemplated, the Government might have demonstrated its will to victory and thereby appeased its carping critics by various moves which it considered repugnant, unwarranted, or both. It might have issued directives to round up the vast numbers of un-naturalized (or even, as some suggested, naturalized) Germans and Austrians resident in the kingdom, or at least it might have kept closer surveillance over their activities; that, however, would have penalized the innocent many for the sake of the dangerous few, and Asquith was 'entirely unconvinced' by Hankey's admonitions on the subject. Or the Government might have tightened its blockade of Germany by clamping down on neutral shipping; that, however, would have inflamed opinion in neutral countries, particularly the United States. The war council also considered the possibility of destroying German crops; but that was another dubious proposition, as well as a morally objectionable one. There were those who contended that an all-party coalition might inspire greater confidence or, at any rate, distribute blame more widely; but the majority of Liberals abhorred the idea, which, anyway, the leading Unionists suspected as a trap. Finally, the Government might have capitulated to demands for compulsion; but the natural inclination of most ministers was against this 'illiberal' step which, Kitchener and other reputed authorities assured them, would result in the dislocation of industry and a superfluity of men for the fighting forces.

Appointed as a figurehead who would confer military prestige on an otherwise civilian Government, Kitchener soon revealed himself to be inestimably more than the 'great poster' which the Asquith women caustically took him for. He got off to a bad start. 'Lord K has rather demoralised the War Office with his bull in the china shop manners and methods, and particularly his ignorance of & indifference to the Territorials', Asquith wrote to Miss Stanley on 12 August 1914. Unable to comprehend the intricacies of the system at his disposal, much less to cope with the awesome details of departmental administration, Kitchener time and again proved true Margot Asquith's prophecy that he 'would be a terrible muddler'. Nevertheless, he performed one indispensable service: as L. S. Amery resentfully put it, he provided his Liberal colleagues with a 'splendid Kitchener umbrella' beneath which they could take shelter from the winds and rain of political adversity.

Asquith, while by no means oblivious to Kitchener's manifold shortcomings, prized him as a special asset. 'The unattackable K', as Runciman dubbed him, fascinated Asquith by demonstrating an 'undisguised contempt for the "public" in all its moods & manifestations' which the self-same 'public', curiously enough, accepted as reassuring. Furthermore, although secretive by nature, he was steadfastly loyal. His inflated reputation was effectively invoked to curb agitations within the Government as well as outside. At a Cabinet on 26 August 1914, for example, 'Winston indulged ... in a long and rhetorical diatribe on the subject' of compulsory service.

'But', Asquith informed Miss Stanley, 'he got very little help from K., who is all for proceeding upon our present lines, until (if ever) their failure is demonstrated & complete'. Lord Emmott, who had recently entered the Cabinet as First Commissioner of Works, amplified this account in a diary entry: 'Winston wasted our time most atrociously . . . He was both stupid and boring. Asquith contemptuous at first, but did not bear him down.' Why, after all, should Asquith exert himself when Kitchener could do the job for him? J. A. Pease, another Cabinet diarist, left a similar version of the incident. By his telling, the Prime Minister 'took . . . with patience' Churchill's harangue: 'the matter he said was not urgent'. Besides, Asquith pointed out, 'many of our own men in the H of C would not assent, such a proposal would divide the country from one end to the other'. Thereupon, he politely deferred to Kitchener, who administered the *coup de grâce* by refusing to make any 'appeal for compulsion yet, he had got his 120,000 men & recruiting was still going on although he had only asked for 100,000 – he could not arm more before April.'

Unlike several of his Cabinet colleagues and many of his back-bench followers, Asquith held no doctrinaire attachment to the voluntary principle. Rather, he regarded it, much as he had long regarded Free Trade, as an expedient to be employed only so long as it continued to fulfil its purpose. To jettison traditional procedures would have been premature and potentially disruptive. A week after Churchill's tirade, Asquith told Miss Stanley that

recruiting is going on so fast & furiously (no less than 28,000 came in yesterday) that it is becoming a question whether we should not rather try for the moment to damp it down. It will be very difficult, if possible, to find an adequate supply of instructors, clothing, rifles, guns and &c. for such a huge number if they continue to increase at their present rate.

Asquith was inclined to dismiss Churchill as intemperately bombastic. Instead he chose to rely on the advice of Kitchener, who shared his pew at a funeral service on the morning of 29 October, '& came to see me afterwards'. In contrast to Churchill, with his dire prognostications, 'K thinks now that the war will end sooner than he used to expect – from dearth of ammunition' on the part of the enemy, who 'fire off every day at least 7 *times* as much as in any previous war, and if it goes on at this rate no possible new supply can keep pace with the demand'. Kitchener, soon to revise more realistically his estimate of the duration of the war, may be forgiven his

illusions about a German munitions shortage. It is impossible, however, to excuse his firm assurances to Asquith, who repeated them
publicly in a speech at Newcastle on 20 April 1915, that Britain was
amply provided with munitions supplies.

'My own opinion of K's capacity increases daily', Asquith told his
favourite confidante on 3 November. 'I think he is a really fine
soldier, and keeps his head & temper, and above all his equability
wonderfully, considering how all three are tried.' He was especially
gratified to observe that Lloyd George, who had been quarrelling
with Kitchener, 'is now an enthusiastic K-ite', too. The authority of
the war secretary was augmented, rather than constricted, by the
creation in late November of a war council. With Hankey as secretary, its charter members were Asquith, Grey, Lloyd George,
Kitchener, Churchill, Balfour (the lone Unionist), and various
military and naval officials, including Lord ('Jacky') Fisher, who had
recently resumed his command as First Sea Lord. Within the next
few months, Crewe, Haldane, Harcourt, McKenna, and Sir Arthur
Wilson (who served at the Admiralty without official title) swelled the
ranks of what Asquith had originally conceived as 'a small conclave
on the Naval and Mily situation'. Its functions as indeterminate as
its shape was amorphous, the war council was called into session
irregularly. 'Occasional meetings at intervals of a week or fortnight
will end in nothing', Lloyd George protested to Asquith on 31 December. Edwin Montagu, who replaced the hapless Masterman as
Chancellor of the Duchy of Lancaster, levelled similar criticisms.
'You do not get discussions in the War Council differing materially
from those in the Cabinet', he complained to Hankey on 22 March
1915; 'you have the same protagonists in both, and all you do is to
substitute a different set of spectators.' It was left to Hankey, in a
memorandum to the Prime Minister on 17 May, to sum up the defects
of this new body with the disturbing pronouncement that there was
'literally no one in this country who knows, or has access to, all the
information, naval, military, and political, on which future plans
must be based'.

This vital deficiency in the area of strategic planning compounded
the risks of hazardous ventures. Churchill, whose autumn expedition
to save Antwerp had ended disastrously, pored over his Admiralty
maps to find a new, more fruitful theatre of combat. 'Are there not
other alternatives than sending our armies to chew barbed wire in
Flanders?' he shrilly addressed the Prime Minister on 29 December.
The captive of his vivid imagination, he proposed a naval assault on
Schleswig-Holstein, which

would at once threaten the Kiel Canal and enable Denmark to join us. The accession of Denmark would throw open the Baltic. British naval command of the Baltic would enable the Russian armies to be landed within 90 miles of Berlin; and the enemy, while being closely held on all existing lines, would be forced to face new attacks directed at vital points and exhaust himself along a still larger perimeter.

Lloyd George, not to be outdone, advocated a double-pronged offensive against the soft Slavic underbelly of the Habsburg Empire and, simultaneously, against the Ottoman Empire in Syria. Independently, Hankey had also turned to the eastern zone, but further north. On 28 December, in a closely reasoned memorandum which was circulated at Asquith's suggestion, he maintained that 'the occupation of Constantinople, the Dardanelles, and Bosphorus . . . would be of great advantage to the allies, restoring communication with the Black Sea, bringing down the price of wheat, and setting free the much-needed shipping locked up there.' Churchill, whose 'volatile mind' had earlier been set on 'a heroic adventure against Gallipoli and the Dardanelles' (according to Asquith, who, on 5 December, professed himself 'altogether opposed'), shelved his elaborate plans for the Baltic. In the closing hours of 1914, he consulted with Hankey and advised Asquith: 'We are substantially in agreement and our conclusions are not incompatible.'

The Foreign Office endorsed the idea as one that was likely to tempt the Balkan states into the war on the Allied side. Kitchener, too, welcomed the prospect of 'a demonstration at the Dardanelles' as a means to relieve pressure on Russia, whose imminent collapse was feared. He was, however, reluctant to divert troops from the western front, and demurred at anything more than a naval enterprise. Lloyd George, who also 'hoped that the Army would not be required or expected to pull the chestnuts out of the fire for the Navy', was less than impressed by the proposal; but his alternative scheme, to which Asquith had been partial, was thwarted by the refusal of Greece to permit British troop landings at Salonika. By default, the Dardanelles strategy held the field, with a fading possibility that it would be accompanied by naval offensives in the North Sea and Adriatic. On 13 January the war council discussed preparations 'for a naval expedition in February to bombard and take the Gallipoli peninsula, with Constantinople as its objective'. Asquith, by his own account, 'maintained an almost unbroken silence till the end, when I intervened with my conclusions'. He accepted the Admiralty's case for 'the methodical forcing of the Dardanelles' which, as he visualized two days later, 'might conceivably make a huge & even decisive diversion. It wd. certainly compel Italy to come in.'

Fisher, wedded to the concept of a Baltic strategy, was unbending. On 28 January he and Churchill, unable to resolve their differences, appeared together before Asquith, who listened to their respective arguments and came down on Churchill's side. At the ensuing meeting of the war council, Fisher maintained 'an obstinate and ominous silence'. His resignation was threatened, but not delivered, much to his subsequent regret. 'With extreme reluctance', he reminded Asquith on 12 May, 'and largely due to earnest words spoken to me by Kitchener, I, by not resigning (*as I see now I should have done*), remained a most unwilling beholder (and indeed a participator) of the gradual draining of our naval resources from the decisive theatre of the war.' For the time being, Churchill and Fisher continued to work in tandem, although, as Asquith understated it to Miss Stanley on 30 January, 'F. is still a little uneasy about the Dardanelles'.

Churchill's strategy, along with his temper, was badly strained by his incessant wrangling with Fisher and by the reluctance of Kitchener to back up the proposed naval assault with an adequate military force. Assuring his colleagues that he agreed with them 'in principle', Kitchener proved 'very sticky about sending out there the 29th Division, which is the best one we have left at home', and which he preferred to hold in reserve in case Russia suddenly fell and Germany moved massively westward. Asquith, who chronicled these deliberations in a letter to Miss Stanley on 24 February, proclaimed his conviction that neither effort nor manpower should be stinted:

One must take a lot of risks in war, & I am strongly of opinion that the chance of forcing the Dardanelles & occupying Constantinople, & cutting Turkey in half, and arousing on our side the whole Balkan peninsula, presents such a unique opportunity that we ought to hazard a lot elsewhere rather than forgo it.

Nevertheless, he cowered before Kitchener: 'If he can be convinced, well & good; but to discard his advice & overrule his judgment on a military question is to take a great responsibility. So I am rather anxious.' To his discredit, Asquith shrank from that responsibility. 'We accepted K's view as right to the immediate situation', he wrote to Miss Stanley two days later, 'to Winston's immense & unconcealed dudgeon.' Also to the irreparable detriment of the Dardanelles strategy, he might have added.

Foredoomed by inordinate delays, by irretrievable blunders, and by insufficient men and supplies, the 'absolutely novel experiment' (as Asquith called it) ended as a costly and humiliating fiasco. As late as 5 June, Churchill was still bravely predicting to his constituents at Dundee that British troops at Gallipoli were 'separated only by a few miles from a victory such as this war has not yet seen'. By then, however, he was whistling in the dark, and struggling to save the vestiges of his reputation.

As it faltered, the attack on the Dardanelles gave evidence of Asquith's paralytic dependence on Kitchener, whose ineptitude was exceeded only by his intransigence. In a memorandum dated 10 April, the fourth Marquess of Salisbury, a leading figure among the old-guard Unionists, put the case for drastic change at the War Office: while it might be useful to retain Kitchener for purposes of publicity, it was imperative to shift the burdens of administrative responsibility to a more capable and dynamic under-secretary than the incumbent, H. J. Tennant, who was incidentally Asquith's brother-in-law. Salisbury's scheme, although stillborn, was symptomatic of an intensifying dissatisfaction with the system over which Asquith had presided with increasing difficulty since the outbreak of war. In May the storm broke. Asquith's 'Kitchener umbrella', like the political truce, was much too tattered to afford him any protection.

# 8

## FROM COALITION
## TO COMPULSION

From the beginning of 1915, Asquith's political position was eroded by a series of embarrassments and reverses, some barely perceptible to the public eye. Adapting himself to new circumstances, he managed temporarily to remain the fulcrum in a delicate balance between rival party forces, the arbitrator between ideological camps, and the mediator between overweening personalities. But each victory taxed his resources and, as he appeared the last to realize, his grasp was increasingly less secure.

'As we drove up this morning in the motor,' presumably from Walmer Castle on the Kent coast, 'we had two or three very narrow shaves of collision & disaster', he wrote to Venetia Stanley on 12 January:

And after each, I said to myself – suppose it had gone wrong, and I had (as Browning says) 'ended my cares', what would have been the consequence?

Lots of stuff in the press – a 'nine days' wonder in the country: violent speculation as to who was to succeed me – E. Grey, Ll. George, Crewe & co; many obituary notices; and after a week or 10 days (at the outside) the world going on as tho' nothing had happened: . . . a few ripples, even, if you like, a bit of a splash in the pool – but little or nothing more.

Roy Jenkins has cited these midnight musings as evidence that 'Asquith was never vain or foolish enough to think that the world, or even a small part of it, would stop without him'. More probably, however, Asquith was simply seeking reassurance from Miss Stanley of her concern and devotion.

Despite this 'stupid letter', as its author himself called it in a postscript, Asquith could not imagine anyone with the presumption, let alone the qualities, to replace him. He had had a dream on the subject, the 'dim memory' of which he shared with his confidante, 'in which (with the concurrence of all my colleagues) I was supplanted by Herbert Samuel – as Prince Hal says "a Jew, an Ebrew Jew". Do you think that is going to be my fate? I wonder. I take refuge in the Beatitude: "The meek shall inherit the earth" – and no Jew was ever meek!' Besides revealing a streak of anti-Semitism (the publication of the latest volume in Buckle's life of Disraeli moved him to comment that Disraeli 'was the only Jew of our time who had real courage – both passive & active – a rare quality in that race'), Asquith's dream provides an indication that, wide awake, he did not take seriously any threat to his supremacy. But his friends, while believing that he was indispensable, did not delude themselves that he was invulnerable.

Early in the year, the death of Percy Illingworth necessitated the appointment of a new Liberal Chief Whip. Various candidates were considered. William Wedgwood Benn, who had taken a commission in the cavalry, removed himself from the running. Montagu proposed Donald Maclean, who eventually deputized for Asquith in the Commons, but whom the Prime Minister brushed aside as 'quite an impossible person'. Lloyd George plumped for Neil Primrose, Lord Rosebery's younger son, but Asquith could not fathom 'why Ll. G. is so enamoured of the idea'. J. H. Whitley, whom Asquith regarded with greater enthusiasm, preferred to remain as deputy Speaker with the prospect of ascending to the speakership in due course. Francis Acland, another nominee, was disqualified on two counts: he had a suffragette wife, and he struck Asquith as 'a rather angular man'. By

process of elimination, Asquith settled on the promotion of John
Gulland, who had served under Illingworth as Scottish whip. 'I
should be the chief sufferer', he anticipated to Miss Stanley on
17 January, eight days before the appointment was announced; 'a
daily interview & intimate converse with Gulland has no attraction
and I doubt whether I could rely upon him (as I always could on
Illingworth) to 'stick up' to me when his judgment differed from
mine.'

These qualms proved amply justified. Whereas Illingworth had
been an adept party manager, whose ingenuity went far to compensate for what Montagu deplored as the 'pathetic weakness of our
Whips' Office', Gulland was overwhelmed by the responsibility to
co-ordinate activity first within the parliamentary party and then
within the constituencies. A lacklustre personality, he sorely lacked
the skill to allay tensions among the party leaders. Fortunately,
Asquith himself made a speciality of reconciling the differences that
arose among his subordinates: he mended the rift between Lloyd
George and Kitchener, played honest broker in the 'bad bêtise'
between Kitchener and Churchill, restored calm when Lloyd George
and McKenna 'were fighting like fishwives', and staved off a showdown between Churchill and Fisher. But, as time would show, there
was no one who might mediate in disputes to which Asquith was
himself a party, and who might impress upon him the sentiments of
his followers.

In response to the Government's apparent infirmity of purpose,
the demand for a coalition grew more insistent and vociferous. For
what it was worth, Horatio Bottomley reiterated his plea in *John
Bull* (13 February) for the Prime Minister 'openly [to] invite Opposition leaders to your Councils and share with them the responsibilities of the hour'. An unscrupulous charlatan, Bottomley was more
easily ignored than others, including Churchill, who flirted with the
same idea. Asquith, dead set against it, was pleased to report to Miss
Stanley on 9 February that Lloyd George and Montagu had just

come back from Paris . . . much impressed by the weakness & timidity
of the present French Ministry. It is a kind of coalition Government
of 'all the talents'; its members hating and distrusting one another;
afraid of the Chamber: afraid of the Press: afraid (from the President
of the Republic downwards) of their own shadows. It is (except perhaps the poor fugitive exiled Belges) by far the most unstable
Government among all the belligerent Powers on both sides.

To his relief, the Unionist leaders gave every intimation that they
were no more eager to assume ministerial responsibility than he to

have them. Balfour, a free agent, participated in the deliberations of the war council, at which Bonar Law and Lansdowne made an unusual appearance on 10 March. Five days later, 'Bonar Law came to the P.M.' (who described the interview to Hankey), 'and told him that though they "enjoyed" the meeting . . . it would not be possible for them, for party reasons, to attend in future. If they did so they feared it would weaken their position in the Conservative Party and, as Mr Bonar Law put it, render their future support of the government less effective.' Consequently, Asquith instructed Hankey 'to send them all the papers prepared for the War Council, but not to invite their attendance . . . How astonishing is the influence of party politics', Hankey ruminated in his diary on the 17th. The thought occurred to many people.

With the assistance of Bonar Law, who 'was like heather honey', the Government 'got through our Welsh Church impasse' on 15 March. The Prime Minister 'made a quiet temporising lubricating sort of speech' to a half-empty House, and the leader of the Opposition 'gave . . . his benediction'. Clearly Parliament no longer qualified as an arena for partisan combat. In spite of – or, more specifically, because of – the prevailing calm, actively promoted by party chiefs on both sides, there was deepening resentment within both sets of back benches and unease within the Cabinet.

Writing to Miss Stanley on 21 March, Asquith reported that Montagu had warned him of an intrigue. Balfour was allegedly 'gaining' an 'ascendancy . . . over L.G. as well as Winston', who acquainted him with 'all their grievances against K and the rest of their colleagues'. Montagu regarded 'A J B as secretly but genuinely hostile' to Asquith, who lent sufficient credence to the story to repeat it to his wife. Margot recorded in her diary that day that Asquith denounced Churchill as 'the greatest donkey! he goes gassing about, abusing K to Arthur and I've no doubt abusing me, giving him much too much information. He thinks he knows Arthur Balfour, he has not the foggiest idea of what Arthur really is . . .' According to her, Asquith ridiculed Balfour as a man with a 'futile feminine brain' who, when he runs into trouble, 'takes his hat off, says he is ill and leaves his unfortunate friends to be led by a man of fifth rate quality like Bonar Law'.

These rumours might have been easily discounted, but for the fact that, four days later, Margot received a visit from H. W. Massingham, the editor of the *Nation*, who brought further information, which, he claimed, he could authenticate. Without delay, she carried it to Asquith, who carried it as quickly to Miss Stanley:

. . . Winston is 'intriguing hard' to supplant E. Grey at the Foreign Office & to put AJB in his place. I gave you the other day a milder version of the same story . . . There is no doubt that Winston is at the moment a complete victim to B's superficial charm; he has him at the Admiralty night & day, and I am afraid tells him a lot of things which he ought to keep to himself, or at any rate to his col leagues.

While he wrote this letter, Asquith was interrupted by a visit from Lloyd George. 'I asked him what he thought of the Massingham story', Asquith continued,

& rather to my surprise he said he believed it was substantially true. He thinks that Winston has for the time at any rate allowed himself to be 'swallowed whole' by AJB on whom he, LG, after working with him for a week or two, is now disposed to be very severe.

It is a pity isn't it? that Winston hasn't a better sense of propor- tion, and also a larger endowment of the instinct of loyalty. As you know, like you, I am really fond of him; but I regard his future with many misgivings . . . He will never get to the top in English politics, with all his wonderful gifts; to speak with the tongue of men & angels, and to spend laborious days & nights in administration, is no good, if a man does not inspire trust.

Lloyd George, quick to confirm Asquith's suspicions of Churchill, was himself the subject of similar rumours. On 29 March McKenna brought word to Asquith (who passed on the information to Miss Stanley) 'that Northcliffe (for some unknown reason) has been engineering a campaign to supplant me by LlG! McK is of course quite certain that LlG & perhaps Winston are "in it". Which I don't believe . . .' At lunch that day, Asquith mentioned the incident to Montagu, whose 'loyalty is a certain & invaluable asset', and who put down McKenna 'as a mischief maker'. Nevertheless, Asquith posed the question: 'what wd. happen if the so-called "intrigue" were to come off, & I were supposed to go'. Montagu satisfied his chief by replying 'without a moment's hesitation that the *whole* Cabinet, including LlG & Winston, would go with me, & make any other alternative impossible'. The next day, Asquith brought McKenna face to face with Lloyd George, who accused him of plant- ing an article in the *Daily Chronicle*, as well as the seeds of mistrust among his colleagues. Churchill declined an invitation to join them with the disarming reply to Asquith: 'I feel that my case is safe in your hands'. There the matter was laid to rest.

And yet it continued to rankle. Asquith might exonerate Churchill and Lloyd George, but Balfour's behaviour remained inexplicable. So, too, did the motives of the various press magnates and journalists who were alternately the accomplices and the instruments of competing politicians. Geoffrey Robinson, whom Northcliffe employed as editor of *The Times*, wrote on 22 March to Lord Esher:

We shall come before long to a National Cabinet for the simple reason that the present Cabinet dare not take the necessary action on their own account. Perhaps it may be all the better to have such a change now that we know our mistakes, though I always think that the PM was a fool, from his own point of view, not to do it from the beginning.

His greatest fear, as he underscored it to Esher the next day, was that the Government, anxious to placate its timorous supporters, would '*accept an unsatisfactory peace*', possibly at Belgium's expense. J. L. Garvin, who divided his editorial talents between the *Observer* and the *Pall Mall Gazette*, disclaimed any knowledge of 'a dark intrigue against Mr Asquith . . . So far as we are aware', he stated in the latter journal on the 29th,

the only suggestions that he should be displaced have come from pure Radicals, who have notoriously muttered in their zeal that Mr Lloyd George would make a better Premier. It is a view with which some Unionists would agree on other grounds. They think the Chancellor of the Exchequer alone has the genius [of] popular leadership, the initiative, decision, driving power, required to raise democratic effort to its maximum.

In his ostensible attempt to dissociate himself from attacks on Asquith's leadership, Garvin did his best to ensure that they would continue.

The controllers of the Unionist press, who spoke for their backbenchers against the party's acquiescent leaders, were resolved that the system had to be changed. They could not agree, however, what to install in its place. 'Those *devils* are starting rumours of a Coalition government', Lady Charles Beresford fumed in early April to H. A. ('Taffy') Gwynne, the editor of the *Morning Post*. 'Are we as stupid as that? Our worst enemy is A.B. who is always at the *A*[squith]'s and now has a room at Whitehall.' In her opinion, the 'Mandarins' on the Liberal side were only slightly more culpable than their Unionist counterparts, who had been hoodwinked into submission by the party truce, and whom a coalition would formally bind and gag. She was, of course, preaching to the converted. On 26 March Gwynne had sent Bonar Law a memorandum in which he argued that, whatever the 'shortcomings' of the men in office, 'with a Unionist Opposition we can stir them up – and stir them up with some effect,

but given a Coalition Government we should get callous and care-
less'. Bonar Law, Gwynne recalled in a letter to Maxse on 17 May,
had professed agreement, volunteering the information that he had
already rejected overtures from Lloyd George and Churchill.

As April wore on, the situation became more critical for both sets
of party leaders. Rumours were rife that munitions supplies were
running low. Asquith consulted Kitchener, who, on the 14th, relayed
assurances from Sir John French, commander-in-chief of the Expeditionary Force, 'that with the present supply of ammunition he will
have as much as his troops will be able to use on the next forward
movement'. On the strength of Kitchener's statement, Asquith
delivered his speech at Newcastle on the 20th in which he denied
categorically that there was any shortage. His critics, who had more
reliable sources of information, were not persuaded. The next afternoon, the *Pall Mall Gazette* pointedly contrasted Asquith's performance at Newcastle ('too guarded, discreet, and uninspiring')
with Lloyd George's 'blunt and truthful' address on the drink question at Bangor a month earlier. The May number of the *National
Review* chose to 'make no comment' on the Prime Minister's veracity,
but instead queried whether 'munitions despatched by Mr Asquith
to Sir John French are being surreptitiously diverted to the Dardanelles by some pushful colleague'. Still more belatedly, a leader in
the *Daily Express* on 1 May expressed the opinion that 'such speeches
as that delivered by Mr Asquith at Newcastle, a speech calculated to
lull the nation into a fool's paradise . . ., are mischievous to a degree.
The Country', it declaimed, 'does not yet realise the significance of
the war, and the fault is the Government's.' It was not until 22 May
that Captain George (later Baron) Lloyd, who had taken leave from
Westminster to serve at the Dardanelles, 'read with absolute amazement Asquith's statement that there was not and never had been any
shortage of ammunition for this Army'. The Newcastle speech, he
wrote sarcastically to Austen Chamberlain, provided 'another proof
of the inaccuracy of the "in vino veritas" proverb'.

By then, it was common knowledge that Asquith had been the
victim and, in turn, the unwitting perpetrator of a gross deception.
On 14 May *The Times*, the most authoritative of the anti-ministerial
organs, featured a lengthy dispatch from Colonel Repington, who
ascribed the failure of British troops to pierce the German line to 'the
want of unlimited supply of high explosive'. It was accompanied by
a hard-hitting leader, and followed up by well-documented accounts
of shocking inefficiency in the Glasgow munitions industry.

The effect was thunderous. 'The attack in yesterday's *Times* on the Govt and the statement of its Military Correspondent on which the attack is based is an unparalleled and amazing piece of black-guardism and treachery', John Dillon spluttered in a letter to Birrell, the Irish Chief Secretary, on the 15th. 'How I should like to know did the Censors pass this atrocious statement? . . . It is enough to bring down a Government – and its publication *must* have had that object in view.' Two days later, J. A. Spender, the well-informed editor of the *Westminster Gazette*, dolefully confirmed to Esher that 'Repington has put the Government very nearly between devil and deep sea'. Lord Stamfordham took stock of the situation in a memorandum to the King on the 19th:

The history of Repington's letter about the ammunition is wrapped in mystery: it was censored in France, came to the War Office where the Censor actually erased passages & then sent it on as it was published. So the W.O. is blamed. Before Mr Asquith made his Newcastle speech he asked Lord Kitchener what he might say: Lord K. replied that French, who had been to England a few days previous, assured him that he was perfectly satisfied about ammunition and Lord K. told the P.M. that there were 1000 rounds per gun. Now he hears that the greater amount of these was shrapnel which is more or less useless! On the other hand he [Asquith] wrote to French to rather cheer him up after our recent failure to drive the Germans back and received a letter in the most optimistic key and without any allusion whatever to lack of ammunition.

This, however, was not the limit of Asquith's difficulties. Within twenty-four hours of Repington's disclosures, Lord Fisher made good his threat to resign as First Sea Lord. Citing his inveterate hostility to the Dardanelles enterprise and his inability to work any longer with Churchill, he notified the Prime Minister of his intention to depart immediately for Scotland 'so as not to be embarrassed or embarrass you by any explanations with anyone'. Asquith's daughter, who held firmly to the view that the ensuing crisis was pre-cipitated exclusively by Fisher's megalomania, has recorded that he 'behaved in a lower, meaner and more untrustworthy way than any Englishman since war began'. According to her diary, Fisher 'had simply *run away* from the Admiralty, deserting his post and work, had pulled down all the blinds in his own house and left a red-herring trail in the direction of Scotland'. Her father, she tells us, sent several lieutenants – including Lloyd George – to patrol 'the Continental railway stations' until the truant had been 'found, caught, carried in a retriever's mouth and dropped – bloodshot and panting – at the door of the Cabinet room'. A colourful account, it differs markedly from that provided by the reporter from the *Manchester Guardian*, who kept vigil in Downing Street. When Fisher arrived at Number Ten that Saturday afternoon, he found Asquith nestled in the rear of his motor car, ready to leave for a weekend at The Wharf. Journalists saw nothing unusual in Fisher's appearance, save its timing. Discharging his chauffeur, Asquith returned inside, where he was closeted with Fisher for nearly an hour. Afterwards, he sent for Kitchener, with whom he spent the remainder of the afternoon.

It remains an open question, fiercely debated among historians, whether Fisher's resignation was the cause of the May crisis or merely the pretext for it. Concurrent with the shells scandal, the altercation at the Admiralty doubtless intensified the Government's distress. But ought it to assume equal or, as some would suggest, paramount significance? The historian's task is rendered immeasurably more difficult by the contradictions that abounded in the minds of key participants, and in their communications to their diaries and to one another. Was Fisher's resignation as 'irrevocable' as Asquith inferred, or was Fisher 'curtly dismissed', as he himself insisted in a flurry of indignant letters? 'Kitchener, who can't get a thing right, gets the Order of the Garter and I get the order of the boot', he lamented to Masterman, whom he chanced to meet soon afterwards. He was not alone in his inability to offer a logical explanation for what had occurred. Prominent Liberals could discern no obvious connection between the Admiralty crisis and the subsequent decision to reconstruct the ministry on an all-party basis. 'Why the fact that Winston quarrelled with Fisher should mean your giving up the L[ocal] G[overnment] B[oard]', Masterman wrote to Samuel on the 26th, 'is a *non sequitur* which today and tomorrow will find difficult to understand.'

As recently as 12 May, the question had been put to Asquith by Handel Booth, a Liberal proponent of coalition, 'whether . . . he will consider the desirability of admitting into the ranks of Ministers leading members of the various political parties in this House'. Asquith had replied, without hesitation or equivocation, that such an arrangement was 'not in contemplation'. Yet, a week later, he told the House that precisely these 'steps are in contemplation'. Indeed, he had already requested and obtained the resignations of his Liberal colleagues as the prelude to the formation of a 'broad based government'. Why, and for what purpose?

In his explanation to the King, Asquith acknowledged two 'actual causes' for the upheaval: '(1) Lord Fisher's resignation (2) The Armament Question raised by the recent letter from the Times special correspondent at the front in Flanders'. He did not assign priority to either. As Trevor Wilson has forcefully argued, 'the point that needs to be stressed here is that it was not the actual crises which drove Asquith to form a coalition, but the use which the Conservatives were threatening to make of them'. There is no other way to account for the days that passed before Asquith's precipitous reaction.

On the 14th, the day that Repington's revelations appeared in print, the Unionist 'shadow cabinet' gathered at Lansdowne House to consider a proposal by Lord Robert Cecil that the Opposition should move 'for a Committee on the state of the Nation, with closed doors, in order to discuss freely the action of the Government in regard to several matters in the conduct of the war which are giving rise to much anxiety'. Austen Chamberlain recorded in his diary that the members of the Unionist front bench rejected this strategy and decided instead that they would 'personally urge' the Government to exert greater effort. In the unlikely event that the Prime Minister deemed it 'necessary to employ compulsion . . . either for the army or for the production of munitions of war', he could count upon Opposition support.

Unionist backbenchers and publicists, whose worst suspicions of the Government's incapacity had been confirmed by that morning's *Times*, were furious. They demanded a full and open debate, and – in the words of Professor W. A. S. Hewins, chairman of the Unionist Business Committee – were resolved to 'carry the matter through'. Without consulting Bonar Law, Hewins wrote a 'strong letter . . . to Asquith intimating the attitude of the organised Unionists with whom I act'. Receiving no reply, he then 'sent round to him private notice of a question for the afternoon' of Monday, the 17th. Stiffly informed by the Prime Minister's private secretary that 'the question . . . cannot properly be dealt with at short notice', Hewins concluded 'that there was no other course than to put the question down for Wednesday . . . Against my advice', he wrote in his diary, his confederates approached Bonar Law, who 'gave . . . a private reason for not taking action'. In the meantime, 'we whipped up people of all parties & told the press'. A. G. Robbins, parliamentary correspondent for *The Times*, 'said it was just what headquarters staff desired, that in fact Repington's statement was made with their consent & approval to provoke action in Parliament'. Bonar Law, put on the spot, 'now changed his mind'. On the 17th he wrote to Asquith that he had 'learnt with dismay' about Fisher's resignation, and proposed to raise the matter in parliamentary debate. His biographer, a distinguished advocate of the interpretation that the shells scandal did not yet loom large, has explained that 'Bonar Law had agreed with Asquith and Lloyd George to write such a letter in order that Asquith could show it to his colleagues and make the situation clear to them'. According to Chamberlain, before Bonar Law had had the opportunity to deliver his letter, he was summoned to Downing Street to discuss plans to reshuffle the Cabinet.

Bonar Law and his principal colleagues were no less eager than Asquith to clamp the lid on intra-party disputes. Coalition, there-fore, was a mutual convenience. 'The Liberal newspapers attribute this action to the Opposition *leaders*', Hewins noted with amusement in his diary on the 18th,

though some deny that Bonar Law forced on the change of Govt. Our experience of course is that B.L. & Co. have always – up to the last moment deprecated & discouraged strong action. My inference from the facts I know, wh. may be mistaken, is that Asquith when faced with the determined attitude of the Unionists tried to meet it & prevent attack by put[ting] a few Front Bench Unionists into the ministry & that he had not in view a complete reconstruction.

Hewins had 'no doubt [that] the Fisher-Winston complication made temporising more difficult', but he saw it as a subsidiary factor. 'Of the latter', he recounted, 'I have heard many accounts wh. in the main agree. Bonar Law said on Tuesday that "munitions" was the main cause. The Govt. became aware on Friday that they wd. have to face the music & they cd. not. A debate on munitions wd. have upset the Govt. as Liberals more or less agree.' A debate on the Admiralty crisis, on the other hand, would have been a relatively harmless diversion. That issue consequently became a smokescreen which historians as well as contemporaries have mistaken for the real conflagration.

From Hewins's standpoint, the outcome was disappointing. He had hoped for new men and new measures, including conscription. Instead, the dreaded 'system' was perpetuated, even reinforced, by Bonar Law's pact with Asquith. 'The Radicals don't know how the change has been effected & certainly don't like it', he wrote in his diary on the 20th. 'They regard it as the end of their party, as no doubt it is. Our people have similar feelings in a modified degree.'

What could have induced Bonar Law to come to the rescue of his beleaguered adversaries? As before, his motives were a mixture of the partisan and the patriotic. He did not relish the prospect of forming the first Unionist administration in a decade: not only would it widen and expose ideological cleavages within his party – especially over the vexed issue of national service – but would also make it difficult to implement the drastic policies which could not long be postponed. The nation, particularly the working classes and the Irish, would sooner accept from familiar Liberal hands the bitter medicine which would have to be swallowed if the war was to be won. Bonar Law, in no hurry to take command, was willing to allow the Liberals to bear the brunt of the disapprobation that would inevitably attach to such measures.

His associates went along without enthusiasm. 'If our help is asked by the Gov't. we *must* give it', Chamberlain counselled him on the evening of the 17th. 'God knows each one of us would willingly avoid the fearful responsibility; but the responsibility of refusing is even greater than that of accepting.' Walter Long admitted to Gwynne on the 20th that he 'loathe[d] the idea of a Coalition Government'. Lansdowne regarded the situation as 'intensely disagreeable'. Curzon and Derby emitted similar grumbles.

Asquith's calculations were transparently clear. As the head of a truly 'national' administration, he might harness the leading Unionists to his stalled chariot. 'Although we may find in his solution to the problem the causes of his final defeat and ruin,' Gollin has cautioned, 'we should notice that his actions at this time were those of a strong man, and not the fumblings of a weak one.' Churchill, not without a tinge of bitterness, put the matter bluntly: recalling the lessons of May 1915, he portrayed Asquith among his *Great Contemporaries* as 'a stern, ambitious, intellectually proud man fighting his way with all necessary ruthlessness . . . These were the convulsive struggles of a man of action and of ambition at death-grips with events.'

It has been suggested that Asquith's behaviour, if not his actual decision, was somehow influenced by the fact that he was reeling under the impact of 'a stunning personal blow'. On the 12th, two days before *The Times* published Repington's article and three days before Fisher resigned, Asquith received unexpected word that Venetia Stanley had consented to marry Montagu. 'As you know well,' he told her, '*this* breaks my heart. I couldn't bear to come and see you. I can only pray God to bless you – and help me.' His anguish was real. But surely it is outrageously melodramatic to say – as one recent historian has done – 'that these convulsive struggles were those of a man enduring a private torment'. For one thing, Asquith was always able to divide his public and private lives into separate compartments, which were never permitted to impinge on each other: his glacial exterior was not melted even when his first wife had suddenly died. For another, however deeply he may have suffered in his *crise de cœur*, he soon found new confidantes to whom he was writing with no less frequency, ardour, and indiscretion. His self-pitying phrases and protestations of utter desolation were a form of flattery, like his earlier appeals for Miss Stanley's political guidance, and ought to be taken no more seriously. Before long, the Montagus were Asquith's weekend guests at Walmer. He certainly grieved to lose her 'epistolary friendship' (as Jenkins has primly described it), but he remained thoroughly in possession of his political faculties.

It has been likewise insinuated that Asquith's judgement was clouded and his will enfeebled by excessive drinking. The intermittent occasions when he was conspicuously under the influence of alcohol tended to elicit sharper comment than before the war, when society had been more relaxed. Sir Douglas Haig put the matter in proper perspective: after entertaining the Prime Minister to dinner at Headquarters on 7 September 1916, he wrote to his wife that Asquith 'did himself fairly well – not more than most gentlemen used to drink when I was a boy, but in this abstemious age it is noticeable if an extra glass or two is taken by anyone!' By the end of the evening, he reported, Asquith's 'legs were unsteady, but his head was quite clear . . . Indeed he was most charming and quite alert in mind.' Nevertheless, Asquith's antagonists spread the rumour that he was a hopeless inebriate. Behind his back, he was nicknamed 'Squiff', and Churchill derided him as 'supine, sodden and supreme'. It would not be unfair to point out that, like the elder Pitt, Churchill himself drank heavily without adverse effect on his performance as a wartime leader. Nor would it be illogical to suppose that Neville Chamberlain would have been none the worse for a couple of diurnal brandies.

The trouble with Asquith was not that he imbibed too much, but that it failed to stiffen his backbone. At least at the outset, he appears to have conceived of coalition as a means to relieve himself of Kitchener, a proved liability. His circular memorandum to his Cabinet colleagues on 17 May gave equal weight to Fisher's resignation and to 'the more than plausible parliamentary case in regard to the alleged deficiency of high explosive shells'. The latter, despite the tortuous phraseology, implied a rebuff to the war secretary. Bonar Law returned that day from his conference in Downing Street to tell Chamberlain that Asquith and Lloyd George were agreed that it was 'absolutely necessary to get rid of Kitchener', and that the Prime Minister proposed to appoint Lloyd George to succeed him. Two days later, in a conversation with Riddell, Lloyd George confirmed the plan. J. A. Pease, who held the portfolio for education in the outgoing ministry, quoted Asquith to the effect that Kitchener had not only 'ignored French's demands for more high explosive supplies', keeping the Cabinet ignorant of them, but also had refused to 'allow civilian help' to tidy the mess at the War Office.

Margot Asquith spent a 'sleepless night of misery' after hearing of her husband's intention. At 6.30 on the morning of the 18th, she addressed a distraught appeal to Haldane, whom she begged to acquaint 'not only Ll. George but Henry' with the certainty that 'there [will] be a scream all over, from the King to the Navvy, . . . when the public learn that K. has gone'. Asquith did not require Haldane or anyone else to alert him to the dangers of Kitchener's displacement. He easily persuaded himself, and then his colleagues, that any gain in efficiency would be offset by the consequent loss in popular esteem. Probably he also perceived that Kitchener had not yet outlived his usefulness. Henceforth, he was increasingly to take refuge behind Kitchener's massive index finger that protruded dauntingly from recruitment posters; it is noteworthy that he was not evicted from the premiership until Kitchener was first removed from the scene.

While Asquith must bear sole responsibility for the retention of an unfit war secretary, he himself continued at the helm virtually by default. There was no one else who, at this juncture, commanded both the confidence of the nation at large and the requisite parliamentary majority. 'The real difficulty', Balfour wrote to Esher on the 15th, 'is to find the man. I look round all the conceivable alternatives, and I find him not!' Less modest, Lloyd George could think of no fewer than three candidates, including himself, but he supplied Bonar Law with irrefutable arguments why each was unsatisfactory: the Liberals, he explained, 'would not stand a Unionist Prime Minister, having regard to the relative numbers in the House; . . . Grey's eyesight put him out of the question, apart from the fact that he had even less push and drive than the present Prime Minister; and lastly, that he himself could not think of taking the position as he would be too much exposed to jealousy and criticism.' It was not loyalty, but a realistic assessment of his chances, that kept Lloyd George's ambition temporarily in check.

Not even the Tory diehards could think of a credible alternative Premier. Lord Salisbury nursed vain hopes that some way might be devised 'to plant out Asquith without superseding him (which is impossible) and at the same time to get things into the hands of the younger men of the front benches – I mean comparatively younger'. Writing on the 19th to his brother, Lord Robert Cecil, he proposed to entrust 'the conduct of . . . War business' to a sort of inner cabinet, 'and Asquith would only come in with the rest of the Cabinet to satisfy or reject . . . decisions'. (He was quite sure that 'it would be the former, for they have not got it in them to reject'.) The promulgation of such schemes was not by any means exclusively the pastime of under-employed Unionists. Birrell expressed doubt whether 'a big, loosely constructed Coalition Cabinet will command confidence, and [whether] it will . . . feel any in itself'. It would have been more sensible, he told his under-secretary on the 24th, to 'appoint a *War Committee* of 6 or 8 men – of both parties – & leave the rest of the Cabinet alone to meet once a *fortnight*'.

Asquith, whose overriding concern was political, missed the opportunity to effect any drastic administrative change. Instead he set about forming a Government in which he could achieve what he described to Samuel as a 'balance'. What exactly did this mean? As his fellow-Liberals were predominant in the new regime, it was obviously not a numerical balance that he had in mind. Nor could it have been a balance of power, for the key departments were kept secure in Liberal hands, and scrupulous care was taken to block Bonar Law, a Tariff Reformer, from the Exchequer, the War Office, or the newly created Ministry of Munitions. At one point, the negotiations nearly broke down when Asquith indicated that he would sooner combine the duties of the chancellorship with those of the premiership than allow Bonar Law to assume them. Significantly, however, he raised no objection to the idea of appointing Balfour to the Treasury, and it was Bonar Law who vetoed it by telling Lloyd George that, while the Liberals might regard Balfour 'as one of the Opposition, the latter looked upon him as much more belonging to the Government!' Far from being 'a hastily improvised shuffle of personalities' (as Hazelehurst has argued) or a straightforward attempt at 'preserving the supremacy of the Liberal Party' (as Robert Rhodes James has remonstrated), the allocation of places in the 1915 coalition represented a deliberate effort by Asquith to strike a balance between the intra-party advocates of *laissez-faire* principles and the proponents of more active and far-reaching intervention on the part of the state, to the limit of military and industrial conscription. Balfour belonged to the first contingent, Lloyd George and Churchill to the second. Asquith confidently expected that, with Kitchener's prestige welded to his own, he would be able to tilt the balance as he saw fit.

It was this dominant consideration that determined the distribution of loaves and fishes: the inclusion of certain people, and the

exclusion – or demotion – of others. That, and Asquith's unfailing
instinct for self-preservation. Quite candidly, he admitted to Lord
Stamfordham on the 22nd that 'not in all cases' were individuals
selected on the basis of 'their fitness for office' and that, in fact,
certain ones were chosen because 'they are safer *in* than out of
office!' Harcourt blandly reasoned that, as 'a cook cannot make
omelettes without breaking eggs, so a Prime Minister cannot make a
coalition without breaking colleagues'. Others were less philosophical. 'Of all the detestable features of this detestable business',
Samuel wrote on 26 May to Charles Hobhouse, whom he supplanted
as Postmaster General, 'the replacements of Liberal ministers by
their own colleagues are the worst.' The same day, Runciman contemplated the 'queer unpalatable prospect for those of us who remain
in this mixed company', and consoled Samuel – and himself – that 'at
the worst it cannot last long'. Birrell, who continued undisturbed at
the Irish Office, deprecated the 'twopenny halfpenny coalition', and
confided to Sir Matthew Nathan on 12 June that Asquith 'had
parted (in circumstances which *never* can be reported favourably
upon) with one or two of his closest friends, and he has a Cabinet
composed of warring, uncongenial, and it may be traitorous elements'.

Liberal politicians who enjoyed either Asquith's confidence or
strong support within the party (or preferably both) made the transition from the old Government to the new. The Liberal membership
in the coalition bore a striking resemblance to the rank list ('like a
Tripos at Cambridge') which Asquith had drawn up the previous
February to amuse Miss Stanley: Crewe, Grey, and McKenna had
been assigned top places, followed by Lloyd George, Churchill, and
Kitchener (who 'ought perhaps to be put in a separate class'); then –
in descending order – Harcourt and Simon, Haldane and Runciman,
Samuel, Pease, Beauchamp, Emmott, Lucas, and McKinnon Wood.
Those placed lowest in the 'Tripos' – Wood being an exception – did
not receive office in the coalition.

Asquith's first inclination was to exclude Harcourt, who, he
informed Stamfordham on the 19th, suffered from poor health and
'manages his office well but is of no use in the H. of C. or with regard
to the *War*'. But, by the third of four provisional rosters, Harcourt
was salvaged from the losers' column and assigned the Office of
Works. He was a dependable 'Asquith man' who, moreover, had an
important segment of party opinion behind him. McKenna, whom the
*Scotsman* justly identified as 'the most abused and vilified Minister
of recent days', was raised from the Home Office to the Exchequer.

Fisher congratulated Pamela McKenna 'on our dear Reggie "going up higher" when the intrigue was under weigh for him to "go-out"!' Simon was another Liberal who had been the victim of press attacks, but who survived to take a place – a better one – in the coalition. Runciman's departure, too, had been mistakenly forecast: he stayed on at the Board of Trade. Birrell, another likely casualty, was likewise sustained by personal backing from the Prime Minister, who considered him 'in a class by himself'. Unlike 'some of my pole-axed friends', Birrell confessed to Nathan on the 22nd, he would have been glad to retire; but the appointment to the Irish Office of a lukewarm Home Ruler, much less a Unionist, would have antago-nized the Irish Nationalists. 'My position is odd', he explained. 'They can't touch me. It is not the strength of the garrison, but the invulnerability of the position.' Nevertheless, he knew that 'a Prime Minister making up a new combination is as untrustworthy as a Young Woman making up her mind whether she will have diamonds or rubies in her engagement ring'.

Grey, whose failing eyesight would have given him a good excuse to withdraw, was too valuable for Asquith to dispense with him. So was Crewe, who found suitable accommodation as Lord President of the Council. But Haldane was summarily dropped from the old team. It was said that Asquith bowed to intense pressure from the Union-ists, who made Haldane's exclusion the price for their co-operation. That, however, is a moot point. According to Chamberlain's diary entry for the 17th, it was Asquith who volunteered Haldane's re-moval from the woolsack when he met that day with Bonar Law. The truth of the matter is that, whatever the Unionist attitude, Haldane was eminently expendable. He lacked the resources to strengthen Asquith's position – which, after all, was the object of the exercise – and he could be trusted to go quietly. Rated surprisingly low in the Prime Minister's February 'Tripos', he had clashed over the years with various Cabinet colleagues and was not especially popular among Liberal backbenchers. Vaughan Nash, who was assisting in a secretarial capacity at Number Ten, admitted to Sidney Webb 'that Asquith and other members of the Cabinet found Haldane woolly-headed and troublesome'. As recently as 13 May, in a debate in the Lords on a Bill to amend the Army Act, Haldane had let slip that the Government was prepared, when the need arose, 'to reconsider . . . the voluntary system . . . in the light of the tremendous necessity with which the nation is faced'. At the same time as many Unionists applauded his remarks as a step towards 'the principle of applying compulsion', many Liberal fundamentalists were incensed.

A past advocate of 'efficiency' and a future Labour Lord Chancellor, Haldane did not fit comfortably into Asquith's projected 'balance'.

Neither did Churchill; but he, unlike Haldane, had plenty of nuisance value. It was also said that the Unionists, who resented him as an apostate, demanded his exclusion, but were content to see him shunted to the Duchy of Lancaster, a ministerial back-kitchen. It has been further proposed that, perhaps unfairly, Churchill was saddled with the blame for the misconceived Dardanelles venture. Both factors may have contributed to his fall, but others were vastly more important.

As the unanticipated elevation of McKenna and Simon would testify, Asquith was able to resist Unionist dictation when he was so inclined. His relationship with Churchill had deteriorated markedly since the turn of the year, and he could not afford to ignore the hostility to Churchill that welled within the Liberal ranks. On 19 May Stamfordham transmitted to the King by cypher telegram a statement by Lord Beauchamp that the 'feeling among his colleagues is that [Churchill] is primary cause of trouble and should be first to go instead of others who will lose their seats in Cabinet'. Three days later, the lobby correspondent for *The Times* reported that Liberal M.P.s, 'look[ing] upon Mr Churchill as the author of all their party ills', were 'petitioning their chiefs to exclude [him] from the new Ministry altogether'. Obviously, neither Churchill's Tory antecedents nor his Admiralty policies would have been sufficient to incite such fury. There were other under-currents that merit investigation.

W. M. R. Pringle, a lifelong Asquithian who was then parliamentary private secretary to Runciman, warned Asquith on the 20th that

a number of your supporters have been driven to the conclusion that the present crisis has been brought about by the actions of Mr Churchill. I do not only refer to his differences with Lord Fisher but we believe that he was privy to the intrigue which resulted in the Repington disclosures.

In these circumstances we regard his presence in the Government as a public danger. It is only fair therefore that you should know, before any arrangement is made, that the attitude of a considerable number of members will be determined by this conviction.

On what, besides his own distrust, did Pringle base his assertions?

At the end of April there was a revival of rumours about Churchill's machinations. Buxton, who had been raised to the peerage and packed off to South Africa as Governor-General, heard from Hobhouse that there had been a 'good deal of "inside" trouble caused as you can guess by Winston . . . [who] has been at his old game of intriguing all round'. According to this detailed account, Churchill had combined with Balfour, Lloyd George, and Garvin in an effort to overthrow Asquith and Grey. Unable to recruit Kitchener as an accomplice, they turned against him, hoping to achieve their greater objective by discrediting an equally prominent and far more vulnerable member of the Government. To this end, they enlisted the support of Sir John French, whose rivalry with Kitchener went back to Boer War days. Suspecting the intrigue, Kitchener retaliated with 'a violent attack on Ll. G. . . . in Cabinet' that left most of their colleagues mystified. Hobhouse, yet to obtain 'the key' to events, confessed to mixed feelings: although loyal to Asquith, he was profoundly disturbed by conclusive evidence of Kitchener's ineptitude. 'I gather', he wrote on 30 April to Buxton, 'that the P.M. is alive to what has been going on, but not to the actual details – and is, for him, dissatisfied.'

On 10 June, after the dust had settled, Hobhouse provided Buxton with a second instalment. Churchill and Lloyd George launched 'a joint attack on K. and Grey' at a Cabinet during the first week of May, 'and then W.S.C. went off to France'. On his way back, Churchill spent the weekend of 8–9 May with French at Headquarters. There, he allegedly caballed with Repington, another guest, whose famous dispatch Churchill 'unquestionably inspired'. Hard on its publication, Fisher fortuitously tendered his resignation. 'Then A.J.B. put a pistol at P.M.'s head threatening debates & disclosures at W.O. & Admiralty. The P.M. resists at first, & then (advised by Ll.G. I think, who alone was consulted I know) capitulated . . . It is a disgusting story of weakness and conspiracy.'

Hobhouse's allegations, which presumably were those to which Pringle made oblique reference, did not command universal acceptance: Alexander MacCallum Scott, one of the Liberal M.P.s whom Pringle tried to rouse to action, professed to 'know of no case against Churchill save what is based on the merest gossip & surmise'. Nor has this dramatic account received unanimous support among historians: Hazlehurst has dismissed Hobhouse as 'uninformed and strongly biased', and has vehemently rejected his information as 'patently fragmentary'. There are, however, diverse sources that corroborate Hobhouse's testimony in essence, if not necessarily in detail.

King George, who boasted a network of well-placed advisers, wrote with relief to the Queen from his railway carriage on the 19th that Churchill, 'the real danger', would be ejected from the

Admiralty for 'intriguing with French against K.' Arnold Bennett, whose weekly chores included a column of political commentary for the *Daily News*, recorded in his journal on the 21st that he had 'learnt a lot' from McKenna: 'Crisis made by Repington's article in *The Times*. Churchill with French at same time as Repington. Rep's article "arranged".' ('It will be noticed that Bennett did not say that Repington and Churchill *met* at French's headquarters, merely that they were there at the same time', Hazlehurst has quibbled. 'Nor did Bennett say *by whom* Repington's article was arranged.' But Bennett, after all, was jotting an entry in his diary, not preparing a legal brief.) In addition, French acknowledged in his diary on the 15th that 'there was trouble about Repington's presence at my headquarters', and, three days later, that he had received a sharp rebuke from Kitchener. And Haig caught wind of 'an organised conspiracy . . . against Kitchener . . . [in which] Sir J. French's personal staff are mixed up'.

Margot Asquith lent further weight to the Hobhouse disclosure: 'Our wonderful Cabinet', she wrote to Haldane on the 18th, has been 'smashed! . . . Practically by the man whom I always said *would* smash it – Winston.' True, eight days later she was rhapsodizing about Lloyd George, who 'has the *sweetest* nature in the *world*'. But Margot flitted from subject to subject, and made it a practice to entertain one acrimony at a time. Finally, on the 17th, Gwynne of the *Morning Post* advised Maxse of the *National Review* that Churchill and Lloyd George, brushed aside by Bonar Law, who 'did not like the thing from the beginning and would have nothing to do with it', had entered into collusion with Balfour. Perhaps, as Hazlehurst has suggested, their objective was nothing more discreditable than to promote 'co-operation between Liberals and Conservatives'. We cannot pretend to know for certain.

Whether or not one credits Hobhouse's interpretation, the fact remains that there was a widespread suspicion that clandestine forces were at work. The official explanation, that the fall of the Liberal ministry had been precipitated by the clash of personalities at the Admiralty, failed to carry conviction. It is possible, of course, to conclude that contemporaries, their nerves on edge, looked for hidden explanations where none existed. Usually, however, there is no smoke without fire. And, in any case, what people believe is often as important a historical determinant as what may or may not have occurred.

Liberal opinion, which Asquith attempted to conciliate with a twenty-minute exhortation, *ex post facto*, remained baffled and aggrieved. 'Had the Prime Minister waited,' Massingham wrote in the *Nation* on the 29th, 'the gust of poison gas which threatened Lord Kitchener would have been swept down the wind, the personal trouble at the Admiralty settled to the national satisfaction by the retention of Lord Fisher and the dismissal of Mr Churchill, and a deficient organization of warlike supplies changed and extended.' But, this time, 'Wait and see' had not suited Asquith's purpose. Instead, a general reconstruction promised an easy solution to his immediate problem. With the leading Unionists affixed to the Government, his potential critics would be effectively muzzled. The King was pleased to anticipate on the 19th that 'the Prime Minister is going to have a National Govt., only by that means can we get rid of Churchill from Admiralty'. Three days later, in a letter to Gwynne, Lord Derby angrily put down the whole affair to the fact that 'Asquith was afraid of sacking Winston'. Fisher, hardly a disinterested spectator, recounted to McKenna on that day the 'wonderful story that Winston was cast out by the Prime Minister from the Cabinet and brought back into it by Balfour'. On the 23rd, in a conversation with Riddell, Lloyd George professed to have 'fought' to get Churchill a more glittering prize, perhaps the viceroyalty of India, and he hinted that Asquith had been the stumbling block.

Subject to a degree of modification, Asquith knew whom he wished to put in precisely which places. Among the incoming Unionists, Bonar Law went to the Colonial Office, Chamberlain to the India Office, and Balfour to the Admiralty. Lansdowne, as an elder statesman, was made minister without portfolio; and other assignments were dealt to Curzon, Selborne, Carson, and Lord Robert Cecil. The Labour Party was represented by Arthur Henderson at the Board of Education. The Irish Nationalists declined the opportunity to affiliate. Out of a total of twenty-three Cabinet ministers, nine were Unionists, twelve were Liberals, one was Labour, and one (Kitchener) was a non-party man.

Attention focused on the lord chancellorship, which Haldane had been forced to relinquish. From all indications, the Unionists expected it among their trophies, but Asquith was equally determined to deny it to them. His first inclination (according to Margot) was to appoint 'some neutral judge'; then he offered it to Simon, who replied that he preferred 'the sack rather than the wool sack'. Finally, he selected Sir Stanley Buckmaster, the former Solicitor-General. This odd choice inspired speculation that Buckmaster was a stop-gap, who was keeping the woolsack warm for his chief. 'I hear that the arrangement is that Asquith should retire in 2 months and take Buckmaster's place and Ll. G. become Prime Minister', Hewins noted in his diary on 3 June. 'But', as he knew from recent experience, 'political plans often go wrong.'

The War Office was another trouble spot. Lloyd George confided to Riddell on the 19th 'that the P.M. wanted him to become Secretary for War, but that he did not feel disposed to accept the position . . . He said that Mrs L.G. had begged him not to go to the War Office and that Mrs Asquith had done the same.' To his wife, Lloyd George wrote the next day that the 'Tories want me in War Office – *but I will not go.*' And on the 21st he told her that he had definitely 'declined'. Bonar Law was a willing candidate, but Asquith cited 'the impossibility from a party point of view of both the Admiralty and War Office being in Tory hands'. Meanwhile, a public furore had greeted the news that Kitchener was imminently to be replaced. It was decided to allow him to remain, but to divert the responsibility for the supply of munitions to an entirely new department. Bonar Law was eager to head it, and Balfour and Chamberlain urged him to press his claims; but, again, Asquith out-manoeuvred him. Lloyd George became Minister of Munitions, freeing the Exchequer for McKenna, who went there '*temporarily*', Lloyd George stressed to his wife, until 'I place the other business on a sound footing'.

'No-one knows how much I have suffered,' Asquith lamented to Samuel during an interview on the afternoon of the 26th. 'Very gladly indeed would I have gone. No-one has ever made a greater sacrifice than I have.' In order to persuade Samuel to accept demotion to the postmaster-generalship without Cabinet rank, he doubtless found it useful to dwell upon his distress. But his tribulations were real enough. 'It has been a *serious* and *trying* affair for the Prime Minister', Birrell knowingly informed his under-secretary on 12 June. 'He has felt it keenly.' Lady Essex gave first-hand confirmation: after dinner at Downing Street on 20 May, she reported to Lady Cynthia Asquith 'that at last the poor darling really looks tired and worried, and his bridge – always bad – was an eloquent barometer'. But on 8 June, when Lady Cynthia came to lunch at Number Ten, she found her father-in-law 'looking quite restored and serene again'.

It had been a trial of strength for Asquith, and he had proved his vigour. His place at the top was secure for the foreseeable future, and he had adeptly assembled his team in such a way as to afford him the 'balance' he desired: McKenna, a trusted follower, provided a counter-weight to Lloyd George; Runciman and Simon could be expected to cancel out Long and Selborne; Bonar Law and Chamberlain were sidetracked into imperial affairs; Balfour, Curzon, and Cecil were adjudged to be reasonable men; and Churchill was well out of harm's way.

The question of compulsion was uppermost in every mind. On 19 May, presented with the *fait accompli* of coalition, Runciman expressed grave misgivings to McKenna: 'I feel that we must first know with whom we are asked to associate, and then what demands were made by or assurances given on *policy* to Bonar and his colleagues; in particular if they were told that we had an open mind on compulsory service or taxation or trade policy.' He need not have worried. Lord Willoughby de Broke, one of the hard-line Tories, wrote angrily to Maxse after a Carlton Club caucus on 5 June: 'Nobody could tell me that our leaders had extracted any pledge from Asquith as the price of surrendering their independence beyond asking for a certain number of seats in the Cabinet.' Bonar Law, as he admitted in private conversation and later in public debate, had entertained the vague expectation that a coalition ministry would tackle precisely those questions which neither party could manage single-handedly. Asquith, on the other hand, was confident that coalition would enable him to hold such decisions at bay, perhaps indefinitely.

Among Liberals, Massingham stated in the *Nation* on 22 May, conscription was 'the all-dominating anxiety'. At that early date, he could not 'count more than four members of the new Cabinet (if Mr Churchill is to be one of them) who are ardent for it, and I note some strong opponents, including Mr Henderson'. The outcome, he grimly anticipated, would depend on 'Mr Facing-both-ways [who] will be strongly represented, and he is not the kind of gentleman who stands fast when an issue emerges just transcending the average party problem'. Asquith's task, it soon became clear, was to keep 'Mr Facing-both-ways' on the fence, and he relied on Kitchener to help him do it.

The lines of battle were quickly drawn. 'We are much worried about compulsory service', Montagu (now financial secretary to the Treasury) wrote to Venetia Stanley (now his fiancée) on 27 May. 'It looks as if L.G. may bring about the fall of the Govt. and I suspect the P.M. is worried.' Through the spring and summer months, the Northcliffe press waged a relentless campaign for military conscription; it received new impetus on 20 August from a manifesto, signed by Lord Milner as chairman of the council of the National Service League, demanding 'not merely National Service for home defence, but universal and compulsory military service for the duration of the war'. On 18 August Margot Asquith warned Kitchener of a plot to force the issue, and she implored him to stand by 'Henry, Grey, Crewe, Arthur Balfour, McKenna and Runciman' in order to 'beat Curzon, F. E. Smith, Winston and Ll. George'. A week later, Runciman described to his wife 'concerted measures to confound the conscriptionists' which he and Simon were taking. They received unsolicited assistance from the King who, after a dinner at Windsor on the 28th, took Milner 'aside and explained at length his views on National Service, which amounted in short to a laudation of Asquith and Kitchener and a strong expression of opinion against the agitation . . .' But neither Milner nor his allies inside and outside the Cabinet were deterred.

'When the new Government was formed,' Churchill recalled in a memorandum to his colleagues on 6 October, 'the belief was widely held that some form of national service would be introduced. More than $4\frac{1}{2}$ months have passed and the Cabinet has never yet ventured to discuss the subject.' At a Cabinet six days later, Kitchener affirmed his support of the voluntary system in the face of opposition from Churchill, Lloyd George, Lansdowne, Curzon, and Long. Margot appealed to Hankey on the 15th to 'be brave & go & see Balfour', who seemed to be weakening. And, on the 17th, her husband addressed a 'most secret' letter to Kitchener:

We are (as you realise) in a most critical situation. You and I have since the war began worked in daily intimacy and unbroken confidence. And you know well that in every exigent crisis, I have given you – as you have given me – loyal and unstinting support. I should like you to realise that what is now going on is being engineered by men (Curzon & Ll. George and some others) whose real objective is to oust you. They know well that I give no countenance to their projects and consequently they have conceived the idea of using you against me . . . So long as you and I stand together, we carry the whole country with us. Otherwise, the Deluge! Cannot you say that, while you aim at and would like to obtain 70 Divisions, the thing should be done gradually and with general consent, and that if you can get under the voluntary system (say) 750,000 men by March 31st – without prejudice, should things point that way, to further accretions, you would be satisfied? . . . It is essential that you and I should stand together and that the intrigue which has for its main object both to divide and discredit us both, should be frustrated.

As much in style as in tone, it was an unusual letter for Asquith; but his precious 'balance' was threatening to dissolve, and his own authority with it. He knew of persistent attempts to replace him with Lloyd George, with whom his relations (according to C. P.

Scott's diary entry for 3 September) had become 'very strained'. Scott had interviewed Simon and Henderson, 'both keen against compulsion and full of suspicion and anger against Lloyd George', from whom he learned, among other things, 'that the first which the Prime Minister had heard of Lloyd George's conscription movement was from Bonar Law, who had gone to the Prime Minister and told him he thought it was his duty, if he didn't know, to inform him'. Professing an open mind on the subject, Scott 'put it to Henderson whether organized labour would be irreconcilably opposed to compulsion', and Henderson replied: 'No. He thought that if the Cabinet were unanimous in supporting it and Kitchener recommended it, the workmen would accept it.' But the Cabinet, Scott determined from his meetings, were 'acutely divided'. On 12 October Carson resigned the attorney-generalship as a protest against Kitchener's incompetence. Churchill, after a barrage of memoranda, followed suit: he submitted his resignation on the 30th, but – at Asquith's request – did not make it final until 11 November.

All the while, Asquith was working to avert a more fundamental split. On 5 October he appointed Derby, an avowed conscriptionist, the Director-General of Recruiting with the special brief to propose an alternative to compulsion. It was an astute tactical move which, as Martin Gilbert has recognized, 'completely undermined the position adopted by those who were trying to use Kitchener's faith in voluntary recruiting as a means of ousting him'. Promulgated on the 15th, the Derby scheme provided that, if a sufficient number of eligible men between the ages of eighteen and forty-one came forth to 'attest' their willingness eventually to serve, there would be no conceivable reason to resort to compulsion. Both sides were left to draw antithetical conclusions: the apostles of Liberal individualism, with the exception of ten adamant backbenchers, approved the scheme in the belief that traditional methods would prove their efficacy; their antagonists, who favoured tighter controls, accepted it as the thin end of the compulsionist wedge. For the time being, exactly as Asquith intended, everyone was obliged to 'Wait and see'.

Asquith also acted discreetly to contend with the problem of Kitchener. He told Hankey, who quoted him in his diary on 1 November, 'that the Cabinet were unanimous that Lord K ought to leave War Office, principal reason being that he will not tell them the whole truth'. Not surprisingly, Kitchener took umbrage at the suggestion that he should go off to the Near East as commander-in-chief of all British forces outside France. But he agreed to undertake a fact-finding mission to the Mediterranean. This, Asquith advised

Lloyd George on 3 November, avoided 'the immediate supersession of K as War Minister, while attaining the same result'. In Kitchener's extended absence, Asquith substituted at the War Office and pried into official files which Kitchener had placed off limits to his civilian colleagues. This informal transfer of power seemed to appease Lloyd George, who had said to Bonar Law (as the latter recapitulated) 'that you were satisfied that nothing but disaster lay ahead of us as long as Lord K was War Secretary & that you were going to write to the P.M. that you could not continue to share the responsibility for the continuance of the present arrangement'. Asquith knew that the Government could withstand the loss of Carson and Churchill, but that Lloyd George's departure would be fatal. '. . . I am confident that in the course of the next month I can . . . come to a complete understanding with you on all the important problems which are connected with the design, fabrication & supply of munitions', he promised Lloyd George in his letter of 3 November. 'This is for yourself alone', he added in an emotional postscript. 'I have not said anything to any of our colleagues. But I regard it as of the first moment that in this matter you & I shd. act together.'

Lloyd George reposed no great confidence in his chief, whom he derided to Scott at the beginning of November as 'a soft-nosed torpedo'. He acknowledged, however, that Asquith 'had practically conceded his point and would say', in a public address on the 2nd, 'that if the present recruiting campaign failed "other measures" would have to be taken'. Scott 'gathered that this would be a pretty vague announcement', and so it was. Nevertheless, under the circumstances, it qualified as an important breakthrough.

Throughout these difficult weeks, Asquith conducted much of this business from his sickbed. On 19 October he fell suddenly and seriously ill, and slept for thirty-six hours. 'I never got such a fright in my life', Margot wrote on the 26th to Lady Islington. 'I thought Henry was *absolutely done*. I think he thought so too.' The doctor, she revealed, had diagnosed that 'overwork, hot rooms and no sort of exercise had gripped his liver and driven bad blood all over him'. Although she later insisted that 'Henry is as indifferent to the Press as St Paul's Cathedral is to midges', there were also symptoms that the vituperation to which he was incessantly subjected was getting to him.

Crewe deputized in his absence, and matters got out of control. At a stormy Cabinet on 21 October, Grey was severely criticized 'for offering Cyprus to Greece after consultation only with the Prime Minister and Kitchener'. This, Crewe informed the King, 'led on without any pre-arranged scheme to a discussion of the conduct of war business and the working of the War Council'. Asquith, who would never have permitted such latitude, was acquainted with 'the unanimous view of the Cabinet that the present system is the opposite of effective only owing to the undue size of the Council'. Accordingly, on 11 November, he announced the creation of a new war council of five members: himself, Lloyd George, McKenna, Bonar Law, and Balfour. Kitchener was not included. The Prime Minister's hand had been forced, and he did not like it.

During his convalescence, Asquith sequestered himself at the War Office, where, Margot explained to Rosebery on the 15th, 'his colleagues can't come & jaw to him'. He was sufficiently recovered to attend the Lord Mayor's banquet as guest of honour in early November. As A. G. Gardiner listened to his speech, his 'eye wandered to the statue of Pitt' above the platform, 'and the living voices seemed merged in the great commentary of the past'. Writing in the *Star* as 'Alpha of the Plough', he reflected that Pitt had known 'what it was to have the curs yapping at his heels, slandering his name, impugning his capacity. But he went on his way heedless of the Fat Boys of his day. And in his patient, unfaltering loyalty to the State, and his scorn for the rabble of snarling critics that beset him, Mr Asquith is not unequal to the great example that Pitt has left to the rulers of men.' Like 'A.G.G.', his *alter ego* in the *Daily News*, 'Alpha' went out of his way to pay tribute to Asquith, whom he hoped thereby to bolster against the seemingly ineluctable advance of Lloyd George. In late September, he had been alerted by Vivian Phillipps, a devoted follower of Asquith and later his amanuensis, to the existence of a 'plot' by 'the conscriptionist gang' to remove Asquith, Grey, 'possibly Kitchener and others', and to install Lloyd George in the premiership. So far as Gardiner could tell, Lloyd George neither discouraged this treachery nor even took the trouble to rebuke those who abused Asquith in print.

Whether Gardiner completely believed his own panegyrics is a moot point. Despite his praise for Asquith's self-control, he would have been glad had Asquith shown a little less dignity and a little more defiance. By this time, even the most fervent Asquithians had begun to recoil at the successive indignities to which they were forced to submit. 'There are some of us that would go to hell or any other place of worship for the Prime Minister *himself*', Runciman wrote on 28 October to Gulland (who forwarded a copy to Gardiner), 'but we are not prepared to go in the company of *his* enemies and ours at their bidding.' A few weeks later, walking down the Strand towards

Fleet Street, Gardiner met W. Llewelyn Williams, the Liberal M.P. for Carmarthen, who subsequently recalled 'your woe-begone face ... when you told me – incredulous! – about L.G. and the weakness of Asquith ... That poor weakling of a P.M.!' Williams exclaimed to Gardiner on 29 December. 'It is too pitiful. How can you make an invertebrate stand up?'

Plank by plank, the Liberal edifice was being demolished, and by Liberals themselves. In September McKenna presented his first budget, which contained protectionist duties in the form of surcharges on enumerated 'luxury' imports. Lloyd George, lunching with Scott in mid-November, pointed up the irony: Bonar Law had been barred from the chancellorship because 'we thought ... that he would let us in for tariff reform, ... and now McKenna has given away the whole principle of Free Trade'. Before long, it was McKenna's turn to protest that his Liberal sensibilities were being outraged. On 7 November Asquith conveyed via Chamberlain his approval for the drafting of a Bill based on a compulsory service scheme prepared by Curzon and Amery. At a Cabinet on 28 December, the same day as the war council adopted plans for a major spring offensive, Asquith accepted conscription as a foregone conclusion. 'P.M. dropped on the right side', Lloyd George trumpeted to his wife. 'Compulsion for unmarried men. There may be resignations. Not certain. Simon, Runciman & McKenna threaten – but [I] doubt it.'

Asquith, with good reason, took these threats more seriously. Lady Scott, his latest confidante, returned home that afternoon 'to find the P.M. had been twice ... However, he came again' in his quest 'for wisdom and sympathy'. They had 'a great discussion about conscription', and she found him 'very sad ... How he hates these tussles!' Margot, on her own initiative, tried to dissuade McKenna: 'I cannot believe that you, the most fearless, the most loyal of *all* Henry's colleagues & above all the most intimate & affectionate, are going to desert him because he is in difficulties ... Do you love yr. opinions more than you love him? It makes me weep to think of such a thing ... Do you not see ahead that this skeleton scheme kills conscription?' McKenna saw nothing of the sort. By the next day, he had handed in his resignation, as had Runciman, Simon, and Grey. 'I have always felt', Grey added wearily, 'that I ought to have left the Cabinet when Haldane went in May.' Birrell, without going so far, accepted conscription as 'a disagreeable necessity', yet did not anticipate that he could remain after the others had departed.

Asquith's motives were too transparent for his decision to carry conviction. Playing both ends against the middle, he maintained to his critics on the left that his policy was merely an extension of the Derby scheme, while those on the right were allowed to infer the contrary. 'What a nasty trick Asquith is playing us on the compulsion question', Scott complained on the 30th to L. T. Hobhouse, who contributed leaders to the *Manchester Guardian*. 'It's a duel I believe between him and Lloyd George and he means to dish Lloyd George by accepting compulsion and to prevent successions by making the dose as homeopathic as possible.' Hobhouse took the same view in a letter of encouragement to McKenna: he had been 'often critical of Asquith', he admitted;

I know nothing about him, & am outside all these personal 'interests'. But I have frequently found a difficulty in reconciling his successive statements & actions wh. has, I confess, disposed me to be very watchful of his policy. This last series of incidents is not calculated to alter that disposition . . . I believe this Government will go down [in] history on a par with that of Lord North, even though the country will save itself from final disaster.

Except for Simon, who attended his last Cabinet on the 28th, the anti-conscriptionists were won over by personal blandishment and artful compromise. On the 31st Lady Scott 'got a letter from the P.M. saying that some of the dissentients are going on, and quoting Macbeth, "All our yesterdays have lighted fools the way to dusty death"'. Six days later, Asquith rose in the House to introduce his Military Service Bill. The benches and galleries were packed, and many members appeared symbolically in khaki. He gave, Lloyd George thought, 'an adroit but not very powerful speech for compulsion. Simon', by contrast, delivered 'a very able lawyer's speech' against it. 'The opposition will be but a minority,' Lloyd George confidently predicted to his wife, 'and that not a large altho' [a] very noisy one.'

A forlorn band of Radical, Labour, and Irish members opposed the measure on its first reading; the Irishmen thereafter abstained on the grounds that this was a 'British' matter. Among the thirty-four recalcitrant Liberals was Williams, who did not doubt that '"compulsion of single men" will be used by Ll.G. to justify all-round compulsion later on'. Harold Dore, the lobby correspondent for the *Guardian*, reported to his editor on 15 January that, the previous evening, Simon had 'said in private conversation' to an 'informant (who is quite trustworthy . . .) . . . that the present bill is *intended* for the purpose of industrial coercion', and that 'in the Cabinet there was no pretence of wanting it in order to get men'. In the struggle between 'freedom' and 'control', the latter had won a major battle, if not yet the war.

Privately, the defenders of voluntary recruiting and all that it represented felt grievously betrayed. Publicly, however, they dared not say anything that might further jeopardize Asquith's position. There were not many Liberals, Trevor Wilson has pointed out, who 'could . . . bring themselves to force Asquith from office when the consequence might be even worse than divided government and diluted conscription: the annihilation of the Liberal Party at a "khaki" election, and the accession to office of a Lloyd George-Carson administration capable of much greater inroads on personal liberty.' Gardiner, for one, although he found it strange that the Military Service Bill was prefaced by 'hosannas to the voluntary system' to which it dealt a death-blow, lamely reasoned in the *Daily News* (8 January) that: 'If we are to accept this dangerous innovation in our national life it is better that we should accept it from his [Asquith's] rather than from any other hand . . .' Given time to reconsider, even the stout Williams came to extol the rare qualities of Asquith, whom he described in a letter to the *Manchester Guardian* on 4 December 1916 as 'that brave, patient man, the greatest Englishman of all time'.

Asquith could depend more easily on the loyalty of his disappointed friends than on that of his gratified opponents. His predicament had become, if anything, more acute. Haldane dined at Downing Street early in the new year, and afterwards wrote to his mother that his host 'seems to be tired, and is feeling the strain'. Henderson, as well as both Labour ministers outside the Cabinet, threatened to leave the Government after their National Executive had repudiated the Military Service Bill. After skilfully overcoming this obstacle on 11 January, Asquith presumed that he was 'practically out of the wood'; but, as he told Lady Scott on the evening of the 13th, McKenna thereupon developed second thoughts and, again, 'things could scarcely be worse'. Instead of 'insisting on the pecuniary impossibility of the compulsion bill', the Chancellor was 'adopting the Runciman depletion of industry attitude', much to the consternation of Asquith, who confessed that 'the Dickens is that I so agree with him'.

These differences were ironed out in prolonged and sometimes acrimonious inter-departmental negotiations. 'Asquith is stronger than ever', Churchill bemoaned to Lloyd George on 25 January. Two months later, with Hankey in tow, Asquith embarked for an

Inter-Allied Conference in Paris. He felt sufficiently secure to go on to Rome, where he consulted with Italian officials. A papal audience was an extra bonus. Altogether he was abroad for ten days.

On 25 March, the day of departure, Hankey expressed to his diary misgivings as to whether he should leave London: there was 'a rumour in the wind of a political plot to be got up in his [Asquith's] absence by Lloyd George, Carson and Churchill'. Montagu and Maurice Bonham Carter, Asquith's private secretary and (since November) his son-in-law, implored Hankey 'to stay – though what I can do I don't know'. As a precaution, he 'exposed the whole plot beforehand' to Asquith, who, perhaps for the same reason, insisted that Lloyd George should come along as far as Paris. Hankey reckoned that 'this will keep Ll.G. out of mischief for a day or two, if it be true that he is on mischief bent'.

The conference was hectic, but basically uneventful: Hankey's judgement was 'much froth and little business'. Asquith, however, revelled in the froth, and wrote home to Margot in glowing detail about the 'luxury' of French railway travel. The concluding session was held on the afternoon of the 28th and, that evening, Hankey relaxed at a performance of the Folies Bergères. He returned late to the Hôtel Crillon, where Asquith was waiting up to show him an urgent telegram from Montagu 'to the effect that the conscriptionists were on the war path and I ought to come home instead of going on to Rome with the P.M.'. After due deliberation, Hankey was instructed to reply to Montagu by telegram that 'if we don't have a costly offensive this spring we don't need our men so fast', and that it was therefore possible that the views of 'all parties can be met'.

In the early hours of 7 April, Asquith returned from his travels to confront his restive critics. The previous day, Arthur Lee told his wife of his 'fears that the diabolically clever "Squiff" will probably devise some new "formula" that will avert this crisis, as so many others'. The Prime Minister himself was not half so sure. The situation at Westminster had deteriorated to such an extent that men of conscience, regardless of party label, were filled with disgust. 'There is a cabal every afternoon and a crisis every second day', declared H. E. Duke (later the first Baron Merrivale), the Unionist member for Exeter. 'It is time an end was made to them.' Short of his own resignation, which he seriously contemplated, Asquith could think of no immediate solution.

Along with mounting pressure for compulsory service, there was the overhanging threat of Irish disorders. The Cabinet, badly divided, met on the 14th. According to Hankey's diary, 'Ll. George, who has been sulking for ten days or so and has not attended the War Ctee. on the plea of illness, came . . . in a most furious rage'. Backed by Bonar Law, he refused to accept the report of the military-finance Co-ordination Committee, which had not recommended general compulsion unless it was first endorsed by the Army Council, which was 'bound to "plonk" for it'. Asquith gave way. At a dinner party at Number Ten that evening, he appeared to Clementine Churchill 'quite unconcerned' about the day's events: 'He is like morphia.' Hankey, who saw him the next morning, found him even 'quite cheery'. The crisis still unresolved, Asquith left for a weekend at The Wharf, where the Army Council's predictable decision was forwarded to him that night.

On Monday, the 17th, Asquith was back in town to begin a week of incessant committee and Cabinet meetings. His mood darkened as, one after another, various compromises were rejected. In his opinion, 'the argument ha[d] become purely academic', and the compulsionist clamour was patently manufactured. 'Of course Lloyd George is the villain of the piece', he told Lady Scott on the 18th; 'you know what I think of him.' The following morning, his frock-coat was laid out in readiness for a visit to the Palace, where he expected to tender his resignation that afternoon. Instead a lengthy Cabinet brought a glimmer of hope. Without reconciling their differences, his colleagues agreed that, after the approaching Easter weekend, the House should assemble in a two-day secret session to hear and debate a statement from the Prime Minister.

As yet, Asquith had no idea what he might say. The King gratified him with an assurance 'of my complete confidence in my Prime Minister', and a hundred Liberal M.P.s met to pass unanimously a resolution that 'his continuance at the head of the Government is a national necessity'. These, however welcome, were tokens that could not compensate for a lack of Cabinet solidarity. Henderson came to his rescue on Thursday, the 20th, with a compromise scheme by which married men who had thus far failed to 'attest' would be given additional weeks to volunteer; general compulsion would hang, on the result. With these guidelines, Asquith retired for a 'placid Easter' at The Wharf, where he prepared his speech for the secret session on the 25th.

On Easter Monday, Hankey ('as though I were a "trainer" charged with the duty of bringing "the Bantam" into the ring in the pink of condition') went to fetch him. They left Sutton Courtenay at 10.30 p.m., Asquith being 'very chatty and jolly'. Two hours later, they arrived at Downing Street, where news awaited them of the rebellion in Dublin. With other things on his mind, 'Asquith merely said "Well, that's really something" and went off to bed'.

The next day, Asquith delivered his much-heralded speech. Hankey, who saw him promptly thereafter, described him as 'very flushed' and 'a trifle hesitating' about the effect he had achieved. Although no record was kept of the secret proceedings, one may infer that the House did not respond favourably. On Thursday, the 27th, Long introduced the actual Bill ('very badly', Asquith thought) in open session. Carson ripped it to shreds, and it was hastily withdrawn. Lord Robert Cecil took the view that the time had come 'for the Government to resign or be re-constructed': in a memorandum to the Prime Minister on the 28th, he reasoned that the King would automatically send for Carson, who would be unable to form a ministry, and Asquith could then return triumphant at the head of a full-fledged 'National Government' rather than a motley collection of party representatives. But 'the whole Cabinet', meeting on Saturday morning to weigh alternatives, decided instead to proceed with legislation for immediate compulsion.

Asquith, with Hankey's customary assistance, drafted another speech. He was 'very short', Hankey wrote in his diary, 'and obviously hated the job'. On the afternoon of 2 May, Hankey 'dropped into the House' to watch the performance. The speech itself 'was not a very good one – not so good as the one I gave him', and the atmosphere 'was astonishingly cold. The fact was', he reflected, 'that the people who want compulsory service don't want Asquith, while those who want Asquith don't want compulsory service; so he fell between two stools!' The news from Ireland had stunned the anti-conscriptionists, permitting the substitute Bill to sail through Parliament; on the 25th it received the Royal assent. Asquith could hardly count it as a personal victory.

Stephen Roskill, Hankey's biographer, has provided the definitive assessment of this dismal episode: '. . . For all his qualities Asquith's character was surely flawed by lack of the moral courage to adopt the course in military affairs in which he believed, because of the likely political consequences. And in the end that weakness destroyed both him and the Liberal Party.' On mortgaged principles, Asquith's long premiership was to survive another seven months. It was not a reprieve, only a stay of execution.

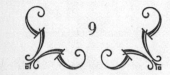

# 9

## FROM DOWNING STREET
## TO
## THE WILDERNESS

Asquith's wartime premiership reached its climax in May 1916, a year after the formation of the first coalition, with the legislation of general compulsion; all that followed was the dénouement. Far from allaying discontent, the halting steps by which he had proceeded to that momentous departure only served to intensify it. The typhoon of parliamentary and press criticism continued to rage and, like Captain MacWhirr, he was 'always facing it'. At this stage, he indeed bore a striking resemblance to Conrad's mariner, who stood transfixed before a barometer whose

fall was of a nature ominously prophetic; but the red face of the man betrayed no sort of inward disturbance. Omens were as nothing to him, and he was unable to discover the message of a prophecy till the fulfilment had brought it home to his very door . . . Having just enough imagination to carry him through each successive day, and no more, he was tranquilly sure of himself.

To some, Asquith's familiar presence at the helm provided a comfort and a reassurance. To others, it became an irresistible provocation. Without conciliating his enemies, he had progressively forfeited the sympathy of many of his friends. On the Sunday after Easter, Margot 'sent over her motor' to Garsington to fetch Philip and Lady Ottoline Morrell for tea at The Wharf. They arrived hoping to confront the Prime Minister on behalf of the conscientious objectors, but he had been called away, presumably to deal with Irish problems. Instead, they spoke to Professor Gilbert Murray, who reported a 'satisfactory talk' with Asquith. Lady Diana Manners (later Lady Diana Cooper) and Violet Bonham Carter were also on hand. The latter, who 'seemed depressed', confided that 'the position of the Government is very precarious'. It was, Lady Ottoline reflected in her diary, a strange entourage: 'All these people seem curiously apart from real life, as if they had no comprehension of what goes on except in their own little Set.'

Transplanted from Bloomsbury to Garsington, Lady Ottoline and her friends saw a good deal of Asquith, whom they regarded with a mixture of disappointment and grudging affection. 'On Sundays', she recalled, he and Violet 'would often come over, sometimes bringing some friends with them, treating us, as I laughingly said at the time, as a convenient and entertaining "side-show" for their guests'. Lytton Strachey, one of the denizens of Garsington, described one such visitation in a letter of 31 May:

. . . As usual, in the middle of the Sunday afternoon torpor, the Prime Minister 'and party' appeared. They *were* a scratch lot: – Lady Robert Cecil, stone deaf and smiling most sweetly at everything she didn't hear, a degraded Lady Meux (wife of Admiral Hedworth) with a paroquet accent, and poor old [Sir Matthew] Nathan, in walrus moustache and an almost Uncle Trevor air of imbecile and louche benignity. I studied the Old Man with extreme vigour; and really he's a corker. He seemed much larger than he did when I last saw him (just two years ago) – a fleshy, sanguine, wine-bibbing medieval-Abbot of a personage – a gluttonous, lecherous, cynical old fellow – ough! . . . I've rarely seen anyone so obviously enjoying life; so obviously, I thought, *out* to enjoy it; almost, really, as if he'd deliberately decided that he *would*, and let all the rest go hang. Cynical, yes. It's hardly possible to doubt it; or perhaps one should say just 'case-hardened'. *Tiens!* One looks at him, and thinks of the war . . . On the whole, one wants to stick a dagger in his ribs . . . and then, as well, one can't help liking him – I suppose because he *does* enjoy himself so much.

Strachey, himself no stranger to hedonism, depicted Asquith as 'a 20th century Silenus'. More commonly and less wittily, the Prime Minister was likened to Nero by others who had the urge 'to stick a dagger in his ribs', and whose weapons were infinitely sharper.

Asquith's handling of the Irish crisis further impaired his credibility. On the one hand, he was assailed for the alleged brutality with which the Dublin uprising was suppressed; on the other, for the Government's failure to have anticipated the rebellion. Birrell's resignation from the Irish secretaryship was accepted 'with infinite regret'. Asquith told the House that 'in the whole of his public life he had not suffered a personal loss which he felt more acutely'. (So much for Haldane.) In the privacy of the Prime Minister's room, the two old friends met for a farewell interview. Afterwards, Birrell could not 'remember what he *said*, but I know he *wept* and stood staring out of the window jingling some half-crowns in his pocket'. That, of course, was an image that Strachey did not see.

To replace Birrell, Asquith turned to Montagu, who (according to Hankey, who was present) 'said he would only take it out of personal loyalty to the P.M. and if he absolutely insisted'. Seeing no practicable alternative, Asquith took on the job himself, and held it until late July, when H. E. Duke was appointed. Besides adding materially to his burdens, his decision obliged him to undertake a tour of Ireland from 11 to 19 May, when his presence was urgently required at Westminster. He found it 'a very curious experience', and an arduous one: 'You never get to the bottom of this most perplexing and damnable country', he wrote to Margot from Dublin on the 16th. As the instrument of his own Irish policy, he inevitably incurred double criticism. The story went about that during an inspection of Irish prisons he had worn a green tie and 'shaken hands with murderers', to whom he reportedly promised to show leniency.

While one side unreasonably accused him of consorting with traitors, loosely defined to include the Irish Nationalist M.P.s, the other attacked him for want of clemency. Sir Roger Casement, smuggled back to his homeland by a German U-boat, was captured, tried, convicted of high treason, and sentenced to death. His infamous diaries, which catalogued his homosexual adventures, were taken into custody with him. Various literary and public figures appealed for his reprieve as much on political as humanitarian grounds. Samuel, the Home Secretary, laid the matter before his Cabinet colleagues, who, after prolonged discussion, took 'the unanimous decision' on 19 July that Casement should be hanged. The Government was indicted not only for its vengeful act, but also for the depths to which it sank in its campaign to discredit the victim's moral character. 'There can be few other examples', Roy Jenkins has expertly reasoned, 'of a Cabinet devoting large parts of four separate meetings to consider an individual sentence – and then arriving at the wrong decision.' As Bernard Shaw had grimly predicted, Casement was to pose a far greater danger as a martyr than he might even have managed as 'a reprieved and probably amnestied man'.

Besides filling in at the Irish Office, which was a thankless task, Asquith also held down the War Office for a period of thirty days. On 4 June Kitchener embarked for a visit to beleaguered Russia. The purpose of the excursion, Asquith gossiped to Lady Scott on the evening of 30 May, was 'to occupy his leisure, incidentally to talk about munitions, finance, etc.', and possibly to escape a drubbing in Parliament. Lloyd George was to have accompanied Kitchener, but changed his plans at the eleventh hour, when he allowed himself to be persuaded to try his hand at an Irish settlement. On Kitchener's second night out, his ship was torpedoed and he was drowned.

The obvious candidate to succeed to the war secretaryship was Lloyd George, but Asquith had cooled to the idea since the previous May. Nor was he keen on appointing Bonar Law to the vacancy. Accustomed to deputizing at the War Office during Kitchener's periodic absences, he informally assumed the duties himself. He may have calculated that, with the passage of time, the way would be cleared for the installation of Derby or Harcourt or some other 'figurehead', who would be more amenable than either of the two front-runners. In any case, this proposed arrangement met with warm support from Lord French and the Army Council, while the King raised no objection.

There was, however, a constitutional obstacle. As Asquith discovered on 20 June, it was an unwritten law that no more than four secretaries of state should sit in the House of Commons. Consequently, it would be necessary either to appoint a peer or to send one of the existing secretaries of state to the Lords. Grey made things easier both for his chief and for himself by volunteering to go to 'another place'. It was not the best solution to have the Foreign Secretary in the upper house; but, under the circumstances, it was a mutually acceptable one.

From 6 June, when Kitchener's death was disclosed, until 7 July, when Lloyd George's transfer was formally announced, Asquith doubled – more literally tripled – as war secretary. It was during his tenure at the War Office that final preparations were made for the battle on the Somme, which began during his final week there. That disaster, therefore, could be held directly against him. Churchill, for one, did not hesitate to do so. 'It was impossible', he proclaimed to the House on 24 July,

that the War Office in time of war should be conducted by the Prime Minister in the odd hours that he could snatch from his own laborious duties, and from adjusting the recurrent crises of the Coalition Government . . . I think it is one of those cases which illustrates the undue importance which is attached at the present time to mere political adjustments as compared with effective, energetic means to prosecute the War.

Doubtless a harsh verdict, it was the sort that Asquith invited by his propensity to collect places.

There is a school of historians that has accepted and propagated the view that Asquith was forcibly evicted from the War Office by an ultimatum from Bonar Law and Lloyd George. Disputing this interpretation, Jenkins has strenuously argued that Asquith meant all along to appoint Lloyd George, but that he delayed in order to mollify the generals and to negotiate satisfactory terms with Lloyd George himself, who 'was playing hard to get'. Nevertheless, the fact remains that he did delay, and his prestige suffered accordingly. For what it was worth, Margot was adamantly opposed to Lloyd George's candidacy: 'We are out,' she declared in her diary on the day that the appointment was made; 'it is only a question of time when we shall have to leave Downing Street.' While it is unlikely that her husband shared her presentiment, he clearly accepted the solution with greater resignation than enthusiasm. 'I took farewell of the War Office this evening', he wrote to his successor on 6 July, 'with much regret on my side, & I think with corresponding feeling on theirs.' Wishing Lloyd George 'with all my heart all success', he took pains to praise the officials whom Lloyd George had disparaged.

It was a cruel irony that Asquith presided at the War Office during the crucial weeks when the Somme offensive was planned. On 15 September his eldest and most promising son was killed in one of its later phases. Asquith intuited the 'terrible, terrible news' of Raymond's death even before Margot had had the chance to break it to him. 'He put his hands over his face,' she recorded, 'and we walked into an empty room and sat down in silence.' It was, as his official biographers (one of them Raymond's brother) put it, 'a maiming blow' from which he recovered slowly. 'Whatever pride I had in the past', he wrote despondently five days after the tragedy, 'and whatever hope I had for the far future – by much the largest part of both was invested in him. Now all that is gone.'

Mourning kept him from several sittings of the Cabinet. Then, on 11 October, he 'braced [him]self up' to make 'a trying and difficult speech' in the Commons. To his relief, 'I got on better than I expected as everyone was very kind and sympathetic'. The solicitude was more apparent than real. On the same day, Gwynne of the *Morning Post* sent warning of 'a sort of plot whose ramifications I am not altogether able to trace'. As he described it to Asquith – and, with greater elaboration, to General Rawlinson – Lloyd George, Churchill, Sir F. E. Smith (now Attorney-General), and French were 'all working hand in hand though with different objects': the first, Gwynne perceived, was 'merely trying to get the Army in the hollow of his hand, and be able to order it about as he did the Ministry of Munitions. The others want to get rid of D. H[aig], but do not have any anxiety about the outcome.'

The self-appointed guardian of military interests against civilian encroachment, Gwynne had momentarily discovered hidden virtues in the Prime Minister. The strains of wartime produced other, equally incongruous alliances. As early as December 1915, Lord Mersey, the eminent jurist, had learned of 'a meeting' at which Lords Loreburn, Milner, St Aldwyn, Midleton, 'and others' had assembled 'to devise means for displacing the ministry or at all events Asquith, Grey and *Lloyd George*'. The following May, Hankey transmitted word of an intrigue masterminded by Leo Amery, 'the very soul of the Unionist War Committee', whose principal accomplices were Milner, Carson, and Geoffrey Robinson of *The Times*. Along with Waldorf Astor, who provided hospitality, these men formed the nucleus of a 'Monday night cabal' which, by autumn, counted Lloyd George among its regulars.

Such clandestine activity worried Asquith far less than did the possibility of a more direct threat to his waning authority. In particular, he kept a nervous watch on Lloyd George, whose virtual prisoner he had become. In the aftermath of the conscription crisis, Lloyd George had reminded C. P. Scott that he reserved the right 'to resign on the conduct of the war'. Throughout the summer and autumn the probability increased. Although he shared responsibility for the formulation of Cabinet policy, he was openly critical of it in his public speeches. Bonar Law noted the paradox that, 'at the same time', Lloyd George was 'the right hand man to the Prime Minister and', to all intents and purposes, 'the leader of the Opposition' as well.

Lloyd George's 'Eastern' strategy pitted him against the professional soldiers, who were 'Westerners' and who moreover bridled at his unorthodox administrative methods. His call for the conscription of munitions workers and for the extension of the compulsory principle to Ireland brought him into conflict with his fellow-ministers. Asquith tried to minimize these differences so as to preserve a semblance of unity. After all, Lloyd George was not the only one whose wishes had to be taken into account, and Asquith could not appease him without incurring protest from other quarters. On 30 October he wrote to Lloyd George, 'under stress, as I have had today something like 6 threatened resignations from colleagues, who are wanting in the sense of proportion'. When ground had to be given, it was usually Asquith himself who gave it. As he informed the King on 6 November, 'The Cabinet resolved (the Prime Minister dissenting) to introduce a Bill to compel the enlistment of un-naturalised aliens of allied countries (mostly Russian Jews) giving them at the same time the option to emigrate . . .'

By this time, the offensive on the Somme stood revealed as a staggering fiasco, and on every front the war was going badly. During the first week of November, there were no fewer than five 'really dreadful' meetings of the war committee, according to Hankey, who was left feeling like 'a squeezed lemon'. The toll on Asquith was even greater. On the evening of the 8th, he 'reviewed his eleven years in office', and told Lady Scott that he was 'heartily sick of it. It was all very well when one had five years in and five years out, taking stock and having no responsibilities, and talking only occasionally and when one liked. That was a gentlemanly life. But eleven years with no spell off was too much.' Lady Scott 'reminded him that five or six years ago he had said to me, "I'm like a rat in a trap." He said, "Yes, and that was before the war."' She then 'asked him point-blank whether he would really like to go'. Asquith gave the equivocal reply 'that he could imagine that, if he kept his faculties and his activity, it might be an irritation to want to do things and to be powerless to do them'. In other words, although 'heartily sick', he was not yet ready to abandon his position.

A few hours earlier, a vote in the Commons had implicitly demonstrated the weakness of that position. On the relatively minor issue of whether enemy property confiscated in Nigeria should be placed on open sale, Carson led sixty-four Unionists into the Opposition lobby. Far from being a dispute over commercial procedure, it was a premeditated assault on Bonar Law, who was resented as Asquith's buttress. The division lists have been carefully scrutinized by Barry McGill, who has evaluated the significance of the Unionist split:

Among the Carsonites were all the officers of the Unionist War Committee, many who had voted against parliamentary salaries in April, and such malcontents as Hewins and Joynson-Hicks . . . In addition to the Unionists, there were a dozen Liberals and forty-one Irish Nationalists. The defecting Liberals included four officers of the Liberal War Committee and Churchill . . . The intention of these defecting Liberals was the same as Carson's. By toppling Bonar Law from the Unionist leadership, they hoped to oust Asquith's government.

Significantly, Lloyd George abstained from the vote. It was his turn to 'Wait and see'.

The storm signals had been hoisted, and Bonar Law could not afford to ignore them. Anxious to save his own political skin, he showed no particular concern for Asquith's. Yet it was still not obvious how he might best serve his personal and party interests. Six days after the Carsonite insurrection, he sought advice from his close friend, Sir Max Aitken (soon to be exalted as Lord Beaverbrook). Whereas the existing arrangement had its distinct disadvantages, he admitted, 'least of all did it appear that to satisfy Lloyd George's aspirations was to supply the remedy'. In fact, Beaverbrook subsequently disclosed, 'Bonar Law had formed the opinion that in matters of office and power Lloyd George was a self-seeker and a man who considered no interests but his own'. Always glad to pull wires, Aitken soon helped to effect a reconciliation.

While Bonar Law pondered his dilemma, Asquith crossed the Channel on the 14th to attend an allied conference. Lloyd George and Hankey were among his companions in what the latter described as 'an extraordinarily harmonious and almost hilarious party which travelled that day to Paris'. Asquith availed himself of Lloyd George's assistance in drafting a speech for delivery to the conference, but expunged Lloyd George's sarcastic references to military personnel. Lloyd George accepted the cuts with resignation. What he could not abide, however, was the cloud of pessimism, even defeatism, that hung over the entire Paris proceedings. After the final session, when Asquith had 'retired to his usual rest before dinner', he and Hankey took a leisurely stroll through the Paris streets. Lloyd George indicated his intention to withdraw from the Government, and Hankey tried to dissuade him. 'You ought to insist on a small War Committee being set up for the day-to-day conduct of the War, with full powers,' he suggested. 'It must be independent of the Cabinet. It must keep in close touch with the P.M., but the Committee ought to be in continuous session, and the P.M., as Head of the Government, could not manage that.' Lloyd George, who had been thinking along similar lines, listened attentively. He was undoubtedly taken with Hankey's stipulation that 'the Chairman must be a man of unimpaired energy and great driving power.' Who could rival him in that respect? Certainly not the old man who, by his telling, lay fast asleep back at the Hôtel Crillon. Without delay, Lloyd George wired Aitken to fix an interview with Bonar Law.

The Unionist leader was predisposed to caution, all the more when he discovered the extent of collusion between Lloyd George and Carson. Gradually, with prodding from Aitken, he lent an approbatory ear to Lloyd George's scheme for a reconstituted war council with himself in the chair. On Monday evening, 20 November, he dined at the Hyde Park Hotel with Lloyd George, Carson, and Aitken. 'Still hostile to Lloyd George', he surmised that 'his plans boiled down to one simple proposal to put Asquith out and to put himself in.' Nothing less would have satisfied Carson, who had vowed never again to serve under Asquith. On Tuesday the so-called 'Triumvirate' met at the House, and Bonar Law and Lloyd George returned on their own to the Hyde Park Hotel for dinner. Further deliberations followed, and by the weekend the trio were agreed on a strategy. Aitken contributed his journalistic skill to the drafting of a document which Bonar Law brought to Asquith on Saturday, the 25th. His bags packed for his customary weekend at The Wharf, Asquith promised to give the 'paper note' his thoughtful consideration, implying to Bonar Law that he was not 'altogether opposed to the idea' put before him. Evidently, he did not yet fully appreciate the implications. His reply, dated the 25th and addressed to Bonar Law 'for your eyes alone', was received two days later. Courteous to a fault, Asquith professed gratitude for Bonar Law's 'frankness and loyalty' and even 'the greatest personal regard' for Carson. 'As to Mr Lloyd George', he went on, 'you know as well as I do both his qualities and his defects . . . There is one construction, and only one, that could be put on the new arrangement – that it has been engineered by him with the purpose, not perhaps at the moment, but as soon as a fitting pretext could be found, of his displacing me.' In conclusion, Asquith rejected 'the plan' as one which 'could not, in my opinion, be carried out without fatally impairing the confidence of loyal and valued colleagues, and undermining my own authority'.

Exactly as intended, Asquith's response divided the would-be triumvirs, who were left unsure of the next step to take. Behind the scenes, Carson worked to intensify the newspaper campaign against the Prime Minister, whom Northcliffe's *Daily Mail* picturesquely likened to a limpet. Lloyd George retreated into a sullen quiescence, while Bonar Law belatedly summoned his Unionist colleagues for consultation. Assembled on the afternoon of the 30th, they heard for the first time about the pact between Lloyd George and Carson, and about the terms which Bonar Law had communicated to Asquith. According to Chamberlain, writing to Lord Chelmsford on 8 December, Bonar Law gave the impression that he remained in favour of Asquith's retention of the premiership. But Lord Robert Cecil, who saw matters more clearly, rebuked him for 'dragging the Conservative Party at the coat-tails of Lloyd George'. It was the first of many times that this charge was to be levelled.

Meanwhile, Asquith was not inactive on his own behalf. On the 28th, he sent for Milner, one of his most implacable critics, and offered him a place as 'Food Dictator' in the tottering ministry. The next day, implored by Margot to 'shake Henry up', Hankey engaged him in a long discussion on the relative merits of the Lloyd George proposals. From all indications, the Prime Minister was edging towards a compromise. On the 30th, Hankey next recorded, there was 'an epoch making meeting' of the war committee at which 'several of us combined to make the P.M. take hold of the Committee and get decisions taken promptly'. At this critical juncture, Runciman interposed a formal request that Hankey, as secretary, should enter into the official 'record the fact that I was not present when the decision on industrial conscription or compulsory service was discussed' and that 'as at present advised I am unable to concur'. Six months later, Hankey minuted the opinion that, 'though denied by Mr Asquith, . . . this letter precipitated the crisis which ended in the fall of the Asquith Government' in that it 'exasperated Lloyd George into taking action'. In any case, Lloyd George had been poised to strike, and one excuse was as good as another.

Harold Wilson, who incidentally recalls Asquith by his dextrous juggling of great issues and Cabinet factions, has observed that a week in politics is a long time. Perhaps no political week was ever longer than the one that began on 1 December 1916. Certainly none has been more exhaustively chronicled, day by day, hour by hour. Consequently there is no need here to present more than an outline of events which have been dissected time and again.

Early on the afternoon of the 1st, when the war committee met, Hankey 'noticed that the P.M. was rather piano'. The fall of

Rumania, which was not unexpected, surely weighed less heavily on him than did an ultimatum delivered that morning by Lloyd George, who 'practically threaten[ed] to resign unless the War Ctee. was reconstructed with himself as Chairman'. Lloyd George further demanded that Carson should replace Balfour at the Admiralty. All expectations to the contrary, Asquith proved moderately receptive. 'Though I do not altogether share your dark estimate & forecast of the situation, actual and perspective [*sic*]', he replied later that day, 'I am in complete agreement that we have reached a critical situation in the war, and that our own methods of procedure, with the experience which we have gained during the last few months, call for re-consideration and revision.' Accepting in principle the formula for a select and semi-autonomous war committee, he nevertheless refused to contemplate anyone but himself at its head. After all, he reasoned to Hankey, 'if he is not fit to run the War Ctee. he is not fit to be Prime Minister'.

Not surprisingly, Lloyd George considered 'entirely unsatisfactory' the counter-proposals which Asquith submitted to him. Thereupon, as Hankey noted in his diary, 'the political crisis became very serious. The morning papers' on Saturday, the 2nd, 'contained a deal of information obviously inspired by Ll. George.' Hankey promulgated a possible solution: 'The obvious compromise is for the P.M. to retain the Presidency of the War Ctee. with Ll. George as chairman, and to give Ll. G. a fairly free run for his money.' But Asquith would not hear of it. After lunch, he left Downing Street for Walmer Castle. 'It was very typical of him', Hankey thought, 'that in the middle of this tremendous crisis he should go away for the week-end. Typical both of his qualities and of his defects; of his extraordinary composure and of his easy going habits.'

Margot, however, was more jittery. At her bidding, Hankey went to sound out Bonar Law, who had seen Lloyd George the previous evening. He learned that a meeting of Unionist ministers had been called for Sunday, and deduced that Bonar Law's primary consideration was to avoid the appearance of acting as the factotum of Lloyd George. Bonar Law volunteered to postpone the Unionist meeting if Lloyd George would hold back his proffered resignation 'and so give the unfortunate Prime Minister time to think it out'. Lord Reading, who kept a foot in both camps, prevailed upon Lloyd George to delay for twenty-four hours; but that 'was not enough' for Bonar Law, who went ahead with his plans. Bonham Carter was hurriedly dispatched to bring his father-in-law back from Walmer. At the end of a hectic day, Hankey 'walked home' with Reading, who agreed that the crisis is intolerable. There is really very little between them. Everyone agrees that the methods of the War Ctee. call for reform. Everyone agrees that the P.M. possesses the best judgement. The only thing is that Ll. George and Bonar Law insist that the former and not the P.M. must be the man to win the war . . . The irony of it all is that if there is a split, as seems almost inevitable, Ll. G. will stump the country with hysterical speeches, and give away an enormous lot to the enemy, encouraging him beyond measure, and every sort of national unity will be broken . . . It is Ll. G.'s publicity and press methods which are so intolerable. Meanwhile the P.M., as usual in the moment of crisis, is cheery and imperturbable.

On Sunday morning, the 3rd, the Unionist ministers met and passed a convoluted resolution of no-confidence in Asquith. According to Hankey, 'no-one seemed to regard it as more than a bluff to force the P.M. to give Lloyd George the chairmanship of the War Ctee.' That, to be sure, was how Asquith himself regarded it. To Pamela McKenna, he grumbled that he had been 'forced back' to London ('as you know my Sabbaths are rarely spent in this most damnable town') in order to 'grapple with a "Crisis" – this time with a very big *C*'. Thereafter, he had 'spent much of the afternoon in colloguing with Messrs Ll. George & Bonar Law, & one or two minor worthies', with the 'result' that the '"Crisis" shows every sign of following its many predecessors to an early & unhonoured grave'. In the process of laying it to rest, he had reluctantly assented to the joint demands of Lloyd George and Bonar Law. He would continue undisturbed as premier, but without a seat on the smaller war committee over which Lloyd George would preside. It was further established that, so as to facilitate the necessary exchange of offices, 'the Cabinet should resign and the Prime Minister should reconstruct on the basis of the Lloyd George plan'. Hankey, who narrated these decisions, soundly disapproved. 'The new War Ctee. is really ridiculous', he wrote. 'It is a mere political expedient of the most transparent kind to tide over a difficult crisis.'

More quickly than Hankey would have dared to anticipate, the scheme came to grief. On Monday morning, the 4th, *The Times* featured a leader that was guaranteed to infuriate Asquith by its blunt pronouncement that the new body was to be 'fully charged with the supreme direction of the war', and that he was disqualified from membership 'on the ground of temperament'. Hankey regarded it as 'intolerable, one-sided, and obviously inspired' by Lloyd George who, it was known, had received Northcliffe at the War Office the previous evening. Leaping to the same conclusion, hardly an unreasonable one under the circumstances, Asquith reversed himself and repudiated the terms by which, as he informed Lloyd George, he would have been 'relegated to the position of an irresponsible spectator of the War'. Lloyd George disclaimed responsibility for the leader in *The Times*, which, it turned out, had been instigated by Carson. But the damage was done.

Invited to stay to lunch at Number Ten on Monday, Hankey found Asquith 'outwardly cheerful but ... noticed his hand trembled a bit, and no wonder ... The P.M. talked in half jest about where he would go for his "holiday" on Wednesday, if he was out of office.' That afternoon, Hankey 'talked out the situation very fully' with Lord Stamfordham, who, like his royal master, seemed 'intensely indignant with Ll. G.'. Stamfordham inclined to the view that Asquith ought to throw down the gauntlet by resigning, 'the idea being that Bonar Law would be asked to form a Govt. and would fail; then Ll. G. would try and would fail; so that the P.M. would come back stronger than ever, and Ll. G. would be discredited'. Later on, Hankey again saw Asquith, who had since taken counsel from Grey, McKenna, and Runciman, and who 'had decided either to resign himself or to call for Lloyd George's resignation'. Taking for granted that the ministerial Unionists would back him up, Asquith 'seem[ed] to think that Lloyd George and Carson have compounded with the Irish, and that if Ll. G. cannot get his way about the War Ctee., he will form a hotchpotch Govt. of Carsonite Unionists, Ll. G. liberals, [Irish] Nationalists, and Labour, who will be bribed by several seats in the Cabinet'. It was Asquith's mistaken presumption of official Unionist support that proved his undoing.

How could he have made so fatal a miscalculation, especially in the light of the hostile resolution which the Unionist chiefs had passed on Sunday morning? Henderson, the lone Labour representative in the Cabinet, had tried to disabuse him of his illusion. On 17 April 1917 Henderson recalled to Robert Donald of the *Daily Chronicle* (who, a week later, transmitted 'a brief statement' for Beaverbrook to add to his 'collection') that he had arrived late for a meeting of Liberal ministers on 4 December 1916: 'When he entered Mr Asquith explained briefly what had happened and said that the general opinion seemed to be that Mr Lloyd George would not succeed in getting the Conservatives, except Mr Bonar Law, to join a Government.' Henderson took issue with the supposition, but failed to shake Asquith, who continued to bank on Unionist loyalty. Perhaps Asquith was led astray by ambiguity on the part of Bonar Law (who communicated verbally the gist of the Unionist resolution, but, by his own admission, 'forgot to hand him the actual document'), or by the disingenuousness of Curzon and several others. Perhaps, as some sources later claimed, he was let down by Gulland who, as Liberal Chief Whip, should have acted to mend the breach with Lloyd George. Perhaps, as others have alleged, he was betrayed by McKenna, who played Iago to his Othello. Perhaps, too, his self-esteem made it impossible for him to conceive that his colleagues might carry on without him.

'It would take a combination of Meredith, Browning, & Henry James to give you the story of our change of Govt.', J. A. Spender soon asserted to a correspondent. Despite a veritable outpouring of memoirs, biographies, and monographs, discrepancies persist. 'It is inevitable, I suppose', Chamberlain wrote on 30 June 1931 to Beaverbrook, with whom he traded recollections of the 1916 Cabinet crisis, 'that no two accounts of these events will exactly coincide, even though everyone concerned was acting in good faith and tells the truth to the best of his ability.' Nevertheless, with regard to Asquith's career, the basic facts are easily ascertained.

At seven o'clock on Tuesday evening, the 5th, Asquith tendered his resignation to the King, to whom he explained that 'he had tried to arrange matters with Lloyd George about the War Committee all day, but was unable to. All his colleagues both Liberal and Unionist', he reported, 'urged him to resign as it was the only solution to the difficulty.' There were those like Arthur Lee who suspected 'that "Squiff" only resigned as a tactical move and that he and his friends are moving heaven and earth to make it impossible for either B.L. or L.G. to form a Government'. Beaverbrook later gave currency to this interpretation by conjecturing that Asquith, believing himself to be 'the only and inevitable Prime Minister', had stepped down expressly to inflict on his challengers 'the humiliation of being unable to form a Government'. That, however, is extremely unlikely. The pair of letters which Asquith had received that day from Balfour, who wrote from his sickbed, and his chilly interview that afternoon with the 'three C's' – Curzon, Chamberlain, and Cecil – would have dispelled any lingering doubts of Lloyd George's chances of success. 'His resignation', Trevor Wilson has incisively argued, 'was not a manoeuvre to strengthen his hold on office, but a despairing act of recognition that the process of retreat and surrender could go no farther, and that the time had come to abandon a position from which dignity and authority had already departed.'

What other options were open to him? 'Had he acted resolutely in his own interest he could have clung to the premiership and restored his waning influence', Cameron Hazlehurst has suggested. The second inference does not follow logically from the first: Asquith might have 'clung to the premiership' only by accepting dictation from Lloyd George and thereby further humbling himself. Alternatively, he might have sought a dissolution of Parliament. But, as recently as 17 August, he had remonstrated to the House of Commons that the country would not abide a general election during wartime. In more recent days, Samuel had speculated that Lloyd George would not undertake to form a Government without first obtaining the promise of a dissolution, and Asquith apprehended 'a great disaster'. In the event, Lloyd George made no such request and managed comfortably on the basis of an inherited Parliament.

Following constitutional convention, the King sent directly for Bonar Law, whom he invited to take command. From the Palace, the Unionist leader went to see Lloyd George, and at dinnertime he called on Asquith, whom he asked to serve under him, presumably as Lord Chancellor. Like the title character of Trollope's *The Prime Minister*, Asquith 'did not smile now . . . "I don't think I could do that,"' he might well have replied. '"Caesar could hardly have led a legion under Pompey."' Nor would Asquith countenance the proposal that he should join the others in a Balfour administration.

He did, however, accept an invitation to attend a conference at the Palace the next afternoon. Lloyd George, Bonar Law, Balfour, and Henderson were also present. According to Lloyd George's retrospective testimony, 'we expressed our readiness to serve under Mr Balfour – all of us except Mr Asquith', who 'broke up the conference' by exclaiming in egotistical outrage: 'What is the proposal? That I who have held first place for eight years should be asked to take a secondary position.' This dialogue was not corroborated by Stamfordham, whose lengthy memorandum quoted Asquith as being 'thankful to feel he was a free man'. At the close of a fruitless session, Balfour enumerated the possible alternatives: Asquith could not retain office without the backing of Bonar Law and Lloyd George, which was clearly not forthcoming; Bonar Law, mindful of his parliamentary minority, was not prepared to assume office unless Asquith 'would agree to accept a subordinate place'; last, but not least, Lloyd George might 'endeavour' to form a Government without Asquith, who, having rebuffed Pompey, was not likely to take a commission from Brutus.

A more conscientious party manager than Bonar Law, who usually consulted no one but Aitken, Asquith delayed his final decision until he had the opportunity to solicit the opinions of his faithful Liberal associates. Except for Montagu (who was closest among them to

Lloyd George) and Henderson (who belonged to a separate category), his lieutenants advised him to hold aloof. What difference would it have made had they recommended otherwise? 'My colleagues today were unanimous in thinking – what seems obvious to me – that it is not my duty to join this new Government in a subordinate capacity', Asquith wrote that evening to Pamela McKenna. 'Apart from the personal aspect of the matter, it would never work in practice.'

Asquith revealed his decision in a letter which Curzon collected at six o'clock and delivered to Bonar Law. Within the hour, Bonar Law appeared at the Palace and, having been unable to secure Asquith's adherence, gave up his attempt to construct a ministry. The King, whose antipathy to Lloyd George was well enough known, had no choice but to send for him. It remained to be seen whether Lloyd George could assemble a viable team from the disparate elements at his disposal.

After dinner, Asquith took refuge in his correspondence. He tried to distract himself by 'using up my stock of official paper' in a spate of letters to his various confidantes, each of whom had hastened to console him. 'I am fighting with beasts at Ephesus', he informed Lady Scott. 'Whether, as Browning says, "God is in his heaven" is given to very few to know. Release, or at any rate relief, is a priceless boon, but one would have liked to complete one's task . . .' To Mrs McKenna, he feebly jested that 'we are all likely to be out in the cold next week. We think of living under Violet's roof on Cy's salary, wh. he has just begun to earn at the Ministry of Munitions!' And to Mrs Harrisson, he wrote four days later from Walmer: 'I am glad you are reading the Book of Job; I think I must refresh my memory of it.'

His financial predicament, to which he jocularly alluded, was no laughing matter. Evicted from Downing Street, the Asquiths took shelter at a borrowed address in Belgravia until March, when their own town house was ready to receive them. It was Haldane's considered judgement that they 'would have done better to let or sell 20 Cavendish Square, and move into a smaller house. But', he reminded his mother on 27 January, 'Margot wants many things.' Although they were far from impecunious, it was not easy for Asquith to maintain his wife – and himself – in the style to which they were both accustomed. For that reason, there was recurrent speculation that he would welcome an appointment as Lord Chancellor, which carried, along with its dignity, a salary of £10,000 and an annual pension of half that amount. But, however tempting, the opportunity was resisted.

While Asquith philosophized, Lloyd George scurried to line up support. His major *coup* was to get Balfour to take the Foreign Office, which Curzon had coveted. Churchill, sketching his *Great Contemporaries*, likened Balfour – in his passage 'from one Cabinet to the other, from the Prime Minister who had been his champion to the Prime Minister who had been his most severe critic' – to 'a powerful graceful cat walking delicately and unsoiled across a rather muddy street'. By nightfall on 7 December, Lloyd George was able to submit to the King 'the proposed names of his colleagues'. George V, scanning the list, was satisfied that 'he will have a strong Government'.

Dr Thomas ('Tom') Jones spent that fateful evening at the Reform Club, where 'the whole atmosphere was very electric', and 'the prevailing feeling . . . was against L.G. and pro-Asquith'. Around ten o'clock, the ticker-tape brought word 'that L.G. had been asked to form a government with the cooperation of Bonar Law'. There was considerably less exultation at the Reform, a bastion of Liberalism, than at the Carlton nearby. The new administration was, quite predictably, a preponderantly Tory assemblage. Bonar Law, at long last, realized his ambition to become Chancellor of the Exchequer. He and Lloyd George, together with Curzon, Milner, and Henderson, constituted a five-member War Cabinet. Carson, unexpectedly excluded from this inner circle, nevertheless went, as expected, to the Admiralty. Long was shifted to the Colonial Office and Derby to the War Office. Chamberlain, Cecil, and Smith kept their former places.

With the single exception of the Prime Minister himself, there were no Liberal survivors from the wreckage of the *ancien régime*. In order to obtain a token Liberal presence, Lloyd George had to make do with men who were not so much untried as unknown. Dr Christopher Addison, who had assiduously canvassed Liberal support for Lloyd George, was named Minister of Munitions. H. A. L. Fisher interrupted a distinguished academic career to take charge at the Board of Education. Lord Rhondda (formerly D. A. Thomas) and Sir Albert Stanley (later Lord Ashfield) were tapped to serve, respectively, at the Local Government Board and the Board of Trade.

Churchill and Arthur Lee were among the hopefuls who came away empty-handed: the former (according to Beaverbrook) 'blazed with righteous anger'; the latter retired with a case of influenza. Montagu, who had shuttled back and forth in a desperate attempt to mediate between the two Liberal leaders, was offered a post, and reportedly a good one, but did not feel free to accept. 'I know that you desired nothing better than to continue to work with Asquith', he told Lloyd George on 13 December: 'I know that you know that throughout the war I have tried to promote the mutual confidence which would have assured this, and very nearly succeeded on Sunday week. But you were pulled apart by the fact that you both had friends who disliked and distrusted the other, and they prevailed.' Although a sense of prudence compelled him to stand out, Montagu looked forward to 'an early opportunity of assisting you', and promised that 'I have not the slightest intention of appearing even in tempered opposition to your Government'. The following July, he entered the Cabinet as Secretary of State for India, and his erstwhile associates responded violently by branding him a traitor.

As Montagu's experience would illustrate, there were strong moral pressures brought to bear on any of the Asquithian regulars who might be disposed to traffic with the enemy. On 7 December 1916 Runciman insisted to an interrogator that 'it was untrue that Asquith had suggested that his colleagues should not join Lloyd George; [he] had left them free to do as they chose'. Yet, a year later, Buckmaster verified that 'the Liberal members of the late Government' had decided 'as a body not to serve under George' out of consideration for Asquith, who did not deserve 'to bear alone the reproach of inefficiency in the conduct of the war which was the ground for the movement against him'. This self-denying ordinance could not have mattered half so much as the fact that Lloyd George was not eager to have them.

Public opinion responded to the news of Asquith's supersession with a mixture of bemusement, alarm, and satisfaction. 'Asquith must have had the surprise of his life when he saw the rejoicing in the British and Allied Press over his resignation', Lady Carson gloated to the Lees on 8 December. 'He had expected it could cause an uproar in Europe and a panic in the Allied and neutral Bourses; instead of which the Mark has gone down and the Pound has gone up.' There were others who employed a less material standard. In D. H. Lawrence's novel *Kangaroo*, Richard Somers (whom Stephen Spender has identified as the author's 'fictitious alter ego') walked through the moors and heard a voice saying: 'It is the end of England. It is finished. England will never be England any more.' In real life, the young Harold Macmillan was more torn:

For me – much as I admired Asquith's intellectual sincerity and moral nobility – Lloyd George was the rebel, the revolutionary; and, above all, the man who would get things done. Asquith represented, as it seemed to me, the qualities, but also the faults of the old world.

Above all, he had tolerated too long the mistakes of the High Command.

Yet, as Macmillan was eventually obliged to admit: 'It is true that Lloyd George disappointed me by his general agreement to such battles as Passchendaele and his apparent inability to control the generals in high places.' Perhaps, therefore, Haldane was right when he confided to Edmund Gosse on 7 December that, 'to tell the truth', he did 'not think that the new Govt. will make as much difference, one way or the other, as people think. Only it is very low class', he snobbishly complained. To this, Gladstone's daughter offered an implicit rejoinder. Her father, she recalled in 1924, had once said:

Up to this time, men have been chosen, as a rule, for the Government, by reason of their high character, their honourable estate, birth, and upbringing, and not only for their capacity. But it remains to be proved whether men inferior in position, in birth, and education and culture, men more accustomed to the practical side of life, might not conceivably prove themselves the fittest to govern the country.

The Grand Old Lady of the Liberal Party added: 'Since Christmas, 1916, often have these words come back to me.'

It was inevitable that Asquith and Lloyd George should have been compared and contrasted, invariably at each other's expense. On the day the second coalition was forged, Haldane met Lord Buckmaster in St James's Park, and acknowledged that 'Asquith is a first class head of a deliberative council. He is versed in precedents, acts on principles, and knows how and when to compromise. Lloyd George', on the other hand, 'cares nothing for precedents and knows no principles, but he has fire in his belly and that is what we want.' This conversation, later recalled by Buckmaster to Haldane's official biographer, exemplifies a view which was widely held at the time (as Macmillan's reminiscences would indicate) and which has been handed down to posterity. It became increasingly common to put down Asquith as a pitiably inadequate wartime leader who, whatever his merits during calmer days, ought to have stepped aside gracefully before it ultimately became necessary to topple him.

In outward manner, Lloyd George and Asquith could not have been more dissimilar. And, after December 1916, the dissimilarity constantly emphasized itself. That they had been collaborators long before they were antagonists tended to be forgotten. That they shared many characteristics, successes, and even failings tended to be glossed over. Although different, their talents were not disjunctive; although distant, their personal relations were not discordant. As the 'honoured grey-haired old Premier', Asquith had had the aura of Trollope's Mr Mildmay; and Lloyd George was comparable to Mr Gresham,

on whose shoulders it was thought that the mantle of Mr Mildmay would fall, – to be worn, however, quite otherwise than Mr Mildmay had worn it. For Mr Gresham is a man with no feelings for the past, void of historical association, hardly with memories, – living altogether for the future which he is anxious to fashion anew out of the vigour of his own brain. Whereas, with Mr Mildmay, even his love of reform is an inherited passion from an old-world Liberalism.

Only with the benefit of hindsight does it become obvious that the paths of Lloyd George and Asquith were fated to diverge.

Sixty-four years old and out of office, Asquith was despised in some quarters, adulated in others. While the press attacks did not abate, and indeed soon intensified with the publication of the Dardanelles Report, he was revered by many as 'the last of the Romans', surrounded by predatory Goths. On 8 December the Liberal Party accorded him a resounding vote of confidence. A few days later, the executive committee of the National Liberal Federation, purporting to speak for 'all the Liberal Associations of the country', unanimously passed a resolution in his support. Sir John Brunner, its venerable president, was authorized to convey personal assurances that this resolution 'only faintly represents the warmth of our feelings towards you as our Leader, or the depths of our regret that circumstances have led you to resign the Premiership.' Like innumerable prewar critics, Brunner had come to idealize Asquith as the repository of discarded virtues.

Asquith's official attitude towards the new Government was essentially one of benevolent neutrality. 'He did not cause Lloyd George a tenth of the trouble that Lloyd George, outside, would have caused him', Jenkins has safely guessed. His partisans in Parliament and the press emulated his example, partly out of a genuine concern for national solidarity, and partly to prove themselves more responsible than their blackguardly opponents. He encouraged them to show restraint and, if possible, generosity. 'As you will no doubt remember,' Strachey of the *Spectator* wrote to him on 16 October 1917, 'I thought the methods by which the present Government came into office abominable; but, following your advice, I thought the only thing to do, pending the War, was to support the Prime Minister "de facto" though not "de jure": i.e. to be loyal to the usurper on public grounds.' Gardiner executed the same editorial policy in the *Daily News*, where he declared on 9 December 1916: 'Mr George's Government must, at all costs, have fair play from the

Press and goodwill from all. He must not live under those screaming placards and those hysterical headlines that have made the past eighteen months a nightmare of shame and disaster.' And Donald of the *Daily Chronicle* professed similar sentiments in reply to a party organizer on 17 April 1917: 'Our attitude towards Mr Lloyd George's Government is precisely that of Mr Asquith; we give it support in prosecuting the war; but, unlike Mr Asquith, we occasionally criticise some of its actions.' By this time, as Donald's letter implied, the Asquithians along Fleet Street were beginning to strain at the bit. Within the year, many of them had completely lost patience with their fallen leader, who seemed to have given up the fight. 'I do not understand Asquith's attitude', Edward Cadbury, chairman of the *Daily News* board, wrote in utter exasperation to his editor on 13 April 1918. 'I think he should be ready to sacrifice future position for present danger. We can do no more.'

Like Peel in 1846 (as opposed to MacDonald in 1931), Asquith remained in undisputed control of the party machinery. He carried with him into the wilderness what Gladstone had described in Peel's case as 'the Official Corps': the vast majority of office holders, the managers of electoral affairs, and a near monopoly on intellectual talent. 'Peel', as Robert Blake observed in his 1968 Ford Lectures, 'occupied an ambivalent position. He had no intention of retiring. He bitterly resented the tactics' of those who had pulled him down. 'On the other hand he never seems to have contemplated any serious attempt to reunite the party.' The same can be said, word for word, about Asquith seventy years later.

'It was an impossible and unsatisfactory situation', Blake has recognized. 'Peel would neither lead a party nor allow others to lead it.' So, too, with Asquith. 'Political activity in the constituencies, largely by Asquith's own wish, was at a standstill', Jenkins has pointed out. At Westminster, where there was one Liberal Party equipped with two rival sets of whips, Asquith tended to be elusive and his statements elliptical. In March 1917, when Lloyd George defied Liberal principle by introducing a protective tariff for Indian cotton manufactures, Asquith failed to take a stand. In a by-election soon afterwards, he went so far as to appeal to voters 'to preserve national unity by returning the official candidate to support the Government in a resolute prosecution of the war to victorious issues'. He made no protest when the overseas sales of the *Nation* were proscribed, and abstained in the division on the controversial Corn Production Bill. In the stormy debate on Irish conscription, he played (as the *Manchester Guardian* complained on 10 April 1918) the role of 'a moderating influence or a "wet blanket", according to the view you take of any particular issue'. In short, he was consistently reticent and mediatory, even when Liberal stalwarts in and out of office were voicing strong opposition to Lloyd George.

He attended an occasional meeting of the Writers' Group, a dining society of journalists and intellectuals who dedicated themselves 'to give expression to Liberal views on the war and still more on the peace to follow'. At Haig's invitation, he toured the Western Front in September 1917. The next month, he delivered a public address at Liverpool, and over the next year he spoke twice more, at Birmingham and Manchester. It was hardly a strenuous schedule. He expended far greater effort in the preparation of the Romanes Lecture which he gave at Oxford in June 1918. Lytton Strachey, to whose *Eminent Victorians* he paid generous tribute, was in the audience, but did not return the compliment. His companion, Lady Ottoline Morrell, was even less impressed by Asquith's presentation: 'I was astonished that anyone with the excellent brain should have been content with giving such a dull address', she wrote in her journal. 'However, all the old dons were enthusiastic about it and thought it "very fine".'

In the Commons, where his attendance was sporadic, Asquith reserved his oratory for occasions that were largely ceremonial. On 18 April 1917 he welcomed the United States into the European war. He endorsed female suffrage, which could no longer be resisted, and also a blueprint for a League of Nations, which he had previously derided to Venetia Stanley as one of President Wilson's 'chimerical ideals'. The advocates of either policy did not consider him sufficiently sincere or energetic. Haldane tried to enlist his support for educational reform, but sadly perceived that 'the ex-PM is not now an enthusiast', and consequently decided that 'I must pursue my own path', which eventually led him into the Labour Party. Invited to lunch at Cavendish Square in April 1917, Haldane arrived to find 'a number of other guests' who made 'it impossible to get any good done . . . I think time has changed the outlook on life of the ex-PM & that he is no longer keenly interested.' Others, from different perspectives, reached exactly the same conclusion.

Perhaps, to give him the benefit of the doubt, Asquith was making an effort to steer clear of any subject that might widen the rift in Liberal ranks. Scott, visiting the metropolis on 4 May 1917, made an appointment for an interview at Cavendish Square. 'Asquith, at first a little icy, thawed rapidly when he found I had something serious to say and aimed at conciliation', he recorded. Coming 'solely on my

own initiative', Scott inquired whether Asquith would be willing to
meet Lloyd George on the worsening Irish situation. Asquith stiffly
replied that Lloyd George 'had not done him the honour to consult
him either directly or indirectly on the subject', but that he was
nevertheless available for discussion. On the 10th, Scott informed
Lloyd George of Asquith's 'placable disposition', and was deputed to
arrange a meeting, which took place at Montagu's house within the
next few days. Scott was curious to know the outcome. 'What about
Asquith? Was he any good?' he asked Lloyd George on the 15th.
'Oh!' Lloyd George scoffed, 'he's perfectly sterile.' Scott further
noted that 'George did not conceal his disgust and said that Montagu
had also been struck with Asquith's total failure to give any help or
suggestion'.

That, however, did not deter either Scott or other concerned individuals from striving anew for Liberal reunification. 'There is a very
disquieting movement going on in certain quarters to insinuate that
it would be an excellent combination if Asquith were to unite with
D. & there were to be a joint Premiership', Frances Stevenson, Lloyd
George's private secretary and mistress, wrote in her diary on 19 May.
'I think it would be fatal to take Asquith back in any position', she
stated. 'The extraordinary thing is that people like Lord Murray of
Elibank are keen about it, but I do hope D. will be quite resolute in
sticking out against it.' On 14 November Murray 'lunched at
Cavendish Square', and the next day he addressed Lloyd George:
'Now that I am out of politics (with the exception of personal attachment to old friends with whom I have worked in the past), I can see
more clearly than ever . . . that the general position to-day more
insistently demands closer co-operation between you and A, if only
it could be accomplished.'

Before the year was over, Scott again tried his hand. 'Hitherto',
he minuted on 20 December,

Asquith has been more extreme than Lloyd George, though a large
part of his followers are semi-pacifist. Lloyd George distrusts Asquith
and would rather not see him, but has agreed to see Buckmaster
with whom I have had several conversations, but wishes that I should
be present. Buckmaster agrees, if Asquith gives permission, so it is
provisionally arranged that he and I are to breakfast with Lloyd
George on Friday in next week.

On the morning of the 28th, Buckmaster and Scott came to breakfast
at Number Ten, where they stayed until 12.30, laying the groundwork for a meeting between their host and Asquith on 5 January.
As an afterthought, Grey was to be included. Buckmaster sub-

sequently told Scott that, on leaving Downing Street, he had
gone

straight to Cavendish Square to ring up Asquith at his place in the
country but by ill-luck tumbled on Mrs Asquith ('Margot') who
insisted on ringing him up herself and then stayed in the room while
he spoke and finally [demanded?] to know who were the people whom
he wanted Asquith to see . . .

Under these circumstances, and Asquith not being at all responsive, he decided to see Asquith and went down that evening and
spent several hours with him. He began by reading him the exact
terms of the memorandum which he had drawn up at the breakfast
with Lloyd George stating the purpose and reasons for which George
wished to see him and Grey. Asquith was extremely unwilling to meet
George. He gave no reason for this and said no word against George
which his best friend could have resented, but it was evident to
Buckmaster that it was his strong personal feeling against George
which moved him. It was only on Buckmaster's strong representation that, under the critical circumstances existing, it was his duty to
comply, that he finally consented to do so, but he made it a condition
that Buckmaster should say that he would see George if he regarded
it as 'important in the national interest' that he should do so.

Each side childishly insisted that the other had taken the initiative. Margot attached particular importance to this petty detail.
'Don't fail to let the political world know that Ll. G. went to *my*
husband – Asquith did not go to 10 Downing Street', she instructed
Gardiner on 7 January. 'It sounds a small thing', she admitted, 'but
it is all important in connection with the 2 meetings', of which Buckmaster and Scott had planned only one. 'The first', by Margot's
account, occurred on Thursday, the 3rd, 'when Ll. G. came to 20 Cav.
Sq. to lunch alone. The 2nd was Sat. à trois with Grey at breakfast in
20 Cav. Sq. My husband said he was amazed at Ll. G.'s deferential
manner to him!' she broadcast. 'It is quite clear Ll. G.'s violent curve
is to escape from his lot & regain ours. This was certain to happen: I
betted on it coming sooner.'

Needless to say, Lloyd George gave a contradictory rendering.
'This morning I breakfasted with Asquith. Very pleasant both', he
jotted to his wife on 5 January so hurriedly that he not only dated his
letter with the wrong year, but also neglected to mention Grey. Three
days later, he treated Scott to a more coherent report at breakfast.
'Asquith's reluctance' to co-operate, he revealed, 'was nothing'
compared to that of Grey, who had to be coaxed to emerge from his
Northumberland retreat. 'I saw Asquith first and then insisted that I
must see Grey also', Lloyd George related. 'I got on all right with
Asquith when we met and with Grey also.' Scott was anxious to

learn whether the others 'had agreed in substance' to the statement
on war-aims which the Prime Minister had delivered to the Trades
Union Congress on Saturday. 'In substance!' Lloyd George swag-
gered. 'I read every word to them and then I told them that I should
state publicly that they approved.' Margot painted a different picture, no less highly coloured. 'I am keen it shd. be known that Ll. G.
did not write *one* line of the document' on war-aims, she told
Gardiner. 'Bob Cecil & Smuts & Henry's corrections did the trick.
Also', she claimed, 'L.G. showed it to *no* colleague till he showed it to
H. & tho Bob Cecil & Smuts saw it, Balfour did not.'

A coolness prevailed between the two Liberal leaders, neither of
whom was prepared to risk a formal rupture. F. E. ('Freddie') Guest,
who served Lloyd George as Chief Whip, considered the anomalous
position of the Prime Minister vis-à-vis his own parliamentary party,
and concluded in a fourteen-page memorandum on 3 December 1917
that 'the time to challenge Mr Asquith's leadership of the Liberal
Party is not yet come and that to do so now is unlikely to lead to
success'. It was his contention that only a third of the Liberal M.P.s
could be counted as 'absolutely reliable' to Asquith, but that
Asquith was nonetheless preferred as party leader even by many who
favoured a Lloyd George premiership. If there was no direct confrontation, it could be assumed that 'the reversion of the [party]
leadership rests with the Prime Minister'.

By contrast, those closest to Asquith were obsessed by the fear
that their cause was steadily losing credibility. In the constituencies
and, more dramatically, in the press, support for the independent
Liberals was slipping away. It was getting difficult to take seriously
an Opposition that did not oppose. Lord Lansdowne's celebrated
letter on the subject of a negotiated peace, published in the *Daily
Telegraph* on 29 November 1917, raised the possibility that he might
combine with Asquith in a new political constellation likely to regain
the centre ground. The hope persisted long after Asquith, speaking
at Birmingham on 11 December, had responded cautiously to Lansdowne's proposals. On 13 February 1918, writing to his sister, Haldane took stock of Lloyd George's difficulties and stated that 'in the
main . . . I should deplore a Lansdowne–Asquith Govt.' for which
'Margot is intriguing busily. The old lot are hoping for it.' Five days
later, he alerted her to new developments: 'There is a grand political
row now on. Margot is up to her elbows in intrigues and actually (do
not mention this) had Gwynne of the *Morning Post* at Cavendish
Square today! But', he accurately predicted, 'the Liberals are too
pacifist . . . to get a vote of no confidence in Ll. G.'

To the disappointment of his followers, Asquith did not so much as try. It had been widely expected that he would exploit the opportunity created by the replacement of Sir William Robertson as Chief of the Imperial General Staff. In that case, he would have been assured of assistance from those, like Gwynne, who unfailingly upheld the claims of the military authorities. But instead of mobilizing his forces, Asquith retreated quietly from the fray.

Informed sources did not doubt that, sooner or later, Asquith would attack. 'He is hard pressed by his adherents', Lord Esher wrote to Sir Henry Wilson on 1 May, 'and one of these days he may yield.' They did not have long to wait. On 7 May *The Times* published a letter from Major-General Sir Frederick Maurice, who defied the sacred canons of military discipline by accusing the Prime Minister of having misrepresented to Parliament the number of British troops deployed in France during the recent German offensive. Two days later, Asquith moved from a select committee to ascertain the validity of Maurice's charge. Although Lloyd George warned that he would regard approval for such an inquiry as a vote of censure, the Opposition divided the House (unsuccessfully) against the Government. The *Manchester Guardian* did not think that Asquith had ever 'before taken so positive a step in opposition'; and *The Times* hailed it as 'the *début* of an organised Opposition'. On 8 May Haldane lunched with Morley, who prematurely speculated on the allocation of places in the next Liberal administration. 'But I am not sure,' Haldane confessed to Gosse, 'although the Conservatives are much aloof from Ll. G.' He appended a postscript that 'Asquith has been screwed up to vote on his motion of censure'.

Yet Asquith categorically denied that his motion constituted any such thing. In his 'innocuous contribution to the debate' (as Trevor Wilson has aptly called it), he went to great lengths to deny either hostility to the Government or, necessarily, acceptance of Maurice's allegations. His purpose, he solemnly averred, was merely to secure a proper investigation of the merits of the case. 'People do not understand this legalistic attitude to affairs of life and death', the *Manchester Guardian* tartly commented on the 10th. The same day, its editor wrote privately to Lord Courtney that the entire 'Maurice affair is something of a mystery . . . Asquith is discredited'.

Asquith had wished to push matters far enough to embarrass Lloyd George but evidently not so far as to challenge him directly and thereby precipitate a general election. A muddled strategy, it was foredoomed to failure. Nevertheless, it had restored him to the limelight, which he had been shunning. Before the uproar had died down, he was embroiled involuntarily in a different sort of controversy. Noel Pemberton Billing, a Titus Oates figure who sat as the independent member for East Hertfordshire, cited the Asquiths among the 47,000 British public figures whose names were inscribed in a 'Black Book' in Berlin as having been sexually corrupted by German agents. A protégé of Horatio Bottomley, Billing published his revelations in the *Vigilante*, a gutter journal which he edited. He was prosecuted for libel in the infamous 'Salome trial', which he interrupted with the sensational disclosure that the presiding judge was another of those tainted. Margot, who considered the affair the dirty work of Lloyd George and Beaverbrook, was close to hysteria: 'Truth *used* to "prevail sooner or later" but now it *never prevails*', she commiserated with Haldane, who was, predictably enough, another victim. 'It is as out of fashion as Christ's teachings.'

Neither Billing's scurrilous accusations nor, more seriously, Asquith's performance in the Maurice debate disqualified him from receiving fresh overtures from Lloyd George. Over the Whitsun weekend, Lord Reading came to see him and broadly 'hinted ... that I cd. have any post I chose, except that of head of the Govt.' Asquith, who did not normally keep memoranda, committed to paper his conversation with Reading on 28 May:

I answered that I must use perfectly plain language since he had raised the subject. I was quite ready to go on giving the Govt. full support, so long as they carried on the war in the proper spirit, & to use my influence with my party, & in the country, in the same sense. But he & others had better understand clearly, & at once, that under no conditions wd. I serve in a Govt. of wh. Ll. G. was the head. I had learned by long & close association to mistrust him profoundly ... In my judgment he had incurable defects, both of intellect and character, wh. totally unfitted him to be at the head.

In the early autumn, Murray made another approach, only to be told that 'in no circumstances whatever' would Asquith consent to serve under Lloyd George. 'The inwardness of Mr A's attitude', Murray perceived, 'is that he does not really trust either Lloyd George or Balfour, and could not therefore serve in the Government with them.'

'If a leader of the Opposition had any function at all in time of war it would be difficult to imagine a more moderate and conciliatory manner of discharging it', Asquith's official biographers have written with particular reference to their hero's performance in the Maurice debate. Celebrating as Asquith's sovereign virtue what others have diagnosed as his crippling inertia, they were too much inclined to credit procrastination as patriotism. While the war continued, Asquith might well have exerted himself far more vigorously. Now that the war was nearly won, he lost any excuse for temporizing. If, as he assured Lord Reading, he 'was quite ready to go on giving the Govt. full support', there was no logical reason why he should have stood outside; if, however, he sincerely believed that Lloyd George was morally objectionable, he ought not to have supported him in any capacity; or else he should have made way for someone with fewer inhibitions. Asquith was acting out of pique, which he asked his contemporaries to accept as principle.

As the nations lurched towards peace, Asquith, like everyone else, turned his thoughts to the postwar order. 'The question of War after War, under various disguises (tariffs etc.) will (I foresee) be very troublesome', he wrote on 1 October to Lord Bryce. 'Whether we shall be forced into an election is, I fancy, a pure question of gambling.' The two topics could not be separated. Lloyd George's hand would doubtless be strengthened by an early election, but at the cost of inciting passions of chauvinism and Germanophobia. The proponent of the 'knock-out blow' was not likely to help realize the Wilsonian ideal of 'peace without victory'. Nor, by the same token, could he be expected to show magnanimity to his parliamentary critics. The Asquithians, recalling the plight of their party at the polls in 1900, had every reason to dread a 'snap' appeal to an electorate that had yet to shed its khaki and recover its equilibrium. But, perhaps with the same precedent in mind, Lloyd George sprang an election within hours of the armistice.

Asquith was given a last chance to reconsider. Scott, on a visit to Downing Street in late October, was taken aside by Lloyd George, who 'said there could be no question of a combination at a General Election between his party and the Liberal Opposition, but only between the Coalition Government and the Opposition. Asquith could not enter the Government as its head, but he might have a great place in it – say as Lord Chancellor.' Fearing the virtual obliteration of Liberalism as he had known it, Murray also resumed his diplomacy. 'I have seen A. on two occasions since that special talk of which you are aware', he informed the Prime Minister on 30 October. 'I by no means despair of the arrangement I had in view.' But, whether or not Asquith could be induced to accept office, Murray hoped somehow to avert the impending smash:

There are . . . many who now support your leadership who are, at the same time, convinced that the slower moving A. Government in the early days prepared the way, in its skilful handling of an equally slow moving nation, for the vigorous methods which you inaugurated. The prospect or possibility at a coming election of having to select between two Statesmen who have unitedly done so much for the common cause, is positively nauseous to many quiet thinking Liberals who count.

Within a few days of the armistice (the exact date is unclear), Asquith was summoned to a tête-à-tête in Lloyd George's room at the House. 'Upon his return', he divulged to Margot 'what had occurred': Asquith, she in turn confided to her diary, 'had been received with a friendliness which amounted to enthusiasm and [was] asked where he stood'. Phrasing the question in the negative, Lloyd George began: 'I understand you don't wish to take a post under the Government.' Asquith confirmed 'that that was so; and added that the only service he thought he could render the Government would be if he were to go to Versailles' for the peace conference. 'At this Mr Lloyd George looked a little confused', continued Margot, who vividly portrayed the scene:

He was walking up and down the room, and in knocking up against a chair a pile of loose books were thrown upon the ground. Hastily looking at his watch and stooping down to pick up the books, he said he would consider my husband's proposal. Nothing more was said; the interview was over, and my husband never heard another word upon the matter.

A year later, Lloyd George complained to Sir Donald Maclean that 'Asquith and three or four of his colleagues had refused to join the Cabinet' at the end of the war. But Asquith heatedly disputed this account. 'All that had passed', he assured Maclean, 'was that Ll. G. had said to him . . .: "I suppose you would not care to take office", and Asquith replied that was true, he did not wish to take office but was not at all averse to going to Paris as a British representative.' In his mind, the two assignments were mutually exclusive; in Lloyd George's, they were mutually contingent. Although various people, including the King and Churchill, urged Lloyd George to include Asquith in the British delegation to Versailles, he refused to do so.

After a haphazard fashion, candidates who supported the coalition were awarded the joint endorsement of Lloyd George and Bonar Law. There were 159 Liberals who carried this seal of approval, along with 364 Unionists and eighteen candidates of the right-wing National Democratic Party. Asquith contemptuously referred to this commendation as the 'coupon', and the epithet stuck. In a speech at Newcastle on 29 November, Lloyd George defensively claimed that he and his partner had used the Maurice debate as the yardstick by which they measured candidates' loyalties. But, as scholars have recently demonstrated, the allocation of coalition favours was a good deal more arbitrary.

To add to the confusion, Asquith waged a circumspect campaign. On 18 November, in his first major election address, he identified himself as a Liberal 'without prefix and suffix, without label and hallmark of any sort and description'. His fire, insofar as he showed any, was concentrated on the Tory element in the coalition. Gradually, goaded by Lloyd George's blistering invective and by angry demands from his own rank and file, he grew more forceful in his denunciations of the 'blank cheque' which the Government solicited. Yet it remained all too apparent that his heart was not in a struggle that offered no better prospect than an extended period of futile opposition. 'There was no question, of course, of displacing, or of attempting or desiring to displace, the present Government', he conceded to his constituents at East Fife on 11 December. His message was hardly calculated to kindle enthusiasm and, indeed, he himself could not muster any. 'I doubt whether so far there is much interest in the elections', he wrote to Mrs Harrisson on 25 November, 'despite the efforts of the newspapers to keep the pot boiling. The whole thing is a wicked fraud which will settle nothing.'

Although Asquith accepted a landslide victory for the coalition as a foregone conclusion, it never occurred to him that he stood in any personal danger. In his memoirs, he was moved to 'confess that I felt so little apprehension for my seat that I spent most of my time . . . in visiting and addressing other constituencies'. At the beginning of the campaign, he was designated one of five 'outstanding' personalities (Pemberton Billing was another, making it a dubious honour) in whose constituencies the coalition would not intervene; but, in contravention of instructions from headquarters, the local Unionist association adopted a candidate to stand against him without benefit of the coupon.

Churchill, winding up his own campaign for re-election at Dundee, reported to his wife on 13 December that 'Asquith is having a very rough time in East Fife, and is subjected to abominable baiting by a gang of discharged soldiers. I do hope it will be all right for the poor old boy.' Asquith was incensed to 'hear . . . that the London papers have been publishing a tissue of absurdities about my reception in Fife', and he called on Gardiner to contradict these malicious rumours:

I was only there for 2½ days, in the course of which I addressed 21 meetings in different towns and hamlets. At every one (with a single exception where there was a large majority for us), I had a unanimous vote of confidence. Perhaps the best of them all was at St Andrews, where, after one or two drunken hooligans had been turned out, I spoke for $\frac{1}{2}$ an hour in such silent attention that you might have heard a pin drop. I have never had such enthusiastic & crowded gatherings, and the women, who at the day meetings were often in the majority, were even more friendly & demonstrative than the men. The heckling was for the most part of the feeblest and most contemptible kind.

The gift of realistic appraisal had deserted him.

Polling took place on the next day, but counting was delayed for a fortnight to allow for the collection of the military vote. During the tense interval, the two Liberal leaders met accidentally when Lloyd George escorted his youngest daughter to Paddington Station on the 19th. 'When I got there I saw the Asquiths, Elizabeth & Puffin on the border of the crowd', he wrote to his wife. 'I went back & fetched them forward on the platform. Poor old Asquith was very touched. I am glad I did it. I asked Mrs A. whether she would like to come forward. She replied "I should like it very much if I am allowed to".'

Nine days later, Asquith and Lloyd George were seated not far from each other at a Mansion House luncheon in honour of President Wilson. Before the meal was over, the early returns began to trickle in. Margot strained to overhear them: 'Herbert Samuel, McKinnon Wood and Runciman are out . . . McKenna is beat . . .' The Liberal Opposition was being utterly routed.

The Asquiths pressed through the crowd to their waiting car, then 'shot down the streets with our minds set and stunned'. Back at Cavendish Square, Asquith retired to his library while his wife 'rang up 21 Abingdon Street (the Liberal headquarters) from the telephone in my boudoir'. By a margin of nearly 2,000 Asquith had lost the seat he had held for thirty-two years. Only twenty-nine uncouponed Liberals (not all of whom qualified as Asquithians) survived the massacre, which had wiped out the Opposition Liberal front bench. Asquith reportedly professed gratitude: 'with all the others out', his own success would have been intolerable. 'Asquith beat? . . . Thank God', Margot recalled having exclaimed at the news of her husband's defeat. Lloyd George, one imagines, knew better than to assign credit to the Almighty.

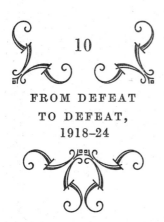

## 10

## FROM DEFEAT
## TO DEFEAT,
## 1918–24

For Asquith and his stricken party alike, the general election of 1918 was an unmitigated disaster. That the un-couponed Liberals had fully expected to suffer a defeat was clear enough from their half-hearted campaign; but the result, declared on 28 December, exceeded their worst apprehensions.

Along with a chorus of lamentations came a litany of post-mortems. Reginald McKenna, rejected by the electors of North Monmouth-shire, whom he had served since 1895, ventured a 'personal opinion' on the situation. There were, he told A. G. Gardiner on the 29th, 'two outstanding reasons' for the débâcle, 'apart from the losses caused by three-cornered fights' in which independent Liberal candidates were simply overwhelmed: on the one hand, as indicated by 'the small poll all over the country', the Liberal machine had been allowed to rust during the 'long years of political truce', with the result that traditionally 'Liberal voters were apathetic and even resentful'; on the other hand, 'anti-Germanism and the desire for revenge were strong among large numbers of people who voted for the Government in the belief that they would get all the indemnities Germany could pay and more'. McKenna's second point, that 'the Liberals are not thought as a party to be sufficiently venomous', was illustrated at East Fife by placards that bluntly proclaimed: 'Asquith nearly lost you the War. Are you going to let him spoil the Peace?'

Hoping that the weakness of Liberalism (as he defined it) in the new Parliament would not be permitted to obscure the fact that it remained 'really strong in the country' (as he gauged it), McKenna preached the necessity 'to make up for 4 years of neglect and get to spade work in the constituencies'. At least in his mind, there was no doubt that this objective could best be achieved by finding 'a name, a formula and a man to unite Liberal and Labour. There is no difference in our immediate political programme', he insisted. If he were in Asquith's shoes, he would 'call an early meeting of the Executive of the National Liberal Federation . . ., place my resignation in their hands, ask for the appointment of a special emergency committee to consider the whole position, and promise assistance in carrying out such recommendations as they might make.'

But that was far too much to ask of Asquith, who had neither the desire to add to the general confusion nor, for that matter, unqualified confidence in the collective wisdom of the N.L.F. Instead, he handpicked Sir Donald Maclean to deputize for him as 'chairman' of the non-coalition Liberals in the Commons. It was decidedly a holding action, intended to last only until Asquith had negotiated a safe return to Westminster. Maclean, for one, understood this perfectly. He responded stiffly when, on 13 November 1919, Bonar Law chaffed that Asquith would never 'come back to this House'. A God-fearing Presbyterian, Maclean put aside his scruples and bet sixpence that Asquith would secure a seat 'before February'. He lost the wager, but only by a few weeks.

Who, in fact, were the non-coalition Liberals? 'We often call them "Asquithians", as if they were distinguished by some strong personal allegiance to their Leader – but nothing of the kind was true', Roy Douglas has discerned. 'Some were very soon reconciled to Lloyd George and estranged from Asquith.' Others, both in doctrine and in spirit, were akin to Labour, and accordingly gravitated in that direction. As Gulland admitted to Runciman on 4 January, the problem of classification 'is not an easy one. It is very difficult to draw accurately a list of the free men, and to differentiate between the Coalition Liberals and the others.' Sooner than try, he and Asquith hopefully awaited 'an early issue that would bring men definitely to our side'. Meanwhile, *The Times* reckoned that fourteen M.P.s could be counted as loyal followers of Asquith.

Only three of the twenty-nine uncouponed Liberals who had scraped through the ordeal could lay claim to ministerial experience even at the junior level. According to Trevor Wilson's tally, two of them – Francis Acland and William Wedgwood Benn –

were radicals who regarded Asquith as too much of a 'whig', while the third, George Lambert, belonged on the right of the party but inclined towards the coalition. Similar differences over leadership and policy were evident throughout the group. Maclean and George Thorne were attached to Asquith, Hilton Young to Lloyd George, and [J.M.] Hogge and [Josiah] Wedgwood to neither.

Sir T. A. Bramsdon, an Asquithian *malgré lui*, related to Maclean on 19 January that, during his contest at Portsmouth Central, 'I was repeatedly asked if elected whether it was my intention to support [Asquith]. Had I replied in the affirmative I should not have attained the unique victory I did.' On the grounds that 'Mr Asquith has entirely lost the confidence of the public', Bramsdon protested that it was 'inconsistent . . . for him to guide the independent Liberals from outside'. There were other so-called Asquithians who shared his disaffection.

Had Lloyd George forced the issue, he might easily have got himself elected to the leadership of the parliamentary Liberal Party; but he held back, obviously reluctant to alienate support among the Unionists. Asquith's status was even more anomalous. He had no seat and no immediate prospect of getting one. Acland, whose own return at North-West Cornwall was admittedly 'rather a fluke', expressed to his unfortunate chief on 29 December the 'wish' that his 'seat was safe for Liberalism against all comers, for of course then I should be delighted to stand down so that you could take it, but it is not'. Asquith, aware that another humiliation would render his position completely untenable, had no choice but to sit on the sidelines.

His colleagues, scrambling to pick up the pieces before Lloyd George might pocket them, were annoyed by his reticence. 'The old man is stoical to the point of indifference', McKenna wrote to Runciman on 4 January, 'but he hasn't the slightest intention to resign.'

Sir Robert Hudson, who doubled as secretary of the National Liberal Federation and honorary secretary of the Liberal Central Association, saw Asquith during the last week of January and afterwards complained to Maclean that 'he had nothing particular to say on any subject'.

On 3 February there was a meeting of twenty-three Liberal M.P.s who were opposed to the coalition, if only by reputation. After a good deal of bickering, the group constituted itself a Free Liberal Party (familiarly known as the Wee Frees, after the Scottish sect) and endorsed Asquith's designation of Maclean as 'sessional chairman'. There was stronger opposition to Thorne, whom Asquith had nominated to succeed Gulland as Chief Whip; as a compromise, he was appointed in tandem with Hogge, whom Asquith and Maclean were inclined to regard as unsuitable. The Free Liberals thereby gave notice that they were likewise free from Asquith's control.

Two days later, there was another, larger meeting to which Liberal M.P.s of all denominations were invited. Maclean was a conspicuous absentee. An eight-member committee was established, with equal representation for the Asquithians and the Lloyd Georgeites, to explore the possibilities for reunion or, at any rate, co-operation. By 6 March the task was given up as hopeless. All but three of the anti-ministerial Liberals boycotted the meeting on the 27th which had been called to elect a chairman. Lambert, one of the mutinous trio, was chosen without opposition and, consequently, was disowned by the Free Liberal rump. The divorce was finalized on 4 April, when the Wee Frees, formally and corporately, disavowed the Government whip, which had been indiscriminately extended to them. All the same, there were individuals among them who continued to straddle the thin line that separated one Liberal camp from the other.

A series of by-election victories augmented the Asquithian representation at Westminster and sparked vain hopes of a sustained revival. Layton West, where there had been a two-to-one Unionist majority at the general election, was captured on 1 March. Even more spectacularly, Hull Central was won on a swing of 32·9 per cent by J. M. Kenworthy on the 28th. Finally, in a three-way battle, Central Aberdeenshire and Kincardine fell to an independent Liberal challenger on 16 April. Thereafter, the initiative quickly passed to Labour, with Asquithian candidates usually placed a sorry third.

Late in the year, a contest at Spen Valley commanded exceptional interest. The death of its Coalition Liberal M.P. produced a vacancy which many observers expected Asquith himself to try and fill. In a memorandum dated 17 November, Maclean recorded that Bonar

Law had recently 'asked me whether Asquith was going to stand for Spen Valley. I said I did not know but I hope[d] he would.' The same day, Haldane informed his sister that the 'Labour people' had vowed 'to oppose HHA ... hotly ... & he will need to be propped up by the Coalition if he is to get in'. Perhaps it was this threat that frightened Asquith off.

Instead Simon was proposed and unanimously adopted by the local Liberal association, which was keen on running an independent Liberal this time around. Hitherto, without hesitating to back a Coalition Unionist against an Asquithian, Lloyd George had declined to involve the two wings of the party in a direct confrontation. At Spen Valley, for the first time, a Coalition Liberal entered the field against an Asquithian. Several prominent coalitionists regretted Lloyd George's action as pointless and provocative. With no real chance of success, the Lloyd George man siphoned enough support from Simon to deliver the seat to Labour on a minority vote.

Asquith was probably glad that he had resisted the temptation to offer himself. Or perhaps he had not felt any. From all indications, he was in no hurry to emerge from his prolonged hibernation. Jenkins, citing 'the small signs of public recognition' that gratified Asquith during the dark months of 1919, has overlooked the recrudescence of innuendoes – not only in the press, but also in parliamentary debate – about Germans who allegedly found shelter in Downing Street early in the war. These calumnies, 'public recognition' of another type, were doubtless calculated to discourage Asquith from returning to the mud-spattered arena.

He followed closely the proceedings of the peace conference at Paris, which he had aspired to attend. To Lord Bryce, he sent a 'line' on 21 May 'to say that I share to the full your apprehensions as to the terms and spirit of the Treaty, though of course in a public speech I could only hint, & that vaguely, at the most general considerations'. He confessed that he was 'much disappointed with [President] Wilson: from the other three nothing different was to be expected'. Although, as his official biographers have pointed out, his exclusion from the conference table 'left him free to take the independent line on the Peace Treaty and Reparations', he did not (as he self-consciously acknowledged to Bryce) avail himself of that opportunity.

In August, he was asked to chair a Royal Commission on Oxford and Cambridge universities, their financial resources, and their internal structures. 'I am disposed to accept', he wrote on the 25th to Maclean, assuring him that 'the work would in no way interfere with my political activities', such as they were. Professor Gilbert Murray encouraged him to undertake the assignment, but other dons were less enthusiastic. 'Several people here have expressed a wish that you were its chairman instead of Asquith', Sir Charles Firth, the Oxford historian, told Haldane on 21 January 1920, when the Commission had opened hearings. 'My impression is that Asquith's views on higher education are those prevalent at Balliol in 1870, and that he has learnt nothing about it since.'

By then, Asquith was deeply involved elsewhere. Early in the new year, Sir John McCallum ('a dear old Scot', as Acland described him) died. At the previous general election, he had held Paisley, a heavily industrialized constituency in Lanarkshire, by the narrow margin of 106 votes. The Free Liberals were determined to retain the seat, and Asquith accepted the challenge to stand.

Why, after passing by more promising opportunities, did he choose Paisley as the place to attempt a comeback? On the face of things, Spen Valley or North Edinburgh (where Runciman had fought a close fight in April) were each more attractive. At Paisley, he had to contend not only with a powerful Labour opponent, but also with a belligerent coalitionist faction within the constituency: the executive of the local Liberal association adopted him by a vote of twenty to seventeen, and the full membership divided 92 to 75 in his favour. Afterwards, the Liberals at Paisley closed ranks and issued a unanimous invitation to Asquith, who knew how to interpret it.

Hardly a safe seat, Paisley was the only one available at the moment, and Asquith could not afford to delay. Many of his most devoted followers were impatient with him; others, like Wedgwood, had lost hope and quit the party. Discontent with 'leaders who refused to lead' had been building up steadily. Back in April, Asquith had delivered his first post-election address, a spiritless appeal to Liberal candidates. 'If Father had been there,' Viscount Gladstone remarked, 'my word, what a time we should have had!' On 15 May Asquith was scheduled to give a major address at Newcastle. 'If his speech . . . is not a punching *fighting* speech', Margot predicted that day to J. A. Spender, 'he will fail. *However fine* – (that it will be probably), however *wise*, however *perfect* it may be – if he shows no indignation, no snap, he is done.' Yet neither indignation nor snap were much in evidence at Newcastle. Hogge, who shared the duties of the Free Liberal whipship, was increasingly outraged by his leader's studied passivity. 'What is Asquith going to do?' he asked Maclean in early September. 'It is now in all conscience long enough since he was defeated and we can't have another annual meeting of the "Wee Frees" without a decision of some kind.' He proposed to give Asquith 'until the Manchester Meetings' of the N.L.F. in November either to declare war or to surrender. 'After that I promise you (with many apologies) to become very restive.'

.At Newcastle, incited by his audience to 'Hit out', Asquith showed something of his old fervour. Nevertheless, the movement against him was assuming menacing proportions. It operated at different levels. On 19 November Haldane reported to his sister a visit from Wedgwood Benn, who came 'at his own request' and 'in despair about the prospects of Liberalism'. A ginger group of 'Independent Lib. MPs & others' was to be established, and Haldane was invited to address it. He accepted, although he 'fear[ed] HHA will not be pleased'. Wedgwood Benn's backbench activities could not have caused Asquith half so much worry as plans which were being floated for a new centre party. Lord Robert Cecil, a leading proponent of the scheme, regarded Asquith as a stumbling-block. 'If the latter were a Gladstone, and glowed with sympathy and indignation and creative genius, I believe R.C. would cooperate with him', Runciman advised Maclean on 30 December, 'but he [Cecil] seems to dislike the Cavendish Square atmosphere, and his own interests are more profoundly or (perhaps it would be fairer to say) more *obviously* human, & stirred by sentiment than Asquith's.' There was serious talk, which persisted through the summer, that Cecil might combine with Grey to lead a new opposition to which moderate men of all parties might adhere. Where would that leave Asquith? According to Haldane, Grey was 'evidently attracted' to the idea, despite his near blindness. An obvious distance had developed in his relations with Asquith. In August 1919, when Grey was dispatched to Washington as ambassador on special mission, he was wounded to receive no message of good wishes from his old friend. 'He never writes to me. He is no good at writing', Grey sulked on 13 September to Gilbert Murray, who insisted that, on the contrary, Asquith was always a prompt correspondent. 'Yes,' Grey retorted, 'but rather as Ld. Salisbury used to make appointments by return of post, to avoid being troubled with them . . .'

At the beginning of 1920, Asquith had a clear-cut choice: either he might return to the House of Commons at the earliest oportunity to resume command of his depleted forces, or he might abdicate in favour of one or another pretender. The gossip, as Lloyd George heard it from 'Freddie' Guest on 16 January, was 'that Messrs Hogge and Company' had presented an 'ultimatum' to Asquith: 'in effect, that if he will not risk election at a by-election he will be repudiated as nominal head of the Independent Liberal Party'. Matters need not have gone so far to convince Asquith that time was running out.

'I don't look forward with much pleasure to the adventure, which however has to be faced', Asquith admitted to Mrs Harrisson on 22 January. 'For one thing I am not very fond of going back to Scotland, for another the issue is extremely doubtful, notwithstanding that the press is practically all with us.' The enthusiasm of his followers, particularly his elder daughter, compensated for his own ambiguity. 'Keep your eye on Paisley', Gardiner urged the readers of the *Daily News* on the 24th. In his weekly column, which survived his editorship, 'A.G.G.' anticipated that Asquith's triumphant return would focus 'national resentment against that criminal hoax', the coupon election, 'and all its disastrous consequences'.

Asquith was not nearly so presumptuous, yet gained confidence as the campaign progressed. Accompanied by Margot, Violet, and Vivian Phillipps, he took the night train to Glasgow on Monday, the 26th. 'We are having a wonderful time here', he wrote four days later to Mrs Harrisson, 'and if outward enthusiasm were a reliable index we should not have much doubt as to the result. But', as he knew from sad experience, 'street crowds and photographers and meetings are most untrustworthy guides.' There were two unknown quantities in the Paisley electorate. The first was the presence of 'about fifteen thousand women on the Register – a dim, impenetrable, for the most part ungettable element – of whom all that one knows is that they are for the most part hopelessly ignorant of politics, credulous to the last degree, and flickering with gusts of sentiment like a candle in the wind.' The second was a community of 'some thousands of Irish, who have been ordered by their bosses to vote Labour – as if Labour had ever done or was ever likely to do anything for them.

At the general election, a couponed candidate of the National Democratic Party had run a close third with 7,201 votes. At the by-election, the coalition put up 'a foul-mouth Tory', whom Asquith did not expect to fare nearly so well. A more formidable opponent, as well as a worthier one, was J. M. Biggar, who had almost won the seat for Labour in 1918 and who had since nursed the constituency. The Webbs told Haldane that they were 'not sure about Paisley at all, but they incline to believe that Biggar will be in'. It was a common assumption.

Haldane's personal attitude towards the Paisley contest was the subject of controversy and recrimination. Without weighing his words, he mused in an interview that Liberalism was a spent force and that it was 'with Labour that the hope lies for tomorrow'. To his consternation, this vague statement was taken to imply an endorsement of Biggar, and Haldane was unwillingly bracketed with the nine former Liberal M.P.s who had indeed sent messages of support to Asquith's Labour opponent. The truth of the matter was that Haldane, although disappointed by Asquith's refusal to diverge from 'the old lines', sincerely hoped to see him restored to an active political life. 'Paisley is too uncertain to speculate on', he told his sister on the 29th. 'On *personal* grounds there is good reason for electing HHA. But will they elect him?' Margot, however, was easily roused to fury. 'What a strange man your son Richard!' she protested to Haldane's aged mother in a letter from Paisley on 7 February. 'And he chooses this moment to stick a knife into Henry. What odd people God makes! To think that your son & Ll. George should hunt in couples!' Haldane, trying to ease his way out of the embarrassment 'without qualifying a word I have said before', paid no attention to Margot and 'just let her talk'. Her husband's successive biographers, who would have done well to follow Haldane's example, have misguidedly parroted her accusation.

Paisley went to the polls on 12 February. That day, Haldane wrote to his mother:

I hope Asquith gets a seat. But I do not feel that it will do much good. Parties will have to be re-cast and their scope enlarged before a proper alternative government can be formed ... Meantime Margot is tiresome because she is ignorant. She has done much to make it difficult in the years gone by for Asquith to rise to the occasion.

Again, Asquith was kept on tenterhooks for a fortnight before the result was declared. This time, he made sure to return to Scotland for the tally. The effort was handsomely rewarded. As he described the occasion to Mrs Harrisson, 'it was clear after the first half-hour that we had won, but the majority steadily increased as fresh ballot boxes were opened till it mounted to close upon 3,000'. On a high turnout, he had polled 14,736 votes, as compared to 7,542 for McCallum at the general election. Biggar was soundly repulsed, although his total increased from 7,436 to 11,902. Best of all, the Coalition Unionist trailed with 3,795 votes, and had the humiliation of forfeiting his deposit.

After 'a gigantic farewell meeting – nearer 5,000 than 4,000 – in the early evening', the Asquiths left Paisley. They returned to London by the night train from Glasgow and, despite police protection, Margot 'was knocked on to the railway line at St Enoch's

Station by the rush of my husband's admirers seeing him off . . .' The next morning, 'another tumultuous greeting' awaited them at Euston. After a late breakfast at Cavendish Square, they celebrated Elizabeth's birthday at a matinée performance of Shaw's *Pygmalion* 'with Mrs Campbell and Marion Terry in the chief parts'.

There was no public reaction and, needless to say, no private letter of congratulation from Lloyd George. But Frances Stevenson commemorated the event in her diary on 25 February:

Well, so Asquith is in! I wonder how the Liberals will like his having got in with *Unionist* votes – and with the help of the Northcliffe press, too! The two very things they can never forgive the P.M. for. D. was not very depressed at the result – he had accustomed himself to the idea, I think . . . Personally, I think when the *fact* of Asquith's having got in is over, it will be all the better for D. As D. himself says, he will be able to get at him in the House, & they will come to grips & I will back D. any time.

On Monday, 1 March, Asquith took his seat. That morning, according to Miss Stevenson, Lloyd George was tempted to play truant, fearful that 'Asquith would get a great reception'. But she persuaded him that

it would be better if he faced the music, as then no-one would accuse him of being afraid or bitter, & everyone would think it more chivalrous of him. So he made up his mind to go, fully expecting it to be a disagreeable incident. To his surprise, however, Asquith had a most feeble reception . . . D. came back very pleased.

Asquith confirmed that the House had greeted his return with 'stony silence'. But he consoled himself with the 'tumultuous but most enthusiastic procession' that accompanied him from Cavendish Square to Westminster. His daughter, too, contrasted the 'thin cheer raised' in the chamber by the 'little gallant handful' of Free Liberals to 'the great voice of the crowd' outside. Gardiner was among the throng that lined the pavements to applaud Asquith as he passed. As 'Alpha of the Plough', he described the joyful scene in the *Star* on 4 March, and brooded on the fickleness of the 'crowd', from which the best men always suffered most. Two days later, as 'A.G.G.' in the *Daily News*, he berated the Coalition Liberals no less for their muted welcome to Asquith than for providing the 'camouflage' behind which Lloyd George 'has completed his deal with reaction and the vested interests'.

Among the faithful, Asquith's campaign at Paisley was seen as a new Midlothian, the dawn of a Liberal renaissance. Asquith, as always, was wary of false expectations. 'I share your hopes, and shall

do what I can', he replied with due humility on 28 February to a
congratulatory letter from Dr R. F. Horton, the eminent Congre-
gational divine; 'but the driving power must come from the inspira-
tion and concentration of a regenerated Liberalism.' In the pitch of
excitement, there were many who entertained the hope that Asquith
would work miracles. Painfully aware of the size of his parliamentary
flock, he knew better than to try.

Even so, he proved distressingly restrained. 'Today was to be the
first sparring contest between D. and Asquith,' Miss Stevenson wrote
in her diary on 15 March:

> The debate was on 'high prices' . . . Everyone expected an attack
> from A. against the Government; indeed it was rather a good op-
> portunity for him. But it was a 'damp squib'. So far from attacking
> he practically apologised for making the speech & made it quite
> clear that he was in no sense criticising the Government. So harmless
> a speech was it that D. could find nothing to answer in it & conse-
> quently did not speak at all, much as he wanted to.

Three days later, she ventured the opinion that Asquith was 'finished . . ., that he has no fight left in him'. More grudgingly, others
reached the same conclusion.

Lord Rothermere, whose newspapers had boomed Asquith's
candidacy at Paisley, admitted to Lord Murray on 1 April that his
'editors and political writers are astounded at Mr A's obvious inadequacy for the position he is expected to fill'. Six weeks later,
Murray's brother recounted in his diary a conversation with Grey,
who lamented that 'Asquith cuts no ice. He is using the machine of
a great political brain to re-arrange old ideas.' *Punch* mocked him as
'the reluctant thruster'; and Sir William Robertson Nicoll, writing
in the *British Weekly* on 25 May, demanded to know 'Who is the
leader of the Independent Liberals?' – Asquith, Grey, or Lord
Robert Cecil? Scott spoke to Cecil in mid-July, and found him more
anxious than ever

> for *a new alignment* of political parties. Asquith though admirable in
> his personal relations as a chief and still influential in the country,
> was no longer capable of giving an effective lead. He had no initiative,
> no sound policy. He was mildly in favour of the League of Nations,
> but 'not red hot' which was essential. *Grey* was his solution.

On the same visit to London, Scott compared notes on 'the present
state of Lib[eral]ism & its Leadership' with Henry Cadbury, manag-
ing director of the *Daily News*. Like 'practically every Liberal whose
opinion I had asked', Cadbury professed dissatisfaction with Asquith,
but appreciated that 'it was extremely difficult to dispossess an

ex-Prime Minister from the leadership of a party except w[ith] his own good-will which at present appeared in A.'s case to be not forthcoming'.

Asquith was acutely sensitive to these criticisms, yet strangely unable to reply to them. 'After his election for Paisley', as Jenkins has noted, 'he spoke in the House of Commons far more frequently than ever previously when he was not a minister', and he appeared prominently on platforms throughout the country. His name headed the list, drawn up by the Chief Whip in June 1921, of Free Liberal M.P.s who had done service for the party. That, he boasted, was 'a complete refutation of the silly legend that I have lost "grip and keenness".' Nevertheless, quantity was no substitute for quality, nor erudition for pugnacity. Asquith recognized as much, but felt trapped. '. . . If one tries to strike a bold true note', he asserted defensively on 24 October 1920, 'half one's friends shiver and cower, and implore one not to get in front of the band: in other words, to renounce both the duties and the risks of leadership.'

Hogge, who had yet to hear the resonance of 'a bold true note', appealed to Maclean to resume the command which, by prior arrangement, he had handed back. 'With a punch in both your hands you could knock Asquith into the middle of next week & create a party if you cared to', he stated on 31 August 1920. Asquith, he concluded, 'never will' succeed, '& this incessant rubbish that Margot churns out is making another term at No. 10 absolutely impossible for him'. Privately, as well as publicly, Asquith seemed incapable of taking a firm stand against his successor. Maclean, who accompanied him to a confabulation in the Prime Minister's room on 10 August, marvelled at the sight of the two of them together: 'There was no constraint of any kind, they chatted freely and L.G. was not only courteous but deferential in his manner, and I could see them slipping back, sub-consciously, to the old days when Mr "A" was P.M. and L.G. his Chancellor.' But, if 'Mr A' had mellowed, 'Mrs A' had lost none of her ferocity. The following February, she took issue with Maclean's statement that political conflict ought not to degenerate into 'a personal affair':

How can it be otherwise? Two men who were for 9 years together: one mean & a fighter – the other magnanimous, not young & not a fighter – are now opposed to each other. Can you keep kid gloves on in behaving like great gentlemen & hope to win anything? *NO*. Every glove must be off & every weapon used & every string pulled.

Hogge, for one, would have seconded her proclamation.

Asquith was pulled in two directions. Before Paisley, he had accepted the premise (as Maclean spelled it out to Henry Cadbury on 16 January 1920) that the next Government would be an amalgam of independent Liberals and Labour. While many of his supporters continued to work towards this objective, Asquith had come to despair of its chances. His position on the Russo-Polish conflict was strongly condemned by Labour spokesmen, who regarded him as singularly unfit to lead a radical revival. Harold Laski, in a letter to the editor of the *Nation* on 21 May 1921, summed up the Labour case against Asquith: his 'Paisley policy' was an affront to the trades unions; his proposals on education and the mines were sadly deficient; and, not least, he bore the blame for the secret treaties that allegedly provoked the war, for 'the treatment of the Easter Rebellion in Ireland', and for assorted instances of wartime repression.

Rebuffed by Labour, Asquith was encouraged to seek alliances elsewhere. Several of his top-ranking associates hankered after a centre party, that perennial will-o'-the-wisp. As a preliminary step, Asquith renewed his ties with Grey, who had involuntarily assumed a strategic importance. On 8 November 1920 Phillipps heard that Grey was coming to town that week, and he instructed Maclean to bring him to 44 Bedford Square, where Asquith had recently moved his smaller family for reasons of economy. 'We don't want him to slip away back to the North without seeing Mr A.' The following summer, with the impending crack-up of the coalition, negotiations entered a more serious phase. On the morning of 29 June 1921, Grey 'came . . . by appointment' to see Asquith, with whom he agreed that 'a strong alternative government . . . could only be provided by the Liberal Party re-inforced by such men as Lord R. Cecil, and perhaps with an infusion of moderate Labour'. Six days later, they were joined in further discussions by Cecil, Maclean, Runciman, and Crewe. Cecil took the unalterable view that Grey must lead. It was not, as Jenkins has suggested, that 'he considered Asquith more committed in a party sense'; rather, as he had once told Runciman, he 'doubted [Asquith's] earnestness'. Maclean dutifully protested that such an arrangement 'would take the life and heart out of the Liberal rank and file'. In any case, Asquith was no more disposed than previously to serve under a former lieutenant. At lunch on 9 August, he assured Scott that Grey, 'though he was willing and able to take once more an active part in politics, . . . would not "take the first place"'. At tea that afternoon, Scott mentioned this pronouncement to Maclean, who replied 'that it was all right that Asquith should think so, but as a matter of fact the question was an open one'. As it proved, it was also an academic one. The differences between Asquith and Cecil were too substantial, 'moderate Labour' declined to respond, and Grey preferred the company of his beloved ducks at Fallodon.

That left Asquith where he began as the leader of a Liberal remnant that followed him with varying degrees of allegiance. On a single issue, that of 'the hellish policy of reprisals' in Ireland, he demonstrated force as well as foresight. A few dissidents, including the young Oswald Mosley, were profoundly impressed. But his passion was too quickly dissipated.

Frances Stevenson, whose diary then consisted of a catalogue of Lloyd George's political troubles, was pleased to record that Asquith was similarly plagued. She gloated on 24 June that 'the Wee Frees are making frantic advances to D. – lunches – dinners, etc.', and described second-hand a meeting on the 22nd,

when they discussed their position, & *all but four* voted for taking D. as their leader (with certain conditions of course). The four opponents were Asquith, Maclean, Wedgwood Benn & Thorne. Hogge has given an interview to The Evening Standard saying they are willing to join D. – with certain conditions . . . What a change of front from 6 weeks ago, when they were hauling down D.'s portrait from the walls of the Nat. Liberal Club. But they find Asquith is no leader, & they have no hope or trust in him.

Her partisan account was partially corroborated on the 29th by *The Times*, whose parliamentary correspondent reported a tempestuous luncheon the previous day at which 'the young Liberals made it clear that they are dissatisfied with the want of leadership of a rather forlorn, if gallant, band, 30 strong, but that in no circumstances, no circumstances whatever, could they adopt Mr Lloyd George for their leader'. It was not only the younger men who felt perplexed and despondent. Maclean, 'though entirely loyal', confided to Scott on 9 August 'that he had evidence that [Asquith] was not gaining but losing ground in the country. He had missed a great and unique opportunity by his failure to make any figure in Parliament since his return.' Scott wondered whether it was consideration for Maclean or simply 'indolence' that governed Asquith's behaviour. 'Something of both said Maclean, but he evidently thought that the first was only a cover for the second.'

During the second half of 1921, while Lloyd George's relations with his coalition colleagues steadily deteriorated, Asquith's relations with the independent Liberals were further strained. Their respective predicaments did not bring the two men closer together, although their women were somewhat reconciled. At a royal garden party on 21 July, Miss Stevenson 'was introduced to Mrs Asquith, above all people', and 'was agreeably surprised by her. She does not repel: on the contrary she rather attracts. She is a sort of kind Nancy Astor, whereas Nancy A. is a good looking Mrs A.' The only sour note in their conversation was struck when Margot mentioned Megan, Lloyd George's youngest daughter, and Frances 'said the P.M. always said how kind Mrs A. was to her. "Not as kind as my husband was to him", was her retort.'

In the closing hours of the year, the Asquithians were galvanized by the announcement that the Coalition Liberals were planning a rally early in 1922 at the Westminster Central Hall. Phillipps, covering every contingency, took an option on the same premises for four different nights in January in order to obtain equal attention for the Wee Frees. 'A dramatic stroke of fighting leadership of this kind will thrill our people as nothing else would', he prophesied to Maclean on 31 December: 'What is more, the fact that Mr A. is to reply within 48 hours from the same platform will hang over [Lloyd George] throughout his speech and cannot fail to cramp his style . . . I feel convinced that we ought to take this chance of a real fighting go at Ll. G.' Phillipps explained that Asquith was willing, but was unsure whether Grey would participate. In the event, Grey accepted an invitation to speak, but Gladstone had to invest 'a very rough unpleasant $\frac{1}{2}$ hour' on 19 January to persuade Asquith to make 'the max. reference possible' to Grey's co-operation. Gladstone wrote in his diary that, although he had 'stuck to my views like a brick', Asquith's proposed text was 'clearly not all I wanted'. Haldane proved even more difficult. Invited to grace the platform at the demonstration but not to address the audience, he refused on the grounds that his dedication to 'the cause of education' was not accommodated within 'the programme of official Liberalism'. An exchange of letters followed, and extracts from it appeared in the press. Asquith and Haldane each disclaimed responsibility and blamed the other for the leakage.

The National Liberal Council, as the Lloyd Georgeites styled themselves, held their rally on 20 January, and even before the sound of cheering had died away the independent Liberals struck back. Laski was there 'to hear Asquith inaugurate the election campaign against Lloyd George', and described the occasion to Oliver Wendell Holmes on 4 February:

As a speech giving ideas it was nothing; but as a speech to give a call to followers to battle it was a very great work of art. What impressed me was the dexterity of light and shade, the skilful way in which you were made to wait eagerly for the end of sentences, and the definite choice of always the exact word that was required.

Churchill, who had delivered a featured address on the first night, carried the rivalry to a meeting of the 1920 Club five days later. Again, he pleaded eloquently for the maintenance of the coalition, and castigated the Asquithians, who

told us how badly we have done, and told us how much better they could have done it themselves. (Cheers.) But they do not stop there. They leave events and address themselves to personalities. They tell us how much better men they are than we are, how much more consistent. All this they repeat with an air of indescribable impudence (Laughter and cheers) to carefully selected audiences, the bulk of whom, like them, in peace or in war, have stood carefully aside from the burden and heat of the day.

His imputations were rejected by his wife, who, on holiday in the south of France, read the speech in *The Times*. To say that the Asquithians had 'stood aside' during the war, she scolded him on 28 January, was 'not quite fair, becos' the Liberals (nearly all) behaved splendidly in the War which is more a credit to them than it is to the Tories who revel in slaughter & the Army etc. Think of Raymond and Oc Asquith', she implored. Churchill, replying to her on 4 February, admitted that his phrase was 'unfortunately turned', and related that his sister-in-law 'tells me the old man is very upset and in fact, in accepting her invitation to dinner next week, stipulated that he should not meet me'. But he was otherwise unrepentant:

I have always been very courteous and considerate to the old man and looked after Oc for him to the best of my ability in the war. All the same, I cannot forget the way he deserted me over the Dardanelles, calmly leaving me to pay the sole forfeit of the policy which at every stage he had actively approved. Still less can I forget his intervention after I had left the Government to prevent Bonar Law giving me the East African command and to deprive me of the Brigade to which French had already appointed me. Lastly, there was the vacancy in 1916 at the Ministry of Munitions, when he could quite easily have brought me back, as Lloyd George urged him to, but when he preferred to put his money on Montagu.

Professing himself 'not the least vindictive', Churchill gave conclusive evidence of the extent to which old wounds continued to fester.

As Churchill's official biographer has politely put it, 'Clementine Churchill was not entirely convinced by her husband's explanations.' She replied from Cannes on the 7th, still 'a little sad about the Asquith episode' and distressed by the offending sentence in his speech of 25 January. 'Everyone is conscious of his limitations', she argued compassionately,

& I daresay that in his dreams & lonely thoughts the old man goes over his war days & tries to prove to himself that he could not have been more energetic. He was as energetic as he could be, but he is not energetic by Nature. He was more energetic then than he is now to get himself back to office.

It is quite a different thing to criticise his unhelpfulness to the Government after the War; but really he would be inhuman if he did not now & then rouse up & try & put a snag in their path. Oh Darling do be a dove & put it right – to please me & to please yourself. People will only say 'Look how nice Winston is'.

I do not mind hard hitting (at least much) but I do think it is so cruel to say anything about a man's war record. And he has suffered more than we have by the War, by Death.

Churchill, resigned to the inevitability that political controversy would become 'more disagreeable, and not less disagreeable, up to the time the Election takes place', brushed aside his wife's advice.

Indeed, as the election neared, rancour increased on all sides. Among the Unionists, there was widespread discontent with Lloyd George, his Irish and foreign policies, and the shamelessness with which he hawked honours. Among the Coalition Liberals, there was anxiety that the Unionists would abandon them to an uncertain fate. Among the independent Liberals, Asquith was regarded – more than ever – as a liability. On 13 September 1922 Maclean gave Laski a 'melancholy' account of the situation: 'Asquith devoted to bridge and small talk, doing no real work, and leaving the party leaderless. I gather', Laski wrote the next day to Holmes, 'that they all want him to go, and see no means of explaining to him how much he stands in the way.'

To all intents and purposes, Asquith was more a name than a presence, but, as such, no less divisive a force. Late in 1921, the National Liberal Federation had adopted an industrial programme without his encouragement and, one may infer, against his inclination. In mid-March 1922 he approved Gladstone's letter to the *Yorkshire Evening News* on the subject of Liberal reunion, but himself took no initiative. 'Over the summer of that year', Jenkins has written, 'Asquith's interest in politics was lower than at any time since his return to the House of Commons.' Why, then, did he hang on?

Unfortunately, Asquith's interest in fashionable society suffered no comparable slump. Churchill, in a postscript to a letter of 16 July, informed his wife that, the previous week, 'the old boy turned up

... vy heavily loaded' at a party given by Philip Sassoon. 'The P.M. accompanied him up the stairs & was chivalrous enough to cede him the bannister. It was a wounding sight. He kissed a great many people affectionately. I presume they were all relations.' As if that were not sufficiently discreditable, Asquith also 'turned up', thinly disguised, in the pages of Aldous Huxley's novel *Crome Yellow*. Lady Ottoline Morrell was 'horrified' by the way in which Huxley had portrayed 'with contempt and ridicule' the friends to whom she had innocently introduced him at Garsington: 'Poor Asquith was depicted as a *ci-devant* Prime Minister, an old man, feebly toddling across the lawn after any pretty girl.' Finally, Asquith's reputation was not enhanced (although his bank account was replenished) by the publication of the first of Margot's two volumes of candid reminiscences, and by her American tour to boost sales. 'It is the first time that the wife of a Prime Minister has appeared on the platform as a public entertainer and it will do her husband great harm', Laski wrote to Holmes on 22 January 1922. 'As Morley said to me, if he wants money he should go back to the Bar.'

Asquith, who had read approvingly Margot's book in draft, was not so much indifferent to the aspersions cast upon him as blissfully unaware of their existence. The story circulated among members of the Reform Club, where he often came to browse or doze in the library after lunch, that he had put down a novel by his younger daughter, Elizabeth (Princess) Bibesco, and sighed: 'Another nail in the Asquith coffin.' Frank Swinnerton, an *habitué* of the Club, asked Phillipps whether the story was true. Phillipps, Swinnerton has recalled, 'laughed and replied "Mr A. doesn't know there *is* an Asquith coffin"'. So it must have seemed to many who worked faithfully to salvage Asquith's political fortunes, while he allowed them to slip irretrievably.

In October, Asquith was distracted from his own literary pursuits – he was preparing the manuscript of *The Genesis of the War* – by the Unionists' decision to withdraw their vital support from Lloyd George. Bonar Law, who emerged from the shadows to form a caretaker ministry, promptly dissolved the 'khaki' Parliament. In the ensuing general election, the two Liberal factions fought separately and, however ingeniously each tried to camouflage the result, fared poorly. The National Liberals fielded approximately 160 candidates as compared to some 320 Asquithians. In various cases, it was impossible to differentiate between Liberals of one stripe and the other, owing to what *The Times* described as 'the confused state of Party politics resulting from the break-up of the Coalition'. It has been ascertained, however, that there were no fewer than twenty-four Asquithians who challenged Liberal supporters of the late coalition, while five independent Liberal M.P.s were opposed by Liberals bearing the 'National' prefix.

The atmosphere was further clouded by the ambiguous response of both Liberal leaders. Lloyd George, determined not to prejudice the chances of restoring his alliance with the Unionists, was unusually inhibited. 'He offered no positive programme, and he carefully avoided defining his relations with the other parties', Chris Cook has observed. Asquith likewise tried his best to hedge his bets. His wife, glad to pay any price for Lloyd George's removal, rashly promised Bonar Law on 24 October 'no lack of generosity in my husband if and when he has to criticise'. Although not responsible for his wife's indiscretions, Asquith irritated officials at Liberal headquarters by entertaining Sir George Younger, the Unionist chairman, at lunch on 6 November. 'It set people talking', Hudson complained to Maclean two days later, 'and we had our work cut out to contradict the foolish rumours wh. grew out of it.'

These 'foolish rumours' were lent verisimilitude by the performance of McKenna. Having embarked on a second career in commercial banking, he declined Bonar Law's surprising offer of the chancellorship, but addressed a Unionist meeting during the campaign. With Lloyd George out of the way, Asquith too might have been able to achieve some limited accord with the Unionists, if only for immediate electoral purposes. Or, like some of his radical supporters, he might have looked forward to an accommodation with Labour. Last, but by no means least, he might have hoped to absorb the chastened National Liberals. The fluidity of the situation presented options which Asquith was in no hurry either to exercise or to relinquish.

Until Lloyd George came to realize that the Tories (with a few prominent exceptions) meant to uphold their party's declaration of independence, he shied away from the independent Liberals. 'All this stuff that is being put about . . . about reunion should not be treated too seriously', Asquith cautioned Maclean on 29 November. 'I am told that at the Peers' meeting this afternoon, Ll. G. almost foamed at the mouth at the mention of Grey's name.' By then, of course, Lloyd George was embittered by defeat. Only fifty-three National Liberals had been returned, with Churchill and Guest among the casualties. The Asquithians did comparatively better, gaining forty-three seats (ten from National Liberals) and losing fourteen (including Maclean's) for a net total of sixty-two. Given the number of candidates they had adopted, the victory scarcely admitted of celebration.

At Paisley, where he 'had been assured that all was more than safe', Asquith defended his seat against Biggar, who was standing for a third time. On 15 November he 'went to the counting . . . shortly before midnight . . . and watched the process until about 1.30 a.m. when the result was declared'. As he described it to Mrs Harrisson two days later,

I was not a little surprised to find when I arrived that it was beginning to look like a neck-and-neck affair. I had quite an exciting hour while the numbers fluctuated up and down, keeping on the whole almost even: indeed it was not until the last quarter of an hour that we forged ahead, and proceeded to win (as the racing people say) 'cleverly'.

His majority was a modest 316. 'I polled more votes than I did three years ago', he consoled himself,

and the drop in the majority was entirely due to the enormous addition to the Labour vote, owing to the 5,000 unemployed in Paisley (of whom there were none in 1920) and the sullen anti-bourgeois feeling which is swelling up like a tidal wave over the whole of the West of Scotland.

Asquith shared the common delusion that these factors were local and transitory. The massive advance of Labour, which more than doubled its parliamentary representation to qualify as the official opposition, should have given him greater pause.

If the writing was on the wall, it was not yet easily decipherable. With 29·1 per cent of the aggregate vote, the two Liberal parties were only a hairbreadth behind Labour, whose share had increased to 29·4 per cent. Moreover, it has been calculated that, had the Liberals abstained from competition among themselves, they would have secured fourteen seats that fell to their opponents (ten to Labour) on minority votes; in that case, the combined Liberals would have garnered 134 seats, thereby eclipsing Labour and retaining the status and psychological satisfaction of being the official opposition.

These arguments implicitly assume that the division between Liberals was no deeper than the labels affixed to them, and that, all things considered, they had more in common with one another than with politicians of the other parties. A year later, after Stanley Baldwin (who had succeeded to the premiership) raised the spectre of Protection, this might well have been true. But at the time of the

1922 election the rivalry between the two Liberal camps was intense and seemingly ineradicable. To speak of 'combined' Liberal strength in this context is to beg the issue.

It was only in the aftermath of the election that Liberal attitudes began to soften, at least among the backbenchers and in the constituencies. With a mixture of sarcasm and incredulity, Asquith reported to Mrs Harrisson on 28 November that there had been

a kind of 'fraternity' gathering last night in one of the Committee rooms between the rank and file of our lot and the ex-Coalie Liberals. The latter seem prepared to 're-unite' on almost any terms . . . Meanwhile Ll.G. is evidently dallying with visions of reconciliation. He took Hogge . . . into his room last night and talked to him for an hour and a half in his most mellifluous vein. Amongst other things he declared that he was quite ready to serve with and under me (!), with whom he had never had a quarrel and whom he had never ceased to admire and respect!

In March 1923, a petition for speedy and effective reunion, circulated exclusively among Liberal backbenchers, collected seventy-three signatures. The *Daily Chronicle*, whose editorial policy was dictated by Lloyd George, promoted the idea. The *Liberal Magazine*, controlled by the Asquithian section, fulsomely reciprocated its sentiments.

Nevertheless, there were obstacles, strategically placed, on both sides. The flames of mutual recrimination, which might have been expected to die down, were assiduously fanned by the men and – especially – the women who were devoted to one leader or the other. 'He never saw a belt without hitting below it', was Margot's familiar dictum on the man who had unforgivably deposed her husband from the premiership. The ladies in Lloyd George's entourage replied less wittily, but no less virulently.

The feud was likewise perpetuated by trusted cronies who fortified each leader against the other. The Asquithians pointed to the sinister influence of Guest and Churchill, both soon to defect to the Tories, and accused Lloyd George of having conspired to defeat Maclean at the general election. Lloyd George, in turn, complained to Scott on 15 March that 'the leaders of the Independent Liberals are determined that [reunion] should not occur. Simon is working against it; the Whips are whipping against it; Lord Gladstone and Geoffrey Howard are using every endeavour to persuade members of the party not to encourage it.' By appointing Vivian Phillipps as Chief Whip (replacing Thorne, who had retired, and superseding Hogge, who was suspected of being in Lloyd George's pay), Asquith and Maclean can

hardly be said to have spurred reunion. Masterman warned Scott
that, if Lloyd George returned to the fold, 'he and plenty of others
would go out'. Massingham and Gardiner joined in his threat, the
latter insisting in the *Nation* on 30 June that Lloyd George was 'the
heaviest political liability that any party, especially any party that
claims to rest on a moral basis, can assume'.

In May, Bonar Law resigned from office for reasons of health. Like
Curzon, Lloyd George waited for a call that never came. The age of
Baldwin had dawned, leaving Lloyd George all the more isolated and
eager to redeem his Liberal credentials. The question remained: on
what – or whose – terms was reunion to be achieved? Lloyd George
had the funds, Asquith the titular position and the control of the
party machinery. Who was to capitalize on whose assets?

Scott, whose integrity (if not his judgement) was above reproach,
acted as intermediary. On 1 July, he had 'a long talk with Lord
Gladstone (at his request) at his house . . . in Cleveland Square'.
Gladstone, an experienced hand at party management, had taken
charge of the Liberal Central Office. He spoke with unimpeachable
authority. 'To begin with,' he told Scott, 'one point must be regarded
as fixed and irrevocable: for whatever reason . . . [Asquith] was resolved never again to accept Lloyd George as a colleague.' Scott
professed that he 'already understood this', but asked 'what exactly
did that imply?' He surmised 'that Asquith was not unwilling to
confer with Lloyd George and had often done so on the day to day
procedure and tactics in the House'. Gladstone confirmed that such
conferences had taken place and that Asquith and Lloyd George had
'met on quite friendly terms'.

Pressed by Scott, Gladstone became more specific:

What Asquith refused to do was to admit Lloyd George into the
'inner council' of the party. This by custom consisted, when the
party was in opposition, of such persons as the leader of the party
chose to summon and was a matter within his absolute discretion,
just as the membership of the Cabinet, when the party was in office,
was within the Prime Minister's discretion. A theory had been
advanced that all ex-Cabinet Ministers had a right to be summoned,
but that was not so.

Gladstone cited the precedents established by his father and by
Campbell-Bannerman, who had excluded the Liberal Imperialists –
including Asquith – from discussions 'on vital matters of policy'.
Scott followed the argument, but disputed 'the importance attached
to this inner council' at the present juncture:

Lloyd George was already consulted on a good many matters

involving policy: why should he not be consulted on all matters of immediate or prospective practical importance? There was in his case no question of difference on policy as there was in that of the Liberal-Imperialists. He was as good a Liberal as any of the leaders of the Independent Liberals, or perhaps rather a more advanced one.

Gladstone 'admitted this', and was forced to concede that 'more was involved'. The paramount consideration was that of the succession. 'It was generally recognised that Asquith was no longer effective as an active leader.' Lloyd George, 'if once accepted and recognised as a full member of the party', would, 'by force of personality and past position', resume the right of reversion to the leadership. 'That', Gladstone maintained, 'would disintegrate the party.' The Asquithians, Scott was astounded to learn, favoured Simon or even Pringle as crown prince.

Admittedly, however, the Asquithians were strapped for funds, while Lloyd George's resources were variously estimated at between one and three million pounds. What did Lloyd George intend to do with this money? Was it to be his dowry in the prospective union? 'I don't see that we could accept it even if it were offered', Gladstone self-righteously informed Scott. 'It is the proceeds of corruption and we have protested against corruption.' Others, unhampered by Gladstonian scruples, were prepared to welcome the prodigal son with open arms and outstretched palms.

Before a marriage settlement could be negotiated, the matter was settled, shotgun-style. In October, Baldwin embraced the policy of protective tariffs as a means to combat unemployment. An early general election was inevitable. Asquith and Lloyd George joined in defence of Free Trade, virtually the only standard to which all Liberals could rally. Parliament was dissolved in mid-November for an appeal to the nation on 6 December. On 13 November Asquith and Maclean met Lloyd George and Sir Alfred Mond, and drafted a proclamation that (1) 'all candidates will be adopted and described as Liberals, and will be supported by the whole strength of the Party without regard to any past differences' and (2) 'Liberal candidates will go to the poll in such numbers as to make united Liberalism a practical alternative to the present Government'. It was privately agreed that Lloyd George would contribute £100,000 from his political fund towards party expenses. Baldwin, by his maladroit tactics, had succeeded where men with better intentions had failed.

The Liberals hastily promulgated a Free Trade manifesto that appeared over the signatures of Asquith and Lloyd George, in that order. A second, more general manifesto enumerated proposals for public works, land valuation, and the stimulation of 'co-operation between employers and employed'. It was the consensus at the meeting of the 13th 'that nothing corresponding to a "Newcastle programme" could or ought to be attempted' at such short notice, 'but that what we wanted was a limited number of bold but effective pronouncements'.

At Paisley, Asquith faced a third challenge from Biggar. But his chances were improved considerably by the intrusion of a renegade socialist who split the Labour vote. A Unionist also stood. Taking no chances, Asquith tended his constituency. His campaign received a fillip from Lloyd George, who 'arrived with his Megan' on 24 November to celebrate 'the rites of Liberal Reunion . . . at an enthusiastic meeting in the Town Hall'. To Mrs Harrisson, Asquith wrote the next day that

I have rarely felt less exhilaration than when we got to the platform amid wild plaudits and a flash-light film was taken, 'featuring' me and Ll. G. separated only by the chairman – an excellent local Doctor. I spoke for about quarter of an hour, and Ll. G. then plunged into a characteristic speech – ragged and boisterous, but with quite a good assortment of telling points. He was more than friendly and forthcoming, and the meeting was full of demonstrative fraternity.

Violet, his mainstay on these occasions, capped the evening by referring to the Biblical image of 'the lion lying down with the lamb': 'I can only say, for myself,' she jested, 'that I have never seen Mr Lloyd George look less voracious or my father more uneatable.' At close range, Margot, too, saw Lloyd George as a lion, toothless if not quite tame. 'I don't think Ll.G. will ever have any power in this country again as *no* one trusts him', she wrote on 2 December to St Loe Strachey, who defended Free Trade from a Tory position. 'Unity has done our party infinite good', she boasted, '& tho I *hoped* it wd. come without Ll.G., he won't do us as much harm as Birkenhead is doing you.'

While Lloyd George tried to rouse Scotland and the north of England, Asquith spoke at Nottingham ('a terrific affair') and Manchester. Lord Rothermere, whose electoral forecasts were usually reliable, sent word to Lloyd George that he anticipated a Liberal 'landslide' of 230–240 seats. Asquith, four days before polling, took a more sober view. 'I have been going through the general list of candidates', he told Mrs Harrisson, 'and I cannot for the life of me see how we are to come back more than 200 strong, it may be less. Labour is the dark horse. The result which I should welcome would be that we should exceed Labour and Baldwin find himself with a majority of 30 to 40 – useless for his purpose, but sufficient to compel him to go on with the Government.' The returns were discouraging. Out of 457 candidacies (thirty more than Labour), the Liberals managed to win 158 seats (thirty-three fewer than Labour). It has been estimated that a quarter of their seats were held by majorities under a thousand. With 258 seats, the Conservatives remained the largest party in the House, but no longer enjoyed an overall dominance. With 191 seats, Labour had pulled ahead of the Liberals.

But, if nothing else, Lloyd George and Asquith were back together, and their collaboration momentarily inspired feelings of confidence and relief. Laski attended 'a dinner at the Asquiths' where they discussed the election': his hostess, he informed Holmes on 13 December, was

full of energy and vigour, finding consolation for the small numbers in the fact that they held the balance; guessing that the nation even yet must turn to [Asquith]; contemptuous of all their opponents and prepared only to defend her suppliants. He, on the other hand, weary of politics, turning to me with eagerness to know why I preferred Catullus to Horace, insisting that (you would agree) the majesty of *Prometheus Vinctus* is unapproachable and urging, *me dissentiente*, that Lytton Strachey is the greatest thing since Sainte-Beuve. It was like stepping into an XVIIIth century salon before the Revolution.

Among the other guests was Lloyd George, who seemed to Laski 'distressed and subdued and ill at ease'; he had obviously been invited to Bedford Square – and had obviously accepted – 'out of courtesy alone'.

There were further meetings between the new allies. On 14 December Lloyd George 'came up . . . for a chat with Asquith', who struck him as 'most friendly and helpful'. He was not surprised. 'The old boy & I get on well together always when mischief makers are kept out', he wrote to his wife. The so-called 'mischief makers' did not trust Asquith to withstand Lloyd George's blandishments and to strike the best bargain. 'H.H.A. is not Ll.G.-proof by any means', Maclean reminded Gladstone on the 29th. 'We must not let L.G. alone with H.H.A. more than we can help.' Gladstone concurred; in his reply the next day, he cited the Liberal showing in the recent election as 'a triumph for H.H.A.' that augured well for the party's recovery. As a rule, candidates of an Asquithian cast had done better than those who were tainted by the coalition brush. 'L.G. knows that apart from the Election costs, he cannot claim any material share in our success', Gladstone ungenerously asserted.

The question of election costs was itself a sticky one. Gladstone complained that, as late as 30 November, Lloyd George had handed over only £30,000. Liberal headquarters eventually put his total donation at £90,000, which fell short of his pledge. But Lloyd George maintained that he had allocated £160,000, much of it directly to candidates and their agents. In any case, he had neither deposited a lump sum nor agreed to amalgamate his assets with those of the party. It was 'not only a question of merging funds', Gladstone insisted to Maclean. 'L.G. seems unable to carry on without his . . . saloon, his attendants, his horrible publicity arrangements.' For that reason, control over finance had to be wrested from him so as to protect the party from his image no less than from his whims.

This problem unresolved, Asquith and Lloyd George turned their attention to arrangements at Westminster. Here, they enjoyed less room for manoeuvre than they supposed or many historians have assumed. For different reasons, each of them was prepared to allow Ramsay MacDonald to form a minority Labour Government. Perhaps Lloyd George nursed a vague ambition to lead a Lib-Lab alliance. Possibly, too, he appreciated better than Asquith the dangers of the moment. Yet, beyond any doubt, he gave full and necessary approval to Asquith's strategy.

'Asquith rejected the idea of playing for a Liberal administration', Roy Douglas has stated. 'Why he did so must remain a mystery; and it is arguable that this decision was the most disastrous single action ever performed by a Liberal towards his Party.' His indictment is grossly unfair. True, there was no majority party in the newly elected Parliament; but the Liberals were the smallest of the three minority parties, hardly in a position to impose their will. Asquith, naturally averse to the idea of coalition, ruled out a 'bourgeois' alliance with the protectionist Tories. The Labour Party executive had proclaimed its readiness, given the opportunity, to form an independent administration, and Asquith reasoned that 'if a Labour Government is ever to be tried in this country, as it will be sooner or later, it could hardly be tried under safer conditions'. The possibility of an Asquith–Grey ministry, he affirmed on 28 December, was no more than 'an amusing whirligig'. If anyone could stop Labour, it was not Asquith but Baldwin, who (as Asquith wrote to Pringle on 10 January 1924) 'could easily have snapped his fingers at the no confidence amendment' carried against him, 'and announced that, as leader of much the largest section of the House, he had better moral authority than anyone else to carry on the King's Government until he was absolutely blocked.' But Baldwin rejected schemes (advanced by Sir Robert Horne and others) for a 'working arrangement' with the Liberals, and, as Cook has put it, was 'determined that Ramsay MacDonald should form a government and the Conservatives go into opposition without any collusion or pre-arranged intrigue with the Liberals'.

With 'hearty concurrence' from Lloyd George and Simon, Asquith put his case to a meeting at the National Liberal Club on 18 December. In the days that followed, his 'postbag' was filled with 'appeals, threats, prayers from all parts, and from all sorts and conditions of men, women, and lunatics' who implored him 'to step in and save the country from the horrors of Socialism and Confiscation'. Several of these entreaties came from Liberal politicians (including Mond and Churchill, who did not even have seats) who were ravenous for a taste of office. To his credit, Asquith discounted the threat of guillotines in Trafalgar Square. To his peril, he failed to anticipate the unfilial attitude of MacDonald towards the Liberals. But, as Lloyd George argued in his defence in the *Daily Chronicle* on 1 November, after Labour had left office: 'How could [Asquith] have conjectured that the Leader of a great party would have behaved like a jealous, vain, suspicious, ill-tempered actress of the second rank?'

The first Labour Government came to power on 23 January 1924 and, on Liberal sufferance, lasted for nine months. In its ranks was Haldane who, on the eve of his return to the woolsack, wrote touchingly to Asquith, with whom he now severed the last of his political ties. Asquith replied with equally fond allusions to their past associations, but tittered in his diary that Haldane 'will have a hellish time in the House of Lords'. He doubted that the new ministers, 'for the most part a beggarly array', possessed either the inclination to inflict damage or the ability to deal constructively with pressing problems. At a Grillion's Club dinner in March, he 'was extraordinarily at his ease, and talked with copious indiscretion' to Edmund Gosse, who recounted the conversation to Haldane on the 29th:

He does not love your Government, but he says he would not lift a finger to turn you out. He considers R.M.'s whole policy 'woolly' and 'fallacious'. 'He (Ramsay M.) clings to the edge of the cliff, with all his wild men underneath, longing to get their fangs into him.' Asquith would not 'rob the poor man of an hour of his brief rule; let him enjoy it while he may, for once out, and he will never be heard of again'.

Confident that the Labour experiment would be judged a failure Asquith trusted that, if the Liberals continued their revival, their turn might yet come.

The 'balance' which the Liberals held in the Commons proved a singular misfortune. Liberal votes were required to sustain Mac-Donald in office and, with increasing reluctance, these were duly forthcoming. But Labour, far from showing gratitude, acted to slough off the vestiges of its long tutelage. The intervention of a Labour candidate in a June by-election at Oxford handed the seat to the Conservatives. Phillipps, the Liberal Chief Whip, described the restlessness of his M.P.s in the face of 'a constant stream of ill-natured criticism and frequently abuse of the Liberal Party'. The *Manchester Guardian*, admitting (as did Asquith) to admiration for MacDonald's conduct of foreign affairs, complained on 3 October that 'the Prime Minister, who can be so sweet to the foreigner from whom he differs most widely, has nothing but unconcealed dislike and exaggerated suspicion for those who in this country stand nearest to him in politics'.

MacDonald's ultimate act of ingratitude was to call a general election that took place twenty-three days later. It was intended to lay flat the Liberals, and so it did. Liberal headquarters was desperately short of time and, still more, of money. Although Asquith and Lloyd George had co-operated publicly during the last session, they were privately engaged in a tug-of-war over financial control. 'It seems clear to me', Maclean told Gladstone on 10 January, 'that if we submit to the periodic contribution, with no Election Fund in hand, we shall be completely at the mercy of Ll.G., who is, it would seem, all-powerful in financial as well as other matters.' Lloyd George held tightly to his purse-strings, determined to obtain value for money. Regarding a Liberal victory at the next election, which could not be long postponed, as 'impossible', he argued that the party should field fewer candidates 'and save money for a better opportunity'. Accused by the Asquithians of maintaining a 'dole' system, he retorted that the 'rottenness' of the party organization made him loath to throw good money after bad. On 4 July Hudson begged leave to second Gladstone's resolution: 'D— L.G.' He and Maclean had had '40 minutes talk with him [that] was so poisonous that I took to my bed with a temperature the next afternoon, & the Dr has kept me until this morning'.

Lloyd George was obviously stalling and, under the circumstances, who can blame him? He had presented a demand for a drastic over-haul of the Liberal machine, including the appointment of two of his deputies to the whips' office. His plea unheeded, he withheld his pecuniary assistance. 'He thought for the first time Asquith's "Wait and see" was the only thing to do, or rather "Watch and see",' he declared on 5 February to Lady Scott, who had switched her allegiance from Asquith to him. On 1 June, she baited him: '"Isn't the Liberal Party ready for real leadership?" He said he thought it was; and I asked "Isn't it ready for *your* leadership?" to which he replied, "Oh, no, no. I couldn't do that. I mustn't think of usurping Asquith's position. I must try, if it's possible, to carry him along".' On 14 September Lloyd George conferred at The Wharf with Asquith, Maclean, and Mond, and pointedly alluded to the probability that, in the next election, Asquith would lose Paisley. Secure in his own constituency, he could then expect the parliamentary leadership to fall to him. For that eventuality, he intended to keep a free hand and as much capital as possible.

Lloyd George's differences with the Asquithians were not, however, exclusively financial. Asquith held to the nineteenth-century view that politicians out of office ought not to be too specific about the policies they proposed to pursue. There was no harm in having 'policy . . . expounded in generalities', but too precise a statement ran the dual risk of opening party wounds and alienating potential support in the country. Lloyd George disagreed, and wished to launch an ambitious programme with as much fanfare as possible. Denied the subsidies which they considered their due, the Asquithians resented Lloyd George's lavish expenditure on a new land campaign, for which he was laying the groundwork. On 10 October a 'meeting of leaders' was hastily summoned to draft a manifesto for the fast approaching election. It was particularly urgent to incorporate some measure of Lloyd George's land policy, but how much? According to W. McG. Eager, who took notes for Lloyd George, the most strenuous resistance came from Mond, who insisted 'that he was not really so much against the policy as against the difficulty of explaining it in the limited time available'. Lloyd George was permitted to add a brief preface to the preamble, drawn up by Masterman, and it was further agreed that, 'on the land question, paragraphs not inconsistent with Mr Lloyd George's policy should be inserted'. But the primary purpose of the document, reflecting the sense of panic that inspired it, 'was to show why the Liberals put the Labour Government out rather than to explain why they ever put it in'.

Haldane, too, had heard 'that Paisley is now unsafe for H.H.A. But he is sure to fight it', he predicted on 26 September, 'and if he is turned out I doubt his wishing to go on.' It was that on which Lloyd George banked. Seventy-two years old, Asquith was spared opposition from the Conservatives, and stood against a single Labour

challenger, Rosslyn Mitchell, a Glasgow solicitor and a former
Liberal. Margot, four days before polling, remarked that she had
'never seen H. in such amazing form!' But more objective sources
described him as languid to the point of indifference. 'What is that
melancholy dirge they are crooning now?' he asked his daughter,
when his audience drowned him out with the familiar strains of 'The
Red Flag'. Thereupon, she wrote in her diary, 'he would evince mild
interest, then lean back in his chair again with a sniff and a shrug and
resume his own train of thought'.

Margot, who gave Mitchell credit for good looks and sartorial
splendour, predicted that 'he may run us very close'. When the votes
were counted, he led Asquith by 2,228, and awkwardly apologized:
'I'm so sorry, so terribly sorry this has happened.' His sympathy was
genuine. 'I only hope', he told a Labour rally soon afterwards, 'that
when my turn comes to be cast aside, I shall be able to accept my
rejection with the courage and dignity which was shown by that
great gentleman.' At the Paisley Liberal Club, the faithful Scots
broke into an inevitable rendition of 'Will ye no' come back again?'
But everyone knew that he never would.

All over the country, the results were much the same. Of the 340
Liberal candidates, only forty were returned. Lloyd George, pinning
the blame on headquarters, fumed that the party 'went into action a
disorganized rabble'. Gladstone countered 'definitely and without
reserve that we at Abingdon St were not responsible for the Election
of 1924 and its disastrous results'.

On the morning of 31 October, Hudson 'went up to Bedford
Square . . . & had a longish talk with H.H.A. while he consumed his
breakfast'. Maclean was present, 'no one else'. Asquith appeared 'fit
enough & unabashedly cheerful', Hudson informed Gladstone the
next day. He 'pictured with some sarcasm our contingent on the
Front Bench of the new House: "L.G. flanked by Simon & Runciman. I have no particular desire to join them – but we can see about
that later on."' Hudson and Maclean strongly 'urged that . . ., as
soon as possible, he should summon his colleagues, including L.G. of
course, for consultation: he firmly taking the chair, & (after private
consultation with L.G.) that he should nominate the new chief whip'
to replace Phillipps, who had lost his seat. They proposed the names
of Wedgwood Benn and Sir Godfrey Collins, both of whom Lloyd
George was known to dislike.

Another, more formal conclave was held at the same address on
the morning of 5 November, the day before Asquith left on a seven-
week visit to Egypt. 'About a dozen' elder statesmen attended, and

the outcome, Hudson told Gladstone, was 'thoroughly unsatisfactory'. Lloyd George vetoed a proposal to call a Liberal convention 'of MPs *plus* defeated candidates, clearly fearing that such a joint meeting wd. turn into a pro-Asquith Demonstration'. With some misgiving, he accepted a compromise by which Asquith would address Liberal M.P.s over lunch at the Reform Club, while Lord Beauchamp would give a private reception at which Asquith would deliver 'a second but secondary speech' to Liberal M.P.s, peers, and candidates. Asquith, knowing that 'I shall have to think over these allocutions rather carefully', was compliant. Corroborating Hudson's account, he wrote to Mrs Harrisson that he had found Lloyd George 'at first very intractable', although eventually 'more reasonable'. The next morning, he went on holiday, carrying with him the King's offer of a peerage, to which he promised to give 'mature and deliberate consideration'.

Margot, who stayed behind in London, grieved bitterly. 'In the country our Party is alive but in the H. of C. it is a painful sight, & I am glad Henry is out of it,' she wrote on Christmas Day to Strachey. 'Ll.G. has been the curse of our Party & but for Baldwin wd. have ruined yours.' That she was to become a countess offered scant satisfaction. 'It is a hard wrench', she confessed a month later to Gardiner:

I have wept many times at leaving the H. of Commons, but there is *no* safe Liberal seat & he must lead his shattered Party from the Lords. The alternative was retirement from public life wh. wd. have killed him . . . Nor do I see him happy muddled up with 3 men who detest one another – Ll. G., Simon, & Runciman (of these, Simon has the best brain). Ll.G. will never lead anyone anywhere & has been our curse.

Quite obviously, at this point, her husband was not going to lead anyone anywhere either.

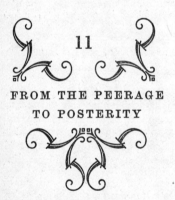

# 11

## FROM THE PEERAGE
## TO POSTERITY

Early in 1925, after an extended holiday in the Middle East, Asquith returned to London to find the situation much as he had left it. He had no seat in the House of Commons, and not even a remote chance of getting one. 'I'd sooner go to hell than to Wales', he reportedly proclaimed to C. F. G. Masterman, who would have been grateful for a constituency anywhere. He doubtless noticed, however, that no one in Wales was inviting him, least of all the triumphant member for the Caernarvon Boroughs.

On 15 January Lloyd George called on him in Bedford Square, and pronounced him 'much better & fitter' than when they had last met in November. Asquith imparted some 'Interesting news. Very confidential': he had decided to accept the offer of a peerage. Lloyd George respected the confidence to the extent that he communicated the information to his wife in Welsh.

Writing to the King five days later, Asquith ended his long 'suspense of judgment' and submitted a 'definite reply': 'If it should be your Majesty's pleasure, in accordance with precedent, to confer upon me the dignity of an Earl, I should propose to take the title of Oxford, which has fine traditions in our history, and which was given by Queen Anne to her Prime Minister, Robert Harley.' The King was amenable, but others thought Asquith rather too presumptuous in his choice. 'It is like a suburban villa calling itself Versailles' was the riposte of the future Lady Salisbury. There were those who fretted about the possibility of confusion in the House of Lords between the new earl and the Bishop of Oxford, who was himself unconcerned. The descendants of Robert Harley, faithful to their family's Tory antecedents, issued a stiff protest. Taking such arguments into account, the College of Heralds saddled Asquith with a double-decked title: as the Earl of Oxford *and Asquith*, he made his début in the Lords on 17 February. St Loe Strachey, who shared his sense of history, accompanied his congratulations with a quotation from Swift's diary (25 May 1712): 'My Lord Oxford can't yet abide to be called my lord; and when I called him my lord, he called me Dr Thomas Swift.' Asquith accepted his change of status with a comparable lack of enthusiasm.

His projected ennoblement had raised immediate and fundamental questions about the party leadership. Lloyd George, he had confided to Mrs Harrisson on 5 November, 'evidently thinks that over forty MPs are for the most part his men, and there was a great deal of friction between him and Simon and D. Maclean'. Was Lloyd George going to permit Asquith, transplanted to 'another place', to retain titular control?

As Roy Douglas has observed, Lloyd George 'was determined to hold the substance of power, if not the shadow'. It mattered little to him whether Asquith pretended to lead the Liberal Party from the upper House, even if Asquith appointed the new Chief Whip. There were greater issues at stake, and, for a while longer, Lloyd George could expect more as Asquith's legitimate heir than as a successful rebel.

On 29 January 1925 the Liberals opened a two-day London convention to revive the party's spirit and to launch an appeal for a million pounds to be raised through the constituency associations. While certain party officials hoped for a generous subvention from the Lloyd George fund, others conceived of the 'Liberal Million

Fund' as a means to release the party from its debilitating bondage to Lloyd George. Lady Scott, who had expected a display of fireworks, came away disappointed on the second day: 'The debate on the leadership fizzled out', she recorded in her diary, because 'few cared to be rude to Mr Asquith. Oh dear! how I wish he could have died when he should in 1916. What a great name my beautiful friend would then have left.'

With a greater name or, at any rate, a more cumbersome one, Asquith (as we shall continue to call him) embarked on a sort of life after death. His public position had become still more incongruous. Although he sat beside Lloyd George on the convention platform, his presence could not disguise the fact that the parliamentary party, in its shrunken state, remained hopelessly divided: some M.P.s, like Simon, swore fealty to him; the bulk were devoted to Lloyd George (who was elected, twenty-six votes to seven, to lead the Liberals in the Commons); and a third component, under Runciman, had constituted itself a Radical Group. Asquith, warned off by Lloyd George, remarked to Phillipps that he 'was certainly not going to put his head into that hornets' nest'.

Behind the scenes there were frenetic efforts to devise some common policy. Various committees and commissions were set up, most of them amply endowed by Lloyd George. He and Asquith vied to pack them with their respective nominees. The Asquithians, entrenched at party headquarters and in the executive of the National Liberal Federation, wanted Lloyd George's money, preferably in one deposit. Lloyd George, for his part, sought party approval and facilities for his scheme of land nationalization, soon elaborated in his 'green book', *The Land and the Nation*. Mond and Runciman were downright hostile to Lloyd George's land proposals, and Asquith 'was not enthusiastic'. He resented the costliness of the land inquiry and, in particular, the self-glorification that Lloyd George got out of it. 'All this Press pushing of Ll.G. & his "policies" is "Pretty Fanny's way",' he wrote scathingly to Maclean on 12 September:

He has got poor Francis Acland well into the net. He (F.A.) wrote to me a week or two ago to ask me to give a good 'Kick-off' to the much boomed demonstration which is to be held at Killerton shortly – regardless of expense & with infinite touting, as I am informed in an angry sputtering letter from C. Hobhouse. I replied to Acland that there was no greater adept in the art of 'Kicking-off' than his present hero, and that I observed that all the sackbuts & psalteries were being turned up for the advertised descent of Moses from the Mount.

The National Liberal Federation, having played no part in the formulation of Lloyd George's land policy, declined to put its organization at his disposal. Lloyd George thereupon set up his independent Land and Nation League, with himself as president. During the summer and autumn months, there was the growing threat of a formal rupture. Deputations shuttled back and forth between Lloyd George's house at Churt in Surrey and Asquith's residences in Bedford Square and Berkshire. W. McG. Eager, who served as secretary to Lloyd George's land inquiry and subsequently to his industrial inquiry, was dispatched to 'prejudice' Asquith 'in favour of the Policy': in a briefing session on 7 July, Lloyd George instructed Eager to 'show him reports' by certain authorities (not by others), and to 'work out sums . . . Lord Oxford likes sums.' Eager eventually recalled to 'Tom' Jones (1 May 1945) how he 'went through the flirtations and engagements and disengagements of Ll.G. and the Asquithians, even to the extent of being Ll.G.'s emissary to Asquith, which gave Margot the chance of being rude to me at her own lunch table, and some priceless cracks from Oxford himself.' Finally, at a parley on 2 December, a tentative agreement was reached: Asquith, to the dismay of his associates, acceded to Lloyd George's land proposals in principle, if not necessarily in detail. On 17 February 1926 he joined with Lloyd George to present them to a special conference at the Kingsway Hall under the auspices of the N.L.F.

Frances Stevenson reproved Lloyd George for being 'far too trustful' of the Asquithians. 'The Old Man counts for nothing,' she warned on 12 August 1925, '& if he is decent about things it doesn't carry any weight. If you are not careful that section of the party is going to be like an old man of the sea about your neck.' Her fears were reciprocated by Maclean, among others, who believed that Lloyd George was trying to subvert the fund-raising appeal. 'And this was not the worst', he told Scott, whom he saw at Manchester on 19 October. 'He was at his old game of intrigue with the Tories' in the hope of resurrecting his coalition. Scott 'asked about Asquith', and Maclean 'admitted that there was no real reconciliation. Asquith's language in private about Lloyd George was lurid.'

Asquith's acolytes, always *plus royalistes que le roi*, tried to translate his private sentiments into public policy. On 25 November they held a war council in Carlton House Terrace at the house of Lord Cowdray, one of their most generous benefactors. Those present included Asquith, Grey, Maclean, Gladstone, Simon, Runciman, Sir William Plender, and Sir Godfrey Collins, now Chief Whip. It was 'the general view to break with Ll.G. on the financial opening', but

Asquith 'said he could not "rush" it & wanted time to think it over'. The next thing they knew, Asquith – true to form – had backed down. Maclean protested that he had been personally betrayed, and he recounted that Phillipps, as chairman of the Liberal Organising Committee, 'felt that . . . his head had been handed on a charger to Ll.G.'

There was another opportunity for decisive action when the National Liberal Federation met in executive session in December 1925, but Asquith (as Maclean wrote to Gladstone on the 24th) 'knocked the affair end ways' by leaving before the topic came up for discussion. Cowdray, Maclean recapitulated, 'is roused to rage . . . & vows that if a clear issue between Ll.G. & Headquarters is not defined by *Asquith*, he will close his support & allow things to take their course as far as he is concerned'. Shortly thereafter, Maclean heard 'that Asquith says he is going on with the financial severance. I place no reliance on that', he concluded. His scepticism was widely shared. Early in 1926, Mond removed himself to the Conservative camp. 'So the Little Welsher has cost us (or lost us) Alfred Mond', Hudson lamented to Robert Donald on 27 January. 'Nor are the entries on the debit side of that particular a/c *yet ended*. I still hold to my gloomy view that our poor old Party will never have a chance until we have had a sequence of notable public Funerals.'

Asquith was having a difficult time all round. Unlike Lloyd George, whose antipathy to Baldwin was mutual and well known, he appeared to enjoy the Prime Minister's patronage. When Asquith was defeated at Paisley, Baldwin sent him a message of 'real regret'. Soon afterwards, Baldwin had paid tribute in the House to 'the stability of his character, the serenity of his temper, his freedom from jealousies and enmities, the magnitude of his mind and the plenitude of his utterance'. Margot took pains to deny that her husband's earldom was 'a Tory gift' that signalled some tacit understanding: the offer had been made by the King, on his own initiative, 'in Nov. when he had *no* P. Minister', she insisted to Gardiner on 23 January 1925. The following May, Asquith accepted the Garter directly from Baldwin, thereby reviving suspicions in certain minds.

Later that spring, Asquith was embroiled in a political struggle in which he incurred his final electoral defeat. Curzon had died, leaving vacant the chancellorship of the University of Oxford. Asquith could not resist the temptation to offer himself as his successor, although he knew from the start that 'the country clergy' would be 'in full blast' against him, rendering the 'result . . . a foregone conclusion.' Grey, who stood unopposed two years later, graciously withdrew from the race in Asquith's favour; with a far less distinguished academic record, he was estimated to command strong support within the cloisters of Balliol, among the League of Nations people, and, especially, from the women electors.

The Tory faction at Oxford, led by the president of Trinity College, were resolved to stop Asquith, whose candidacy was not helped by Lord Birkenhead's commendation of him in a letter to *The Times* (19 May) as 'the greatest living Oxonian'. Birkenhead had recently spoken slightingly of the League of Nations, and his irreligious views were notorious. Asquith was mischievously depicted as 'a warming pan for Birkenhead & the "anti-clericals"'. An unsuccessful attempt was made to conscript no less a personage than Randall Davidson, the Archbishop of Canterbury, to stand against him. When Davidson proclaimed himself an Asquith supporter, Lord Cave, the Lord Chancellor, was adopted. Aside from Lord Robert Cecil, 'the Cavemen' seemed to Asquith to be 'rather a sorry, scurvy lot'. Nevertheless, they were sufficiently numerous to trounce him by a margin of more than two to one. 'Zadok the Priest and Abiathar the Priest – with their half literate followers in the rural parsonages – were too much for us', Asquith sadly acknowledged on 24 July to Strachey, who had sent him a note of commiseration. Like the fact that his youngest son, Anthony ('Puffin'), only 'got a Second' in Greats, the experience left him 'more disappointed than surprised'.

The response to the 'Liberal Million Fund' appeal, on which so much depended, was again more a disappointment than a surprise. 'The failure of the Million Fund made Oxford's position extremely precarious', his official biographers have stated. Phillipps, who chaired the fund-raising drive, ascribed public indifference to the existence of a separate Lloyd George treasury that discouraged contributions to official party coffers. That explanation, readily accepted by the Asquithians, does not suffice. For one reason or another, many of the wealthy men, including Mond, were lost to Liberalism. Sir Robert Perks received '2 urgent appeals from Asquith to subscribe to his party funds', and told Lord Rosebery on 4 February 1926 that he had replied 'that during the 20 years I was in Parliament I gave between £50,000 and £60,000 to the party, and I think I have done my share. Asquith's fault', Perks asserted, 'is that he does not know how to keep his friends, or how to treat them. The result is that he has few *personal* friends, & is a lonely figure.' He exaggerated, of course. Asquith had many friends, some of whom were fiercely devoted to him politically; but money was not among their attributes.

Public appearances were kept up. On 9 December 1925 Asquith amused Mrs Harrisson with an account of the opening of the Liberal Fair at the Albert Hall, 'in which ceremony Dame Margaret Ll. G. and I sang a dulcet duet in perfect tune'. In private, there was less harmony. Lloyd George was unavoidably re-elected as sessional chairman of the Liberal M.P.s, but, as Maclean observed with satisfaction to Gladstone on 31 January, 'under circumstances of sufficient humiliation to indicate how profound is the distrust of him'. At the Liberal Land Conference on 17 February, Leslie Hore-Belisha, a young Lloyd Georgeite, slapped Pringle across the face for an offensive remark. Asquith, having discharged his platform responsibilities, 'was heard to say that he never wished to hear another word about the Lloyd George Fund'.

The showdown, long postponed, came in May, at the time of the General Strike. The Liberal Shadow Cabinet – to which Asquith and Lloyd George both belonged – met on the 3rd and unequivocally backed the Baldwin Government against the insurgent trades unions. The next day, Asquith spoke to this effect in the House of Lords, and he and Grey contributed articles to the *British Gazette*, the official anti-strike daily. Asquith's unsympathetic attitude was well documented in successive letters to Mrs Harrisson: 'I cannot think that the General Strike will last long: it is very unpopular, and they are short of funds for anything like a severe struggle', he wrote to her on the 4th. His 'young people', he revealed two days later, 'are hard at work in keeping things going': his niece, Kathleen Tennant (later Duchess of Rutland),

who has just been here at lunch, takes out her car every morning at about seven, and fetches shop girls, typists, etc., from the East End to their work in the City. Puffin plies his little car in north London and brings out-patients to and from the hospitals: later in the day, he picks up stray people who are stranded in the streets, and takes them to their homes in the suburbs . . . The whole thing is a piece of criminal folly, which will soon break to pieces.

The break imminent, the Liberal Shadow Cabinet met again at Liberal headquarters in Abingdon Street on the morning of the 10th. As Asquith told Mrs Harrisson the next day, 'there was one notable absentee – Ll.G. – who was in the sulks, and had cast in his lot for the moment with the clericals – Archbishops and Deans and the whole company of the various Churches (a hopeless lot) – in the hope of getting a foothold for himself in the Labour camp.' Lloyd George's intentions were, as always, difficult to divine. Perhaps taken aback by Simon's truculent (and seemingly official) proclamation in the

Commons four days earlier, he had sent word via Collins, the Chief Whip, that he could not endorse any party statement that did not condemn in equal measure the Government's intransigence. Furthermore, in a column for the Hearst syndicate in America, he took what a majority of his colleagues regarded as 'a much too pro Labour line . . . But I did it deliberately,' he assured his wife on 18 May, '& I mean to stick to it'.

Maclean, 'in high hopes', initially presumed that Lloyd George 'was in full cry to join Labour'. But within twenty-four hours he was less sure. Lloyd George, he informed Gladstone on the 11th, had 'sent a message to H.H.A. asking whether he would speak with him at Carnarvon on July 3rd!' Asquith, who reportedly replied 'that he could not consider matters of that kind just now', confirmed the receipt of such a message in his correspondence with Mrs Harrisson. He took it as a sign that Lloyd George 'is already, being a creature of uncertain temperature, suffering from cold feet'. There was, as yet, no indication that he attached any vital importance to this episode.

On the 18th, there was 'a very private confabulation' at Asquith's house in Bedford Square, where he was visited by Simon, Runciman, Maclean, Collins, Phillipps, Hudson, Pringle, and Lords Buxton, Buckmaster, and Beauchamp. The last, who was the only Lloyd Georgeite among them, 'left early', and the 'talk became more free after his departure'. Hudson hastened to inform Gladstone that Asquith had been '*far more* indignant at L.G.'s behaviour than I have ever seen. Runciman, Simon & Buckmaster all declared with emphasis position to be intolerable. Others murmured assent.' It was 'agreed unanimously that H.H.A. should write to L.G. & say flatly that his patience was exhausted'. Asquith concurred, but stipulated 'that any letter he wrote must be so framed as to put L.G. in the wrong if it had to be published'. Hudson, although impressed by 'H.H.A.'s indignation', refused to take anything for granted: 'we shall see *what we shall see!*' But, this time, Asquith did not waver. On the evening of the 20th, he dispatched by hand a letter of rebuke to Lloyd George. 'At last I really think the break has come', Maclean crowed to Gladstone with incredulous delight. 'I never thought he would come right up to it, but he has.' Phillipps, too, was ebullient: 'I did not expect such a deliverance from him as he has produced', he confessed late the same evening to Gladstone. 'All my advices from the country are that Ll.G.'s stock was never lower than it is at the present moment.'

The next day, Lloyd George left London to join his family in Wales. He travelled a roundabout route through Manchester, where he broke his journey to confer with Scott at the Midland Hotel. As Scott's son later recalled, Lloyd George 'submitted with extra-ordinary good humour' to his father's blue pencil. Together, they prepared a lengthy document that defended Lloyd George's plea for moderation during the strike and 'effectively countered' the suggestion that his absence from the Shadow Cabinet was tantamount to an act of resignation. J. L. Hammond and, more interestingly, Masterman were also consulted. On the 24th, Lloyd George wrote to Miss Stevenson from Criccieth, and vented the spleen which Scott had prevailed upon him to suppress:

Asquith has as usual been badly advised & when he listens to those poor creatures he has a weakness for gathering around him he generally makes a fool of himself. He did so in 1916 – afterwards in 1918 when he refused the chancellorship. In 1922 when he declined to extend to the Liberal Coalitionists the right hand of fellowship. 1924 when he put Ramsay into office without conditions – & now when he overestimates my unpopularity through my strike attitude & thinks he is now strong enough to force me out. In spite of great gifts he is a silly old man drunk with hidden conceit. He believes any fool who exaggerates his power & influence. Anyhow he has committed a bad miscalculation this time & committed it at least a fortnight too late to give it a chance . . . They are really 'beat'. Dirty dogs – & *bitches* . . .

Miss Stevenson was relieved to hear that, in his speech at Llandudno on the 26th, Lloyd George had shown 'restraint'. The next day, he returned to London, 'outwardly very cheerful & determined, but inwardly trembling with excitement . . . and deep down hurt, almost like a child unjustly punished, at the treatment he had received . . . The rumour', she recorded in her diary on the 30th, 'is that Oxford will not reply to D.'s letter, but that they intend to ignore him – more easily said than done.'

Lloyd George's reply was circulated at a meeting of the Shadow Cabinet on the 31st. 'There never was any hope of any meeting, nor any wish for compromise. I was alone', Lord Beauchamp reported back to him. Asquith answered in a letter which he formally addressed to the Chief Whip (the recipient of Lloyd George's communication of 9 May) on 1 June: 'If the leaders of the Liberal Party as a body had adopted Mr Lloyd George's view', he reasoned, 'we should have been doing our best to weaken the authority of the Government, which was for the moment the embodiment and organ of the national self-defence against the gravest domestic danger which has threatened the country in our time.' He had personally 'sat in many Cabinets under various Prime Ministers', he attested, and he had 'not known one of them who would not have treated such a communication from a colleague, sent at such a time, as equivalent to a resignation'. (Did he recall how leniently he himself had treated certain refractory colleagues in the early days of August 1914?) Lloyd George, his denials notwithstanding, 'was not driven out, he refused to come in', Asquith concluded.

If Asquith's hand was not exactly forced, his elbow was jogged by a letter he received the same day from twelve of the eighteen members of the Shadow Cabinet. Reciting a long list of grievances against Lloyd George, his correspondents collectively affirmed that 'we cannot feel surprised at your feeling that confidential relations are impossible with one whose instability destroys confidence'. Yet there was no denying that a majority of the Liberal M.P.s, as opposed to their nominal leaders, took Lloyd George's part in the dispute. Where did this leave matters?

Asquith, in the so-called reply he had written to the Chief Whip, had put on record that 'I will not continue to hold the leadership for a day unless I am satisfied that I retain in full measure the confidence of the party'. His lieutenants anticipated no difficulty, but they were soon proved mistaken. The parliamentary party, outraged and humiliated by 'the publicity given to the differences between the Liberal leaders', among whom they continued to count Lloyd George, expressed 'the earnest hope that our leaders will use their best endeavours to restore unity in the ranks of the Party'. Beyond Westminster, the cry reverberated.

In the closing days of May, the executive of the National Liberal Federation convened to plan the agenda for its annual session, scheduled for 17 June at Weston-super-Mare. Of the twenty-four members present, sixteen were identified by Eager as Asquithians, eight as followers of Lloyd George. Maclean moved – and Hudson seconded – a resolution of 'unabated confidence in Lord Oxford as Leader of the Liberal Party'. There followed 'a good deal of discussion as to the terms of this resolution', and Walter Layton delivered the minority opinion that the executive ought not to adopt 'any motion which would imply a vote of censure on Mr Lloyd George'. Various amendments were proposed, and Maclean and Hudson consented to append to their original resolution an expression of 'hope that as speedily as possible a united Liberal Party may be able to discharge its vital functions in the interests of the community'. It was logically asked 'whether this meant with or without Mr Lloyd George, and Sir Robert Hudson made it quite plain that it was without Mr Lloyd George'. It being 'obvious there could be no agreement', Layton moved – and Ernest Brown seconded – that a decision should be postponed until a deputation had seen Asquith to 'ascertain his views on the form of words suggested'. Except for 'the absolute "diehard" element' (Maclean, Hudson, Phillipps, R. D. Holt, Layland Barratt, and Lady Violet Bonham Carter), there was substantial sympathy among the majority for 'the plea that individual members of the Committee and the rank and file of the Party as a whole ought not to have been put in the position of having made an apparent choice between Lord Oxford and Mr Lloyd George'.

Times had changed and, for that matter, so had his favourite confidante; but Asquith was once again 'fighting . . . with the beasts at Ephesus', who were the same. He took time off on 3 June to tell Mrs Harrisson that 'the air is clearing now, and all the people I care for have been wonderfully affectionate and loyal'. Six days later, he waxed even more optimistic: 'The "Liberal split" is running its course to its goal not far off: a dissolution of partnership between Ll. G. and myself, with all my respectable and capable colleagues.' But, writing to her on the 11th, his mood was darker:

The squalid controversy about our Party 'splits' still goes on. I have too much sympathy with our honest, hardworking, ill-informed rank and file to be hasty in dispelling their visions and aspirations after 'unity'. But unless they are prepared to give me a wholehearted and unreserved vote of confidence, I shall in the course of the next three days tell them (with equal unreserve) God's truth about Ll.G. As you know, it would be nothing but a relief to me to wash my hands of the whole thing.

The next day, which was five days before the National Liberal Federation was due to assemble, Asquith was incapacitated by a stroke. 'God's truth about Ll.G.', which he had threatened to divulge, was safe with the Almighty, who was frequently invoked by Asquith's forlorn supporters. 'The Lord alone knows where we stand as regards W super M now that H.H.A. is ill!' Hudson wrote in acute distress to Gladstone on the 14th. Although the delegates to the Federation, with only one dissenting vote, passed the resolution of 'unabated confidence' in Asquith's leadership, it was devoid of any practical significance. There was an assurance from the chair that it implied no censure on Lloyd George who, in robust health, was accorded a rapturous welcome at Weston-super-Mare. More seriously, the Liberal Candidates' Association, in defiance of its Asquithian officers, called upon the ailing leader to receive Lloyd George back into the fold. Asquith adamantly refused and, in the face of determined opposition within the party, he tendered his own resignation the following October.

Before taking that momentous step, he was said to have repented of his precipitous action the previous May. On 29 September, while he attended to business in London, Margot motored over from North Berwick to visit Lord Balfour at Whittinghame. On her arrival, she found one of her distant relations, Mrs Winifred Coombe Tennant, to whom she admitted that she and Asquith 'had made a dreadful mistake over the whole business' of the General Strike. 'We were entirely misled', she reportedly averred. 'Certain prominent rich Liberals came to Herbert & said "we shall not give a shilling to the Liberal Fund until you have got rid of Lloyd George".' Fortified by assurances that 'people in the country overwhelmingly agreed', Asquith had then seized 'the opportunity' fortuitously offered by the Strike, and 'wrote the disastrous letter'. He was now, by his wife's description, 'miserable over the whole business'. Aside from the incidental fact that Margot would never have referred to her husband as 'Herbert', the story (which Mrs Coombe Tennant recounted to Lloyd George on 30 September) rings true.

On 15 October Asquith announced his retirement in a succinct public letter. Grey and 'the faithful' had approved the strategy and the text, he told Mrs Harrisson on the 13th, 'and a wagon-load of them' had promised to accompany him to Greenock to 'make a brave show' on the night of its publication. It is perhaps surprising that he chose Greenock as the place to hold his farewell meeting. But it had the attraction of being close to Paisley, which permitted 'a lot of my old and trusty friends' to attend, and it was not too far from North Berwick, where he went afterwards for some golf on 'our old, familiar links at Archerfield'. The presence on the platform of Grey, Simon, Runciman, and Maclean helped to make the occasion 'unique in my experience, at moments thrilling in its intensity . . . I have not a doubt', he told Mrs Harrisson on the 17th, 'that I have taken the only wise & honourable course, and I was sure that you would agree with me.'

He lived sixteen months longer, but there was not much left to his public life: a few speeches in the House of Lords (the 'Charnel House'); some nostalgic visits from Balfour and other companions from the past (including Venetia Montagu, now a widow); an appearance at Oxford, where the city council had elected him high steward, and another at York, where he received the freedom of the city.

From a safe distance, he followed developments in the Liberal

Party, where his disciples continued to wrestle with Lloyd George over finances. He did not, 'of course, go to the Grey dinner' on 13 December 1926, but was able to 'gather that it was a great success'. All the same, he wrote to Mrs Harrisson two days later, he did not expect it 'to arrest our weaklings who are going a-whoring after Ll.G.' Early in 1927, the administrative committee of the Million Fund accepted, by a close vote, Lloyd George's offer of support and the terms that attached to it. The members of the Asquithian minority were either deposed (as was the case with Hudson and Collins) or withdrew to form a new agency, the Liberal Council. Grey was its president, and Lady Violet Bonham Carter bestowed the stamp of Asquithian approval as one of its vice-presidents. They did not, however, carry all of Lloyd George's opponents with them: Simon ominously declined to affiliate; and Wedgwood Benn, like Kenworthy before him, switched to Labour sooner than accept Lloyd George as his chief.

Asquith played no part in these convulsions. During the third week of the new year, he suffered a second stroke. He was taken by Margot to recuperate at Cannes, where he kept 'aloof (as it is easy to do) from the madding crowd, which gambles and races and plays tennis'. Towards the end of February, he returned to Bedford Square, sufficiently recovered to speak twice the next month in the House of Lords, where he 'had the unusual compliment, an audience (such an audience!) of 100 peers'. Thereafter, his strength ebbed, and he was confined to a wheelchair during the spring and summer months.

Problems of health, which were new to him, were compounded by problems of money, which were sadly familiar. On 5 May 1927 Margot wrote a sorrowful letter to Maclean, to whom she revealed their financial predicament. 'H. has lost confidence to a degree I cd. not have believed possible', she also admitted. 'To see him now . . . like a helpless giant is terrible for me. I pray that retribution will come to Ll. G.' The next day, she wrote again to refute the popular notion that her mindless extravagance was to blame:

I made £18,000 out of my books & another 10,000 out of various writings & write from 6 A.M. to 11 (often 5 A.M.) every day. I made 7000 this year by writing. No one can say I have not contributed *all* I've got to the family fortune. I have just pawned my pearls for £2000 to Cartier to pay immediate household bills. I am neither selfish or mercenary but we have always lived on the same scale. Had we changed after 1916 – wh. I asked H. if we sd. do – we sd. not have been in this quandary. He said 'no'. For myself, I mind *nothing*; but I do mind for him & for the world at large. I married a man who might have made 50,000 £ a year at the Bar: he gave it all up for his Party & of course to lead it. We have been the making of *half* the rich men we know. It cannot be very long for either of us now & I think for whatever we owe – I think about 15,000 £ – it wd. be strange if none of those we have done so much for wd. not help us now.

On 30 July *The Times* helped to launch a public fund for Asquith, which Lord Reading organized. Lord Beaverbrook was among the first and most generous contributors, and Margot contrasted his munificence with 'the behaviour of our Liberal *friends* – men who owe us not only their political reputations but their political salvation'. Asquith, on 3 August, also penned a note of gratitude to Beaverbrook who, obviously moved, replied three days later that he welcomed the 'opportunity . . . of doing Lord Oxford a service – however small', and that, if 'the question had been put to the House of Commons', M.P.s 'would have gladly voted to Lord Oxford a sum far more commensurate to his public service than a few private individuals can subscribe'. Until she died in 1945, Margot received periodic allotments from Beaverbrook that supplemented her income from occasional forays into journalism, from fees she obtained for advice to 'clients upon matters of taste in furniture colour and decoration', from advertising Wix cigarettes, and from the pencilled IOUs which she distributed widely. Her husband, she revealed to Beaverbrook on 7 December 1929, had left her a mere £300, 'because the only money he had from his life insurance he had to leave to his 5 children'.

In the later months of 1927, Asquith's physical condition deteriorated rapidly. On 3 December he dictated to his wife an unsigned preface to the published report of the Liberal Industrial Inquiry (the spelling of 'enquiry' was amended to avoid an unfortunate acronym), which had been commissioned during palmier days with 'the active cooperation of Mr Lloyd George'. After a third stroke, his mind was usually too cloudy for him to attend to political affairs or even to keep up his intimate correspondence. On 21 January 1928 Phillipps paid him a visit during a lucid interval. 'You will come and see me again – right to the end', Asquith instructed him as they parted. 'I mean right on to the end of this Parliament', he quickly added. He died on 15 February.

With his distinguished daughter to keep vigil at his shrine, his memory was kept alive. It lingered over the successive crises that continued to afflict his party. Each glimmer of a Liberal revival has enhanced his historical stature, if only as the victim or agent of the Liberal decline.

Long, eventful, and complex, Asquith's career does not admit easily of a summing up. The problem with his critics and panegyrists alike, whose perspectives have lurched with the passing decades, has been their inexorable reluctance to take account of the weaknesses along with the strengths, the victories along with the defeats. Asquith's failings were no less manifest than his achievements, and perhaps no less a part of his legacy; if it were otherwise, he would not have excited the passions that persist to this day.

# BIBLIOGRAPHICAL NOTES

These notes concentrate on material published or made available since the publication of Roy Jenkins's biography in 1964. The principal collection of Asquith's private papers is on deposit at the Bodleian Library, Oxford.

## Introduction

Harold Nicolson's opinions were expressed in his *Diary and Letters* (ed. Nigel Nicolson), II (1967), and in the *Observer*, 12 October 1958. A copy of Haldane's letter to an unidentified correspondent, 26 September 1924, is among the Haldane Papers (National Library of Scotland, Edinburgh).

## Chapter 1

In addition to the standard autobiographical and biographical works, to which references are made in the text, information and interpretations have been drawn from a variety of sources. J. F. Glaser provides important background in

'English Nonconformity and the Decline of Liberalism', *American Historical Review* lxiii (1957–8). On the Baines family and its connections, there is much to be gleaned from H. J. Hanham, *Elections and Party Management* (1959), Donald Read, *Press and People* (1961), and John Vincent, *The Formation of the Liberal Party 1857–1868* (1966). Geoffrey Faber has written 'a portrait with background' of *Jowett* (1966), generally less illuminating than Melvin Richter's study, *The Politics of Conscience: T. H. Green and His Age* (1964). Other glimpses of Balliol society and its leaders are to be found in the Earl of Midleton's *Records and Reactions* (1939), in A. M. Gollin's masterly life of Milner, *Proconsul in Politics* (1964), and in G. Kitson Clark's thoughtful examination of *Churchmen and the Condition of England 1832–1885* (1973). Anthony Sampson brings the subject up-to-date in *Anatomy of Britain* (1962). And Wilson Harris, in a brief memoir of J. A. Spender (1946), offers some interesting sidelights on the Balliol mind of one of Asquith's official biographers.

R. B. Haldane's *Autobiography* (1929) contains some shrewd and candid observations; these have been supplemented with material from various books on Haldane, particularly the present author's *Lord Haldane, Scapegoat for Liberalism* (1969), and from an article, 'Haldane and Asquith', by William Verity in *History Today* xviii (1968). Keith Robbins has written a lively biography of Sir Edward Grey (1971) that supersedes G. M. Trevelyan's 1948 work. Margot Asquith has yet to receive the biographical attention that is her due; but Mark Bonham Carter has contributed a perceptive introduction to an abridged edition of her *Autobiography* (1962), and she enlivens the pages of many books written by and about her contemporaries. C. M. Bowra includes a vivid portrait of her, late in life, among his *Memories* (1966). Daphne Bennett's *Margot* (1984) is a curiously dour exercise.

## Chapter 2

New interpretations and a wealth of new evidence are to be found in a number of recent works that deal with the decade after 1885. Walter L. Arnstein, in his expert unravelling of *The Bradlaugh Case* (1965), makes pointed reference to Asquith's involvement. The Cabinets and Parliaments of 1885–6 are microscopically studied by A. B. Cooke and John Vincent in *The Governing Passion* (1974). *The Diaries of Sir Edward Walter Hamilton*, edited by Dudley W. R. Bahlman (2 volumes, 1972), are indispensable to an understanding of Gladstone. Michael Hurst, *Joseph Chamberlain and Liberal Reunion* (1967), analyses the party split and the unsuccessful efforts to mend the rift.

Beatrice Webb's diaries were consulted both in the original (Passfield Papers, British Library of Political and Economic Science) and in Margaret Cole's two-volume edition (1952, 1956).

The Vizetelly case is discussed by Samuel Hynes in *The Edwardian Turn of Mind* (1968). On the all-important Irish problem, F. S. L. Lyons has written a valuable account of *The Fall of Parnell* (1960), and an article, 'The Irish Question and Liberal Politics, 1886–1894', in the *Historical Journal* xii (1969). J. L. Hammond's 1938 classic, *Gladstone and the Irish Nation*, has been made available in a new edition (1964). It is usefully supplemented by L. P. Curtis Jr, *Coercion and Conciliation in Ireland 1880–1892* (1963), and by material in S. H. Zebel's *Balfour: a Political Biography* (1973).

H. C. G. Matthew provides an introduction to Asquith's parliamentary circle, and neatly disposes of Jenkins's argument that Asquith was 'a natural "Rose-beryite"' in *The Liberal Imperialists* (1973). Peter Stansky, *Ambitions and Strategies* (1964), gives the best rendering of the Newcastle Programme and the leadership struggles of the Nineties. Robert Rhodes James has produced the definitive biography of Rosebery (1964), and D. A. Hamer has done justice to Morley (1968), whose actions are further examined in Koss, 'Morley in the Middle', *English Historical Review* lxxxii (1967). Hamer has also offered an overview of *Liberal Politics in the Age of Gladstone and Rosebery* (1972). Sir Philip Magnus's assessment of Asquith as Home Secretary is in *Gladstone: A Biography* (1954). John Grigg, *The Young Lloyd George* (1973), criticizes Asquith, perhaps misguidedly, on the issue of Employers' Liability. Finally, the Welsh Disestablishment Bill as a prelude to the fall of the Rosebery Government is illuminated by Kenneth O. Morgan in his book *Wales in British Politics 1868–1922* (1963; rev. ed. 1970), and in his edition of the Lloyd George *Family Letters* (1973).

*Chapter 3*

Material for this chapter has been drawn from a number of manuscript collections: the Lyttelton and Roskill papers at the library, Churchill College, Cambridge; the Haldane and Rosebery papers at the National Library of Scotland, Edinburgh; the Harcourt, Bryce, and Asquith papers at the Bodleian Library, Oxford; the Spencer papers at Althorp, Northamptonshire; the Perks papers (by courtesy of Sir Malcolm Perks); the Viscount Gladstone, Balfour, and Campbell-Bannerman papers in the British Library; the Gardiner papers at the British Library of Political and Economic Science, London; and the Strachey papers in the Beaverbrook archive, transferred to the House of Lords Record Office.

Several published sources, mentioned in the notes for earlier chapters, yielded further information: Stansky, *Ambitions and Strategies*; Hamer, *Liberal Politics in the Age of Gladstone and Rosebery*; Matthew, *The Liberal Imperialists*; James, *Rosebery*; and Robbins, *Sir Edward Grey*.

John Wilson has written a new life of Sir Henry Campbell-Bannerman, *CB* (1973), as solid – and in some respects as artless – as its subject. Jeffrey Butler has provided a first-rate account of *The Liberal Party and the Jameson Raid* (1968). Bernard Semmel has investigated the intellectual link between *Imperalism and Social Reform* (1960). G. R. Searle has documented *The Quest for National Efficiency* (1971), in which the Liberal Imperialists took a prominent part.

Gollin's *Proconsul in Politics* (1964) is complemented by two articles: Eric Stokes, 'Milnerism', in the *Historical Journal* v (1962); and H. W. McCready, 'Sir Alfred Milner, the Liberal Party and the Boer War', in the *Canadian Journal of History* ii (1967).

Peter D. Jacobson has taken a fresh approach to 'Rosebery and Liberal Imperialism, 1899–1903', in the *Journal of British Studies* xiii (1973). A religious component of Liberal Imperialism is explored in Koss, 'Wesleyanism and Empire', in the *Historical Journal* xviii (1975).

Asquith's attempt to come to terms with the Unionist Free Traders is treated in Richard A. Remple, *Unionists Divided* (1972), and in Julian Amery's volumes V and VI of *The Life of Joseph Chamberlain* (1969). Nonconformist opposition to Asquith's effort, and his own part in the agitation over the Education Act of

1902, are discussed in Koss, *Nonconformity in Modern British Politics* (1975).

## Chapter 4

In addition to the principal manuscript collections consulted for the previous chapter, two memoranda are quoted from the Herbert Lewis papers in the National Library of Wales, Aberystwyth.

In addition to the above-mentioned biographies of Campbell-Bannerman, Grey, Haldane, Milner, and Rosebery, information has been culled from the following studies: A. M. Gollin, 'Asquith: A New View', in Martin Gilbert (ed.), *A Century of Conflict 1850–1950* (1966); J. F. Harris and C. Hazlehurst, 'Campbell-Bannerman as Prime Minister', in *History* xv (1970); A. F. Havighurst, *Radical Journalist: H. W. Massingham* (1974); and Koss, *Fleet Street Radical: A. G. Gardiner and the 'Daily News'* (1973).

On the formation of the 1905 Government and the ensuing general election, the standard works have been usefully supplemented by several recent publications: A. K. Russell, *Liberal Landslide* (1973); T. Boyle, 'The Formation of Campbell-Bannerman's Government in November 1905: A Memorandum by J. A. Spender', *Bulletin of the Institute of Historical Research* xlvi (1972); Trevor Lloyd, 'The Whip as Paymaster: Herbert Gladstone and Party Organization', *English Historical Review* lxxxix (1974); and P. F. Clarke, 'Electoral Sociology of Modern Britain', *History* lvii (1972).

Electoral statistics here and elsewhere have been taken from the indispensable volume by David Butler and Jennie Freeman, *British Political Facts 1900–1968* (1969).

On the personnel, problems, and personalities of the Campbell-Bannerman administration, there is an iconoclastic study by Peter Rowland, *The Last Liberal Governments: The Promised Land 1905–1910* (1968), which sometimes strains for its effects. A more sympathetic treatment is to be found in Roy Douglas, *The History of the Liberal Party 1895–1970* (1971). Asquith's daughter, Lady Violet Bonham Carter, has afforded some illuminating glimpses of *Winston Churchill as I Knew Him* (1965).

## Chapter 5

Among the collections of private papers consulted for this chapter were those of Bryce (Bodleian Library, Oxford), Haldane (National Library of Scotland, Edinburgh), Lloyd George and Strachey (Beaverbrook archive, House of Lords Record Office), Brunner (by courtesy of Sir Felix Brunner), and the diary of Sir F. A. Hirtzel (India Office Library, London).

Joseph ('Jo') Grimond has contributed an adulatory portrait of Asquith to an anthology, *The Prime Ministers* (ed. H. Van Thal, 2 volumes, 1974–5), in which Norman Gash's appraisal of Lord Liverpool also appears. A querulous view of Asquith as premier is provided by Cameron Hazlehurst in the *English Historical Review* lxxxv (1970).

Various quotations on the subject of Asquith's social life have been taken from Michael Holroyd, *Lytton Strachey*, II (1968); Peter Stansky and William Abrahams, *Journey to the Frontier* (1966); S. D. Waley, *Edwin Montagu* (1964); C. M. Bowra, *Memories* (1966); and Sir Oswald Mosley, *My Life* (1968).

On questions of social reform, there are important interpretations offered by Bentley B. Gilbert, *The Evolution of National Insurance in Great Britain* (1966); José Harris, *Unemployment and Politics* (1972); and H. V. Emy, *Liberals,*

*Radicals and Social Politics 1892–1914* (1973). J. R. Hay has provided a useful bibliographical survey, *The Origins of the Liberal Welfare Reforms 1906–1914* (1975), which contains many distinctive arguments, largely sustained by Bruce K. Murray, *The People's Budget* (1980). P. F. Clarke has tested historiographical orthodoxies in his magisterial study, *Lancashire and the New Liberalism* (1971).

On the intra-party disputes over foreign and defence policy, there is information to be gleaned from A. J. Marder, *From the Dreadnought to Scapa Flow*, I (1961); A. M. Gollin, *The Observer and J. L. Garvin* (1960); Koss, *Sir John Brunner, Radical Plutocrat* (1970); Peter Fraser, *Lord Esher* (1973); Nicholas d'Ombraine, *War Machinery and High Policy* (1973); and A. J. A. Morris, *Radicalism Against War 1906–1914* (1972). Morris has also edited a volume of essays, *Edwardian Radicalism 1900–1914*, in which there are several relevant pieces. It is from his essay on C. P. Trevelyan that the letter from Trevelyan to his father has been drawn.

### Chapter 6

As indicated in the text, quotations have been drawn from a number of manuscript collections, including the McKenna Papers at Churchill College, Cambridge. Copies of Asquith's extraordinary letters to Miss Venetia Stanley (later Mrs Edwin Montagu) were made available by Michael and Eleanor Brock, whose edition of this correspondence appeared in 1982; extracts from these letters are also to be found among the papers of Lord Beaverbrook, who was given them by Mrs Montagu, and who quoted from them extensively (and without attribution) in his volumes on politics during the First World War.

Roy Jenkins, *Mr Balfour's Poodle* (1954), presents a detailed 'Account of the Struggle between the House of Lords and the Government of Mr Asquith'. It is complemented and, in some respects, superseded by Neal Blewett, *The Peers, The Parties and the People: The General Elections of 1910* (1972).

The second volume of Randolph S. Churchill's official biography of his father, *Winston S. Churchill* (1967), together with its companion volumes, yields a considerable amount of evidence. There is also Henry Pelling's one-volume assessment of Churchill (1974), neither as succinct nor as spirited as Kenneth O. Morgan's one-volume *Lloyd George* (1974).

On the labour unrest of the period, Pelling has written *A History of British Trade Unionism* (1963) that provides a balanced narrative and valuable statistical tables. E. H. Phelps Brown, *The Growth of British Industrial Relations* (1959), is indispensable; and some stimulating perceptions are offered by J. M. Winter in the introductory chapters to his *Socialism and the Challenge of War* (1974).

Andrew Rosen, *Rise Up, Women!* (1974), and David Morgan, *Suffragists and Liberals* (1975), are the best in the recent outpouring of works on their provocative subject. A. T. Q. Stewart, *The Ulster Crisis* (1967), similarly counterbalances Patricia Jalland, *The Liberals and Ireland* (1980).

Reference must also be made to *A Good Innings: the Private Papers of Viscount Lee of Fareham* (ed. A. Clark, 1974); to Lucy Masterman, *C. F. G. Masterman* (1935); to Lady Diana Cooper, *The Rainbow Comes and Goes* (1958); and to Philip Magnus, *King Edward the Seventh* (1964).

### Chapter 7

Further archival sources consulted for this chapter include the Grey and

Kitchener collections, both in the Public Record Office, the Runciman Papers in the University Library at Newcastle upon Tyne, and the Maxse Papers in the County Record Office, Chichester. Sir Geoffrey Harmsworth kindly made available a copy of Repington's letter to Buckle (8 February 1912) from the Northcliffe Papers. Walter Long's memorandum of 27 January 1915 is to be found among the Balfour Papers; Lord Salisbury's memorandum of 10 April 1915, among the papers of Lord Robert Cecil, also in the British Library.

On the conduct of British foreign policy before the war, special reference must be made to A. J. P. Taylor's monumental work, *The Struggle for the Mastery of Europe* (1957). The relevant sections of Peter Rowland, *The Last Liberal Governments: Unfinished Business 1911–1914* (1971), tend to be rhetorical and redundant. *British Foreign Policy under Sir Edward Grey* (ed. F. H. Hinsley, 1977) and Paul Kennedy, *The Rise of the Anglo German Antagonism* (1980) abound in insights.

Biographical works that help to illuminate the period include Robert Blake's portrait of Bonar Law, *The Unknown Prime Minister* (1955), F. S. L. Lyons's *John Dillon* (1958), the first of Stephen Roskill's three distinguished volumes on *Hankey, Man of Secrets* (1970), and the third instalment – by Martin Gilbert – of the official life of Churchill (1971). In addition, Trevor Wilson has meticulously edited the *Political Diaries of C. P. Scott* (1970).

First aired in a lecture to the British Academy, Taylor's seminal theory on the wartime conflict between Freedom and Control is most readily available in his collection of essays *Politics in Wartime* (1964). Gollin has added depth and substance to the argument in his political biography of Milner, *Proconsul in Politics* (1964), and in an article, 'The Unmaking of a Prime Minister', *Spectator*, 28 May 1965; the latter triggered off a public correspondence with Robert Rhodes James that ran into July. In *Politicians at War* (1971), a curious compound of painstaking research and strident argument, Cameron Hazlehurst has plunged peremptorily into the fray.

*Chapter 8*

Materials from the Royal Archives at Windsor are quoted by gracious permission of Her Majesty The Queen. Other manuscript collections consulted for this chapter (and not previously enumerated) include the Austen Chamberlain Papers (University Library, Birmingham), the Gwynne Papers (by courtesy of Vice-Admiral I. L. T. Hogg, C.B., D.S.C.), the Esher Papers (now on deposit at Churchill College, Cambridge), the Buxton Papers (by courtesy of Mr and Mrs J. Clay), the Hewins Papers (University Library, Sheffield), the Samuel Papers (House of Lords Record Office), the Simon Papers (by courtesy of Viscount Simon), the Scott Papers (British Library), the Milner and Nathan Papers (Bodleian Library, Oxford), and Arnold Bennett's journal (City Museum, Stoke-on-Trent).

Copies of items in the *Guardian* archives were kindly provided by David Ayerst, whose 'biography' of that newspaper (1971) fills in the background to Scott's *Political Diaries* (1970). Geoffrey Harmsworth and Reginald Pound, *Northcliffe* (1959), is similarly useful.

Trevor Wilson, *The Downfall of the Liberal Party* (1966), spans the period from 1914 to 1935 with clarity and vigour.

John Rae, *Conscience and Politics* (1970), deals with the conscription controversy from the perspective of the problem posed by the conscientious objectors. Gilbert, *Winston S. Churchill*, III (1971), and Roskill, *Hankey*, I (1970), make available extensive documentation.

Barry McGill has examined 'Asquith's Predicament, 1914–1918' in the *Journal of Modern History* xxxix (1967). The Hobhouse conspiracy theory was first aired in the same journal in Koss, 'The Destruction of Britain's Last Liberal Government', xl (1968).

Lady Cynthia Asquith's *Diary 1915–1918* (1968) contains some pertinent entries. Lady Scott (later Lady Kennet) included copious extracts from her own diary in her memoirs, *Self-Portrait of an Artist* (1949). Robert Blake has edited *The Private Papers of Douglas Haig* (1952). John Jolliffe has poignantly portrayed Raymond, Asquith's eldest son (1980).

## Chapter 9

Additional manuscript collections consulted for this chapter include the J. A. Spender Papers (British Library), the Edmund Gosse Papers (Brotherton Collection, University Library, Leeds), and the Courtney Papers (British Library of Political and Economic Science). The Beaverbrook Papers contain his research notes on the 1916 Cabinet crisis, his correspondence with participants, various memoranda and copies of letters from Robert Donald, and copies of two letters which Asquith wrote to Pamela McKenna and which Reginald McKenna made available to Beaverbrook.

Extracts from Lady Ottoline Morrell's diary are to be found in R. Gathorne Hardy (ed.), *Ottoline at Garsington* (1974). Lytton Strachey's letter of 31 May 1916 is included in *The Really Interesting Question and Other Papers* (ed. Paul Levy, 1972).

In his biography of *Hankey, Man of Secrets*, Roskill restores those portions of his subject's diary which Hankey suppressed in his two-volume work, *The Supreme Command* (1961), and which consequently were not available to Asquith's previous biographers. Thomas Jones, *Whitehall Diary*, I (ed. K. Middlemas, 1969), covers the years 1916–25.

Asquith's letters to Mrs Hilda Harrisson, edited by Desmond MacCarthy, have been published as *H.H.A.: Letters of the Earl of Oxford and Asquith to a Friend* (2 volumes, 1933). 'The editing of these letters has been of course a great blow to us and I fear to many others', Lady Violet Bonham Carter lamented to A. G. Gardiner on 4 December 1933.

Reference is made in this chapter to Robert Blake's 1968 Ford Lectures, *The Conservative Party from Peel to Churchill* (1971).

Half melodrama and half farce, the Pemberton Billing case (Rex v. Billing, 1918) is deftly examined in Joseph Dean, *Hatred, Ridicule or Contempt* (1953).

## Chapters 10 and 11

Asquith's postwar career, to which his previous biographers gave short shrift, has recently been the subject of scrutiny and reappraisal. In part, this historiographical development reflects the availability of new documentary materials: the Lloyd George Papers (now transferred to the House of Lords Record Office), the Maclean Papers (Bodleian Library, Oxford), a further deposit of the Viscount Gladstone Papers (British Library), and the papers of Lord Murray of Elibank (National Library of Scotland, Edinburgh); to these must be added the Gilbert Murray Papers (Bodleian Library) and the W. McG. Eager Papers (Reform Club Library, London). In part, too, this development reflects a renewed attempt to comprehend the reasons for the decline of the Liberal Party: the above-mentioned studies by Trevor Wilson and Roy Douglas are cases in point.

The fourth volume of the official biography of Winston S. Churchill, written by Martin Gilbert (1975), contains a good many revelations. Frances Stevenson's published diary (1971) has been rounded out by a volume of her correspondence with Lloyd George, *My Darling Pussy* (1975), both edited by A. J. P. Taylor. *The Holmes-Laski Letters* have been edited in two volumes by M. DeWolfe Howe (1953).

Maurice Cowling, *The Impact of Labour 1920–1924* (1971), offers interpretations guaranteed to stimulate, to provoke, and even to infuriate. Michael Kinnear, *The Fall of Lloyd George: the Political Crisis of 1922* (1973), affords some new perspectives on electoral questions. Chris Cook, *The Age of Alignment: Electoral Politics in Britain 1922–1929* (1975), is rather less declamatory. John Campbell has considered 'The Renewal of Liberalism: Liberalism without Liberals' in G. Peele and C . Cook (eds.), *The Politics of Reappraisal 1918–1939* (1975), and Michael Bentley has analysed 'The Liberal Response to Socialism, 1918–29' in K. D. Brown (ed.), *Essays in Anti-Labour History* (1974).

Asquith's letter to Dr R. F. Horton (28 February 1920) was kindly made available by Mrs I. V. Horton. Correspondence relating to Asquith's candidacy for the chancellorship of Oxford University is to be found among the Davidson Papers (Lambeth Palace Library).

Rosslyn Mitchell's tribute to Asquith, whom he defeated at Paisley in 1924, was recounted by John Tristram in a letter to the editor of the *Guardian*, 6 November 1965.

Frank Swinnerton communicated his reminiscences about Asquith in a letter to the author on 8 August 1973.

# INDEX

Abbott, Edwin, 4

Abrahams, William, 288

Acland, Sir A. H. D., 23, 26, 31, 32, 35, 38, 43, 72

Acland, Sir Francis, 176, 241, 244, 272

Acton, Lord, 36

Addison, Christopher (Viscount Addison), 224

Admiralty crisis (May 1915), 182–3, 185, 194

Agadir crisis, 143, 145–6

Aitken, Sir Max: *see* Beaverbrook, Baron

Algeciras conference, 143

Allard, William, 57

'Alpha of the Plough': *see* Gardiner, A. G.

Amery, Julian, 287

Amery, Leo, 62, 74, 169, 202, 213

Anglo-Russian Convention, 159

Anne, Queen, 126, 128, 164, 271

Anti-Corn Law League, 3

Antwerp, expedition to, 171

Army Council, 206, 211

Arnstein, W. L., 286

Articles Club, 24

Askwith, G. R., 129

Asquith, Anthony (son), 91, 238, 275, 276

Asquith, Arthur (son), 11, 82, 92, 254

Asquith, Lady Cynthia (daughter-in-law), 141, 161, 196, 291

Asquith, Cyril (son), 11, 23, 92, 223. *See also* Spender and Asquith

Asquith, Elizabeth (daughter; Princess Antoine Bibesco), 91, 238, 248, 256

Asquith, Emily Willans (mother), 3, 4

Asquith, Helen Melland (first wife), 10, 11, 14–15, 29

Asquith, Herbert (son), 11, 92

Asquith, H. H. (Earl of Oxford and Asquith):

   *personal:* as a biographical subject, vii–ix; religious and social background, 2–4; education, 4–5, 9; first visit to House of Commons, 4, 101; quotes the classics, 4, 32, 119, 263; quotes Browning, 176, 223; financial worries, 9–10, 13, 43, 223, 256, 282–3; plays golf, 7, 14, 94; plays bridge, 94, 155, 196, 255; worse for drink, 139–40, 187, 255–6; mixes in society, 2, 9, 15–16, 87, 93–94, 160–61, 255–6; travels, 11, 122, 140, 141, 153, 205, 215, 229, 268, 270, 282; first marriage, 10, 14–15, 29; second marriage, 14–16, 39; goes from Herbert to Henry, 17; relationship with Venetia Stanley, 126, 140–41, 186–7; suffers anguish during war, 165, 213–14, 255; visits Garsington, 209–10, 256; health, 200, 280, 282; death, 283

   *early career:* develops political ambitions, 11; friendship with Haldane, viii–ix, 12–14, 15–16, 22; elected to Parliament, 12; maiden speech, 13, 20; 'goes into House of Commons shape', 21; stands up to Chamberlain, 21, 39; devoted to Gladstone, 22–3; at the Bar, 26, 28–29, 43, 44, 74; favours 'better kind of Radicalism', 26; on Parnell commission, 27–8, 29; defends seat (1892), 30; moves motion of no-confidence, 31; kisses hands, 32; at Home Office, 15, 33–7, 38, 114; defends seat (1895), 41; on Liberal Unionism, 42; on Liberal Imperialism, 37, 42, 45, 49, 63; connections with Rosebery, 38, 42, 51; defers to Campbell-Bannerman, 44–5; on South African affairs, 46, 48; critical of Campbell-Bannerman, 50, 54, 55; difficulties with Rosebery, 51, 52, 56, 58, 68; defends seat (1900), 52; never calls himself a Liberal Imperialist, 56; leads Liberal Imperialists, 57–8; defends Free Trade, 59–60, 67; disavows Milner, 61–2; accepts Exchequer, 67

   *1905–1914 (July):* improved relations with Campbell-Bannerman, 61, 69; subscribes to Relugas strategy, 65–9; pays tribute to Haldane, 73; reputation in debate, 74–5; in 1906 campaign, 76; response to Labour, 42, 77; on South African settlement, 78, 79; policies at Exchequer, 2, 79ff, 103; friction with Lloyd George, 83–4; distinguishes between socialism and social reform, 81, 103; bids farewell to Campbell-Bannerman, 86; ascends to premiership, 87–8, 89–90; likened to Peel, 88, 228; mixes metaphors, 90, 104; reconstructs government, 95–6, 128–9, 145, 146–147, 159–60; tendency to collect offices, 97–8, 137; characteristics as Prime Minister, 98–100; debt to Gladstone, 101–2; commitment to social reform, 100–101, 103; resists women's suffrage, 102, 130, 131–2; contends with labour unrest, 102, 129–30, 132–4; introduces 1908 budget, 105; takes up House of Lords reform, 85, 106–7, 110; effects naval compromise, 108–9; indispensable to Lloyd George, 113–15; critical of Churchill, 114; 'Wait and see', 115, 161–2; misunderstands Unionists, 115, 126; during Jan. 1910 campaign, 116–18,

125; has 'no plan of any kind', 119;
reasserts control, 121; seeks inter-
party accommodation, 122–3;
solicits royal 'guarantees', 124–5;
during Dec. 1910 campaign, 125–6;
respects Balfour, 126, 180; shouted
down in Commons, 127, 137; faces
Ulster crisis, 135–8; attends all-
party conference, 138; on foreign
policy, 143–5; ties with Lloyd
George, 145, 156; avoids commitment to France, 147–8; seeks
improved relations with Germany,
146, 149, 151–2; considers dissolution, 150–51, 154–5; builds
bridges between colleagues, 152,
153, 177; faces international crisis,
154–5

*1914 (August) to 1916:* holds
together his Cabinet, 157–8, 279;
receives Unionist pledge, 158–9; as
war leader, 160–61, 164–5, 208–9;
exercises dominance in Cabinet,
161; likened to Kaiser, 166; war
strategy, 168; relies on Kitchener,
169–70, 173, 174, 183, 188, 189,
198; accepts Dardanelles strategy,
172–3; weakened position, 174–5;
rumours of intrigues against, 178–
180; suffers press attacks, 180, 181,
200, 217, 227, 243; alleged
indifference to press attacks, 168,
200; denied munitions shortage,
181, 182; forms coalition, 183–6,
189–92, 195; strikes a 'balance',
189–90, 196–7; relations with Lloyd
George 'very strained', 198–9;
substitutes at War Office, 200;
addresses Lord Mayor's banquet,
201; accepts conscription as foregone conclusion, 202–3; devises
compromise on conscription, 204;
contemplates resignation, 205, 206;
legislates compulsory service, 207;
fills in as Irish secretary, 210, 211–
212; warned of a plot, 213; reviews
eleven years in office, 214; receives
terms from 'Triumvirate', 216;
offers office to Milner, 217; submits
to Lloyd George proposals, 218–19;

banks on Unionist support, 220–21;
resigns premiership, 88, 97, 221

*later career:* 'thankful to feel he
was a free man', 222; fights with
'beasts at Ephesus', 223, 280;
mentioned as a Lord Chancellor,
223, 235, 278; public response to his
fall, 224, 225–6; adopts benevolent
attitude to successor, 225, 227–8;
contrasted with Lloyd George, viii,
225, 226–7; reticent, 228–9, 233,
234–5; delivers Romanes Lecture
(1918), 102, 229; confers with Lloyd
George, 230, 231, 236; response to
Lansdowne letter, 232; in Maurice
debate, 233, 234; discusses war
aims, 235; aspires to attend Peace
Conference, 236; during 1918 campaign, 237–8; loses seat at East
Fife, 238, 240; sits on the sidelines,
241; chairs Royal Commission, 243–
244; incited to 'Hit out', 245–6;
stands in Paisley by-election, 244,
246–7; returns to Commons, 248–9;
visits Lloyd George, 250; opposed
by Labour, 251; loses ground, 252;
addresses Wee Free rally, 253–4;
differences with Haldane, viii–ix,
253, 265; incurs Churchill's resentment, 254; regarded as a liability,
255; literary pursuits, 256; during
1922 campaign, 257–8; moves
towards reunion, 259–62; 'weary of
politics', 263; receptive to first
Labour Government, 264, 265–6,
278; friction with Lloyd George,
266, 269, 271; loses seat at Paisley,
267, 268, 274; takes peerage, 269,
271; private resentment of Lloyd
George, 272, 273; pressed to break
with Lloyd George, 273–4, 279;
stands for Oxford chancellorship,
274; rebukes Lloyd George, 277–9;
resigns Liberal leadership, 280–81
Asquith, Joseph Dixon (father), 3
Asquith, Katharine Horner
(daughter-in-law), 92
Asquith, Margot (second wife;
Countess of Oxford and Asquith):
ambitious for Asquith, 14–15; per-

Asquith, Margot – *cont.*
sonality, 16–17; extravagant tastes,
43–4, 223; recites her address, 47,
59; 'a lost soul', 60; promotes
Asquith premiership, 62, 65;
admires her husband, 70; left on
doorstep, 72; mixes in society, 74,
92–3; finds House 'sadly
unfamiliar', 78; discusses Relugas
Compact, 82; on Asquith's personality, 90, 91; as stepmother, 91–
92; 'an effort', 98; jealous of Lloyd
George, 117, 118; hears Asquith
shouted down, 127; opposes
'petticoat politics', 131; denounces
the Tories, 137–8; lavished
enmities, 154; talks loosely, 165;
hears of plot, 178; spends 'sleepless
night of misery', 188; blames
Winston, 194; reveals Asquith's
intentions, 195; counsels Lloyd
George, 196; appeals to Hankey,
198, 217; warns Kitchener of plot,
198; reports Asquith's illness, 200;
appeals to McKenna, 202; opposes
Lloyd George at War Office, 212;
jittery, 218; an obstacle to Liberal
accord, 221; 'up to her elbows in
intrigues', 232; names in 'Black
Book', 234; thanks God for
Asquith's defeat, 238; hopes
Asquith will show 'indignation',
244; denounces Haldane, 247;
denounces Lloyd George, 250, 259,
269, 273, 282; meets Miss Stevenson, 253; promises 'generosity' to
Bonar Law, 257; during 1924 campaign, 268; 'glad Henry is out of
it', 269; writes off Lloyd George,
262, 269; repents, 281; reveals
financial plight, 282–3; her diary
quoted, 66, 69, 71, 201; mentioned,
42, 123, 141, 157, 159, 209–10, 246,
274
Asquith, Raymond (son), 7, 11, 15, 30,
44, 59, 92, 212–13, 254
Asquith, Violet (daughter): *see* Bonham Carter, Lady Violet
Asquith, William Willans (brother), 3,
4, 7

'Asquith Committee', 57
'Asquithians', defined, 240
'Asquithism', Harcourt opposes, 25,
30
Astor, Waldorf (Viscount Astor), 213
Athenaeum, 68
Ayerst, David, 290

Bagehot, Walter, quoted, 75, 128, 141
Baines, Edward, 3–4, 4–5, 101–2
Baldwin, Stanley (Earl Baldwin of
Bewdley), 98, 258, 261, 262, 264–5,
269, 274, 276
Balfour, A. J. (1st Earl of Balfour):
lays wager with Brodrick, 6; as
Irish Secretary, 21; counsels
Asquith, 31; as Prime Minister, 59,
61, 62, 64, 65, 76, 106; resigns
premiership, 67, 69; loses seat, 77;
attends constitutional conference,
123; misrepresented, 124; tries to
forget, 128; on war council, 171,
178; reputed influence over Churchill, 178–9; in May 1915 crisis, 188,
189, 193, 195, 196; intimacy with
Asquith, 180, 197; supports
voluntary recruiting, 198; movements to oust, 218; gives notice to
Asquith, 221, 222; crosses
'delicately and unsoiled', 224;
Asquith distrusts, 234; Margot
visits, 281; mentioned, 24, 39, 44,
48, 94, 117, 127, 139, 201, 232
Balliol College, Oxford, 2, 5–8, 244,
275, 286
Barratt, Layland, 280
Beauchamp, 7th Earl, 129, 140, 159,
190, 192, 269, 277, 278
Beaverbrook, Baron (Sir Max Aitken),
215, 216, 220, 221, 222, 224, 283,
289, 291
Belgium, neutrality of, 156, 158, 159,
180
Bell, Vanessa, 93
Benn, William Wedgwood (1st
Viscount Stansgate), 176, 241, 245,
252, 268, 282
Bennett, Arnold, 194
Bentley, Michael, 292
Beresford, Lady Charles, 180

Beresford, Lord Charles, 167

Biarritz, royal interview at, 88, 95, 97

Bibesco, Princess Antoine: *see* Asquith, Elizabeth

Diggar, J. M , 246, 247, 258, 262

Bigge, Sir Arthur: *see* Stamfordham, Baron

Billing, Noel Pemberton, 234, 237

Birkenhead, 1st Earl of: *see* Smith, F. E.

Birrell, Augustine, 74, 83, 96, 100, 106, 123, 153–4, 182, 189, 190, 191, 196, 202, 210

Blake, Robert (Baron Blake), 228, 290, 291

Blewett, Neal, 116, 117, 289

Blue Posts, 24

Boer War, 42, 80, 114, 193. *See also* South Africa

Bonar Law, Andrew: 'very vicious', 134–5; attends all-party conference, 138; pledges support, 158, 162; likens Asquith to Kaiser, 166; co-operates with Liberals, 178; dislikes coalition idea, 180–81; in May 1915 crisis, 184, 185, 187, 194, 195; kept out of Exchequer, 189, 202; kept out of War Office, 196, 211; his expectations, 197; relations with Lloyd George, 206, 213–14, 215, 216, 218; consults Unionist colleagues, 217, 218–19; deals with Asquith, 220, 222; takes Exchequer, 224; lays wager with Maclean, 240; becomes premier, 256; resigns premiership, 260; mentioned, 188, 200, 201, 254

Bonham Carter, Mark, ix, x, 218, 286

Bonham Carter, Sir Maurice, 92, 205

Bonham Carter, Lady Violet (Baroness Asquith of Yarnbury): as guardian of her father's reputation, ix, 283; birth, 11; recalls Margot, 91–2; inspects No. 10, 92; promotes Churchill's cause, 97; her health, 117; opposes 'petticoat politics', 131; reports Fisher's resignation, 182; 'very depressed', 209; campaigns at Paisley. 246; on Asquith's return to the Commons, 248; opposes Lloyd George, 280, 282; mentioned, 2, 93, 166, 223, 288, 291

Booth, Handel, 183

Booth, 'General' William, 91

Bottomley, Horatio, 177, 234

Bowen, Charles (Lord Bowen), 9, 10, 11, 24, 34–5

Bowra, C. M., 93, 286, 288

Boyle, T., 288

Bradlaugh, Charles, 11, 22

Bradley, Andrew, 6

Bramsdon, Sir T. A., 241

Brassey, Lord, 51, 57

Bright, John, 3

*British Gazette*, 276

*British Weekly*, 249

Broadhurst, Henry, 20

Brock, Michael, ix, x, 289

Brock, Eleanor, ix, 289

Brodrick, W. St John, Earl of Midleton, 5, 6, 53, 213, 286

Brown, Ernest, 280

Browning, Robert, 176, 221, 223

Brunner, Sir John, 23, 93, 103–4, 108, 110, 150, 227

Bryce, James (Viscount Bryce), 50, 51–2, 60, 73, 74, 99, 126, 130, 235, 243

Buchan, John (1st Baron Tweedsmuir), 59

Buchanan, Mrs T. B., 71

Buckle, G. E., 148, 176

Buckmaster, Sir Stanley (1st Viscount Buckmaster), 161, 195, 225, 226, 229–30, 277

Budget Protest League, 114

Budgets: (1894), 35; (1906), 79–80; (1907), 80, 81–2; (1908), 98, 105; (1909), 94, 109, 110, 111–15, 118, 121, 138; (1911), 130; (1915), 202

Burns, John, 27, 73, 83, 95–6, 116, 146, 154, 158, 159

'Business as usual', 164

Butler, David, 288

Butler, Jeffrey, 47, 287

Buxton, Sydney (Earl Buxton), 23, 26, 32, 38, 47, 73, 109, 129, 132, 192, 193, 277

Buxton, Mrs Sydney (Lady Buxton), 15, 109

Cadbury, Edward, 228
Cadbury, Henry, 249–50, 251
Cambon, Paul, 158
Campbell, John, 292
Campbell, Mrs Patrick, 248
Campbell-Bannerman, Sir Henry: at
    the War Office, 35; in 1895 election,
    41; as possible leader, 42, 43, 44;
    elected party leader, 46, 103, 104,
    260; on South African affairs, 47,
    49, 50, 53–4, 58; in 1900 election,
    51–2; opinion of Asquith, 55, 57, 60;
    might bow out, 61, 62; shows
    renewed determination, 65, 66–7;
    takes office, 68–9, 98, 143; peerage
    proposed for, 70, 86; forms govern-
    ment, 71–2, 73–4; differences with
    Asquith, 76, 83; as architect of
    South African settlement, 78–9; on
    House of Lords reform, 84, 85, 117,
    120, 121; illness, 86, 87; compared
    to Asquith, 89–90; his foreign
    policy, 144, 145; mentioned, 88, 95,
    131
Campbell-Bannerman, Lady, 70, 79
Canning, George, 79
Canterbury, Archbishop of: *see*
    Davidson, Randall
Carlton Club, 197, 224
Carlyle, Thomas, quoted, 21
Carnarvon, 4th Earl of, 9
Carrington, Earl, 73
Carson, Sir Edward (Baron Carson),
    24, 134–5, 138, 167, 195, 199, 200,
    204, 205, 207, 213, 214–15, 216, 218,
    220, 224
Carson, Lady, 225
Casement, Sir Roger, 210–11
Cave, Viscount, 275
Cawdor, 3rd Earl of, 123
Cecil, Lord Hugh, 127, 139
Cecil, Lady Robert, 209
Cecil, Lord Robert (Viscount Cecil of
    Chelwood), 184, 188, 197, 207, 217,
    221, 224, 232, 245, 249, 251, 275
Central Aberdeen, by-election (1919),
    242
'Centre Party', proposals for, 245,
    251–2
Chamberlain, (Sir) Austen, 87, 105,
    123, 181, 184, 186, 191, 195, 196,
    197, 202, 217, 221, 224
Chamberlain, Joseph, 19–20, 21, 24,
    39, 46, 47, 48, 51, 53, 59–60, 102,
    155
Chamberlain, Neville, 187
Chelmsford, Viscount, 217
Chinese labour, 61–2, 76
Churchill, Clementine (Baroness
    Spencer-Churchill), 127, 166, 206,
    254–5
Churchill, Lord Randolph, 7, 24, 27,
    28, 74, 97, 134
Churchill, Randolph S., 97, 289
Churchill, (Sir) Winston: enters 1905
    government, 74; on South African
    affairs, 79, 82; likens Asquith to
    Peel, 88; ambitions in 1908, 97;
    alleged to 'push along' Asquith,
    100; supports miners' Bill, 105; as
    Radical economist, 108; 'furious' at
    the Lords, 109; Asquith rebukes,
    114; in Jan. 1910 campaign, 117; on
    House of Lords reform, 119, 121;
    pays tribute to Asquith, 125–6, 153;
    decries Unionist behaviour, 127; at
    Home Office, 129; as Home Ruler,
    135; in Ulster crisis, 136; his *World
    Crisis*, 142; becomes 'warlike', 146,
    147, 148, 149–50, 152, 155, 157;
    affection for Lloyd George, 153;
    advocates conscription, 169–70;
    seeks new strategy, 171–2; favours
    Dardanelles enterprise, 172–4; calls
    for coalition, 177, 181, 189, 197,
    198; quarrels with Fisher, 177, 182,
    183, 185, 192; 'the greatest don-
    key', 178; portrays his *Great
    Contemporaries*, 186, 224; dis-
    parages Asquith, 187, 212; loses
    Admiralty, 192, 197; provokes
    distrust, 192–5; leaves office, 199,
    200; implicated in intrigues, 205,
    215; anticipates Asquith's defeat,
    237; resentful of Asquith, 204, 254–
    255; reports Asquith 'heavily
    loaded', 255–6; loses seat, 257;
    mentioned, 1, 2, 95, 128, 139, 141,
    154, 236, 265
City Liberal Club, 55–6

City of London School, 4–5, 8
Clark, G. Kitson, 286
Clarke, P. F., x, 288
Cluer, A. R., 7
Coal Mines Regulation Act, 105–100
Coalition: moves towards, 169, 177, 180–81; created by Asquith, 183ff; created by Lloyd George, 223ff; break-up of, 256
Coalition Liberals, 241, 243, 253, 255–257, 278
Cobden, Richard, 3
Collings, Jesse, 20, 31, 167
Collins, Sir Godfrey, 268, 273, 277, 278, 282
Committee of Imperial Defence, 128, 144–5
Compulsion: demands for, 169, 184, 197–8, 205; Haldane seems to endorse, 191–2; divides Cabinet, 198–9; Runciman opposes, 217
Congregationalism, 2, 3. *See also* Nonconformists
Conrad, Joseph, quoted, 208–9
Conscription: *see* Compulsion
Conservative Party: *see* Unionist Party
Cook, Chris, x, 257, 265, 292
Cooke, A. B., 286
Cooper, Lady Diana (Lady Diana Manners), 141, 209, 289
Cooper, Sir Richard, 167
Corrupt Practices Act (1883), 12
'Coupon Election': *see* General elections (1918)
Courtney, 1st Baron, 233
Cowdray, 1st Viscount, 273, 274
Cowling, Maurice, 292
Crewe, 1st Marquess of: Asquith's esteem for, 72, 96, 145, 190, 191; accepts office, 73; deputizes for Asquith, 117, 200–201; on House of Lords Reform, 119, 120; mentioned, 9, 123, 128, 147, 158, 171, 176, 198, 251
Cromer, 1st Earl of, 67
Curragh 'mutiny', 98, 136–7
Curtis, L. P., Jr, 286
Curzon of Kedleston, 1st Marquess, 6,

21, 128, 186, 195, 197, 198, 202, 221, 223, 224, 260, 274

*Daily Chronicle*, 39, 152, 179, 220, 228, 259, 265
*Daily Express*, 137, 151, 167, 181
*Daily Mail*, 217
*Daily News*, 8, 60, 90, 118, 148, 151, 164, 194, 201, 204, 227–8, 246, 248, 249
*Daily Telegraph*, 232
Dalmeny, Lord, 82
Dardanelles, 172–4, 181
Davidson, Randall T. (Archbishop of Canterbury), 166, 275
Dean, Joseph, 291
'Death duties', 35
Derby, 14th Earl of, 79
Derby, 16th Earl of, 163, 186, 195, 199, 211, 224
Derby scheme, 199, 203
Diamond Jubilee (1897), 47
Dicey, A. V., 94
Dilke, Sir Charles W., 102
Dillon, John, 153, 182
Disraeli, Benjamin (Earl of Beaconsfield), 1–2, 9, 52, 78, 79, 99, 111, 154, 176
'Ditchers', 127
Donald, Robert, 220, 278, 291
Dore, Harold, 203
Douglas, Roy, 240, 271, 288, 292
Dreadnoughts: *see* Naval estimates
Drew, Mary Gladstone, 16, 226
Duke, H. E. (1st Baron Merrivale), 205, 210

Eager, W. McG., 267, 273, 279
Earlsferry, Asquith's speech at, 68
East Fife: Asquith adopted at, 12; Asquith defends, 30, 41, 52, 76; Asquith loses, 237
*Economist*, 10, 141, 149
Edinburgh Philosophical Institution, viii
Education: 1902 Act, 59, 83, 114; 1906 Bill, 83, 204; 1908 Bill, 106
Edward VII, 66, 69, 86, 88, 95, 98, 105, 115, 121, 122, 127
Eighty Club, 21, 22, 37

Elgin, 9th Earl of, 73, 79, 95, 96, 97
Ellis, J. E., 42, 49
Ellis, T. E., 23
Emmott, Lord, 170, 190
Employers' Liability Bill, 35, 36
Emy, H. V., 288
*Enchantress*, 122
Ensor, Sir Robert, 35, 44–5, 75
Entente Cordiale, 143
Esher, 2nd Viscount, 98, 108, 144,
    152–3, 180, 188, 233
Essex, Lady, 196
*Evening Standard*, 252

Faber, Geoffrey, 286
Fabian Society, 13, 24, 26
Fashoda, 47–8
Fawcett, (Dame) Millicent, 132
Featherstone, 34–5
Fenwick, Charles, 49
*Fifty Years of Parliament* (1926), 19,
    22, 131
First World War, 13, 96, 142ff
Firth, Sir Charles, 244
Fisher, Baron (Admiral Sir John
    Fisher), 80, 108, 171, 173, 177, 182ff,
    193, 195
Fisher, H. A. L., 224
Fowler, Henry (1st Viscount
    Wolverhampton), 35, 43, 49, 51, 53,
    57, 74, 87, 95, 129
Free Churches: *see* Nonconformists
Free Liberal Party, founded, 242. *See
    also* Independent Liberals
Free Trade, viii, 67, 76, 102–3, 150,
    164, 170, 202, 261, 262
'Freedom *v.* Control', 164
Freeman, Jennie, 288
French, Sir John (1st Earl of Ypres),
    181, 188, 193, 194, 211, 264

Gardiner, A. G., 8, 54, 60, 70, 72, 79,
    90, 95, 118, 164, 201, 204, 227–8,
    232, 237–8, 239, 246, 248, 260, 274,
    291
Garibaldi, Giuseppe, 4
Garvin, J. L., 124, 126, 180, 193
Gash, Norman, 99, 288
General elections: (1880), 21; (1885),
    12, 13; (1886), 12, 18; (1892), 30, 74;

(1895), 40, 41; (1900), 50, 51–2;
    (1906), 76–7; (Jan. 1910), 116–19,
    125, 126; (Dec. 1910), 116, 125–6,
    139; (1918), 235, 236–8, 239; (1922),
    256–9; (1923), 261–3; (1924), 266,
    267–8
General Strike (1926), 276–7, 281
*Genesis of the War, The* (1923), 109,
    256
George V: succeeds to throne, 122; in
    constitutional crisis, 123, 124–5,
    126, 128; presses for all-party con-
    ference, 138; suggests dissolution,
    154; 'very anti-German', 160; in
    May 1915 crisis, 183–4, 193–4, 195;
    expresses confidence in Asquith,
    206; antipathy to Lloyd George,
    220, 223; in Dec. 1916 crisis, 221,
    222, 224; offers Asquith peerage,
    269, 274; mentioned, 129, 136, 153,
    182, 188, 200, 211, 236
Germany: naval expansion of, 108,
    149; in Moroccan crises, 143, 145;
    on eve of war, 155, 158; Britain
    declares war on, 160. *See also* First
    World War
Gilbert, B. B., x, 288
Gilbert, Martin, 199, 254, 290, 291,
    292
Gladstone, Herbert (Viscount Glad-
    stone): as chief whip, 49, 58, 61, 68,
    77; at Home Office, 70, 73, 105;
    bursts into Margot's boudoir, 72;
    quarrels with Ripon, 95; leaves
    Home Office, 129; critical of
    Asquith, 244, 261; urges co-
    operation with Grey, 253; explores
    possibility of reunion, 255, 259,
    260–61; distrusts Lloyd George,
    263, 264, 266, 273; mentioned, 38,
    50, 52, 268, 269, 274, 277, 280
Gladstone, W. E.: commends Asquith,
    11, 22; appoints Asquith to Cabinet,
    15; preaches to Margot, 16; ends
    third government, 19; Asquith's
    devotion to, 20, 21, 22, 95, 153;
    accepts Newcastle Programme, 29–
    30; begins fourth premiership, 31;
    retires, 36–7; Bagehot on, 75; as
    Chancellor, 79, 80, 97; denounces

House of Lords, 84; favours Spencer, 64; Asquith's debt to, 101, 102; Asquith compared to, 244, 245; mentioned, 1, 2, 14, 39, 156, 260

Glaser, J. F., 280

Gollin, A. M., x, 53, 67, 164, 286, 287, 288, 290

Gosse, Edmund, 226, 233, 265

Gore, Charles (Bishop Gore), 7

Gough, Brig.-Gen. Hubert, 137

Graham, R. B. Cunninghame, 26, 33

Green, T. H., 6, 81

Greenock, Asquith's farewell at, 281

Grey, Sir Edward (Viscount Grey of Fallodon): at Balliol, 6, 275; friendship with Asquith, 13, 68, 73; admires Asquith, 13–14; meets Margot, 15; takes office, 31, 32; follows Asquith, 31, 32, 44; relations with Rosebery, 51, 52, 56, 69; as a Liberal Imperialist, 49, 53, 55, 57, 58, 73; quarrels with Campbell-Bannerman, 50, 55, 58; subscribes to Relugas Compact, 65–69; appointed to Foreign Office, 14, 71; on 1906 election, 76–7; on domestic policy, 84, 85, 108, 119, 120, 133; mentioned as possible premier, 87, 176; at the Foreign Office, 96, 143, 144, 145, 155–6; on Anglo-German relations, 147–8; on 1910 election results, 118; seeks inter-party accommodation, 123; defends Asquith, 127; favours dissolution, 154; threatens to resign, 157, 158, 202; addresses House, 159; lectures Asquith, 165; attempts to oust, 179, 193, 201, 213; personal deficiencies, 188; Asquith's trust in, 190, 191; supports voluntary system, 198; criticized over Cyprus, 200; takes peerage, 211; counsels Asquith to resign, 200; confers with Lloyd George, 230, 231; nominated to lead Centre Party, 245, 251, 252; post-war relations with Asquith, 245, 249, 251; addresses Wee Free rally, 253; urges break with Lloyd George, 273; favoured for Oxford chancellorship, 274–5; attends Asquith's farewell, 281; dinner for, 282; mentioned, 22, 23, 24, 26, 30, 38, 131, 132, 139, 149, 150, 163, 171, 257

Grey, Lady, 15

Grigg, John, 141, 287

Grillion's Club, 265

Grimond, Joseph ('Jo'), 101, 123, 288

Guest, F. E., 232, 245, 257

Gulland, John, 177, 201, 221, 241, 242

Gwynne, H. A., 180–81, 186, 194, 195, 213, 232, 233

Haig, Sir Douglas (1st Earl Haig), 187, 194, 213, 229

Haldane, R. B. (Viscount Haldane of Cloan): friendship with Asquith, 11, 12–14, 15–16, 20, 22, 23; friendship with Grey, 13, 68, 73; critical of Margot, 15–16, 223; collectivist tendencies, 26, 133; legal career, 29; aspires to office, 31; as special commissioner, 34–5; denied office, 32, 38; loses confidence in Rosebery, 39; as a Liberal Imperialist, 49, 53, 57, 58; arouses Campbell-Bannerman's suspicions, 55; party to Relugas Compact, 65–9; at War Office, 71, 72, 80, 82, 96, 107, 108; metaphysical digressions, 74; anticipates Asquith premiership, 61, 86; proposes a strategy, 109–10; on House of Lords reform, 119, 121; becomes Lord Chancellor, 129; on foreign policy, 143, 148–9, 156; urges Admiralty reforms, 146, 147; relations with colleagues, 147, 150, 154; takes charge at War Office, 160; allegedly pro-German, 165, 167; excluded from Cabinet, 191–2, 195, 202, 210; on Lloyd George premiership, 226; estranged from Asquith, viii–ix, 204, 229, 245, 252; affiliates with Labour, 243, 246–7, 265, 267; mentioned, 27, 44, 50, 87, 131, 136, 140, 145, 150, 171, 233, 234, 244

Halévy, Élie, 144

Halley's Comet, 122

Hamer, D. A., 45, 287

Hamilton, Sir Edward, 38

Hammond, J. L., 278, 286

Hanham, H. J., 286

Hankey, Sir Maurice (1st Baron Hankey), 169, 171, 178, 198, 199, 205, 206, 207, 214, 215–16, 217, 218, 219

Harcourt, Lewis (1st Viscount Harcourt), 38, 39, 74, 108, 119, 120, 129, 144–5, 146, 150, 167, 190, 211

Harcourt, Sir William: relations with Asquith, 20, 25, 31, 43; praises Asquith, 21, 39; opposes 'Asquithism', 25, 30; at Home Office, 33, 35; quarrels with Rosebery, 33, 37, 114; at Exchequer, 35; 'an almost impossible colleague', 38; advocates dissolution, 40; loses seat, 41; resigns leadership, 44; as a Little Englander, 47–8, 49, 51; mentioned, 42, 52, 53, 57, 74

Hardie, Keir, 130

Harley, Robert (1st Earl of Oxford), 271

Harmsworth, Sir Geoffrey, 290

Harris, José, 288

Harris, Wilson, 286

Harrisson, Mrs Hilda, 141, 223, 237, 246, 247, 258, 259, 262, 269, 271, 276, 277, 281, 291

Havighurst, A. F., 288

Hay, J. R., 288

Hazlehurst, Cameron, 139, 189, 193, 194, 221, 288, 290

Henderson, Arthur, 197, 199, 204, 220, 222, 223, 224

Hewins, W. A. S., 167, 184, 185, 215

Hirst, F. W., 149, 150

Hobhouse, (Sir) Charles, 55, 190, 192–193, 194, 272

Hobhouse, L. T., 77, 203

Hogge, J. M., 241, 242, 244, 245–6, 250, 252, 259

Holmes, Oliver Wendell, 253–4, 255, 256, 263

Holroyd, Michael, 288

Holt, R. D., 280

'Holy Warriors', 163

Home Office, Asquith's tenure at, 31–40

Home Rule, 12, 19, 22, 28, 30, 36, 50, 107, 116, 122, 134, 137, 152, 154, 162, 166. See also Ireland

Hore-Belisha, Leslie, 276

Horne, Sir Robert, 265

Horner, Frances (Lady Horner), 5, 15, 30, 32, 72

Horton, R. F., 249, 292

Houghton, 1st Lord (R. Monckton Milnes), 9

House of Lords: Conservative control of, 33; subverts Liberal legislation, 36, 83, 84, 85, 101, 104, 106, 107, 109; bows to labour interests, 105, 106, 133; Asquith denounces, 106–107, 110; rejects 1909 budget, 111ff; reform of, 30, 115–16, 119–20, 138, 150; passes People's Budget, 121; as a campaign issue, 125

Howard, Geoffrey, 259

Huddersfield College, 4

Hudson, Sir Robert, 242, 266, 268, 269, 277, 279, 280, 282

Hull Central, by-election (1919), 242

Hurst, Michael, 286

Huxley, Aldous, 256

Hynes, Samuel, 286

Illingworth, Percy, 165, 176, 177

Imperial Federation League, 25

Imperialism, 24, 25. See also Liberal Imperialists

Independent Liberals, 253–4, 255, 256–7. See also Free Liberal Party

Ireland: coercion of, 20; Liberal policy on, 154; threat of disorders in, 205; Easter Rebellion in, 98, 207, 251; extension of compulsion to, 214, 228; Asquith opposes reprisals in, 252. See also Home Rule

Irish Nationalist Party, 19, 114, 119, 120, 121, 122, 126, 150, 203, 210, 215, 220

Isaacs, Sir Rufus (1st Marquess of Reading), 125, 129, 139, 218–19, 234, 235, 283

Islington, Lady, 200

Jacobson, P. D., 287

James, Sir Henry (Lord James of Hereford), 11, 20, 21, 42, 60

James, Henry, 221

James, Robert Rhodes, 40, 189, 287, 290

Jameson, Leander Starr, 46, 47

Jameson Raid, 47

Jenkins, Roy: as Home Secretary, 35; as Chancellor of the Exchequer, 81; as Asquith's biographer, vii, ix, 6, 7, 9, 11, 15, 17, 25, 33, 39, 42, 44, 47, 52, 55, 60, 76, 93, 115, 127, 138, 140, 176, 187, 211, 212, 227, 228, 243, 250, 251, 255, 285, 286, 289

*John Bull*, 177

Jones, Thomas ('Tom'), 224, 273, 291

Jowett, Benjamin, 5–6, 8, 9

Joynson-Hicks, William (1st Viscount Brentford), 167, 215

Kenworthy, J. M., 242, 282

Kiderlin-Wächter, Alfred von, 146

Kimberley, 1st Earl of, 38

Kinnear, Michael, 292

Kitchener of Khartoum, 1st Earl: becomes War Secretary, 159–60; Asquith relies on, 170, 173, 174, 183, 188, 189, 200; stands against compulsion, 169–70; offers assurances on munitions, 170–71, 181, 182; accepts Dardanelles strategy, 172, 173; quarrels with his colleagues, 177; 'in a separate class', 190; attempts to remove, 187–8, 199–200, 201; ineptitude, 193; remains at War Office, 195; supports voluntary system, 198, 199; drowns, 211

Knollys, 1st Viscount, 66, 86, 87, 124

Koss, S. E., 286, 287, 291

Labouchere, Henry, 26, 38, 47, 49, 51

Labour Party: emerges in 1906, 77–8; opposes 1907 budget, 81; wins by-elections, 81, 104; satisfied with 1908 budget, 105; demands Veto Bill, 119, 120; in 1910 elections, 122, 126; Asquith placates, 130; resistance to mines legislation, 133;

Lloyd George's ambitions to lead, 153, 220, 257; accepts party truce, 162; Haldane gravitates towards, 192, 229; joins 1915 coalition, 195; opposes conscription, 203, 204; postwar relations with Liberals, 240, 242, 243, 246, 251, 252; in 1922 election, 258; in 1923 election, 262–263; forms government, 264ff; defeats Asquith at Paisley, 267–8; Liberal recruits to, 282

Labour unrest, Asquith contends with, 34, 102, 129–30, 132–4

Lambert, George, 241, 242

Land and Nation League, 273

*Land and the Nation, The* (1925), 272

Land Purchase (Ireland) Bill (1888), 23

Lansdowne, 5th Marquess of, 6, 114, 123, 127, 176, 186, 195, 198, 232

Laski, Harold, 251, 253–4, 255, 256, 263

Lawrence, D. H., 225

Lawson, Sir Wilfrid, 50, 52

Layton, (Sir) Walter, 279, 280

Layton West, by-election (1919), 242

League of Nations, 229, 249, 275

Lee, Arthur (Viscount Lee of Fareham), 107–8, 139, 205, 221, 224, 225

*Leeds Mercury*, 4

Lewis, Herbert, 83, 85

Liberal Candidates' Association, 280

Liberal Central Association, 12, 242

Liberal Council, 282

Liberal Imperialist League, 58

Liberal Imperialists, 37, 42, 45–63 *passim*, 73–4, 98, 145, 260

Liberal Industrial Inquiry, 283

Liberal League, 58–9, 62, 73, 109

*Liberal Magazine*, 259

Liberal Million Fund, 271–2, 275, 281, 282

Liberal Organising Committee, 274

Liberal Party: split over Home Rule, 12, 18–20; adopts Newcastle Programme, 29–30; in 1895 election, 41; 'painfully difficult years', 45; 'nearing its final cataclysm', 49; in 1900 election, 52; fights 'war to the knife and fork', 54–5; in 1906

Liberal Party – *cont.*
  election, 76–8; in 1908, 89; as a
  Nonconformist party, 93; embraces
  social reform, 100–101; by-election
  losses, 104, 106, 137, 149; in 1910
  campaigns, 116–17, 126; divides on
  women's suffrage, 130; policy on
  Ireland, 154; in possible 1914
  election, 155; at outbreak of war,
  156; accepts party truce, 162; bleak
  prospects, 204; supports Asquith,
  206, 227; destruction of, 207;
  divided at Westminster, 228; in
  1918 election, 236, 238, 239; in 1924
  election, 266, 268; 'ready for real
  leadership', 267; shattered, 269;
  holds London convention, 271–2;
  during General Strike, 276–7;
  further convulsions in, 280, 282;
  Asquith's legacy to, 283–4
Liberal Unionists, 19, 42. *See also*
  Unionist Party
Liberal War Committee, 215
Liberation Society, 59
Licensing: 1904 Act, 106; 1908 Bill,
  84, 85, 106, 109–10; as campaign
  issue, 116
Lichnowsky, Prince Karl Max, 158,
  165
Lincoln's Inn, 9
Liverpool, 2nd Earl of, 99
Lloyd, George (1st Baron Lloyd), 181
Lloyd, Trevor, 288
Lloyd George, David (1st Earl Lloyd-
  George of Dwyfor): compared with
  Asquith, viii, 1, 2, 74, 93–4, 141,
  225–7; Asquith's early relations
  with, 39, 40, 51, 60, 96, 113–14, 130;
  as a pro-Boer, 50, 52, 53; defends
  Nonconformist interests, 59, 83–4;
  at Board of Trade, 73; praises
  Campbell-Bannerman, 79; critical
  of government policy, 85–6, 145;
  mentioned as possible premier, 87,
  139; appointed to Exchequer, 97–8;
  alleged to 'push along' Asquith,
  100; on 1908 budget, 105; as a
  Radical economist, 108, 109, 147,
  149–50; frames his People's Budget,
  112–13; in 1910 elections, 117–18;

on House of Lords reform, 119;
  urges coalition, 123; negotiates
  with miners, 132; as a Home Ruler,
  135; speaks at Mansion House, 145–
  146; consulted by Asquith, 150–51;
  relations with Churchill, 152–3, 154;
  relations with colleagues, 120, 154,
  177; becomes 'the crucial figure',
  156; 'all for peace', 157–8; supports
  war, 159; on war strategy, 168, 171,
  172; credits story of plot, 179;
  dislikes McKenna, 179, 202;
  praised by Garvin, 180; favours
  coalition, 181; as possible war
  secretary, 187–8, 196; his ambition
  held in check, 188; supports conscription, 189, 198, 199, 205–6;
  allegedly involved in plot, 193–4;
  becomes Minister of Munitions, 196;
  relations with Asquith 'very
  strained', 198–9; threatens
  resignation, 200; considered
  disloyal, 201, 202, 204, 205, 206;
  succeeds to War Office, 212;
  opposes government from within,
  213–14; threatens to resign, 215,
  218; in Dec. 1916 crisis, 215–27;
  Asquith shows benevolent neutrality towards, 227–9; confers with
  Asquith, 230, 231–2; overtures to
  Asquith, 234; calls 1918 election,
  235; distributes 'coupon', 236–7;
  dependent on Unionists, 241;
  opposes Simon at Spen Valley, 243;
  'not very depressed' by Paisley,
  248; meets Asquith, 250; political
  troubles, 252; falls from power, 256;
  in 1922 election, 257; has 'visions of
  reconciliation', 259; financial
  assets, 260, 261, 263–4, 266, 271,
  272, 275, 282; moves towards
  reunion, 259–61; joins with
  Asquith, 261–2; in 1923 election,
  262–3; defends Asquith, 265;
  criticizes Liberal headquarters, 266,
  268; adopts land policy, 267, 272–3;
  friction with Asquith, 269, 270–71;
  elected chairman in House, 272;
  antipathy to Baldwin, 274;
  responds to General Strike, 276–9;

replies to Asquith's rebuke, 278–9;
attempted censure of, 279–80;
mentioned, 54, 94, 122, 131, 171,
176, 182, 211, 247, 254

Lloyd George, (Dame) Margaret, 196,
202, 203, 238, 276, 277

Lloyd George, (Lady) Megan, 238,
253, 262

Lloyd-George, Countess: *see* Stevenson, Frances

London County Council, 25

London dockers' strike (1912), 133

London School of Economics, 81

Long, Walter (1st Viscount Long of
Wraxall), 167, 186, 198, 207, 224

'Lord Rosebery's Escape from
Houndsditch', 63

Loreburn, 1st Earl of (Sir Robert
Reid), 73, 78, 79, 87, 96, 129, 146,
157, 213

Lough, Thomas, 95

Lowe, Robert (Viscount Sherbrooke),
4

Lucas, 8th Baron, 190

Lucy, (Sir) Henry W., 43, 54

Lupton, Arnold, 77

Lymington, Lord: *see* Portsmouth,
6th Earl of

Lyons, F. S. L., 29, 286, 290

Lyttelton, Alfred, 21, 42, 61, 85

McCallum, Sir John, 244, 247

McCallum, R. B., vii

McCready, H. W., 287

MacDonald, C. J., 28

MacDonald, J. Ramsay, 9, 77, 228,
264, 265, 266, 278

McGill, Barry, 291

McKenna, Pamela, 141, 161, 219, 223,
291

McKenna, Reginald: boycotts
Asquith dinner, 55; at Admiralty,
96, 97, 108, 109, 146–7, 148;
Asquith defends himself to, 100; at
Home Office, 129; opposes naval
estimates, 150; distrusts Churchill,
154; responds to war, 158; disapproves of Asquith's social life,
161; tempted to hit Bonar Law,
166; suffers press attacks, 167;

friction with Lloyd George, 179;
raised to Exchequer, 190–91, 192,
196; supports voluntary system,
198; presents 1915 budget, 202;
threatens resignation, 202, 203,
204; counsels Asquith to resign,
220; blamed for misleading Asquith,
221; loses seat, 238; surveys
electoral wreckage, 239–40; critical
of Asquith, 241; addresses a
Unionist meeting, 257; mentioned,
106, 120, 139, 171, 201, 291

McKenna, Stephen, 138–9

Maclean, Sir Donald, 176, 240, 241,
242–3, 244, 250, 251, 255, 261, 263,
264, 266, 267, 268, 269, 273, 274,
276, 277, 279, 280, 281

Macmillan, Harold, 225–6

McNeill, Ronald, 167

Mafeking, 50

Magnus, Sir Philip, 33, 287, 289

Mallock, W. H., 7

*Manchester Guardian*, 87, 148, 151–2,
156, 157, 182–3, 203, 204, 228–9,
233, 266

Manchester South, by-election (1900)
50

Manners, Lady Diana: *see* Cooper,
Lady Diana

Mansion House, 146, 238

Marconi scandal, 138, 151

Marlborough, 9th Duke of, 135

Mary, Queen, 193

Massingham, H. W., 39, 51, 152, 178,
179, 195, 197

Masterman, C. F. G., 109, 119, 121,
137, 167, 171, 183, 260, 267, 270, 278

Masterman, Lucy (Mrs C. F. G.
Masterman), 109, 119, 120, 121, 289

Matthew, H. C. G., 25, 57, 286

Maurice, Maj.-Gen. Sir Frederick,
233, 234

Maurice debate, 233, 236

Maxse, Leo, 82, 90, 158, 165, 166, 167,
181, 194, 197

Melland, Frederick (father-in-law), 10

Melland, Helen (first wife): *see*
Asquith, Helen Melland

*Memories and Reflections* (1928), 2

Merchant Shipping Act (1906), 85

Meredith, George, 221
Mersey, 1st Viscount, 213
'Methods of Barbarism', 53–4, 58
Meux, Lady, 209
Midleton, Earl of: *see* Brodrick, W. St
John
Military Service Bill (1916), 203–4
Milner, 1st Viscount (Sir Alfred
Milner), 6, 7, 11, 48, 53, 58, 82, 197–
198, 213, 217, 224
Miners' Federation, 132
Miners' Minimum Wage Act (1912),
133
Minto, Earl of, 88, 96
Mitchell, Rosslyn, 268, 292
Monckton Milnes, R.: *see* Houghton,
Lord
Mond, Sir Alfred (1st Baron Melchett),
261, 265, 267, 272, 274, 275
Monger, G., 290
Montagu, Edwin, 93, 140, 171, 176,
177, 178, 186–7, 197, 205, 223, 224–
225, 230
Montagu, Venetia (Mrs Edwin
Montagu): *see* Stanley, Venetia
Morgan, David, 289
Morgan, Kenneth O., 113–14, 287, 289
Morley, John (Viscount Morley of
Blackburn): early ties with Asquith,
21, 23, 25, 31, 43; assesses party
prospects, 26; interprets 1892
results, 30; in leadership struggles,
33; loses seat, 41; follows Harcourt,
45; in 1900 election, 50, 51–2;
critical of Asquith, 57, 68, 75; at
India Office, 73; predicts tie in
1906, 76; discomfort in Commons,
78; 'would *like* to be Prime
Minister', 87; on Asquith's ascent,
88; takes peerage, 96; purveys
gossip, 98, 149; threatens to resign,
100, 120–21; as a Radical economist,
108, 109, 150; leads in the Lords,
128; in C.I.D., 144, 145; resigns,
157, 159; prophesies Asquith's fall,
160; mentioned, 24, 46, 47–8, 49,
53, 54, 74, 133, 136, 146, 154, 233
*Morning Post*, 180, 194, 213, 232
Morocco crisis: (1906), 143; (1911): *see*
Agadir crisis

Morrell, Lady Ottoline, 209, 229, 256,
291
Morrell, Philip, 209
Mosley, Sir Oswald, 91, 252
Munitions, shortage of, 181–2, 183,
184–5, 188
Munro Ferguson, R. C. (1st Viscount
Novar), 23, 24, 32, 52–3, 57, 61, 82,
87
Murray, Alexander, Master of Elibank
(1st Baron Murray of Elibank), 119,
121, 138, 230, 235–6, 249
Murray, A. C., 249
Murray, Gilbert, 209, 244, 245

Napier, Mark, 11
Napoleon III, 5
Nash, Vaughan, 98, 184, 191
Nathan, Sir Matthew, 190, 209
*Nation*, 148, 152, 195, 197, 228, 260
National Democratic Party, 236, 246
National Insurance Act, 147, 149, 151
National Liberal Club, 24, 106, 125,
252
National Liberal Council, 253
National Liberal Federation, 21, 29,
125, 148, 149, 151, 227, 240, 242,
245, 255, 272, 273, 274, 279, 280
National Liberals: *see* Coalition
Liberals
National Reform Union, 53, 54
*National Review*, 90, 158, 161, 181,
194
National Service League, 197–8
Naval estimates, Radical opposition
to, 93, 107–9, 112, 145, 149–50, 152
Newcastle Programme, 29–30, 45, 58,
102, 262
*News of the World*, 137
Nicholas II, Tsar, 163
Nicoll, Sir William Robertson, 249
Nicolson, Sir Harold, viii, 285
Nigeria debate, 214–15
*Nineteenth Century*, 63
Nineteen-Twenty Club, 254
Nonconformists, influence within
Liberal Party, 3, 19, 59, 60, 76, 83–
84, 87, 93, 120, 122, 135, 148, 149,
150, 152, 276
North, Lord, 99, 203

North Edinburgh, by-election (1919), 244

Northcliffe, 1st Viscount (Alfred Harmsworth), 179, 180, 197, 217, 219

Northcliffe press, 197, 248

North-East Lanark, by-election (1901), 57, 58

*Observer*, 180

O'Connor, T. P., 153

Old-age pensions, 80–81, 103, 105, 112

Orange Free State: *see* South Africa

Osborne judgement, 120, 130

O'Shea, William, 29

Oxford, Bishop of, 271

Oxford, by-election (1924), 266

Oxford Union, 5, 7, 9

Oxford University, 243–4, 274. *See also* Balliol College.

Paget, Lt-Gen. Sir Arthur, 136–7

Paisley: by-election (1920), 244, 246–247; Asquith defends (1922), 258; Asquith defends (1923), 267; Asquith loses (1924), 267–8; proximity to Greenock, 281

'Paisley Policy', 251

*Pall Mall Gazette*, 180, 181

Palmerston, 3rd Viscount, 112, 118

Pankhurst family, 132

Parliament Act (1911), 110, 120, 124, 126–7, 128, 135

Parnell, Charles Stewart, 27, 29

Parnell Commission, 27, 120

'Parnellism and Crime', 27, 34

Party truce, 162, 163, 166, 167, 168

Patents Act (1907), 85

Paul, Herbert, 7

Peace Conference, 236, 243

Pease, J. A. (Lord Gainford), 170, 187, 190

Peel, Sir Robert, 35, 79, 88, 99

Pelling, Henry, 104, 289

Pentland, 1st Baron: *see* Sinclair, John

People's Budget: *see* Budgets (1909)

Percival, Spencer, 88

Perks, Sir R. W., 51, 54, 57, 58, 60, 77, 97, 117–18, 275

Phelps Brown, E. H., 289

Phillipps, Vivian, 201, 246, 251, 253, 256, 259, 266, 268, 272, 274, 275, 277, 280, 283

Piggott, Richard, 28

Pitt, William (1st Earl of Chatham), 135, 187, 201

Plender, Sir William, 273

Ponsonby, Arthur (1st Baron Ponsonby of Shulbrede), 98, 157

Portsmouth, 5th Earl of, 8–9

Portsmouth, 6th Earl of (Lord Lymington), 8, 95

Potter, Beatrice: *see* Webb, Beatrice

Pound, Reginald, 290

Primrose, Neil, 176

Pringle, W. M. R., 192, 193, 261, 276, 277

Protection: *see* Tariff Reform

Proust, Marcel, 91

*Punch*, 249

Radical Group, 272

Rae, John, 291

Rawlinson, Gen. Sir Henry, 213

Read, Donald, 286

Reading, 1st Marquess of: *see* Isaacs, Sir Rufus

Redmond, John, 34, 119, 120, 121, 127, 134, 160

Reform Club, 45, 55, 103, 224, 256, 269

Reid, Sir Robert: *see* Loreburn, 1st Earl of

*Religio Milneriana*, 52

Relugas Compact, 31, 65–9, 86

Remple, R. A., 287

Repington, Charles à Court, 148, 181–182, 184, 192

*Review of Reviews*, 74

Rhodes, Cecil, 47

Rhondda, Viscount (D. A. Thomas), 224

Richter, Melvin, x, 286

Riddell, 1st Baron (Sir George Riddell), 79, 137, 187, 196

Ridley, Sir Matthew White (Viscount Ridley), 35

Ripon, 1st Marquess of, 73, 76, 95, 105, 115

Robbins, A. G., 184

Robbins, Keith, 13, 69, 286, 290

Robertson, Edmund, 95

Robertson, Sir William, 233

Robinson, Geoffrey (later Geoffrey Dawson), 180, 213

Rollitt, Sir Albert, 34

Romanes Lecture (1918), 102

Rosebery, 5th Earl of: 'man of the future', 24; weighs Asquith's prospects, 31; as Foreign Secretary, 32, 37; quarrels with Harcourt, 33, 37, 43, 114; on good terms with Asquith, 38; as premier, 39, 40; observes 'smash up', 41–2; leads Liberal Imperialists, 45–6; views 1900 election, 50, 51–2; 'ploughs his furrow alone', 55–6; speaks at Chesterfield, 57–8; and Liberal League, 57, 59; sulks, 61; 'out of the running', 62, 65; repudiates Home Rule, 68; Grey's devotion to, 69; forsaken, 73; criticizes Asquith's budget, 81; nurses resentment, 82; understands Asquith's problems, 103; mentioned, 21, 36, 44, 49, 72, 87, 101, 103, 118, 165, 201, 275

Rosen, Andrew, 289

Roskill, John, 28, 48

Roskill, Stephen, 207, 290, 291

Ross, Robert ('Robbie'), 93

Rothermere, 1st Viscount (Harold Harmsworth), 249, 262

Rowland, Peter, 80, 288, 290

Royal Commission on Oxford and Cambridge Universities, 243–4

Royal Declaration, 122

Runciman, Walter (1st Viscount Runciman of Doxford): expects Asquith premiership, 88; as education minister, 106; on House of Lords reform, 120; quarrels with Lloyd George, 154; at Board of Trade, 159; disapproves of Asquith's social life, 161; wary of political truce, 163; on war strategy, 168; nicknames Kitchener, 169; retains office, 191; fits into 'balance', 196, 198; criticizes Asquith, 201; opposes conscription,

202, 204, 217; counsels Asquith to resign, 220; supports Asquith, 225; loses seat, 238; stands in by-election, 244; attracted to Centre Party, 245, 251; survives 1924 election, 268, 269; heads Radical Group, 272; urges break with Lloyd George, 272, 277; attends Asquith's farewell, 281; mentioned, 140, 144, 190, 192, 241

Russell, A. K., 288

Russell, Sir Charles (Lord Russell of Killowen), 27, 28

Russell, George, 38

Russell, Lord John (1st Earl Russell), 118

Russia, British alliance with, 159

Ryan, A. P., 115

St Aldwyn, 1st Earl (Sir Michael Hicks-Beach), 213

Salisbury, 3rd Marquess of, 20, 31, 40, 42, 94, 245

Salisbury, 4th Marquess of, 174, 188–9

Salisbury, Lady, 271

'Salome Trial', 234

Sampson, Anthony, 8, 286

Samuel, Herbert (1st Viscount Samuel), 8, 139, 158, 176, 183, 190, 196, 210–11, 222, 238

Sassoon, Philip, 256

Savoy Hotel, 24, 122

Scott, Lady (later Lady Kennet), 141, 202, 204, 206, 214, 223, 267, 272, 291

Scott, C. P., 87, 156, 198–9, 202, 203, 229, 230, 235, 249, 251, 252, 259, 260–61, 273, 278

Scott, Ted, 278

Searle, G. R., 287

Seely, J. E. B. (1st Baron Mottistone), 98, 129, 136, 137, 140

Selborne, 2nd Earl of, 195

Semmel, Bernard, 287

Shaw, Bernard, 87, 211, 248

Shaw-Lefevre, J. G., 38

Sheffield, Lord (Lord Stanley of Alderley), 126, 137

Shells scandal: *see* Munitions

Simon, Sir John (1st Viscount Simon),

129, 140, 153, 157, 159, 167, 191, 192, 195, 196, 199, 202, 203, 204, 243, 259, 261, 268, 272, 273, 276, 281
Sinclair, John (1st Baron Pentland), 74, 120
Smith, F. E. (1st Earl of Birkenhead), 127, 135, 198, 213, 224, 262, 275
Smith, Goldwin, 87
Smuts, Jan Christiaan, 48, 78, 232
Socialism, 52, 77, 81
Solomon, Sir R., 79
South Africa, 46, 47, 48, 78–9. *See also* Boer War
South Africa Committee, 47, 48
South Essex Liberal Association, 54
*Spectator*, 10, 62, 103
Spen Valley, by-election (1919), 242–243, 244
Spencer, 5th Earl, 25, 37, 43, 52, 62, 64, 65
Spender, Harold, 120, 149
Spender, J. A., 23, 79, 100, 118, 182, 221, 244. *See also* Spender and Asquith
Spender and Asquith, as official biographers, vii, 9, 10, 11, 20, 34, 60, 91, 107, 212, 234, 275
Stamfordham, 1st Baron (Sir Arthur Bigge), 124, 182, 190, 192, 220, 222
Stanhope, Philip, 48, 49, 52, 53
Stanhope amendment, 50
Stanley, Sir Albert (Baron Ashfield, 224
Stanley, Venetia (Mrs Edwin Montagu), ix, 96, 126, 133, 137, 139, 140–41, 152, 154–5, 156, 158, 159, 160, 161, 165, 166, 168, 169, 170, 171, 172, 174–5, 177, 178, 179, 186–187, 190, 197, 229, 281, 289
Stansky, Peter, x, 44, 287, 288
*Star*, 201
Stead, W. T., 74
Steiner, Zara K., 290
Stevenson, Frances (Countess Lloyd-George), 230, 248, 252, 253, 273, 278, 292
Stewart, A. T. Q., 289
Stokes, Eric, 287
Stopford Green, Alice, 26

Strachey, Lytton, 93, 94, 209–10, 229, 263, 291
Strachey, St Loe, 62, 103, 118, 158, 211, 227, 262, 269, 275
Suffragettes, 102, 116, 134, 136, 176. *See also* Women's suffrage
Swinnerton, Frank, 256, 292

Taff Vale, 83
Tariff Reform, 59–60, 107, 151, 189, 235, 258, 261
Taylor, A. J. P., x, 164, 290, 292
Tennant, Sir Charles ('The Bart'), 16, 44, 58
Tennant, H. J., 174
Tennant, Kathleen (Duchess of Rutland), 276
Tennant, Lillian, 141
Tennant, Margot: *see* Asquith, Margot
Tennant, Winifred Coombe, 281
Tennyson, Alfred, Lord, 24
Thorne, George, 241, 242, 252, 259
*Times, The*, 21, 27, 28, 34, 48, 52, 55, 58, 59, 62, 70, 72, 107, 120, 148, 181–2, 183, 184, 192, 213, 219–20, 233, 241, 252, 254, 256, 283
Tonypandy, 129
Toynbee, Arnold, 7
Trades Disputes Act (1906), 83
Trades Union Congress, 232
Trafalgar Square, right of assembly in, 33–4
Transvaal: *see* South Africa
Tree, Lady, 165
Trevelyan, C. P., 106–7
Trevelyan, G. M., 14, 286
Trollope, Anthony, quoted, 91, 222, 227
Tweedmouth, 2nd Baron, 74, 95, 96
Two-Power Standard, 107, 108

Uganda, 37
Ulster crisis, 102, 132, 138, 150, 155, 166
Unionist Business Committee, 184
Unionist Party: in 1886 election, 19; in 1900 election, 52; split over tariffs, 59–60; smashed in 1906, 77; split within, 150–51; accepts party truce, 162, 163, 167; joins coalition,

Unionist Party – *cont.*
  195, 197; no confidence in Asquith,
  219, 220; backs Asquith at Paisley,
  248; tires of coalition, 255, 256, 257;
  in 1923 election, 263
Unionist War Committee, 213, 215
United States: labour problems in,
  130; neutrality of, 169; enters war,
  229

Verity, William, 286
Versailles, Treaty of, 243
Victoria, Queen, 32–3, 34, 65
*Vigilante*, 234
Vincent, John, 286
Vizetelly, Henry, 27

'Wait and see', 115, 161–2, 195, 199,
  266
Waley, S. D., 288
Walton, Sir John Lawson, 79
War aims, 232, 235
War committee, 214, 218
War council, 201
Warren, Herbert, 6
Watson, Robert Spence, 49
'Wayfarer, A': *see* Massingham, H. W.
Webb, Beatrice (Mrs Sidney Webb),
  13, 24, 26, 38, 47, 48, 51, 56, 57, 73,
  167, 246
Webb, Sidney (Baron Passfield), 38,
  56, 57, 63, 191, 246
Webster, Richard, 27
Wedgwood, Josiah, 241, 244
Wee Frees: *see* Free Liberal Party *and*
  Independent Liberals
Welsh disestablishment, 30, 39, 107,
  114, 117, 135, 150, 162, 167

West, Sir Algernon, 36
*Westminster Gazette*, 70, 118, 157, 182
'Whig revolt' (1886), 19, 20
White, Arnold, 167
Whitley, J. H., 176
Wilde, Oscar, 93
Wilhelm II, Kaiser, 146, 163, 166
Willans, John (uncle), 4
Willans, William (grandfather), 3, 4
Williams, W. Llewelyn, 202, 203, 204
Willoughby de Broke, 19th Baron,
  197
Wilson, Admiral Sir Arthur, 171
Wilson, Sir Harold, 217
Wilson, Sir Henry, 233
Wilson, John, 45, 54, 68, 75, 287
Wilson, Trevor, 184, 204, 221, 233,
  241, 290, 291, 292
Wilson, Woodrow, 229, 235, 238
Winchester, 8, 30, 92
Wolverhampton, Viscount: *see*
  Fowler, Henry
Women's Social and Political Union,
  130
Women's suffrage, 102, 130, 131, 138,
  275. *See also* Suffragettes
Wood, Thomas McKinnon, 190, 238
Wright, R. S., 11
Writers' Group, 229

*Yorkshire Evening News*, 255
Young, Hilton, 241
Younger, Sir George (1st Viscount
  Younger of Leckie), 257

Zebel, S. H., 286
Zola, Émile, 27

*Hamish Hamilton Paperbacks*

# QUEEN VICTORIA: Her Life and Times 1819–1861
## Cecil Woodham-Smith

A new conception of Queen Victoria emerged from this biography.
Mrs Woodham-Smith had access to previously unused information
and her book established once and for all the true character of the
young Victoria. Its publication was a landmark in historical
research. Intensely readable and sympathetic, this biography deals
with the Queen's wretched childhood, her passionate nature, her
devotion to the Prince Consort and her native shrewdness in politics.
Sadly the author did not live to complete the second volume of this
life, but her work on the young Queen is unrivalled.

'. . . unlikely ever to be surpassed.' Michael Ratcliffe, *The Times*

'. . . quite indispensable to any student of this peculiar sovereign.'
Paul Johnson, *Guardian*


# VOLTAIRE IN LOVE
## Nancy Mitford

In this very funny book Nancy Mitford writes of the famous love
affair between Voltaire and the beautiful blue-stocking Marquise du
Châtelet. It is rightly regarded as her most successful essay in
history.

'There is not a dull page . . . witty, vivacious, accurate, informative
and a delight to read.' – Harold Nicolson, *Observer*

'A witty and absorbing account of one of the great love stories of the
world.' – Cyril Connolly, *Sunday Times*


# THE DRAGON EMPRESS
## Marina Warner

From 1861 to 1908, the Empress Dowager Tz'u-hsi dominated China.
In this immensely readable biography, Marina Warner lays bare
Tz'u-hsi's complex personality, and portrays a China in rapid decline
as poverty, civil war and foreign exploitation and invasion brought
about the fall of the Ch'ing dynasty.

'A fresh and fascinating account that reveals China's last imperial
reign as surely the most absurd government ever to have had charge
of a major nation. I read every word.' – Barbara W. Tuchman

## Available in Hamish Hamilton Paperbacks